NBER Macroeconomics Annual 2011

NBER Macroeconomics Annual 2011

Edited by
Daron Acemoglu and Michael Woodford

The University of Chicago Press
Chicago and London

NBER Macroeconomics Annual 2011, Number 26

Published annually by The University of Chicago Press.

Standing orders
To place a standing order for this book series, please address your request to The University of Chicago Press, Chicago Distribution Center, Attn. Standing Orders/Customer Service, 11030 S. Langley Avenue, Chicago, IL 60628. Telephone toll free in the U.S. and Canada: 1-800-621-2736; or 1-773-702-7000. Fax toll free in the U.S. and Canada: 1-800-621-8476; or 1-773-702-7212.

Single-copy orders
In the U.K. and Europe: Order from your local bookseller or direct from The University of Chicago Press, c/o John Wiley Ltd. Distribution Center, 1 Oldlands Way, Bognor Regis, West Sussex PO22 9SA, UK. Telephone 01243 779777 or Fax 01243 820250. E-mail: cs-books@wiley.co.uk

In the U.S., Canada, and the rest of the world: Order from your local bookseller or direct from The University of Chicago Press, Chicago Distribution Center, 11030 S. Langley Avenue, Chicago, IL 60628. Telephone toll free in the U.S. and Canada: 1-800-621-2736; or 1-773-702-7000. Fax toll free in the U.S. and Canada: 1-800-621-8476; or 1-773-702-7212.

Special orders
University of Chicago Press books may be purchased at quantity discounts for business or promotional use. For information, please write to Sales Department—Special Sales, The University of Chicago Press, 1427 E. 60th Street, Chicago, IL 60637 USA or telephone 1-773-702-7723.

This book was printed and bound in the United States of America.

ISSN: 0889-3365
ISBN-13: 978-0-226-00214-9 (hc.:alk.paper)—0-226-00216-3 (pbk.:alk.paper)

10   9   8   7   6   5   4   3   2   1

Relation of the Directors to the Work and Publications of the NBER

1. The object of the NBER is to ascertain and present to the economics profession, and to the public more generally, important economic facts and their interpretation in a scientific manner without policy recommendations. The Board of Directors is charged with the responsibility of ensuring that the work of the NBER is carried on in strict conformity with this object.

2. The President shall establish an internal review process to ensure that book manuscripts proposed for publication DO NOT contain policy recommendations. This shall apply both to the proceedings of conferences and to manuscripts by a single author or by one or more co-authors but shall not apply to authors of comments at NBER conferences who are not NBER affiliates.

3. No book manuscript reporting research shall be published by the NBER until the President has sent to each member of the Board a notice that a manuscript is recommended for publication and that in the President's opinion it is suitable for publication in accordance with the above principles of the NBER. Such notification will include a table of contents and an abstract or summary of the manuscript's content, a list of contributors if applicable, and a response form for use by Directors who desire a copy of the manuscript for review. Each manuscript shall contain a summary drawing attention to the nature and treatment of the problem studied and the main conclusions reached.

4. No volume shall be published until forty-five days have elapsed from the above notification of intention to publish it. During this period a copy shall be sent to any Director requesting it, and if any Director objects to publication on the grounds that the manuscript contains policy recommendations, the objection will be presented to the author(s) or editor(s). In case of dispute, all members of the Board shall be notified,

and the President shall appoint an ad hoc committee of the Board to decide the matter; thirty days additional shall be granted for this purpose.

5. The President shall present annually to the Board a report describing the internal manuscript review process, any objections made by Directors before publication or by anyone after publication, any disputes about such matters, and how they were handled.

6. Publications of the NBER issued for informational purposes concerning the work of the Bureau, or issued to inform the public of the activities at the Bureau, including but not limited to the NBER Digest and Reporter, shall be consistent with the object stated in paragraph 1. They shall contain a specific disclaimer noting that they have not passed through the review procedures required in this resolution. The Executive Committee of the Board is charged with the review of all such publications from time to time.

7. NBER working papers and manuscripts distributed on the Bureau's web site are not deemed to be publications for the purpose of this resolution, but they shall be consistent with the object stated in paragraph 1. Working papers shall contain a specific disclaimer noting that they have not passed through the review procedures required in this resolution. The NBER's web site shall contain a similar disclaimer. The President shall establish an internal review process to ensure that the working papers and the web site do not contain policy recommendations, and shall report annually to the Board on this process and any concerns raised in connection with it.

8. Unless otherwise determined by the Board or exempted by the terms of paragraphs 6 and 7, a copy of this resolution shall be printed in each NBER publication as described in paragraph 2 above.

Contents

Editorial

Daron Acemoglu and Michael Woodford

The twenty-sixth edition of the *NBER Macroeconomics Annual* continues with its tradition of featuring theoretical and empirical contributions that shed light on central issues in contemporary macroeconomics. As in previous years, the contributions push the frontiers of macroeconomic work in areas ranging from short-run macroeconomic fluctuations to exchange rates, financial regulation, and political economy. Also as in previous years, the contributions address important policy-relevant questions and open new debates, which we expect to continue in the years to come. As with the previous two volumes in this series, this year's volume features several papers that aim to illuminate the causes of the recent financial crisis and consider policies that might reduce the likelihood of similar crises in the future. These include two papers that analyze the sources of asset market bubbles and their macroeconomic consequences, and two papers that address aspects of financial regulation and their effect on financial markets. In addition, the volume also includes papers on exchange-rate determination and on the macroeconomic determinants of unemployment. Each of the six papers tackles an important area in macroeconomics and advances the literature in several directions. We hope that these papers and the detailed discussions of each paper will provide useful starting points for the further study of these important debates.

The first two papers deal with asset bubbles and possible sources of widespread mistakes in asset valuation during bubble periods. In the first paper, "Natural Expectations, Macroeconomic Dynamics, and Asset Pricing," Andreas Fuster, Benjamin Hebert, and David Laibson propose a theory of "natural expectations" that allows for systematic forecasting errors in sufficiently complex environments, despite considerable sophistication on the part of forecasters. Agents in Fuster et al.'s model forecast on the basis of linear time-series models that may be misspecified as they do not include sufficiently many lags. They show that when confronted with true data-generating processes with high-order autocorrelation, many parsimonious time-series models will be biased in a similar way: they will fail to capture the long-run mean reversion, incorrectly extrapolating short-run momentum into the future. They also argue that US time series for the earnings of capital exhibit this type of long autocorrelation, thus potentially inducing systematic biases in expectations. This kind of bias in earnings forecasts could then give rise to departures of stock prices from fundamental values in a manner consistent with certain stylized patterns: prices are predicted to overreact to changes in fundamentals and hence to be excessively volatile; excess returns should be (negatively) predictable by lagged excess returns and by price/earnings ratios; and equities should be perceived to be highly risky, so that the equity premium is large on average, even though long-run equity returns are only weakly correlated with long-run consumption growth. The paper discusses additional implications of the model for the character of business fluctuations and for the differential behavior of more and less sophisticated investors, and argues that most of its predictions are consistent with US data. This is a provocative hypothesis with broad implications for macroeconomic and financial modeling, and one that is sure to spark considerable further debate.

The second paper, "House Price Booms and the Current Account," by Klaus Adam, Pei Kuang, and Albert Marcet, also considers boom-bust cycles in asset prices and also argues that these must be understood as reflecting departures from correct forecasts of the kind assumed in the theory of "rational expectations." Similar to the previous authors, Adam et al. propose that the errors are endogenous responses to certain histories of fundamentals (rather than being entirely unpredictable or outside the model) and that they arise despite a high degree of rationality on the part of market participants. The approach in this paper is different in that traders are modeled as forecasting future price movements by extrapolating past movements in asset prices, and not simply bidding for assets on the basis of a forecast of future earnings. And perhaps more importantly, Adam et al. assume that forecasts are "internally rational," in the sense that they follow from Bayesian updating given the data (for both prices and dividends) observed thus far, starting from some logically coherent prior beliefs. This implies that boom-bust cycles are consistent with a high degree of sophistication on the part of market participants, though this sophistication ensures internal consistency of traders' beliefs over time than to the relationship between their forecasts and the true data-generating process. The paper also considers the macroeconomic implications of asset booms of this kind, in particular the implications for the current account balance of a housing boom, in a small open economy model in which borrowing is constrained by the market value of housing collateral. The authors argue that a quantitative version of their model successfully explains broad differences in the sizes of the housing booms and current account deficits in several countries over the past decade. An important aspect of this exercise is that, using purely differences in initial conditions of countries at the beginning of the last decade, they can account not only for the correlation between housing booms and current account deficits, but also for the magnitudes of housing booms in the different countries. In the authors' parsimonious model, the housing booms (or non-booms) of each country are due to a single common disturbance, a decline in the world real interest rate (attributed to monetary policy), which has different consequences for different countries only to the extent that market participants have different beliefs in the different countries; and these in turn are different only because the Bayesian updating in the different countries has been based on different pre-2000 data sets. The authors' findings provide important evidence both for the usefulness of their way of modeling expectation formation and for the hypothesis that low real interest rates in the middle of the past decade played an important role in generating the housing bubbles in several countries, the consequences of which remain with us today.

The next two papers both contribute to the broad reconsideration of financial regulation that has been one of the most evident intellectual consequences of the global financial crisis. In "Risk Topography," Markus Brunnermeier, Gary Gorton, and Arvind Krishnamurthy discuss the kind of financial sector data that would need to be collected and disseminated in order to provide a basis both for more effective macro-prudential policies and for improved private-sector risk management. They argue that existing reporting requirements for financial institutions, such as the Call Reports mandated by the National Banking Act, do not provide the kind of information that is needed for effective oversight of modern financial systems, and discuss potential changes in the reporting requirements. Rather than contenting ourselves with simple reporting of balance-sheet quantities at a point in time, the authors discuss the potential effects of requiring systemically important financial institutions to regularly report their estimates of the sensitivity of their balance sheets to a specified list of risk factors and hypothetical scenarios. They note that such reporting would shift toward the assessment of risk exposures, and a uniform reporting format across institutions would facilitate assessment of the extent to which the system as a whole is exposed to particular types of risk. While such data reporting would represent a sharp departure from existing policy, the Dodd-Frank Act has established an Office of Financial Research (OFR) within the Department of the Treasury, tasked with providing information to the Financial Stability Oversight Council, and with the power to require financial institutions to supply data that it requests. The paper essentially offers a potential analysis for what the OFR could do with this authority, drawing upon recent research into the nature of systemic risk and its macroeconomic consequences. This discussion provides an excellent example of the way that scholarly research in economics can be used to inform public policy, as well as an example of the interplay between improved data collection and advances in both theoretical understanding and regulation of the economy.

In the fourth paper, "A Fistful of Dollars: Lobbying and the Financial Crisis," Deniz Igan, Prachi Mishra, and Thierry Tressel discuss another hypothesis about the reason for the failure of financial regulation to prevent the crisis; namely, the role of financial-sector lobbying in shaping regulatory policy. The paper undertakes an empirical analysis of the connection between lobbying by financial institutions and those institutions' mortgage lending; to do so, it constructs a unique, highly detailed data set that matches the lobbying activities of individual institutions (identifying the particular bills targeted by the lobbying) with a variety of information about their lending. They find that institutions that lobbied more about a specific set of issues (such as consumer protection in mortgage lending and underwriting standards) also differed in a number of dimensions in their mortgage lending: their loan-to-income ratios were higher, they securitized a larger fraction of the mortgages that they originated, and their mortgage portfolios grew more rapidly than in the case of institutions that lobbied less. The lobbying institutions also differed in their performance ex post: delinquency rates in 2008 were higher in the areas where these firms concentrated their lending, and the stock valuations of these firms were more sensitive to particular events during the crisis that changed public perceptions of financial-sector risk. These results suggest that lobbying may have contributed to—or at least has been strongly associated with—increased risk-taking by mortgage lenders that paved the way to the financial crisis. These provocative findings suggest that further study and closer monitoring of lobbying activities might contribute to reducing the risk of future crises of a similar nature.

Our final two papers present advances in general methods of macroeconomic analysis. In "Risk, Monetary Policy, and the Exchange Rate," Gianluca Benigno, Pierpaolo Benigno, and Salvatore Nisticò revisit a central issue in open-economy macroeconomics, the influence of monetary policy on exchange rates, with particular attention to the role of time-varying risk in exchange-rate determination. The view that time-varying risk premia are an important factor in the explanation of exchange-rate movements is a familiar one, owing to well-documented anomalies such as the failure of uncovered interest-rate parity to hold; but standard open-economy dynamic stochastic general equilibrium (DSGE) models do not allow for them (except perhaps as adhoc error terms added to the model's structural equations that are not actually connected to risk in the model), as a consequence of the linearization methods used for numerical analysis of the models. An important contribution of this paper is to show how time-varying risk premia can be rigorously incorporated into DSGE analysis through a higher-order perturbation analysis, which the authors show can be made surprisingly tractable under certain simplifying assumptions about the nature of volatility shocks. They illustrate their method by analyzing exchange-rate determination in a two-country DSGE model with nominal price rigidities, national monetary policies described by interest-rate rules, and stochastic volatility in the exogenous processes driving the economy. The exogenous stochastic volatility (which is in turn the source of the time-varying risk premia) is of several sorts: the paper considers the effects of stochastic volatility in productivity, in the central bank's inflation target, and in a transitory error term in the central bank's reaction function. The paper provides new empirical evidence on the effects of each of these types of volatility shocks on exchange rates, and shows that the proposed theoretical model can be specified in a way that yields predictions broadly in conformity with this evidence. It also clarifies the role that particular aspects of the model and of its quantitative specification play in matching particular aspects of the empirical evidence. This paper marks an important advance in open-economy modeling, and is likely to provide a foundation for much further work in this vein.

Finally, our sixth paper, "Unemployment in an Estimated New Keynesian Model," by Jordi Galí, Frank Smets, and Rafael Wouters, extends a standard empirical monetary DSGE model to include an explicit account of variations in the rate of unemployment, and not simply variations in the aggregate labor input, represented as the labor supply of a representative household, as in the first generation of empirical DSGE models. The authors propose a particular, fairly simple model of unemployment determination that allows unemployment to be introduced into the model without greatly increasing the number of variables of the model or its complexity in other respects, and show that estimation of the model with this addition (and requiring it to fit an additional time series, namely unemployment) does not reduce the consistency of the model with aggregate time series. As well as incorporating unemployment as an additional macroeconomic variable, this extension of the standard model can potentially resolve a challenging identification issue. While the standard DSGE model cannot separately identify labor supply shifts from changes over time in the market power of labor despite their very different welfare implications, the authors' approach can do so thanks to the existence of an additional state variable, unemployment, that is differently affected by the two types of disturbances. The authors find that variations in market power do not contribute much to variations in real GDP (contrary to the results of Smets and Wouters for the model without unemployment), but they do find that variations in market power in the labor market are a significant source of secular movements in both unemployment and the inflation rate. The paper's new approach also yields important new measures of variation over time in both potential output and the natural rate of unemployment—two very controversial quantities to measure which are, however, of fundamental importance both for understanding business-cycle dynamics and for assessment of the appropriate stance of stabilization policy—and new evidence on the role of demand as opposed to supply factors in accounting for business cycles. The new model and the account of historical business fluctuations that it contributes are likely to provide the new benchmark for further quantitative analysis of this crucial set of issues.

Finally, the authors and the editors would like to take this opportunity to thank Jim Poterba and the National Bureau of Economic Research for their continued support for the NBER *Macroeconomics Annual* and the associated conference. We would also like to thank the NBER conference staff, particularly Rob Shannon, for his usual excellent organization and support. Financial assistance from the National Science Foundation is gratefully acknowledged. Neil Mehrotra and Dmitriy Sergeyev provided invaluable help in preparing the summaries of the discussions. And last but far from least, we are grateful to Helena Fitz-Patrick for her invaluable assistance in editing and producing the volume.

Endnote

For acknowledgments, sources of research support, and disclosure of the authors' material financial relationships, if any, please see http:// www.nber.org/ chapters/c12403 .ack.

Abstracts

1 Natural Expectations, Macroeconomic Dynamics, and Asset Pricing

Andreas Fuster, Benjamin Hebert, and David Laibson

How does an economy behave if (1) fundamentals are truly hump-shaped, exhibiting momentum in the short run and partial mean reversion in the long run, and (2) agents do not know that fundamentals are hump-shaped and base their beliefs on parsimonious models that they fit to the available data? A class of parsimonious models leads to qualitatively similar biases and generates empirically observed patterns in asset prices and macroeconomic dynamics. First, parsimonious models will robustly pick up the short-term momentum in fundamentals but will generally fail to fully capture the long-run mean reversion. Beliefs will therefore be characterized by endogenous extrapolation bias and procyclical excess optimism. Second, asset prices will be highly volatile and exhibit partial mean reversion—that is, overreaction. Excess returns will be negatively predicted by lagged excess returns, P/E ratios, and consumption growth. Third, real economic activity will have amplified cycles. For example, consumption growth will be negatively auto-correlated in the medium run. Fourth, the equity premium will be large. Agents will perceive that equities are very risky when in fact long-run equity returns will co-vary only weakly with long-run consumption growth. If agents had rational expectations, the equity premium would be close to zero. Fifth, sophisticated agents—that is, those who are assumed to know the true model—will hold far more equity than investors who use parsimonious models. Moreover, sophisticated

agents will follow a countercyclical asset allocation policy. These predicted effects are qualitatively confirmed in US data.

2   House Price Booms and the Current Account
Klaus Adam, Pei Kuang, and Albert Marcet

A simple open economy asset pricing model can account for the house
price and current account dynamics in the G7 over the years 2001–2008.
The model features rational households, but assumes that households
entertain subjective beliefs about price behavior and update these using Bayes' rule. The resulting beliefs dynamics considerably propagate
economic shocks and crucially contribute to replicating the empirical
evidence. Belief dynamics can temporarily delink house prices from
fundamentals, so that low interest rates can fuel a house price boom.
House price booms, however, are not necessarily synchronized across
countries and the model is consistent with the heterogeneous response
of house prices across the G7 following the reduction in real interest
rates at the beginning of the millennium. The response to interest rates
depends sensitively on agents' beliefs at the time of the interest rate
reduction, which in turn are a function of the country-specific history
prior to the year 2000. According to the model, the US house price boom
could have been largely avoided if real interest rates had decreased by
less after the year 2000.

3   Risk Topography
Markus K. Brunnermeier, Gary Gorton, and Arvind Krishnamurthy

The aim of this paper is to conceptualize and design a risk topography
that outlines a data acquisition and dissemination process that informs
policymakers, researchers, and market participants about systemic risk.
Our approach emphasizes that systemic risk (1) cannot be detected
based on measuring cash instruments, for example, balance sheet items
or ratios such as leverage and income statement items; (2) typically
builds up in the background before materializing in a crisis; and (3) is
determined by market participants' endogenous response to various
shocks. Our measurement system asks that regulators elicit from market participants their (partial equilibrium) risk as well as liquidity sensitivities (our response indicator) with respect to major risk factors and
liquidity scenarios. General equilibrium responses and economy-wide
system effects can be calibrated using this panel data set.

4 A Fistful of Dollars: Lobbying and the Financial Crisis
Deniz Igan, Prachi Mishra, and Thierry Tressel

Has lobbying by financial institutions contributed to the financial crisis? This paper uses detailed information on financial institutions' lobbying and mortgage-lending activities to answer this question. We find that lobbying was associated with more risk-taking during 2000–2007 and with worse outcomes in 2008. In particular, lenders lobbying more intensively on issues related to mortgage lending and securitization (1) originated mortgages with higher loan-to-income ratios, (2) securitized a faster growing proportion of their loans, and (3) had faster growing originations of mortgages. Moreover, delinquency rates in 2008 were higher in areas where lobbying lenders' mortgage lending grew faster. These lenders also experienced negative abnormal stock returns during the rescue of Bear Stearns and the collapse of Lehman Brothers, but positive abnormal returns when the bailout was announced. Finally, we find a higher bailout probability for lobbying lenders. These findings suggest that lending by politically active lenders played a role in accumulation of risks and thus contributed to the financial crisis.

5 Risk, Monetary Policy, and the Exchange Rate
Gianluca Benigno, Pierpaolo Benigno, and Salvatore Nisticò

In this research, we provide new empirical evidence on the importance of time-varying uncertainty for the exchange rate and the excess return in currency markets. Following an increase in monetary policy uncertainty, the dollar exchange rate appreciates in the medium run, while an increase in the volatility of productivity leads to a dollar depreciation. We propose a general-equilibrium theory of exchange rate determination based on the interaction between monetary policy and time-varying uncertainty aimed at understanding these regularities. In the model, the behavior of the exchange rate following nominal and real volatility shocks is consistent with the empirical evidence. Furthermore, we show that risk factors and interest-rate smoothing are important in accounting for the negative coefficient in the UIP regression.

6 Unemployment in an Estimated New Keynesian Model
Jordi Galí, Frank Smets, and Rafael Wouters

We reformulate the Smets-Wouters (2007) framework by embedding the theory of unemployment proposed in Galí (2011b, 2011c). We estimate the resulting model using postwar US data, while treating the unemployment rate as an additional observable variable. Our approach overcomes the lack of identification of wage markup and labor supply shocks highlighted by Chari, Kehoe, and McGrattan (2008) in their criticism of New Keynesian models, and allows us to estimate a "correct" measure of the output gap. In addition, the estimated model can be used to analyze the sources of unemployment fluctuations.

1

Natural Expectations, Macroeconomic Dynamics, and Asset Pricing

Andreas Fuster, *Harvard*
Benjamin Hebert, *Harvard*
David Laibson, *Harvard and NBER*

I. Introduction

Most macroeconomic models assume that people know the true model of the economy—that is, rational expectations. In this paper, we follow a different tradition and assume that agents use simple prediction models that are estimated using historical data.[1] In other words, *agents adopt a parsimonious model that fits the available data.* In general, this parsimonious model will not nest the true model (though the true model may nest the parsimonious model). Following Fuster, Laibson, and Mendel (2010), we call the resulting beliefs *natural expectations*.[2] We assume that agents use simplified models because economists and noneconomists— statisticians, professional forecasters, and firms—regularly make such simplifications.

People use simple models for a wide range of good reasons. Simple models are easier to understand, easier to explain, and easier to employ. Simplicity also reduces the risks of overfitting, which is the reasoning that underlies many formal model selection criteria. Whatever the mix of reasons—pragmatic, psychological/suboptimal, and statistical— economic agents usually *do* use simple models to understand economic dynamics.

We study a class of parsimonious models that generates empirically observed patterns in asset prices and macroeconomic dynamics. To illustrate this claim, we study an economy in which fundamentals are hump-shaped, exhibiting momentum in the short run and partial mean reversion in the long run. Hump-shaped dynamics are controversial in the sense that economists continue to debate whether such cyclical dynamics are present in aggregate fluctuations.[3] This debate is consistent with our claims, since we only want to argue that hump-shaped dynamics are plausible. Hump-shaped dynamics match the point estimates from ARIMA (autoregressive integrated moving average) models of various economic time series, though standard errors are large enough that the data do not rule out alternative dynamics.[4]

We will ask: How would an economy behave if (1) fundamentals were truly hump-shaped, and (2) agents adopted a parsimonious model of the fundamental process, fit to the available data?[5] We embed these two assumptions—hump-shaped fundamentals and natural expectations—in a consumption/asset-pricing model.[6] We use a habit model to generate slow adjustment in consumption; however, as we combine habit formation with CARA (constant absolute risk aversion) preferences (Alessie and Lusardi 1997), these habits do not produce countercyclical variation in risk premia.[7]

The following five sets of results emerge from our analysis. Some of these results are comparative: how does equilibrium behavior in an economy with natural expectations compare to equilibrium behavior that would have arisen if agents knew the true model—that is, if agents had rational expectations?

First, simple models robustly pick up the short-term momentum in fundamentals but often fail to capture the full extent of long-run mean reversion. Under natural expectations, beliefs will often be characterized by endogenous extrapolation bias in levels. Forecasts about fundamentals will be too persistent, such that beliefs will be too optimistic in good times and too pessimistic in bad times, relative to the rational expectations benchmark.

Second, under natural expectations, asset prices will be highly volatile (LeRoy and Porter 1981; Shiller 1981) and exhibit partial mean reversion—that is, overreaction. Excess returns will be negatively predicted by lagged excess returns (Fama and French 1988b; Poterba and Summers 1988), price/earnings ratios (Campbell and Shiller 1988b, 2005), and consumption growth. Excess returns will be positively predicted by lagged "cay," a measure of transitory deviations of consumption from wealth (Lettau and Ludvigson 2001).[8]

Third, real economic activity will have amplified cycles. For example, consumption growth will be positively auto-correlated in the short run and *negatively* auto-correlated in the medium run. Consumption growth will be weakly negatively predicted by lagged excess returns and P/E (price/earnings) ratios.

Fourth, the equity premium will be large. Agents will perceive that equities are very risky when in fact long-run equity returns will co-vary only weakly with long-run consumption growth. The covariance of consumption growth and asset returns will be close to zero over short-run horizons (because of slow adjustment in consumption), it will be higher over medium-run horizons (as consumption catches up with asset prices), and it will fall again over long-run horizons (as asset prices and consumption both mean revert). If agents had rational expectations, the equity premium in our economy would be close to zero.

Fifth, sophisticated agents—that is, those who are assumed to know the true model—will hold far more equity than investors with natural expectations. Moreover, sophisticated agents will be "value" investors, following a countercyclical investment policy.

These five sets of predicted effects are qualitatively confirmed in US data. An economy in which agents estimate simple models—for example, an AR(10) in earnings growth, when the data-generating process is assumed to be AR(40)—generates simulated behavior that quantitatively matches the point estimates observed in US data. However, the moments that we study have large standard errors because of the limited span of available data. It is therefore not possible to reject classical models in which excess returns are unpredictable and consumption is consistent with rational expectations.

The body of the paper is divided into six sections; appendices are used for derivations. Section II discusses the econometric and psychological motivations for natural expectations, as well as the related literature. Section III solves and calibrates a consumption-based asset pricing model, which generalizes the model in Fuster, Laibson, and Mendel (2010). Section IV reports model simulations and compares these simulations to the empirical evidence from the United States. We focus on eight moments that summarize the key properties of the model. We show that a parsimonious version of the model matches these moments. Section V discusses the behavior of sophisticated agents. Section VI concludes and identifies directions for future work.

II. The Appeal of Simple Models

The premise of our approach to understanding macroeconomic and financial dynamics is that economic agents tend to make forecasts based on statistical or mental models that are reasonable given the data available to them, but "too simple" to fully capture the long-term dynamics of many economic time series.

In this section, we motivate our assumptions both on statistical and psychological grounds, though we believe that the psychological motivations are more important.[9] We will also discuss how simple models lead agents to overestimate the persistence of shocks when the true process is hump-shaped. Finally, we summarize evidence from different settings that are related to our approach.

A. Statistical Perspective

Choosing the right model to forecast an economic time series is by no means a trivial task, and there is no single generally accepted way of doing so. When choosing how many parameters to include, a modeler faces a trade-off between improving the fit of the model in-sample and the risk of overfitting the available data, which may result in poor out-of-sample forecasts. A number of formal statistical criteria have been proposed to formalize the trade-off between fit and parsimony. The best-known and most popular ones are the Akaike Information Criterion (AIC) and the Schwarz or Bayesian Information Criterion (BIC).[10] These criteria are both asymptotically optimal, but in different ways. If the set of candidate models is not presumed to contain the true model (perhaps because the true model is of infinite dimension), the AIC is *efficient* in that it will select the candidate model with minimum mean squared error distribution with probability 1 as the sample size grows to infinity. If instead the true model is among the set of candidate models, the BIC will select it with probability 1 asymptotically (the BIC is *consistent*), while the AIC will tend to result in an overparametrized model (Hannan 1980).

When the likelihood function is Gaussian, the two criteria can be written as follows:

$$\text{AIC} = \ln(\hat{\sigma}^2) + \frac{2k}{T}$$

$$\text{BIC} = \ln(\hat{\sigma}^2) + \frac{\ln(T) \cdot k}{T},$$

where $\hat{\sigma}^2$ is the error variance estimated by maximum likelihood, k is the number of parameters (including the constant), and T is the number of observations. One is supposed to pick the model with the smallest value of the preferred criterion. Both criteria trade off fit and parsimony: as k increases, $\hat{\sigma}^2$ decreases, but the second ("penalty") term increases. Generally, the BIC imposes a larger penalty for increasing the number of parameters, and thus will tend to select models with fewer parameters than the AIC. A relatively recent literature based on extensive simulation studies has argued that a version of the AIC corrected for small sample sizes, the AICc, tends to perform well (in various senses) and, relative to the AIC, reduces the likelihood of overfitting.[11]

It is not clear which criterion should be preferred. If one believes that the true model is among the candidate models, and as $T \to \infty$, there seems to be a clear case for the BIC. Yet, in practice, these conditions are rarely met, and it appears that which criterion is preferred is to some extent a matter of taste.[12] While strictly speaking, each criterion picks one model, a reasonable pragmatic strategy would be to choose a model that is close to the best model according to different criteria, or perhaps to make forecasts based on averaging the predictions of different models.

For the purpose of our work, what matters is whether a modeler who is presented with a time series of length equal to the typical macroeconomic time series (e.g., 250 quarters) and who relies on (one of) these information criteria will generally pick a model that correctly captures the properties of the data-generating process. In particular, we are interested in time series that feature hump-shaped dynamics, in the sense that they are characterized by momentum (positive autocorrelation in growth rates) in the short run but (partially) revert back to the mean in the long run. To our knowledge, this is not a question that has been formally analyzed in the existing literature, so we now present some suggestive evidence from Monte Carlo simulations to shed light on this question.

Assume that the true data-generating process is an ARIMA(0, 1, 16), and for simplicity assume that the modeler considers univariate models of the ARIMA(p, 1, 0) and ARIMA(0, 1, q) classes. The process we study has a hump-shaped impulse response function with a long-term persistence of 0.5.[13] We draw 100 samples of length 255 (which is the number of observations we will use in the estimation of the aggregate earnings process) and estimate AR(p, 1, 0) models for $p = 1, \ldots, 25$ and MA(0, 1, q) models for $q = 4, 8, 12, 16, 20, 24$.[14]

In our 100 simulations, the AICc selects an AR(1), AR(2), or AR(3) in 60 cases; the BIC does so in all cases. The average estimated long-term persistence of a shock implied by the AICc-selected model equals 1.02, and is below 0.8 only in 25% of cases. For the BIC-selected model, it is never below 1. Thus, in the vast majority of cases, a modeler who considers this set of candidate models and selects based on AICc or BIC would grossly overestimate the persistence of shocks to the process. Note that while it appears difficult to capture the mean-reversion in a sample of this length, it is not impossible: for instance, the implied persistence from an estimated MA(16) (the true model order) averages 0.56 and is below 0.8 in 88% of cases.[15] Yet the improvement that the MA(16) brings in terms of fit relative to, for example, an AR(2) rarely justifies the large increase in the number of parameters (a MA(q) with $q \geq 16$ is selected nine times by the AICc).

In large part, the difficulty that these models have in detecting mean reversion seems due to the relatively short sample length. If we repeat the same exercise but with 1,255 observations instead of 255, the AICc selects the MA(16) in 75% of cases, and the mean long-term persistence of a shock estimated by the preferred model decreases to 0.53; that is, very close to the actual persistence of the data-generating process.

We have conducted similar simulations with other data-generating processes. With somewhat less complicated hump-shape patterns, the AICc often does well in terms of selecting a model that gets the long-term persistence approximately right, while the BIC tends to select low-order models (with 5 coefficients or less) in the vast majority of cases. Overall, our simulations suggest that even a sophisticated modeler who goes through the trouble of estimating and comparing a wide range of candidate models may well end up with a model that vastly overestimates the long-term persistence of shocks.[16] To be clear, we are not claiming that it is impossible to find a model that gets the long-term dynamics right. One could use more sophisticated methods than ARIMAs (e.g., multivariate models), add more ex ante imposed structure to the model, or attempt to form unbiased estimates of long-term persistence at the expense of one-period-ahead forecast accuracy. We argue that these practices are neither straightforward nor widespread.

So far, we have discussed the model selection problem under the assumption that the stochastic process of interest is stable over time and that economic agents should use all the historical data that is available to them in estimating a model, and weigh all observations equally. However, it is possible that the properties of the data-generating process change over time, and so it may well be optimal for an agent to down-weight or discard old data.[17] While we will not attempt a normative analysis of optimal model selection under the possibility that parameters of the data-generating process (such as the mean growth rate of earnings) change over time, it seems intuitive that in such a world, agents would tend to use shorter effective samples to estimate their models, and this would increase the likelihood of picking a low-order model.

B. *Psychological Perspective*

Psychological factors also lead agents to adopt simple models. In fact, we believe that psychological considerations are far more important in driving preferences for simplicity than the statistical considerations reviewed before. Even *if* nonparsimonious, complicated models were statistically optimal, real people would probably not adopt such models.

Constraints on memory and cognition make it difficult for agents to work with complicated models, leading decision makers to adopt simplifications and heuristics (e.g., Tversky and Kahneman 1974; Gigerenzer and Goldstein 1996; Gabaix et al. 2006; Gabaix 2011). Simple models are relatively easy to comprehend, use, revise, and explain. Complicated "black-box" models are viewed with a degree of suspicion; programmers themselves are boundedly rational, so high-dimensional computational models often have subtle programming errors and other unintended or poorly understood features that make such models unreliable. Even when people do use complicated models, the conclusions are rarely taken at face value and usually tempered with "common sense" about how the world works.

The "psychological" motives for simplicity can also be interpreted through a rational lens. If complicated models tend to induce confusion or mistakes, then simple models may be the lesser of two evils. Complicated models also engender high costs for agents with costly cognition,[18] providing another rational explanation for choosing simple models.

There are also specific psychological biases that reinforce our approach. The heuristic of representativeness (Kahneman and Tversky 1973; Tversky and Kahneman 1974) leads people to believe that small samples are representative of the world at large. Representativeness has two implications for our analysis. First, recent observations are viewed as representative of the future. Thus representativeness leads agents to underestimate the degree of mean reversion (Kahneman and Tversky 1973).

Second, representativeness leads agents to mistakenly believe that the properties of population samples will be reliably observed in small samples (e.g., Rabin 2002; Rabin and Vayanos 2010). This is sometimes referred to as the (psychological) law of small numbers. Agents mistakenly believe that the ergodic properties of a time series can be inferred by studying a short subsample (e.g., 20 years of data). In addition, a willingness to rely on short subsamples implicitly reinforces the tendency to rely on models without long lag effects.

The availability heuristic (Tversky and Kahneman 1973) also reinforces our modeling approach. Availability leads people to overweight information that is easily accessible and salient. Hence, availability bias also implies that people will excessively overweight recent data and underweight data from the distant past.

Some observers have argued that related biases play an important role in driving aggregate dynamics. For instance, Reinhart and Rogoff (2009) document how investors time and time again fall prey to the belief that "this time is different" and that this belief causes recurrent financial crises. Relatedly, Shiller (2005) points out the lure of "new era" stories and how they are associated with episodes of bubbles in asset markets. Barberis (2010) notes that overextrapolation of past price changes may have been an important psychological driving force during the run-up to the Great Recession. We now turn to a large body of related economic research.

C. Additional Related Literature

There is a small but growing body of evidence on deviations from rational expectations. For instance, lab experiments in which subjects forecast financial or other time series find that extrapolative expectations or "trend following" provide a good description of observed beliefs (De Bondt 1993; Hey 1994) and may be a driving force behind the bubbles that are observed in asset-market experiments (Haruvy, Lahav, and Noussair 2007; Hommes et al. 2008). On the other hand, Dwyer et al. (1993) finds that subjects' forecasts of a random walk (in which growth has no persistence) do not deviate systematically from the rational expectations forecast. This is consistent with our model, where extrapolation is not "baked in" but depends on the predictions generated by estimating simple models on the available data.

In field data, a number of papers have argued that asset allocation choices are affected by extrapolation of recent price appreciation (Chevalier and Ellison 1997; Sirri and Tufano 1998; Benartzi 2001; Choi et al. 2004, 2009; Benartzi and Thaler 2007; Chalmers and Reuter 2009; Previtero 2010; Malmendier and Nagel 2011). One could argue that biases in expectations have little or no effect on asset prices because investors with biased beliefs are relatively poor, while wealthier market participants may be more rational. However, Vissing-Jorgensen (2003) documents that at the peak of the market in 2000–2001, even wealthy investors expected continuously high stock returns. Bacchetta, Mertens, and van Wincoop (2009) conduct a similar exercise and find that, in several asset markets, (institutional or wealthy individual) investors' expectational errors about future returns are predicted by the same variables that predict excess returns.

One might alternatively think that the expectations held (and made public) by financial analysts, which may have a strong influence on asset prices, are not biased. However, De Bondt and Thaler (1990) argue that security analysts overreact and make earnings-per-share forecasts that are too extreme.[19] Most of the studies on analyst forecasts look at relatively short-run forecasts, while our model mostly has implications for long-run forecasts. Bulkley and Harris (1997) study five-year earnings forecasts for about 500 US companies and report results that are consistent with our model: (1) analysts appear to extrapolate past growth in earnings when forecasting future growth, even though there is pronounced negative serial correlation in earnings growth over five-year periods; and (2) analysts' forecasts and excess returns over the subsequent five years are significantly negatively correlated.[20] Chan, Karceski, and Lakonishok (2003) provide further evidence that there is little predictability of long-term earnings growth rates, but that investors and analysts behave as if recent growth rates were positive predictors of future growth.

A significant literature in behavioral finance has accumulated evidence on cross-sectional stock return patterns that are consistent with such biases in expectations having strong effects on prices: De Bondt and Thaler (1985, 1989) and Lakonishok, Shleifer, and Vishny (1994) are among the best-known examples of such work.[21] Baker and Wurgler (2007) document that empirical measures of investor sentiment predict cross-sectional return patterns and also aggregate returns.

Apart from stock markets, other asset markets may also be influenced by biased beliefs. For instance, Greenwood and Hanson (2010) document patterns in bond risk premia that can be explained by investors extrapolating recent returns or default rates. Periods of high returns on corporate bonds are followed by a decline in issuer quality and low or negative excess returns on corporate debt in a highly predictable manner. Also, biased (extrapolative) beliefs have been advanced as a key explanation behind the recent housing bubble as well as earlier boom-bust cycles (Abraham and Hendershott 1996; Muellbauer and Murphy 1997; Case and Shiller 2003; Gerardi et al. 2008; Goetzmann, Peng, and Yen 2009; Piazzesi and Schneider 2009; Glaeser, Gottlieb, and Gyourko 2010). Finally, Ball (2000) and Tortorice (2011) show that misspecified models can explain empirically observed inflation persistence and unemployment expectations, respectively.

A variety of "behavioral" models have been proposed to explain stock return patterns, including DeLong et al. (1990); Barberis, Shleifer, and Vishny (1998); Daniel, Hirshleifer, and Subrahmanya (1998); and Hong and Stein (1999). Closely related are models in which investors continuously update their belief about future dividend growth or other parameters. This learning, which can be interpreted as behavioral or fully rational (similar to our model), generates predictability in returns as well as excess volatility. Among the best-known papers in this literature are Barsky and DeLong (1993) and Timmermann (1993). While our approach is closely related to these earlier papers, most previous authors consider simpler setups (often partial equilibrium valuation models without consumption) to illustrate the consequences of biased beliefs or learning, and do not study the interrelation between asset prices and other macroeconomic variables. An exception to this, and similar in spirit to our exercise, is a paper by Cecchetti, Lam, and Mark (2000). They show that distorted beliefs about the growth rate of the aggregate endowment can generate high, volatile, and predictable excess returns on equity, as in the data.[22] Similarly, Lansing (2006), Choi (2006), and Adam and Marcet (2010) study economies where some or all investors hold extrapolative beliefs, or learn about the return process, in otherwise standard Lucas tree economies with CRRA (constant relative risk aversion) utility, and show that this can generate realistic asset price dynamics.

More generally, a large literature in macroeconomics and finance, surveyed by Sargent (1993), Evans and Honkapohja (2001, 2011), and Pastor and Veronesi (2009), assumes that agents are rational (in the sense that they form their beliefs in the statistically optimal way) but need to learn the relevant parameters of the reduced form equations governing the economy over time.[23] While the early papers in this literature mostly focused on whether expectations would ultimately converge to the rational expectations equilibrium, more recent work has considered what happens if agents have misspecified models or down-weight older data, and finds that this can generate additional volatility and persistence of shocks in asset prices and/or the economy (e.g., Branch and Evans 2007, 2010; Hong, Stein, and Yu 2007; Huang, Liu, and Zha 2009; Eusepi and Preston 2011). In these models, "misspecification" means that agents omit a relevant variable from their forecasting equation, while in our model, it means that they may not include enough lags of the variable they are trying to forecast.[24]

An alternative modeling approach assumes that agents evaluate different forecasting models' past performance in order to (probabilistically) select among these models. This approach is frequently used in the agent-based literature (for example, LeBaron, Arthur, and Palmer 1999; Tesfatsion and Judd 2006; De Grauwe 2010; LeBaron 2010). An advantage of such models, which are usually analyzed computationally, is that they generate heterogeneity in beliefs across agents, something that is not present in our model. Such heterogeneity allows, for instance, the study of wealth dynamics and trading volume.[25]

Finally, there is a very large literature that studies asset pricing and macroeconomic dynamics under the assumption of perfect rationality and knowledge of the economy's structure.[26] While basic rational models are rather unsuccessful in generating realistic asset pricing patterns, more elaborate versions can generate a high equity premium, volatile asset prices, and predictable excess returns. Perhaps the most successful and influential consumption-based models over the past fifteen years are (a) Campbell and Cochrane's (1999) habit model, which matches many of the main observed empirical asset pricing phenomena through countercyclical and (on average) high effective risk aversion; and (b) the "long-run risks" model by Bansal and Yaron (2004), who engage in an exercise somewhat similar to ours: they assume that the world is characterized by a driving process for which evidence is statistically rather weak (namely, a consumption growth process with a small predictable component as well as time-varying volatility) and study the implications for asset pricing (in their case, using Epstein-Zin-Weil preferences with an elasticity of intertemporal substitution above 1).

III. Consumption Model with Asset Pricing

We now illustrate our approach by characterizing equilibrium in an economy in which agents hold natural expectations. This is an extension of the model analyzed in Fuster, Laibson, and Mendel (2010).[27]

We study an open endowment economy with two assets. The first asset is foreign debt, b_t, which is borrowed at a fixed international (gross) interest rate R.[28] We introduce foreign debt since we do not want a mechanistic linkage between production and consumption. The second asset is a Lucas-style domestic equity tree, which generates a dividend, d_t, that is stationary in first differences. In other words, Δd_t follows an AR(n) process,

$$\Delta d_t = \rho_1 \Delta d_{t-1} + \ldots + \rho_n \Delta d_{t-n} + \sigma \varepsilon_t$$

where ε_t is an iid Gaussian shock with unit variance.[29] We assume that the equity tree must be held by domestic agents.[30] We will distinguish between the "true" data-generating process for dividends, and the perceived data-generating process for dividends. When the true data-generating process matches the perceived data-generating process, agents hold rational expectations. Our focus, however, is on cases in which the perceived data-generating process has fewer lags than the true data-generating processes. As discussed in Section II, this can occur for various reasons, and we will refer to this as "natural expectations."

Our timing conventions and wealth definitions follow. Period t is divided into the following sequential subperiods. We describe the model using a "quarterly" frequency, since this is the calibration that we will use, but the model can be calibrated for any period of observation.

1. On the first day of the quarter (January 1) households start with debt, b_t, and θ_{t-1} units of claims to the risky asset.

2. Time passes and production occurs from January 1 to March 31. Households make no additional choices until the end of the quarter: March 31.

3. At the end of the quarter (March 31) the dividend of the equity tree is realized and paid to households: d_t per unit of claim. So each household receives $\theta_{t-1} d_t$ units of output.

4. The tree is priced (ex-dividend): p_t per unit of claim (where output units are the numeraire). So households can sell the tree for $\theta_{t-1} p_t$ units of output.

5. Wealth, w_t, is measured at the end of the quarter,

$$w_t = -Rb_t + \theta_{t-1} d_t + \theta_{t-1} p_t.$$

Wealth is measured after production has occurred in the period but *before* consumption is chosen.

6. Consumption is chosen: c_t.

7. Asset allocation takes place: agent buys θ_t units of equity at price p_t.

8. End-of-quarter debt, after these transactions, is

$$b_{t+1} = c_t + \theta_t p_t - w_t.$$

9. Households start the next quarter (beginning on April 1, which is period $t + 1$), with this level of debt.

Period $t + 1$ continues and the cycle of subperiods restarts.

A.   Preferences and the Bellman Equation

We have two desiderata for preferences. We want preferences that generate a closed form solution. We also want preferences—or technology—that will generate slow aggregate adjustment in consumption *without* assuming procyclical risk tolerance. For evidence on the slow adjustment of consumption when responding to wealth shocks, see Dynan and Maki (2001), Gabaix and Laibson (2002), Parker (2001), and Carroll, Sommer, and Slacalek (2011).

Motivated by these goals, we use exponential preferences (e.g., Caballero 1990) with habits, as introduced by Alessie and Lusardi (1997):

$$u(c_t, c_{t-1}) = -\frac{1}{\alpha} \exp(-\alpha[c_t - \gamma c_{t-1}]).$$

The parameter $\gamma \in [0, 1]$ reflects the strength of the habit. As we show in the following, in this formulation habits only serve to slow down consumption adjustments. If we did not include habits, our model would imply counterfactually rapid adjustment in consumption. Our habits are not operating as in Campbell and Cochrane (1999), where the habit is constructed in a way that generates countercyclical relative risk aversion.

Utility flows are weighted with discount factor δ, so that lifetime utility is given by:

$$\sum_{s=0}^{\infty} \delta^s u(c_{t+s}, c_{t+s-1}).$$

Lifetime utility is maximized with respect to the dynamic budget constraints summarized earlier. Here is the decentralized Bellman equation, which includes the state variables that we have already introduced as well as the vector of historical dividends, $\vec{d}_t$:

$$V(c_{t-1}, w_t, p_t, \vec{d}_t) = \sup_{\theta_t, c_t} u(c_t, c_{t-1})$$

$$+ E_t[\delta V(c_t, (w_t - c_t - \theta_t p_t)R + \theta_t(d_{t+1} + p_{t+1}), p_{t+1}, \vec{d}_{t+1})],$$

since

$$w_{t+1} = (w_t - c_t - \theta_t p_t)R + \theta_t(d_{t+1} + p_{t+1}).$$

For now, we will not pin down the conditional expectation operator, E_t. It depends only on the perceived data-generating process for dividends. We will study the predictions of the model under rational expectations and a large set of specifications for natural expectations.

The social planner's Bellman equation (which eliminates the asset allocation issue and eliminates price-based wealth measurement) is the following:

$$V(c_{t-1}, b_t, \vec{d}_t) = \sup_{c_t} u(c_t, c_{t-1}) + E_t[\delta V(c_t, (c_t + Rb_t - d_t), \vec{d}_{t+1})],$$

since

$$b_{t+1} = c_t + Rb_t - d_t.$$

B. Value Functions, Policy Functions, and Asset Pricing

We first study the representative household's problem, since we here assume that the economy is populated by homogeneous households. In Section V, we introduce a zero measure of rational expectations agents and study their policy functions.

For the representative agent's problem, we can ignore the asset allocation decision as well as asset pricing. Appendix A shows that:[31]

$$c_t = \frac{\gamma}{R} c_{t-1} + \left(1 - \frac{\gamma}{R}\right) x_t - \psi, \tag{1}$$

where

$$x_t = \frac{R-1}{R}\left[-Rb_t + \sum_{s=0}^{\infty} \frac{E_t d_{t+s}}{R^s}\right]$$

$$\psi = \frac{1}{R-1}\left[\frac{1}{\alpha} \ln(R\delta) + \frac{\alpha}{2} Var_t(\Delta c_{t+1})\right].$$

This implies that consumption is a weighted average of lagged consumption and the (risk-neutral) annuity value of perceived future dividends, x_t, down-shifted by an additive constant ψ (a precautionary savings effect).

For the planner, the value function takes a simple form:

$$V(c_{t-1}, b_t, \vec{d}_t) = -\frac{R}{\alpha(R-1)} \exp(-\alpha[c_t - \gamma c_{t-1}]),$$

where c_t is given by equation (1).

To calculate the equilibrium price of the Lucas tree, we consider the asset-allocation problem (as opposed to the planner's problem). We then solve for the asset price that leads the representative agent to hold one unit of the equity tree. These calculations are provided in appendix B, where we show that the equilibrium price of the Lucas tree is given by:

$$p_t = \sum_{s=1}^{\infty} \frac{E_t d_{t+s}}{R^s} - \frac{R\alpha \times Var_t(\Delta c_{t+1})}{[1 - (\gamma/R)](R-1)^2}.$$

Appendix B also provides a closed form expression as a function of the dividend history. Note that this is not bounded below, since earnings are not bounded below in this arithmetic (exponential utility) model.

Using the asset pricing relationship it is possible to re-express the consumption function in terms of total wealth, $w_t = -Rb_t + d_t + p_t$. Here we are studying a representative agent economy so that $\theta_t = 1$ for all t:

$$c_t = \frac{\gamma}{R} c_{t-1} + \left(1 - \frac{\gamma}{R}\right) x_t - \psi$$

$$= \frac{\gamma}{R} c_{t-1} + \left(1 - \frac{\gamma}{R}\right)\left(\frac{R-1}{R}\right)\left[-Rb_t + d_t + p_t + \frac{R\alpha \times Var_t(\Delta c_{t+1})}{[1 - (\gamma/R)](R-1)^2}\right] - \psi$$

$$= \frac{\gamma}{R} c_{t-1} + \left(1 - \frac{\gamma}{R}\right)\left(\frac{R-1}{R}\right) w_t + \Lambda$$

where

$$\Lambda = \frac{\alpha}{2} \frac{Var_t(\Delta c_{t+1})}{R-1} - \frac{1}{R-1}\frac{1}{\alpha} \ln(R\delta).$$

We can rewrite the value function in the following simplified form (redefining the earlier value function notation):

$$V(c_{t-1}, w_t) = -\frac{R}{\alpha(R-1)} \exp(-\alpha[c_t - \gamma c_{t-1}]).$$

Relative risk aversion is given by:

$$CRRA = -\frac{wV_{ww}}{V_w}$$

$$= w\alpha\frac{\partial c_t}{\partial w_t}$$

$$= w\alpha\left(1 - \frac{\gamma}{R}\right)\left(\frac{R-1}{R}\right)$$

$$\simeq c\alpha\left(1 - \frac{\gamma}{R}\right).$$

C. Calibration

To match historical data, we assume that the quarterly risk free (world) interest rate is $R = 1.0025$, implying that the annualized (net) rate is 0.01. We set the product of the discount factor and the gross interest rate to unity: $\delta R = 1$. The (quarterly) habit parameter is set to $\gamma = 0.9$, implying a half-life of adjustment of about six quarters. Finally, we set the curvature of the utility function so that relative risk aversion (at initialization) is approximately four:[32]

$$\alpha = \frac{4}{d_0[1 - (\gamma/R)]}.$$

The curvature of the utility function only affects three of the moments that we study: the equity premium, the standard deviation of equity returns, and the standard deviation of consumption growth. Hence, this parameter is not important for most of what follows.

The stochastic driving process is exogenous capital income, which is calibrated using real capital income from the National Income and Product Accounts (NIPA).[33] We use capital income from the NIPA because it is seasonally adjusted (unlike corporate earnings) and is not artificially smoothed (like corporate dividends[34]). Figure 1 plots the natural log of real capital income at a quarterly frequency from 1947:1 to 2010:3.

Using this data, figure 2 plots the impulse response functions resulting from estimating a range of ARIMA(p, 1, 0) models, with $p = 1, 10, 20, 30, 40$. We will henceforth refer to these as AR(p) models, omitting the full notation ARIMA(p, 1, 0). Figure 2 reveals that the order of the model is critical in determining inferences about persistence. Low-order mod-

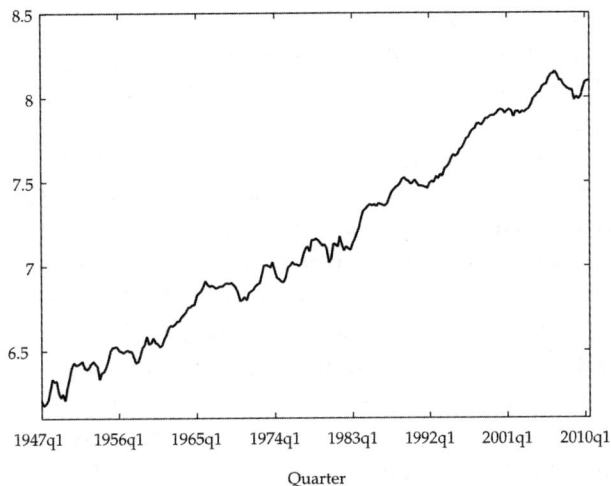

Fig. 1. Log of real net operating surplus ("earnings") of US private enterprises from 1947Q1 to 2010Q3.

Source: US NIPA (Bureau of Economic Analysis), table 1.10, line 12. Adjusted for inflation using the GDP deflator.

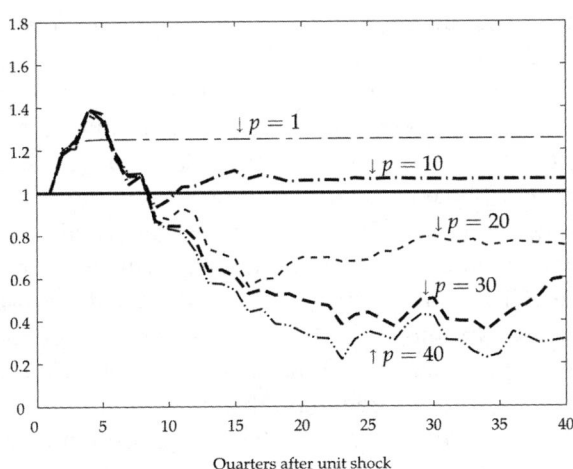

Fig. 2. Estimated impulse response function for earnings (in levels), for different AR(p) models of earnings growth.

els ($p = 1$ and 10) generate persistence estimates that are greater than or equal to 1. As the order of the model increases, estimated persistence falls dramatically. For an AR(40) model, estimated persistence after 40 quarters is about $1/3$.

For AR(p) models with $p \leq 20$, there is a substantial gap between the persistence implied by the estimated model and the persistence implied by what we are assuming to be the true model, the AR(40). Hence, parsimonious AR(p) models yield a form of extrapolation bias in *levels* (not growth rates). In other words, "low-order" AR(p) models imply that shocks are far more persistent than they are actually likely to be; low-order models imply excess optimism in good times and excess pessimism in bad times.

The associated coefficient estimates from the five AR(p) models in figure 2 are reported in table 1. There are few significant coefficients after the 10th lag.[35]

In what follows, we will always assume that the *true data-generating process* is the AR(40) estimated in the final column of table 1 and plotted as an impulse response function in figure 2. We are not loyal to this particular specification. It is merely a convenient way of capturing hump-shaped dynamics: short-run momentum and long-run partial mean reversion. We will assume that this is the true data-generating process because this case is interesting, and not because we believe that there is strong evidence for this specification. We only wish to argue that this hump-shaped process—the point estimate from the AR(40) case—is plausible.

The only remaining task is to specify the beliefs of the agents in the economy. We do not have strong views about this either. We will therefore study the beliefs generated by every AR(p) model with $p = 1, 2, \ldots,$ 40. In other words, we will assume that the true model is the AR(40) estimate in the last column of table 1, but that agents believe some AR(p) model that may not be the AR(40) model. We will study the properties of all of these belief assumptions: $p = 1, \ldots, 40$. When we assume $p = 40$, we are implicitly assuming that the agents know the true model; $p = 40$ is the rational expectations benchmark. When $p < 40$, we are assuming that agents use a simpler model than the true model.

The agents in our model act as if the model on which their beliefs are based is the true model, even though it is actually misspecified. This dogmatic belief in the wrong model is a limiting case of overconfidence (e.g., Lichtenstein, Fischhoff, and Philips 1982). An alternative approach, which would be more realistic and less tractable, would be to

Table 1

Estimated Coefficients from AR(p) Models of Earnings Growth

		AR(1)		AR(10)		AR(20)		AR(30)		AR(40)	
		Coeff.	t	Coeff.	t	Coeff.	t	Coeff.	t	Coeff.	t
Coeff. on lag	1	.201	3.27	.184	2.83	.189	2.80	.182	2.57	.211	2.79
	2			.032	.48	.016	.23	.011	.15	−.049	−.64
	3			.124	1.93	.112	1.64	.157	2.19	.197	2.57
	4			−.101	−1.57	−.080	−1.16	−.079	−1.11	−.128	−1.64
	5			−.149	−2.31	−.162	−2.36	−.191	−2.68	−.106	−1.35
	6			−.090	−1.41	−.028	−.40	−.045	−.62	−.088	−1.13
	7			.118	1.86	.063	.90	.049	.68	.068	.87
	8			−.132	−2.04	−.172	−2.42	−.150	−2.03	−.207	−2.59
	9			.085	1.31	.043	.62	.041	.55	.076	.94
	10			−.013	−.20	.014	.21	−.051	−.69	−.083	−1.02
	11					−.016	−.23	−.020	−.27	−.005	−.06
	12					−.170	−2.48	−.151	−2.07	−.183	−2.32
	13					−.023	−.33	.004	.05	.033	.41
	14					−.010	−.15	−.032	−.43	−.064	−.82
	15					−.057	−.85	−.025	−.34	−.023	−.30
	16					.021	.31	−.025	−.35	−.059	−.75
	17					−.058	−.89	−.072	−.99	−.087	−1.12
	18					.088	1.34	.014	.19	.004	.05
	19					−.023	−.35	−.053	−.74	−.062	−.81
	20					−.091	−1.41	−.062	−.88	−.070	−.92
	21							−.006	−.08	−.006	−.08
	22							−.104	−1.48	−.134	−1.76
	23							.056	.81	.094	1.23
	24							−.040	−.58	−.054	−.70
	25							−.046	−.68	−.035	−.46
	26							−.060	−.90	−.088	−1.15
	27							.019	.29	.032	.41
	28							.047	.71	−.001	−.02
	29							−.020	−.31	−.011	−.15
	30							−.170	−2.62	−.214	−2.95
	31									.055	.74
	32									−.102	−1.39
	33									.056	.78
	34									−.099	−1.39
	35									.144	2.01
	36									−.141	−1.95
	37									−.015	−.21
	38									−.121	−1.71
	39									.086	1.20
Coeff. on lag	40									−.063	−.90
N		253		244		234		224		214	
Adjusted R^2		.037		.087		.087		.084		.074	
Root MSE		.025		.024		.023		.022		.023	
Persistence		1.252		1.062		.745		.548		.445	

Source: US National Income and Product Accounts (Bureau of Economic Analysis), table 1.10, line 12 (adjusted for inflation using the GDP deflator). Data is Log of Real Net Operating Surplus of US Private Enterprises from 1947Q1 to 2010Q3. MSE = mean squared error. "Persistence" is given by $1/(1 - \text{sum of AR coefficients})$.

assume that agents take the possibility of misspecification into account when making decisions (for such an approach, see the literature on robustness; e.g., Hansen 2007; Hansen and Sargent 2007, 2010).

IV.   Simulation and Empirical Evaluation

To characterize the qualitative predictions of our model, we begin by reporting two impulse response functions—one for asset returns and one for consumption—that summarize the key mechanisms in the model. We then describe eight empirical moments that enable us to quantitatively evaluate the model's predictions. These empirical moments characterize the joint evolution of asset prices and consumption. The moments are chosen to test the anomalous predictions that the model makes—for example, cyclical fluctuations in asset returns and consumption growth. We find that these anomalous predictions match the empirical evidence well. Specifically, when agents hold beliefs generated by an AR(p) process with $p \leq 20$, and unlike in the rational expectations benchmark, the model provides a good quantitative fit to the empirical moments.

A.   Impulse Response Functions

We begin by reporting the impulse response function for cumulative excess returns. In our economy with exponential (CARA, contstant absolute risk aversion) utility, the excess return is more naturally expressed as an "excess gain," g_t, which is defined as:

$$g_t = p_t + d_t - Rp_{t-1}. \tag{2}$$

Note that:

$$\frac{g_t}{p_{t-1}} = \frac{p_t + d_t - Rp_{t-1}}{p_{t-1}}$$

$$= \frac{p_t + d_t}{p_{t-1}} - R, \tag{3}$$

which is the standard definition of excess return, since R is the gross risk-free rate. We study g_t, without dividing through by scaling factor p_{t-1} since prices can fall below zero in our CARA economy (assuming no free disposal of negative earnings), so the usual definition of excess return (3) is not appropriate. Henceforth, we will refer to excess gains—

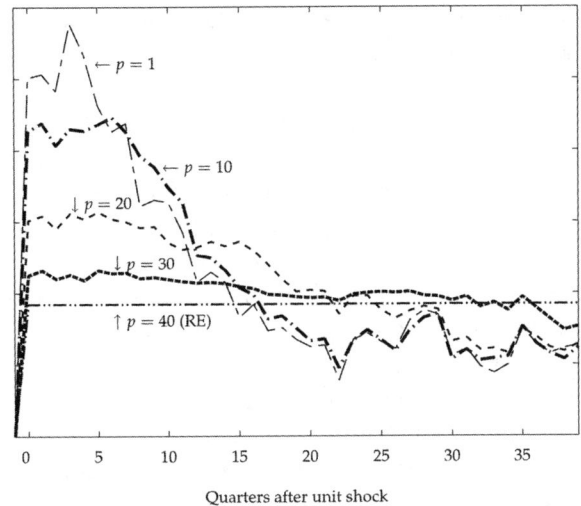

Fig. 3.   Cumulative impulse response function for gains, for different AR(p) models of earnings growth.

equation (2)—when studying asset returns in our model, but the reader should intuitively think of excess gains as excess returns, since excess gains are an appropriately rescaled version of excess returns.

Figure 3 reports the impulse response function for the "cumulative excess gain" following a positive (one-unit) shock to the earnings process at date zero. The cumulative excess gain is defined as:

$$\text{cumulative excess gain } t \text{ periods after the shock} = \sum_{s=0}^{t} g_s.$$

The cumulative excess gain is the CARA analog of the cumulative excess return from date zero to date t.

In figure 3, the impulse response function is reported for five simulated economies. In every case, the *true* process for earnings growth is the same—the AR(40) model described in Section III, subsection C. The economies differ only with respect to the *beliefs* that agents hold. Figure 3 analyzes economies in which agents generate forecasts using the following AR(p) models for earnings growth: $p = 1, 10, 20, 30, 40$.

Since the true data-generating process is an AR(40), let's start with the rational expectations case in which agents use the same model, an AR(40), to form beliefs. The impulse response function in this economy is the flat line in figure 3; that is, the cumulative excess gain jumps up at date zero and immediately plateaus. In the rational expectations case, an impulse at date zero does not forecast additional excess returns in periods after date zero.

When agents generate beliefs from an AR(p) model with $p < 40$, the natural expectations case, excess gains become more volatile and predictable. For example, when agents use an AR(1) model, they mistakenly infer that earnings impulses are highly persistent (see figure 2). This belief in persistence causes the asset price to jump up more than it should at date zero. Thereafter, the asset price tends to decline, and this decline is not foreseen by the agents. This decline is easy to see on the impulse response function, since there is only one impulse at date zero and no impulse at any other point in time. In a full-blown simulation of the economy, the stream of negative excess gains would be largely masked by subsequent shocks in the economy. Hence, the predictable negative excess gains would be hard to infer.

As the order of the estimated AR(p) model rises from $p = 1$ to $p = 40$, the impulse response functions look more and more like the rational expectations impulse response function. As p rises, the initial jump in the asset price becomes smaller, since agents with high-order models correctly anticipate more mean reversion in the true data-generating process. As p rises, the magnitude of the negative excess returns gets smaller.

Hence, models with low levels of p are characterized by a high degree of overreaction in asset prices. Models with p equal to or near 40 are characterized by little or no overreaction and little or no predictability of excess gains.

Figure 4 reports the impulse response function for consumption following a positive (one-unit) shock to the earnings process at date zero, and mimics the reporting conventions of figure 3. Specifically, the impulse response function is reported for five simulated economies. In every case, the true process for earnings growth is the AR(40) model described in Section III, subsection C, while agents generate forecasts using an AR(p) model. We again plot the cases $p = 1, 10, 20, 30, 40$.

Let's again start with the case in which agents have AR(40) beliefs, which is the rational expectations case. In this world, a shock at date zero would forecast a slow rise in consumption because the agents in our setting have a preference for slow adjustment, due to the habit term in their utility function. On the other hand, if the habit parameter, γ, were zero, the consumption series would jump up at date zero and immediately plateau.

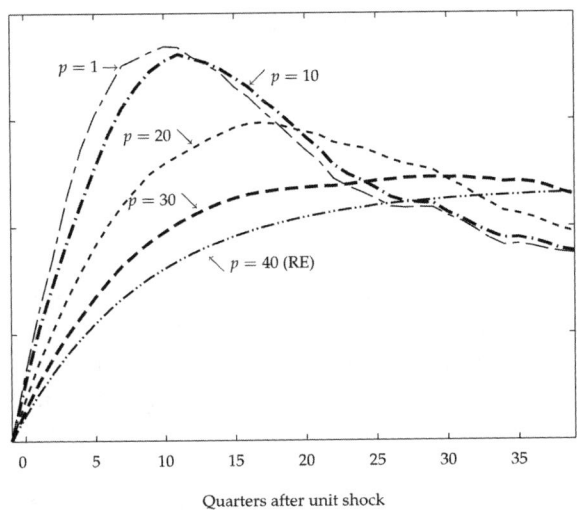

Fig. 4. Impulse response function for consumption, for different AR(p) models of earnings growth.

When agents have natural expectations (i.e., they hold beliefs generated from an AR(p) model with $p < 40$), the impulse response function for consumption tends to become hump-shaped. For example, when agents use an AR(1) model, they mistakenly infer that the earnings impulse is highly persistent, leading them to overreact to the earnings impulse (despite their preference for slow adjustment). About ten quarters after the initial impulse, they realize that they have gone too far and begin to reduce consumption. Over the long run, consumption falls from its peak level as households realize that their wealth is not as great as they initially thought (mirroring the negative excess gains in figure 3). Since the NPV (net present value) of these consumption responses must be the same across the p values—a consequence of the budget constraint—the long-run consumption asymptotes are different, reflecting payback for the short-run overconsumption.

As the estimated AR(p) model rises from $p = 1$ to $p = 40$ in figure 4, the impulse response functions again move toward the rational expectations benchmark. The initial growth in consumption becomes smaller, since agents that use high-p models believe in more mean reversion in the earnings process and therefore do not believe that the impulse to earnings has made them much more wealthy. Therefore, as p increases, the magnitude of the predictable fall in consumption also gets smaller.

In summary, models with low levels of p generate overreaction of consumption. Models with p equal to or near 40 are characterized by little or no overreaction and little or no eventual declines in consumption.

B.   Empirical Moments for Model Evaluation

We use the following eight moments to evaluate the empirical performance of our model under different assumptions. All data is annual, and goes from 1929 to 2010 (we use annual data so we can go further back in time, as the quarterly series in NIPA only starts in 1947). To distinguish this *annual* data from the *quarterly* observation frequency of the model/calibration, we use the new time subscript τ.

The moments reveal evidence for reversals that start around two years after an initial impulse. Our model predicts that these reversals will be delayed for two reasons. First, equity prices will not mean revert until agents start to notice a break between their forecasts and the realizations of earnings (see figure 2). For the simple models that we estimate, this divergence tends to occur about two years after an initial impulse. Second, consumption growth in the short-run is positively auto-correlated because of habits (see figure 4). The presence of habits delays the onset of mean reversion in consumption and slows down the process of mean reversion. Because it takes longer for the consumption dynamics to play out, we always extend the consumption analysis an extra year beyond the window of the asset price analysis. After an initial impulse at date τ, the asset price dynamics are measured from $\tau + 2$ to $\tau + 5$. The consumption dynamics are measured from $\tau + 2$ to $\tau + 6$. The key empirical moments we study are:

1. The correlation between excess returns of equity over the risk-free rate in year τ and cumulative excess returns from year $\tau + 2$ to year $\tau + 5$. This equals -0.22.[36]

2. The correlation between the ratio of S&P price at the end of year τ and average earnings over years $\tau - 9$ to τ (the P/E_{10} ratio) and excess returns from year $\tau + 2$ to year $\tau + 5$. This equals -0.38.[37]

3. The correlation between the one-year change in log consumption (i.e., $\ln(c_\tau) - \ln(c_{\tau-1})$) and cumulative excess returns from year $\tau + 2$ to year $\tau + 5$. This equals -0.30.[38]

4. The correlation between the P/E_{10} ratio and the change in log con-

sumption from year $\tau + 2$ to year $\tau + 6$ (i.e., $\ln(c_{\tau+6}) - \ln(c_{\tau+2})$). This equals -0.17.

5. The correlation between $\ln(c_\tau) - \ln(c_{\tau-1})$ and $\ln(c_{\tau+6}) - \ln(c_{\tau+2})$. This equals -0.25.

6. The mean annual excess return of equity over the risk-free rate (the "equity premium"). This equals 7.44%.

7. The standard deviation of annual excess return of equity over the risk-free rate. This equals 20.83%.

8. The standard deviation of $\ln(c_\tau) - \ln(c_{\tau-1})$. This equals 0.022.

While the directions and magnitudes of the correlations reported under (1) to (5) in the list are suggestive, one has to be careful with the interpretation: as investigated in the finance literature by Stambaugh (1999), Valkanov (2003), and others, predictive regressions in short samples and with overlapping data can yield biased coefficients, and standard statistical inference may not be valid.[39]

To get an idea of the statistical significance of our results as well as the magnitude of a potential bias, we conduct a series of bootstrap exercises (similar to, e.g., Nelson and Kim 1993). For moment (1), we draw repeatedly (with replacement) from the observed realization of excess returns under the assumption that excess returns are not serially correlated, and construct the measure of subsequent cumulative excess returns that we use in the empirical data. We then calculate the correlation between the two series and repeat this 10,000 times for samples of length 75 (corresponding to our empirical sample size), so we can construct a confidence interval under the null of independent returns. For moment (5), we instead assume one-period log consumption growth follows an AR(1) process.[40] We estimate this process and then simulate time series of consumption (of length equal to our empirical sample) by repeatedly drawing from the residuals. From this series, we construct the change in log consumption between years $\tau + 2$ and $\tau + 6$, and correlate it with the one-period change in log consumption. Again, this is repeated 10,000 times, and we construct confidence intervals based on the obtained correlations.

For moments (2) to (4), we proceed in a similar manner: for example, for (2) we assume and estimate an AR(1) process for P/E_{10} (accounting for the small-sample bias in the autoregression coefficient); we assume that excess returns are independently distributed (the null); and draw residual pairs under the null (with replacement), construct the

Table 2
Bootstrap Confidence Intervals (CI) under the Null of No Predictability

		Bootstrap		
Moment	US Data	Mean	90% CI	95% CI
(1) $\text{corr}(XR_\tau, XR_{\tau+2\to\tau+5})$	−.220	−.049	[−.249, .165]	[−.284, .206]
(2) $\text{corr}((P/E_{10})_\tau, XR_{\tau+2\to\tau+5})$	−.377	−.141	[−.432, .192]	[−.478, .249]
(3) $\text{corr}(\ln(c_\tau) - \ln(c_{\tau-1}), XR_{\tau+2\to\tau+5})$	−.297	−.009	[−.267, .254]	[−.313, .297]
(4) $\text{corr}((P/E_{10})_\tau, \ln(c_{\tau+6}) - \ln(c_{\tau+2}))$	−.167	−.022	[−.424, .388]	[−.493, .450]
(5) $\text{corr}(\ln(c_\tau) - \ln(c_{\tau-1}), \ln(c_{\tau+6}) - \ln(c_{\tau+2}))$	−.245	.008	[−.237, .257]	[−.283, .302]

Note: Sources for empirical moments and bootstrap procedures are described in the text.

predicted variable we use in the data (for a sample of equal length to our data), and estimate the correlation between the two series. We again repeat this 10,000 times and construct 90% and 95% confidence intervals for the correlation coefficient.

The results in table 2 show that the correlations (3) and (5) are outside of the 90% confidence interval constructed under the null, but not outside the 95% interval. The "long-horizon autocorrelation" of excess returns (1), as well as the correlation of P/E_{10} with subsequent excess returns (2), are not quite significant at 10%, while the correlation between P/E and subsequent consumption growth (4) is far from significant.[41]

These relatively "weak" results do not come as a surprise, as a large literature in finance has established that predictability patterns that had appeared highly statistically significant in the early (1980s) literature are much less significant once statistical complications are accounted for. That said, our use of annual rather than quarterly data (as is more common in the literature) presumably weakens our statistical power. Furthermore, there exist more sophisticated ways of testing for predictability, and overall the finance literature seems to have concluded that "despite complexities with statistical inference in return predictability regressions, it is difficult to reconcile the historical behavior of the US stock market without admitting some degree of predictability in excess returns" (Lettau and Ludvigson 2010, 620). Finally, even where we cannot reject the null hypothesis of no predictability, we certainly also cannot reject an alternative null with economically high predictability—the currently available data just do not allow us to know.

C.   Asset Return Predictability

For the next eight exhibits, we will illustrate the implications of the model for the full range of natural expectations cases. Specifically, beliefs about earnings are generated for all AR(p) models, for $p = 1, \ldots, 40$. As usual, we always assume that the true model generating earnings is an AR(40). The rational expectations case therefore coincides with the case $p = 40$; natural expectations correspond to the cases $1 \le p < 40$. It turns out that when p is between 10 and 20 the natural expectations model does a good job of matching the point estimates for the eight empirical moments.

In the exhibits that follow, we always study simulations with 328 periods of quarterly data, matching the duration of our available empirical data (annual US data since 1929). We then calculate the eight moments on these 328 simulated periods. We repeat this exercise 200 times and average the eight moments over these 200 (independent) simulations. We match the sample duration of our empirical data and the sample duration of our simulated data to make finite sample biases comparable across the empirical and simulated moments.

Figure 5 studies the correlation between excess returns in year τ and cumulative excess returns from year $\tau + 2$ to $\tau + 5$. The empirical correlation is −0.22. For low values of p, the simulated moment is about −0.3, rising to about −0.15 as p rises to 20. For the rational expectations case, $p = 40$, the correlation is approximately zero.[42]

Similarly, figure 6 studies the correlation between the P/E_{10} ratio at

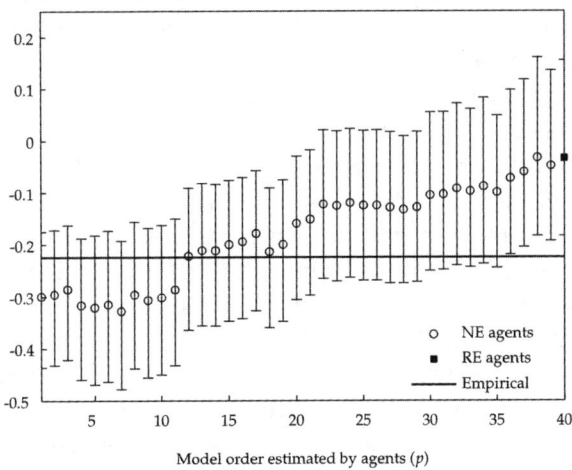

Fig. 5. Correlation of excess returns in year τ with cumulative excess returns for years $\tau + 2$ to $\tau + 5$, for different AR(p) models of earnings growth.

Notes: Circles depict mean correlations over 200 simulations of length equal to the empirical sample, while bars depict the 5th and 95th percentile of simulated values. "NE agents" use models with too few lags (AR(1) to AR(39)), while "RE agents" use the correct (AR(40)) model for earnings growth.

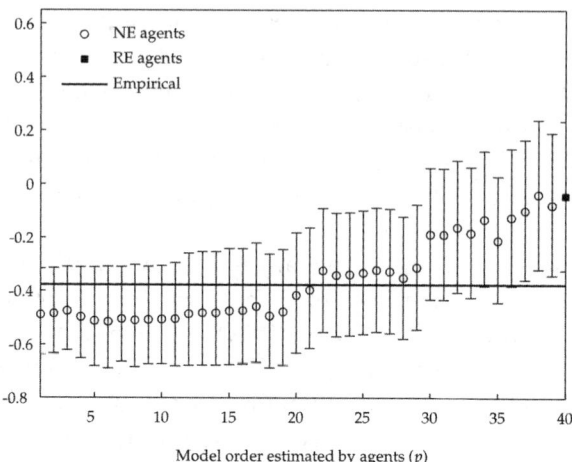

Fig. 6. Correlation of the P/E_{10} ratio in year τ with cumulative excess returns for years $\tau + 2$ to $\tau + 5$, for different AR(p) models of earnings growth.

Note: See notes for figure 5.

year-end τ and cumulative excess returns from year $\tau + 2$ to $\tau + 5$. The empirical correlation is −0.38. For low values of p, the simulated moment is about −0.5, rising to about −0.35 as p rises to 20. For the rational expectations case, $p = 40$, the correlation is again approximately zero.

The natural expectations model matches these moments, because good earnings news at date zero generates overreaction in asset prices (and increase the P/E_{10} ratio, since the denominator is relatively unresponsive given that it is averaged over 40 quarters). Over the next five years, some of that initial return will be reversed as agents discover that the good earnings news was not as persistent as they had anticipated.

In our model, Lettau and Ludvigson's (2001) *cay* variable is positively correlated with excess returns (for the same reason that P/E predicts future excess returns). The *cay* variable is constructed by identifying the co-integration residual between consumption and wealth: $cay_t = c_t - \Psi w_t$. In our model, a positive earnings shock raises asset values but does relatively little to consumption in the short run (due to slow adjustment). Thus a positive earnings shock causes *cay* to fall. Over the next five years, asset returns will tend to be low, due to unanticipated mean reversion in earnings. Hence, our model provides an alternative explanation for the observed positive correlation between *cay* and future excess returns.[43]

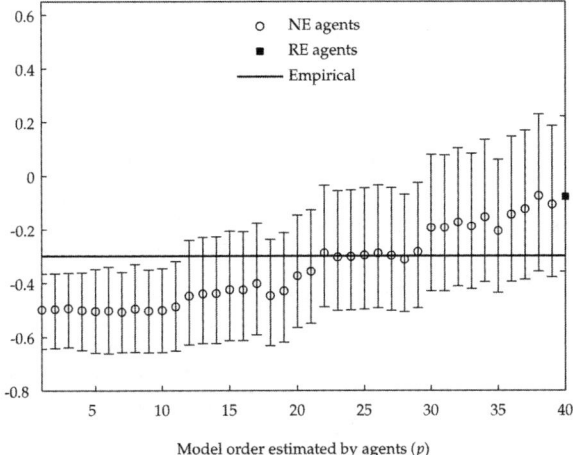

Fig. 7. Correlation of consumption growth in year τ with cumulative excess returns for years $\tau + 2$ to $\tau + 5$, for different AR(p) models of earnings growth.

Note: See notes for figure 5.

Figure 7 studies the correlation between consumption growth at year τ and equity returns from year $\tau + 2$ to $\tau + 5$. The empirical correlation is −0.30. For low values of p, the simulated moment is about −0.5, rising to about −0.35 as p rises to 20. For the rational expectations case, $p = 40$, the correlation is approximately zero.[44] A high level of lagged consumption growth is a proxy for a positive earnings shock (at that date or some preceding date). Natural expectations agents subsequently discover that the earnings news was not as persistent as they had anticipated, leading to below average excess gains/returns.

D.   Consumption Growth Predictability

Figure 8 studies the correlation between the P/E_{10} ratio at year-end τ and consumption growth from year $\tau + 2$ to $\tau + 6$. The empirical correlation is −0.17. For low values of p, the simulated moment is about −0.35, rising to about −0.15 as p rises to 20. For the rational expectations case, $p = 40$, the simulated correlation is approximately +0.25; this large positive value in the rational expectations case is due to habit formation and slow adjustment in consumption. For the natural expectations agents, $p < 40$, the negative correlations arise because unanticipated mean reversion in earnings swamps the effects of habit formation. Good earn-

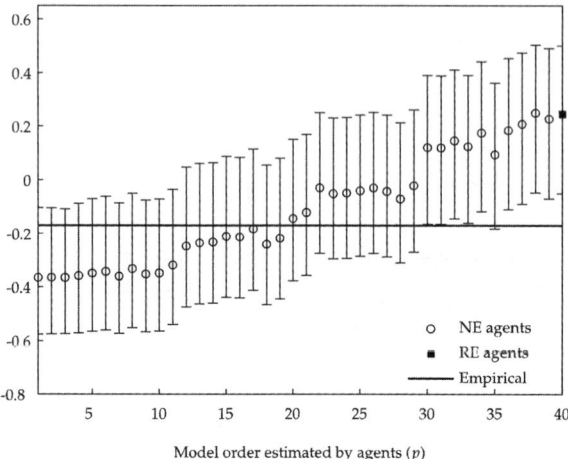

Fig. 8. Correlation of the P/E_{10} ratio in year τ with consumption growth from year τ + 2 to τ + 6, for different AR(p) models of earnings growth.

Note: See notes for figure 5.

ings news increases the P/E ratio, since the denominator is relatively unresponsive given that it is averaged over 40 quarters. Over the next five years, some of that initial return will be reversed as natural expectations agents discover that the earnings news was not as persistent as they had anticipated. This causes consumption to decline from year τ + 2 to τ + 6 for the natural expectations agents. This decline is strong enough to overcome the positive correlation that would otherwise arise because of habit formation. The consumption impulse response function (figure 4) illustrates the effects of the countervailing forces of unanticipated mean reversion and habit formation. For the natural expectations agents, unanticipated mean reversion offsets the pure effects of habit formation.

Figure 9 studies the correlation between consumption growth at year τ and consumption growth from year τ + 2 to τ + 6. The empirical correlation is −0.25. For low values of p, the simulated moment is about −0.3, rising to about −0.2 as p rises to 20. For the rational expectations case, p = 40, the simulated correlation is approximately +0.15; once again, the positive correlation in the rational expectations case is due to habit formation. The consumption of natural expectations agents ($p < 40$) initially overreacts to a positive earnings shock. Subsequently, they realize that the initial positive earnings shock was not as persistent as they had anticipated, which in turn causes consumption to decline

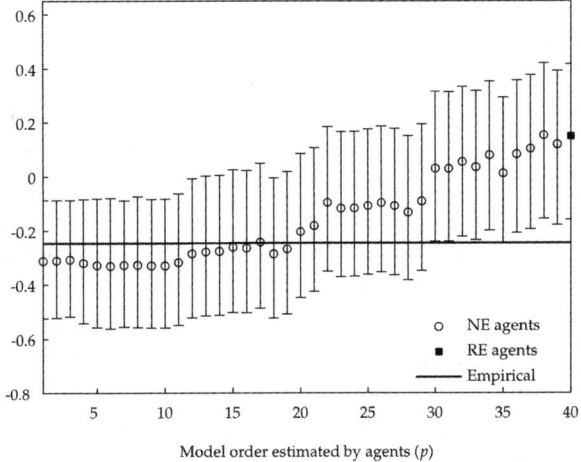

Fig. 9. Correlation of consumption growth in year τ with consumption growth from year $\tau + 2$ to $\tau + 6$, for different AR(p) models of earnings growth.
Note: See notes for figure 5.

from year $\tau + 2$ to $\tau + 6$. This decline is strong enough to overcome the positive correlation that would otherwise arise because of slow habit-based adjustment.

The fact that consumption growth is only relatively weakly predicted by lagged equity prices is a strength of our model.[45] Beeler and Campbell (2009) point out that Bansal and Yaron's (2004) long-run risks model is problematic because it implies much more predictability of consumption growth from lagged price/dividend ratios than is present in the data, while at the same time generating too little excess return predictability.[46] Beeler and Campbell also note the empirical evidence for medium-run mean reversion in the level of consumption, while the long-run risks model implies that all autocorrelations of consumption growth should be positive.

E. *The Equity Premium and Standard Deviations*

In the natural expectations economy, agents perceive that equities are much riskier than they actually are. Specifically, agents with natural expectations *believe* in asset-price dynamics that imply that long-run risk in equity markets, $cov(\Delta_h c_{t+h}, \tilde{R}_{t,t+h})/h$, is an order of magnitude larger than it actually is (for large h).[47] In our calibrated simulations this normalized covariance ($cov(\Delta_h c_{t+h}, \tilde{R}_{t,t+h})/h$) rises steeply for $h \leq 4$, and then falls as h rises beyond this horizon, generating a strong hump-shaped pattern. The normalized covariance falls at long horizons, because earnings mean revert more than anticipated by the agents in the economy. Mean reverting asset prices and mean reverting consumption jointly pull down the long-horizon (large h) normalized covariance. Actual US data also displays a hump-shaped pattern for the normalized covariance.[48] In contrast, in the *rational expectations* version of our economy (with or without habits), the normalized covariance rises monotonically with h, which is empirically counterfactual.

As explained earlier, agents believe that earnings innovations are highly persistent, equity returns arc highly volatile, and consumption growth will therefore co-vary strongly with equity returns in the long run. This leads agents with low values of p to require a high premium to hold equities. By contrast, when $p = 40$ (the rational expectations case) the equity premium is only 1/10 of 1%. Figure 10 plots the (annual) equity premium for different values of p as well as the historical premium of 7.4%.[49]

Finally, we are able to roughly match the equity premium without generating counterfactually high levels of asset return volatility (see figure 11) or consumption volatility (see figure 12). No matter what the

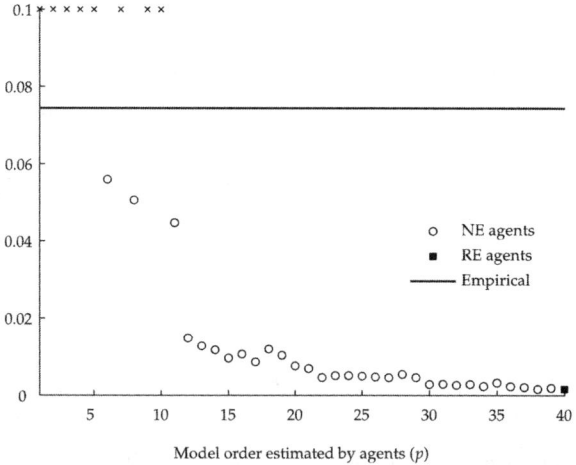

Model order estimated by agents (p)

Fig. 10. Equity premium (= mean excess return of equity over the risk-free rate) for different AR(p) models of earnings growth.

Notes: "x" denotes equity premia above 10%. "NE agents" use models with too few lags (AR(1) to AR(39)) while "RE agents" use the correct (AR(40)) model for earnings growth.

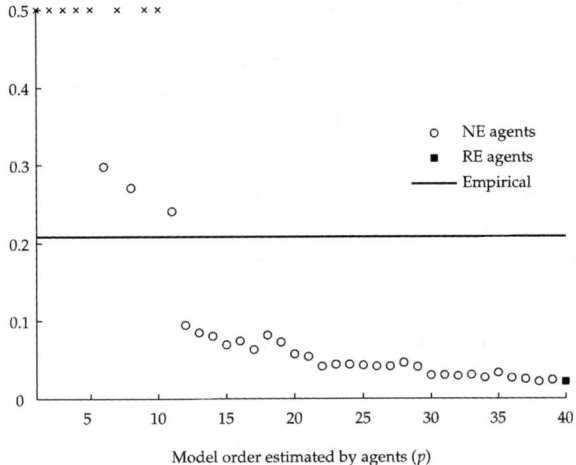

Fig. 11. Standard deviation of excess returns for different AR(p) models of earnings growth.

Notes: "x" denotes standard deviations above 50%. "NE agents" use models with too few lags (AR(1) to AR(39)) while "RE agents" use the correct (AR(40)) model for earnings growth.

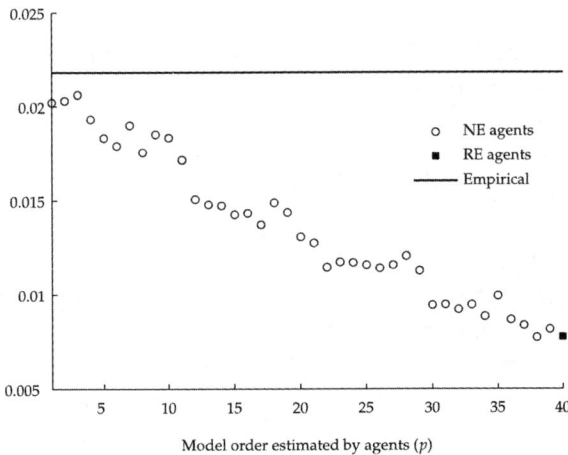

Fig. 12. Standard deviation of consumption growth for different AR(p) models of earnings growth.

order of the forecasting model, the standard deviation of consumption volatility is less than the historical standard deviation of consumption volatility. We do not see this as a substantial problem for two reasons. First, we can raise the standard deviation of consumption changes by lowering the (high) level of the habit: for example, set $\gamma = 0.75$ rather than the calibrated value of 0.9. Second, the post-War variation in consumption is substantially lower than the full-sample variation, which is used to generate the empirical line in the figure.

V.   Agents with Rational Expectations

Starting with the natural expectations economy just described (with $p < 40$), we now add a vanishingly small measure of agents with rational expectations. These "RE agents" know all of the coefficients in the true data-generating process for dividends—the AR(40) model. This perfect knowledge is meant to proxy for the more plausible assumption that these new agents have a high degree of sophistication relative to the agents with natural expectations.

We solve for the behavior of the RE agents, assuming that they have no effect on equilibrium prices. This *small mass* assumption is made for tractability. Future work should consider equilibria in which the rational agents are wealthy enough to influence equilibrium prices. The current analysis is a limit case of the results that will apply in that more realistic case.

Appendix C derives the optimal asset allocation and consumption policy functions of the RE agents. Later in this section, we present the optimal policy rules for the RE agent. Those policy rules take a large set of other objects as inputs. We now discuss and define those inputs before turning to the key result of this section.

Let Φ be the vector of true autoregressive coefficients in the earnings process, which as always is an AR(40) process. Let $\hat{\Phi}$ be the vector of autoregressive coefficients in the earnings process as perceived by the NE (natural expectation) agents. Let σ_ε be the true standard deviation of shocks to the dividend process. Let $\hat{\sigma}_c^2$ be the conditional variance of consumption changes as perceived by the NE agents. Let $e_{1,p} = [1\,0\,0\ldots0]'$ be a standard basis vector of length p. We define the following variables, which will appear in the policy functions:

$$\sigma_g = \frac{R}{R-1}\,\sigma_\varepsilon e'_{1,p}\left(I - \frac{1}{R}\hat{\Phi}\right)^{-1} e_{1,p}.$$

$$\mu = \frac{R\alpha}{[1 - (\gamma/R)](R-1)} \hat{\sigma}_c^2.$$

$$M = \frac{R}{R-1} e'_{1,p} \left[\Phi - \hat{\Phi}\left(I - \frac{1}{R}\hat{\Phi}\right)^{-1}\left(I - \frac{1}{R}\Phi\right)\right].$$

$$B = \frac{1}{2R[1 - (\gamma/R)]\alpha\sigma_g^2} \sum_{k=0}^{\infty} R^{-k}\hat{\Phi}'^k M'M\hat{\Phi}^k.$$

$$A' = \frac{2\mu}{R\sigma_g}\left(\frac{1}{2[1 - (\gamma/R)]\alpha\sigma_g} M + \sigma_\varepsilon e'_{1,p} B\hat{\Phi}\right)\left(I - \frac{1}{R}\hat{\Phi}\right)^{-1}.$$

$$\lambda = \left(1 - \frac{\gamma}{R}\right)\sigma_\varepsilon^2 e'_{1,p} Be_{1,p}$$

$$q = \frac{1 + 2\alpha\lambda}{2(R-1)[1 - (\gamma/R)]\alpha\sigma_g^2}\mu^2 - \frac{\mu\sigma_\varepsilon}{\sigma_g(R-1)} A'e_{1,p}$$

$$+ \frac{1}{2\alpha(R-1)[1 - (\gamma/R)]} \ln(1 + 2\alpha\lambda).$$

We can now describe the policy function of RE agents. We introduce a new variable, θ_t, which is the quantity of units of the Lucas tree held by an RE agent. By comparison, the quantity of units of the Lucas tree held by an NE agent is normalized to one. Hence, when $\theta_t > 1$, each RE agent holds more equities than each NE agent.

Theorem 1. For an agent with rational expectations, the optimal asset allocation, θ_t, is given by

$$\theta_t = \frac{R}{R-1}\frac{1}{\sigma_g}\left(\frac{\mu + M\Delta\vec{d}_t}{[1 - (\gamma/R)]\alpha\sigma_g} + \frac{2\mu\sigma_\varepsilon^2}{\sigma_g}e'_{1,p}Be_{1,p} - \sigma_\varepsilon A'e_{1,p} - 2\sigma_\varepsilon e'_{1,p}B\hat{\Phi}\Delta\vec{d}_t\right),$$

and the optimal consumption rule is given by:

$$c_t = \left(1 - \frac{\gamma}{R}\right)\left(\frac{R-1}{R}\right)w_t + A'\Delta\vec{d}_t + \Delta\vec{d}_t'B\Delta\vec{d}_t + q\right) + \frac{\gamma}{R}c_{t-1}.$$

The proof is provided in appendix C. The consumption policy rule implies that consumption is still a weighted average of the annuity value of wealth and lagged consumption, with weights $1 - (\gamma/R)$ and γ/R. There are two additional terms in the consumption policy, reflecting the impact of dividend shocks beyond their direct effect on prices and hence wealth. These two additional terms represent the ability of the fully informed investor to predict future "returns" (gains), and adjust consumption accordingly. In our setting, the rational agent knows about mean reversion that is not "priced in" to asset prices. In our calibration, the first order effect ($A'\Delta\vec{d}_t$) tends to partially offset the effect of wealth shocks: a rational agent changes his or her consumption *less* than a wealth shock would imply since the agent recognizes that mean reversion will reverse part of the original wealth shock. The second-order effect ($\Delta\vec{d}_t'B\Delta\vec{d}_t$) is strictly positive and increasing in the scale of $\Delta\vec{d}_t$, because the benefit of being able to predict returns is greater when large shocks have occurred in the past.

The asset allocation result is harder to interpret than the consumption rule, though it is also a linear function of the dividend history. However, we can derive a simple lower bound on the average equity holding:

Corollary 2. On average, rational agents will hold a quantity of equities greater than

$$\bar{\theta}_{min} = \frac{\hat{\sigma}_\varepsilon^2}{\sigma_\varepsilon^2}.$$

Note that $\hat{\sigma}_\varepsilon^2/\sigma_\varepsilon^2$ is the ratio of variances of impulses to earnings. The numerator, $\hat{\sigma}_\varepsilon^2$, is the variance perceived by the NE agents. The denominator, σ_ε^2, is the variance perceived by the RE agents. Since the NE agents estimate a simpler model than the (true) model used by the RE agents, it follows that $\hat{\sigma}_\varepsilon^2 > \sigma_\varepsilon^2$.

The average value of θ_t (given in appendix C) includes two terms related to the consumption policy matrices A and B. These terms reflect the contrarian nature of the consumption policy: because dividend shocks have a muted effect on consumption via A, and because shocks of any sort increase consumption via B, the Lucas tree is less risky for the rational investors than would otherwise be the case, and the equilibrium outcome is for them to hold even more equities than the natural expectations agents. Because both of these terms have a positive impact on average equity holdings, discarding them generates the lower bound just described.

The lower bound can also be interpreted as the policy of an agent who knows there is an equity premium, but is not able to time returns. In our framework, this would occur if $\hat{\sigma}_\varepsilon > \sigma_\varepsilon$ but $M = 0$.

In figure 13, we report the average asset allocation, and this lower bound, over different model orders chosen by the NE agents. The ex-

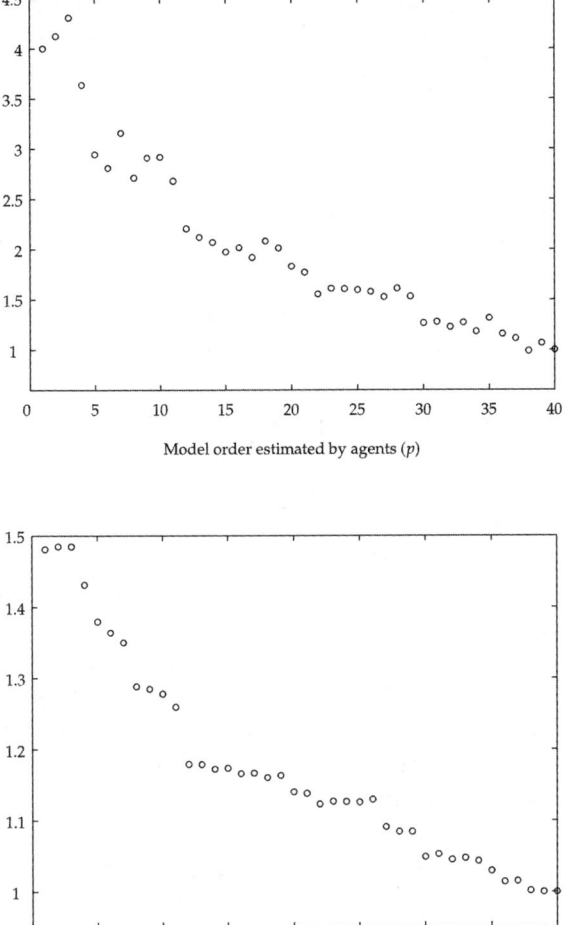

Fig. 13. Equity allocation of rational agents for different AR(p) models of earnings growth held by NE agents: Average (top panel) and lower bound (bottom panel).

tent to which NE agents choose low-order models determines both the excessive variance they perceive and the ability of rational agents to predict returns, and it is therefore unsurprising that the equity holdings for rational agents is generally decreasing in the order of model chosen by the NE agents.

Finally, RE agents will make countercyclical equity investments. Because of overreaction among the NE agents, the (rational) expected return on equities falls after positive shocks, leading the RE agents to lower their equity exposure during good times. Conversely, the RE agents increase their equity exposure during bad times.

VI. Conclusion

This paper examines an open endowment economy in which (a) fundamentals have hump-shaped dynamics (momentum in the short run and partial mean reversion in the long run), and (b) agents do not know these dynamics and generate beliefs by fitting parsimonious models. We show that these two assumptions have a large set of empirically valid implications: endogenous extrapolation bias, procyclical excess optimism, overreaction in asset pricing, mean reversion in returns, amplified dynamics in consumption, cyclical dynamics in consumption, a high equity premium, relatively highly levered equity exposure among sophisticated investors, and countercyclical asset allocation among sophisticated investors. The framework that we have described provides a parsimonious and psychologically plausible explanation for these stylized facts.

We believe that our two assumptions also characterize other "macro" markets. For example, the same approach could be used to study dynamics in housing prices, residential investment, nonresidential investment, inventory accumulation, international capital flows, bond markets, or commodity prices.[50] Wherever our two assumptions apply, markets will be characterized by amplified cycles, overreaction, excess volatility, and asset returns that are negatively autocorrelated over the medium-run.

Finally, we wish to highlight a gap in our analysis. Our model is about belief formation, but all of our evidence about beliefs is indirect— for instance, consumption and asset price dynamics. We believe that researchers should also measure beliefs directly. Some research on bubbles has moved in this direction (e.g., Case and Shiller 2003; Vissing-Jorgensen 2003; Shiller 2005; Piazzesi and Schneider 2009, 2011) and we hope that more will do so in the future.

Endnotes

We are grateful to Daron Acemoglu, Nicholas Barberis, John Beshears, Markus Brunnermeier, John Campbell, James Choi, Larry Christiano, John Driscoll, Emmanuel Farhi, Kenneth French, Xavier Gabaix, Stefano Giglio, Lars Peter Hansen, Blake LeBaron, Greg Mankiw, Joshua Schwartzstein, Andrei Shleifer, Jeremy Stein, Jim Stock, Michael Woodford, our discussants Marty Eichenbaum and George Evans, and seminar/conference participants for helpful comments and discussions. We are indebted to Brendan Price and Fernando Yu for excellent research assistance. David Laibson acknowledges support from the NIA (P01AG005842). For acknowledgments, sources of research support, and disclosure of the authors' material financial relationships, if any, please see http://www .nber.org/chapters/c12404.ack.

1. For example, Barberis, Shleifer, and Vishny (1998); Hong, Stein, and Yu (2007); and Branch and Evans (2010) study settings in which agents estimate a misspecified model and optimize against that model.

2. The current paper is more parsimonious since it zeros out a weighting parameter that is used in Fuster, Laibson, and Mendel (2010).

3. See Campbell and Mankiw (1987); Cochrane (1988); Morley, Nelson, and Zivot (2003); and Perron and Wada (2009) for a range of opinions.

4. Fuster, Laibson, and Mendel (2010) provide some empirical evidence for hump-shaped dynamics in different economic time series.

5. The agents in our model behave as if they thought their model represented the truth; i.e., their decisions do not take into account the possibility of misspecification or display a concern for "robustness" (see Hansen 2007; Hansen and Sargent 2007, 2010). We hope to explore the differences between models with natural expectations and models of robustness in future work.

6. To keep the analysis in our paper maximally tractable, we abstract away from learning and give agents a fixed simple model that is estimated from data available in 2011. Adding learning would complicate the analysis, but not change the qualitative results.

7. In contrast, Campbell and Cochrane (1999) use a habit model that generates counter-cyclical risk premia, thereby explaining numerous asset pricing regularities.

8. When cay is low, wealth is transitorily high. In our economy, this predicts low future excess returns.

9. Brav and Heaton (2002) emphasize that when explaining "financial anomalies," behavioral theories and rational theories with structural uncertainty are often very similar mathematically and also in terms of predictions. We remain relatively agnostic as to whether the reliance on models that fail to capture long-term dynamics is "behavioral" or "rational" in our setting, and focus on the implications.

10. McQuarrie and Tsai (1998) provide an overview of these and other selection criteria.

11. The AICc can be written as $\ln(\hat{\sigma}^2) + [(T + k - 1)/(T - k - 1)]$.

12. McQuarrie and Tsai (1998) indicate that "AIC is probably the most commonly used model selection criterion for time series data" (2). On the other hand, Neath and Cavanaugh (1997) note that BIC "is often preferred over AIC by practitioners who find appeal in either its Bayesian justification or its tendency to choose more parsimonious models than AIC" (559). For an interesting discussion on this topic from an online forum for "statisticians, data analysts, data miners and data visualization experts," see http://stats.stackexchange.com/questions/577/is-there-any-reason-to-prefer-the-aic-or-bic-over-the-other.

13. The MA coefficients are: +0.15, +0.1, −0.02, −0.05, −0.05, −0.05, −0.05, −0.05, −0.06, −0.06, −0.06, −0.06, −0.06, −0.06, −0.06, −0.06. The long-term persistence of an ARIMA$(p, 1, q)$ process is given by $(1 + \text{sum of MA coefficients})/(1 - \text{sum of AR coefficients})$.

14. Estimating MA models with a large number of terms is computationally demanding, which is why we only estimate a subset of the possible models one might consider. In our simulations the maximum likelihood estimation of MA models sometimes failed to converge, or the maximum likelihood estimator of the root (i.e., the negative of the sum of the lagged MA coefficients) "piled up" at a value of 1, which means that the predicted long-term persistence of a shock equaled 0. This pileup occurs because the sample likelihood function is locally flat at an MA root of 1, so that it is a local maximum of the likelihood function and may be the global maximum in finite samples, even if the true MA root is less than unity (see Campbell and Mankiw 1987 or Stock 1994 for discussions). It seems likely that a modeler would be highly skeptical of such a result. Also, our modeler does not consider ARIMA$(p, 1, q)$ models with both p and $q > 0$. While such models are often

estimated in practice, based on our results and some additional smaller-scale simulations, it seems very unlikely that estimating more models would change our qualitative conclusions.

15. For these calculations, we drop simulations in which the sum of MA coefficients equalled exactly −1 (see previous footnote).

16. The spectral formulas derived by Sims (1972) for understanding the consequences of misspecification in regression provide a useful way of thinking about our agents' problem. This point is developed in a note by Lawrence Christiano, available at http://faculty .wcas.northwestern.edu/~lchrist/finc520/note_on_fhl.pdf.

17. A large literature in statistics and economics studies methods to detect regime switching or structural breaks.

18. For example, see Sims (1998, 2003); Gabaix et al. (2006); Woodford (2009).

19. Other studies instead find that analysts underreact. Easterwood and Nutt (1999) argue that analysts overreact to positive information but underreact to negative information. Lim (2001) argues that considering analysts' objective function can "rationalize" their biases.

20. La Porta (1996) finds a negative relation between analysts' long-term growth estimates and future one-year risk-adjusted returns. Bergman and Roychowdhury (2008) document a positive relation between the consumer confidence index (a proxy for market sentiment) and the error in long-horizon earnings estimates of financial analysts, consistent with the idea that when times are good, market participants may insufficiently adjust for subsequent mean reversion.

21. More recently, Chen, Moise, and Zhao (2009) argue that myopic extrapolation can also explain momentum, if investors completely miss the hump-shaped dynamics of firm-specific earnings shocks and simply treat current earnings shocks as permanent. They point out that apart from cognitive biases, the practice of pricing securities using earnings multiples can also contribute to this phenomenon.

22. The type of distortion that Cecchetti et al. focus on has agents *underestimate* the persistence of good and bad shocks to endowment growth (see Gourinchas and Tornell 2004 for a related model in an international finance context), while our "natural expectations" agents will *overestimate* the persistence of shocks to earnings growth.

23. For an early example, see Friedman (1979).

24. The downweighting of old data is often captured by assuming constant gain rather than decreasing gain (least squares) learning. Some papers, such as Marcet and Nicolini (2003), endogenize agents' choice between constant and decreasing gain based on recent prediction errors.

25. See Hong and Stein (2007) for a discussion of models of disagreement in a finance context.

26. See Campbell (2003) and Cochrane (2007) for surveys of the rational asset pricing literature.

27. The current model differs in five ways. We now assume CARA preferences instead of limiting risk neutral preferences (in the quadratic utility class). We now assume a consumption habit. We now assume a general ARIMA(p, 1, 0) process for the dividend tree instead of an AR(2). We also allow our natural expectations agents to have general ARIMA(p', 1, 0) beliefs, instead of ARIMA(1, 1, 0) beliefs. Finally, we introduce a zero measure of agents with rational expectations.

28. In a closed version of our economy, the risk-free rate would also be nearly constant, since, in our preferred calibrations, agents (mistakenly) perceive the endowment to be approximately a random walk with drift.

29. Without loss of generality, we assume that the process has no deterministic drift. Adding deterministic drift would not change any of our results on comovement.

30. If the equity tree were held by foreign investors, this would drastically dilute the associated risk. Domestic ownership can be motivated by home bias.

31. All appendices are available online at http://www.nber.org/data-appendix /c12404/appendix.pdf.

32. At initialization, with $b_0 = 0$, relative risk aversion in our CARA economy is

$$\left(\frac{R-1}{R}\right)w\alpha\left(1-\frac{\gamma}{R}\right) \simeq c_0\alpha\left(1-\frac{\gamma}{R}\right) \simeq d_0\alpha\left(1-\frac{\gamma}{R}\right).$$

33. Specifically, we study the natural log of real net operating surplus of private enterprises as reported in the US NIPA (Bureau of Economic Analysis, 1947:1 to 2010:3). The net operating surplus of private enterprises is reported in NIPA table 1.10, line 12. This definition is net of capital depreciation. To adjust for inflation, we use the GDP deflator.

34. Dividends also have the problem that they miss cash flow that is returned to shareholders through buy-backs.

35. It is well-known that estimating AR coefficients in small samples yields biased coefficients (e.g., Shaman and Stine 1988). Monte Carlo simulations indicate that with our sample size, this does not significantly affect estimated persistence.

36. Excess returns are defined as "the value-weight return on all NYSE, AMEX, and NASDAQ stocks (from CRSP) minus the one-month Treasury bill rate (from Ibbotson Associates)" (source: Ken French's online data library). Early evidence on long-term mean reversion in stock prices was presented in Fama and French (1988b) and Poterba and Summers (1988). The significance of this evidence was subsequently challenged on statistical grounds (e.g., by Richardson 1993). Cutler, Poterba, and Summers (1991) look at a variety of stocks, bonds, and foreign exchange markets and find a relatively slight negative autocorrelation in returns in many markets over a horizon of three to five years. Balvers, Wu, and Gilliland (2000) consider a panel of 18 countries and document strong mean reversion in national equity indices relative to the world index.

37. Data on stock prices and earnings come from Robert Shiller's website. Earnings and dividend yields as predictors of future returns are studied by Campbell and Shiller (1988a, 1988b, 2005) and Fama and French (1988a).

38. For our consumption measure, we use real per capita expenditures on nondurable consumption and services from NIPA. The nominal data on expenditures are in NIPA table 2.3.5, while price indices are in table 2.3.4. The population data come from table 2.1. Consumption growth is a relatively little studied predictor for excess returns. However, in recent work, Moller (2008) and Moller and Rangvid (2011) show that high consumption growth between quarters 3 and 4 significantly predicts low excess returns over the following year.

39. See Lettau and Ludvigson (2010) for an overview of the issues as well as potential remedies.

40. This is the approximate process that consumption growth should follow when a consumer has habit preferences; see, for example, Dynan (2000).

41. The wide confidence intervals for (2) and (4) may seem surprising; they are due to the high persistence of the P/E_{10} and the use of overlapping data for consumption growth and excess returns (see Boudoukh, Richardson, and Whiltelaw 2008).

42. The rational expectations benchmark is slightly below zero due to a variant of Hurwicz bias.

43. The classical explanation, derived from the intertemporal budget constraint, is that rational, forward-looking consumers will consume little today relative to their wealth if they expect future returns to be low. In our model, *cay* correlates with future excess returns only because expectations overreact to shocks; the future returns *expected* by our agents are always constant.

44. Once again, Hurwicz bias lowers the rational expectations correlation below zero.

45. On the other hand, as there is only one source of shocks in our model, equity returns and consumption growth, as well as the P/E ratio and consumption growth, display a higher contemporaneous correlation than in the data. A more realistic model would incorporate other aggregate shocks (e.g., labor income), which would reduce these correlations without qualitatively changing the economy's other properties.

46. For an alternative view, see Bansal, Kiku, and Yaron (2009), who argue that consumption growth becomes much more predictable once additional predictor variables are considered.

47. In this expression, $\Delta_h c_{t+h}$ is the h-year growth rate in consumption and $\tilde{R}_{t,t+h}$ is the h-year excess return.

48. In the annual US data we use throughout, the normalized covariance takes on the following values for h = 1, 2, . . ., 10 years: 0.0006, 0.0015, 0.0019, 0.0013, 0.0007, 0.0002, –0.0004, –0.0006, –0.0006, –0.0006. See related analyses in Parker (2001) and Gabaix and Laibson (2002).

49. See appendix B for the formulae that we use to calculate the equity premium. The "x" marks on the upper edge of figure 10 represent equity premia that exceed the vertical scale of the figure.

50. For some alternative approaches, see, for example, Lansing (2009); Hassan and Mertens (2010); Adam and Marcet (2010); LeBaron (2010); Burnside, Eichenbaum, and Rebelo (2011); and Piazzesi and Schneider (2011).

References

Abraham, J. M., and P. H. Hendershott. 1996. "Bubbles in Metropolitan Housing Markets." *Journal of Housing Research* 7:191–207.

Adam, K., and A. Marcet. 2010. "Booms and Busts in Asset Prices." Bank of Japan Institute for Monetary and Economic Studies (IMES) Discussion Paper Series 2010-E–2.

Alessie, R., and A. Lusardi. 1997. "Consumption, Saving and Habit Formation." *Economic Letters* 55:103–8.

Bacchetta, P., E. Mertens, and E. van Wincoop. 2009. "Predictability in Financial Markets: What Do Survey Expectations Tell Us?" *Journal of International Money and Finance* 28:406–26.

Baker, M., and J. Wurgler. 2007. "Investor Sentiment in the Stock Market." *Journal of Economic Perspectives* 21:129–51.

Ball, L. 2000. "Near-Rationality and Inflation in Two Monetary Regimes." NBER Working Paper no. 7988. Cambridge, MA: National Bureau of Economic Research, October.

Balvers, R., Y. Wu, and E. Gilliland. 2000. "Mean Reversion across National Stock Markets and Parametric Contrarian Investment Strategies." *Journal of Finance* 55:745–72.

Bansal, R., D. Kiku, and A. Yaron. 2009. "An Empirical Evaluation of the Long-Run Risks Model for Asset Prices." Working Paper.

Bansal, R., and A. Yaron. 2004. "Risks for the Long Run: A Potential Resolution of Asset Pricing Puzzles." *Journal of Finance* 59:1481–509.

Barberis, N. C. 2010. "Psychology and the Financial Crisis of 2007–2008." Working Paper, Yale School of Management.

Barberis, N. C., A. Shleifer, and R. W. Vishny. 1998. "A Model of Investor Sentiment." *Journal of Financial Economics* 49:307–43.

Barsky, R. B., and J. B. DeLong. 1993. "Why Does the Stock Market Fluctuate?" *Quarterly Journal of Economics* 108:291–311.

Beeler, J., and J. Y. Campbell. 2009. "The Long-Run Risks Model and Aggregate Asset Prices: An Empirical Assessment." NBER Working Paper no. 14788. Cambridge, MA: National Bureau of Economic Research, March.

Benartzi, S. 2001. "Excessive Extrapolation and the Allocation of 401(k) Accounts to Company Stock." *Journal of Finance* 56:1747–64.

Benartzi, S., and R. H. Thaler. 2007. "Heuristics and Biases in Retirement Savings Behavior." *Journal of Economic Perspectives* 21:81–104.

Bergman, N., and S. Roychowdhury. 2008. "Investor Sentiment and Corporate Disclosure." *Journal of Accounting Research* 46:1057–83.

Boudoukh, J., M. Richardson, and R. F. Whiltelaw. 2008. "The Myth of Long-Horizon Predictability." *Review of Financial Studies* 21:1577–605.

Branch, W. A., and G. W. Evans. 2007. "Model Uncertainty and Endogenous Volatility." *Review of Economic Dynamics* 10:207–37.

———. 2010. "Asset Return Dynamics and Learning." *Review of Financial Studies* 23: 1651–80.

Brav, A., and J. Heaton. 2002. "Competing Theories of Financial Anomalies." *Review of Financial Studies* 15:575–606.

Bulkley, G., and R. D. F. Harris. 1997. "Irrational Analysts' Expectations As a Cause of Excess Volatility in Stock Prices." *Economic Journal* 107:359–71.

Burnside, C., M. Eichenbaum, and S. Rebelo. 2011. "Understanding Booms and Busts in Housing Markets." Working Paper.

Caballero, R. J. 1990. "Consumption Puzzles and Precautionary Savings." *Journal of Monetary Economics* 25:113–36.

Campbell, J. Y. 2003. "Consumption-Based Asset Pricing." In *Handbook of the Economics of Finance*, vol. IB, edited by M. H. George Constantinides and R. Stulz, 803–87. Amsterdam: North Holland.

Campbell, J. Y., and J. H. Cochrane. 1999. "By Force of Habit: A Consumption-Based Explanation of Aggregate Stock Market Behavior." *Journal of Political Economy* 107:205–51.

Campbell, J. Y., and N. G. Mankiw. 1987. "Are Output Fluctuations Transitory?" *Quarterly Journal of Economics* 102:857–80.

Campbell, J. Y., and R. J. Shiller. 1988a. "The Dividend-Price Ratio and Expectations of Future Dividends and Discount Factors." *Review of Financial Studies* 1:195–228.

———. 1988b. "Stock Prices, Earnings, and Expected Dividends." *Journal of Finance* 43:661–76.

———. 2005. "Valuation Ratios and the Long-Run Stock Market Outlook: An Update." In *Advances in Behavioral Finance*, vol. II, edited by R. H. Thaler, 173–201. Princeton, NJ: Princeton University Press.

Carroll, C. D., M. Sommer, and J. Slacalek. 2011. "International Evidence on Sticky Consumption Growth." *Review of Economics and Statistics*, forthcoming.

Case, K. E., and R. J. Shiller. 2003. "Is There a Bubble in the Housing Market?" *Brookings Papers on Economic Activity* 2:299–342.

Cecchetti, S. G., P.-S. Lam, and N. C. Mark. 2000. "Asset Pricing with Distorted Beliefs: Are Equity Returns Too Good to Be True?" *American Economic Review* 90:787–804.

Chalmers, J., and J. Reuter. 2009. "How Do Retirees Value Life Annuities? Evidence from Public Employees." NBER Working Paper no. 15608. Cambridge, MA: National Bureau of Economic Research, December.

Chan, L. K. C., J. Karceski, and J. Lakonishok. 2003. "The Level and Persistence of Growth Rates." *Journal of Finance* 58:643–84.

Chen, L., C. E. Moise, and X. S. Zhao. 2009. "Myopic Extrapolation, Price Momentum, and Price Reversal." Working Paper.

Chevalier, J. A., and G. Ellison. 1997. "Risk Taking by Mutual Funds As a Response to Incentives." *Journal of Political Economy* 105:1167–200.

Choi, J. J. 2006. "Extrapolative Expectations and the Equity Premium." Working Paper.

Choi, J. J., D. I. Laibson, B. C. Madrian, and A. Metrick. 2004. "Employees' Investment Decisions About Company Stock." In *Pension Design and Structure:*

New Lessons from Behavioral Finance, edited by O. S. Mitchell and S. P. Utkus, 121–36. New York: Oxford University Press.

———. 2009. "Reinforcement Learning and Savings Behavior." *Journal of Finance* 64:2515–34.

Cochrane, J. H. 1988. "How Big Is the Random Walk in GNP?" *Journal of Political Economy* 96:893–920.

———. 2007. "Financial Markets and the Real Economy." In *Handbook of the Equity Premium*, edited by R. Mehra, 273–325. Amsterdam: North Holland.

Cutler, D. M., J. M. Poterba, and L. H. Summers. 1991. "Speculative Dynamics." *Review of Economic Studies* 58:529–46.

Daniel, K. D., D. Hirshleifer, and A. Subrahmanya. 1998. "Investor Psychology and Security Market Under- and Overreactions." *Journal of Finance* 53: 1839–86.

De Bondt, W. F. M. 1993. "Betting on Trends: Intuitive Forecasts of Financial Risk and Return." *International Journal of Forecasting* 9:355–71.

De Bondt, W. F. M., and R. H. Thaler. 1985. "Does the Stock Market Overreact?" *Journal of Finance* 40:793–805.

———. 1989. "Anomalies: A Mean-Reverting Walk Down Wall Street." *Journal of Economic Perspectives* 3:189–202.

———. 1990. "Do Security Analysts Overreact?" *American Economic Review* 80:52–57.

De Grauwe, P. 2010. "Top-Down versus Bottom-Up Macroeconomics." Center for Economic Studies (CESifo) Working Paper 3020.

DeLong, J. B., A. Shleifer, L. H. Summers, and R. Waldmann. 1990. "Positive Feedback Investment Strategies and Destabilizing Rational Speculation." *Journal of Finance* 45:379–95.

Dwyer, G. P., A. W. Williams, R. C. Battalio, and T. I. Mason. 1993. "Tests of Rational Expectations in a Stark Setting." *Economic Journal* 103:586–601.

Dynan, K. E. 2000. "Habit Formation in Consumer Preferences: Evidence from Panel Data." *American Economic Review* 90: 391–406.

Dynan, K. E., and D. M. Maki. 2001. "Does Stock Market Wealth Matter for Consumption?" Finance and Economics Discussion Series (FEDS) Discussion Paper No. 2001–23.

Easterwood, J. C., and S. R. Nutt. 1999. "Inefficiency in Analysts' Earnings Forecasts: Systematic Misreaction or Systematic Optimism?" *Journal of Finance* 54:1777–97.

Eusepi, S., and B. Preston. 2011. "Expectations, Learning and Business Cycle Fluctuations." *American Economic Review*, forthcoming.

Evans, G. W., and S. Honkapohja. 2001. *Learning and Expectations in Macroeconomics*. Princeton, NJ: Princeton University Press.

———. 2011. "Learning As a Rational Foundation for Macroeconomics and Finance." Working Paper.

Fama, E., and K. French. 1988a. "Dividend Yields and Expected Stock Returns." *Journal of Financial Economics* 25:23–49.

———. 1988b. "Permanent and Temporary Components of Stock Prices." *Journal of Political Economy* 96:246–73.

Friedman, B. 1979. "Optimal Expectations and the Extreme Information Assumptions of 'Rational Expectations' Macromodels." *Journal of Monetary Economics* 5:23–41.

Fuster, A., D. Laibson, and B. Mendel. 2010. "Natural Expectations and Macroeconomic Fluctuations." *Journal of Economic Perspectives* 24:67–84.

Gabaix, X. 2011. "A Sparsity-Based Model of Bounded Rationality." NBER Working Paper no. 16911. Cambridge, MA: National Bureau of Economic Research, March.

Gabaix, X., and D. I. Laibson. 2002. "The 6D Bias and the Equity Premium Puzzle." *NBER Macroeconomics Annual 2001*, vol. 16, edited by Ben S. Bernanke and Kenneth Rogoff, 257–311. Cambridge, MA: MIT Press.

Gabaix, X., D. Laibson, G. Moloche, and S. Weinberg. 2006. "Costly Information Acquisition: Experimental Analysis of a Boundedly Rational Model." *American Economic Review* 96:1043–68.

Gerardi, K. S., A. Lehnert, S. M. Sherlund, and P. S. Willen. 2008. "Making Sense of the Subprime Crisis." *Brookings Papers on Economic Activity* 2008:69–145.

Gigerenzer, G., and D. G. Goldstein. 1996. "Reasoning the Fast and Frugal Way: Models of Bounded Rationality." *Psychological Review* 103:650–69.

Glaeser, E. L., J. D. Gottlieb, and J. Gyourko. 2010. "Can Cheap Credit Explain the Housing Boom?" NBER Working Paper no. 16230. Cambridge, MA: National Bureau of Economic Research, July.

Goetzmann, W. N., L. Peng, and J. Yen. 2009. "The Subprime Crisis and House Price Appreciation." NBER Working Paper no. 15334. Cambridge, MA: National Bureau of Economic Research, September.

Gourinchas, P.-O., and A. Tornell. 2004. "Exchange Rate Puzzles and Distorted Beliefs." *Journal of International Economics* 64:303–33.

Greenwood, R., and S. G. Hanson. 2010. "Issuer Quality and Corporate Bond Returns." Working Paper, Harvard University.

Hannan, E. 1980. "The Estimation of the Order of an ARMA Process." *Annals of Statistics* 8:1071–81.

Hansen, L. P. 2007. "Beliefs, Doubts and Learning: Valuing Macroeconomic Risk." *American Economic Review* 97:1–30.

Hansen, L. P., and T. J. Sargent. 2007. *Robustness.* Princeton, NJ: Princeton University Press.

———. 2010. "Fragile Beliefs and the Price of Uncertainty." *Quantitative Economics* 1:129–62.

Haruvy, E., Y. Lahav, and C. N. Noussair. 2007. "Traders' Expectations in Asset Markets: Experimental Evidence." *American Economic Review* 97:1901–20.

Hassan, T. A., and T. M. Mertens. 2010. "The Social Cost of Near-Rational Investment." Working Paper.

Hey, J. D. 1994. "Expectations Formation: Rational or Adaptive or . . . ?" *Journal of Economic Behavior and Organization* 25:329–49.

Hommes, C., J. Sonnemans, J. Tulnstra, and H. van de Velden. 2008. "Expectations and Bubbles in Asset Pricing Experiments." *Journal of Economic Behavior and Organization* 67:116–33.

Hong, H., and J. C. Stein. 1999. "A Unified Theory of Underreaction, Momentum Trading, and Overreaction in Asset Markets." *Journal of Finance* 54:2143–84.

———. 2007. "Disagreement and the Stock Market." *Journal of Economic Perspectives* 21:109–28.

Hong, H., J. C. Stein, and J. Yu. 2007. "Simple Forecasts and Paradigm Shifts." *Journal of Finance* 62:1207–42.

Huang, K. X., Z. Liu, and T. Zha. 2009. "Learning, Adaptive Expectations and Technology Shocks." *Economic Journal* 119:377–405.

Kahneman, D., and A. N. Tversky. 1973. "On the Psychology of Prediction." *Psychological Review* 80:237–51.

La Porta, R. 1996. "Expectations and the Cross-Section of Stock Returns." *Journal of Finance* 51:1715–42.

Lakonishok, J., A. Shleifer, and R. W. Vishny. 1994. "Contrarian Investment, Extrapolation, and Risk." *Journal of Finance* 49:1541–78.

Lansing, K. J. 2006. "Lock-in of Extrapolative Expectations in an Asset Pricing Model." *Macroeconomic Dynamics* 10:317–48.

———. 2009. "Speculative Growth, Overreaction, and the Welfare Cost of Technology-Driven Bubbles." Federal Reserve Bank of San Francisco Working Paper 2008–08.

LeBaron, B. 2010. "Heterogeneous Gain Learning and the Dynamics of Asset Prices." Working Paper, Brandeis University.

LeBaron, B., W. B. Arthur, and R. G. Palmer. 1999. "Time Series Properties of an Artificial Stock Market." *Journal of Economic Dynamics and Control* 23: 1487–516.

LeRoy, S. F., and R. D. Porter. 1981. "The Present Value Relation: Tests Based on Implied Variance Bounds." *Econometrica* 49:555–74.

Lettau, M., and S. C. Ludvigson. 2001. "Consumption, Aggregate Wealth and Expected Stock Returns." *Journal of Finance* 56: 815–49.

———. 2010. "Measuring and Modeling Variation in the Risk-Return Trade-off." In *Handbook of Financial Econometrics*, vol. 1, edited by Y. Ait-Sahalia and L. P. Hansen, 617–90. Amsterdam: Elsevier Science B.V. North Holland.

Lichtenstein, S., B. Fischhoff, and L. Philips. 1982. "Calibration of Probabilities: The State of the Art to 1980." In *Judgment Under Uncertainty: Heuristics and Biases*, edited by D. Kahneman, P. Slovic, and A. Tversky. Cambridge: Cambridge University Press.

Lim, T. 2001. "Rationality and Analysts' Forecast Bias." *Journal of Finance* 56: 369–85.

Malmendier, U., and S. Nagel. 2011. "Depression Babies: Do Macroeconomic Experiences Affect Risk Taking?" *Quarterly Journal of Economics* 126:373–416.

Marcet, A., and J. P. Nicolini. 2003. "Recurrent Hyperinflations and Learning." *American Economic Review* 93:1476–98.

McQuarrie, A. D., and C.-L. Tsai. 1998. *Regression and Time Series Model Selection*. Singapore: World Scientific Publishing.

Moller, S. V. 2008. "Consumption Growth and Time-Varying Expected Stock Returns." *Finance Research Letters* 5:129–36.

Moller, S. V., and J. Rangvid. 2011. "The Fourth-Quarter Consumption Growth Rate and Expected Returns." Working Paper, Aarhus School of Business and Copenhagen Business School.

Morley, J., C. Nelson, and E. Zivot. 2003. "Why Are Beveridge-Nelson and Unobserved Component Decompositions of GDP So Different?" *Review of Economics and Statistics* 85:235–43.

Muellbauer, J. N., and A. Murphy. 1997. "Booms and Busts in the UK Housing Market." *Economic Journal* 107:1701–27.

Neath, A., and J. Cavanaugh. 1997. "Regression and Time Series Model Selection Using Variants of the Schwarz Information Criterion." *Communications in Statistics—Theory and Methods* 26:559–80.

Nelson, C., and M. Kim. 1993. "Predictable Stock Returns: The Role of Small Sample Bias." *Journal of Finance* 48:641–61.

Parker, J. A. 2001. "The Consumption Risk of the Stock Market." *Brookings Papers on Economic Activity* 2:279–348.

Pastor, L., and P. Veronesi. 2009. "Learning in Financial Markets." *Annual Review of Financial Economics* 1:361–81.

Perron, P., and T. Wada. 2009. "Let's Take a Break: Trends and Cycles in US Real GDP." *Journal of Monetary Economics* 56:749–65.

Piazzesi, M., and M. Schneider. 2009. "Momentum Traders in the Housing Market: Survey Evidence and a Search Model." *American Economic Review* 99:406–11.

———. 2011. "Trend and Cycle in Bond Premia." Working Paper.

Poterba, J. M., and L. H. Summers. 1988. "Mean Reversion in Stock Prices: Evidence and Implications." *Journal of Financial Economics* 22: 27–59.

Previtero, A. 2010. "Stock Market Returns and Annuitization." Working Paper.

Rabin, M. 2002. "Inference by Believers in the Law of Small Numbers." *Quarterly Journal of Economics* 117:775–816.

Rabin, M., and D. Vayanos. 2010. "The Gambler's and Hot-Hand Fallacies: Theory and Applications." *Review of Economic Studies* 77:730–78.

Reinhart, C., and K. Rogoff. 2009. *This Time Is Different: Eight Centuries of Financial Folly*. Princeton, NJ: Princeton University Press.

Richardson, M. 1993. "Temporary Components of Stock Prices: A Skeptic's View." *Journal of Business & Economic Statistics* 11:199–207.

Sargent, T. J. 1993. *Bounded Rationality in Macroeconomics*. Oxford: Oxford University Press.

Shaman, P., and R. A. Stine. 1988. "The Bias of Autoregressive Coefficient Estimators." *Journal of the American Statistical Association* 83:842–48.

Shiller, R. J. 1981. "Do Stock Prices Move Too Much to Be Justified by Subsequent Changes in Dividends?" *American Economic Review* 71:421–36.

———. 2005. *Irrational Exuberance*, 2nd ed. Princeton, NJ: Princeton University Press.

Sims, C. A. 1972. "The Role of Approximate Prior Restrictions in Distributed Lag Estimation." *Journal of the American Statistical Association* 67: 169–75.

———. 1998. "Stickiness." *Carnegie-Rochester Conference Series on Public Policy* 49:317–56.

———. 2003. "Implications of Rational Inattention." *Journal of Monetary Economics* 50:665–90.

Sirri, E. R., and P. Tufano. 1998. "Costly Search and Mutual Fund Flows." *Journal of Finance* 53:1589–622.

Stambaugh, R. F. 1999. "Predictive Regressions." *Journal of Financial Economics* 54:375–421.

Stock, J. H. 1994. "Unit Roots, Structural Breaks and Trends." In *Handbook of Econometrics*, vol. IV, edited by R. F. Engle and D. McFadden, 2739–841. Amsterdam: Elsevier.

Tesfatsion, L. S., and K. L. Judd, eds. 2006. *Handbook of Computational Economics: Agent-Based Computational Economics*, vol. 2. Amsterdam: North-Holland Publishing Company.

Timmermann, A. G. 1993. "How Learning in Financial Markets Generates Excess Volatility and Predictability in Stock Prices." *Quarterly Journal of Economics* 108:1135–45.

Tortorice, D. L. 2011. "Unemployment Expectations and the Business Cycle." Working Paper.

Tversky, A. N., and D. Kahneman. 1973. "Availability: A Heuristic for Judging Frequency and Probabilities." *Cognitive Psychology* 5:207–32.

———. 1974. "Judgment under Uncertainty: Heuristics and Biases." *Science* 185:1124–31.

Valkanov, R. 2003. "Long-Horizon Regressions: Theoretical Results and Applications." *Journal of Financial Economics* 68:201–32.

Vissing-Jorgensen, A. 2003. "Perspectives on Behavioral Finance: Does 'Irrationality' Disappear with Wealth? Evidence from Expectations and Actions." *NBER Macroeconomics Annual 2003*, vol. 18, edited by Mark Gertler and Kenneth Rogoff, 139–94. Cambridge, MA: MIT Press.

Woodford, M. 2009. "Information-Constrained State-Dependent Pricing." *Journal of Monetary Economics* 56:100–24.

Comment

Martin Eichenbaum, *Northwestern University, NBER, and Federal Reserve Bank of Chicago*

Introduction

This last July marked the fiftieth birthday of John Muth's seminal paper, "Rational Expectations and the Theory of Price Movements." This assumption about how expectations are formed is now the standard approach in modern, quantitative macro. But there is an increasingly important literature which examines the deeper foundations of the rational expectations hypothesis and the assumption that agents have common priors.[1] If we had an empirically convincing model of asset pricing and financial markets that embodied simple forms of rational expectations, I suspect that this literature would be of interest primarily to a small set of decision theorists. As recent events have forcefully brought home, we do not. So we are forced to reassess all of our cherished maintained assumptions. Like Lehman Brothers, the luxury of sacred cows is dead.

Fuster, Hebert, and Laibson take it as a given that it is not reasonable to assume agents have common priors and rational expectations when we try to explain asset prices. They then investigate how the economy would behave if (a) "fundamentals" are hump-shaped, exhibiting momentum in the short run and partial reversion in the long run, and (b) agents forecast fundamentals using "reasonable models that are too simple to capture long-term dynamics of key time series." These forecasts are based on simple univariate time series models and correspond to what the authors call "natural expectations." The associated specification error leads agents to systematically overestimate the persistence of shocks. Fuster and colleagues argue that the natural expectations assumption allows them to "generate examples that are consistent with a host of asset pricing phenomenon," such as the equity premium puzzle and the apparent volatility of asset prices relative to fundamentals.

My discussion of the paper is organized as follows. First, I review the authors' statistical argument in favor of "natural expectations." This argument revolves around the same feature of the data emphasized in the literature that explores the problems of agents who are vitally concerned with the possibility of model misspecification.[2] This feature is that there is an enormous amount of statistical uncertainty about the true data generating process of objects that agents care about. In principle, this observation is very damaging to the Fuster et al. paper. Why would risk-averse agents ever settle on a particular forecasting model, which is very likely to be misspecified and act as if the model is, with, probability one, true?

To explore the seriousness of this problem, I investigate how much agents would pay to know the true model for "fundamentals." To my surprise, I find that the utility cost of specification errors associated with natural expectations can be quite small. This result holds even though the implications of the specification error association with natural expectations for key moments of the data can be quite large. I make this argument using a variant of the simple setup in John Cochrane's classic paper, "The Sensitivity of Tests of the Intertemporal Allocation of Consumption to Near Rational Alternatives" (1989).

Do my misspecification "cost" numbers hold up in the actual Fuster et al. model? I do not know. Absent such a calculation, the authors' statistical results about the difficulty of pinning down the "true" ARIMA (autoregressive integrated moving average) representation of fundamentals can be thought of as evidence *against* the way they model agents' behavior. In fact, for reasons discussed later, I suspect that these costs will be small in their application. The reason might be anticipated from the famous argument of Cochrane (1989) and Lucas (1987) that the welfare costs of business cycles are small. In Cochrane (1989), Lucas (1987), and Fuster et al. model agents respect their intertemporal budget constraints. So in a well-defined sense, their average level of consumption would not be different if we eliminate business cycles (Lucas), or if agents used optimal decision rules (Cochrane), or had rational expectations (Fuster et al.). But as in Cochrane (1989), the change in the decision rule induced by the assumption of natural expectations can have large implications for various moments of the data. If my conjecture is correct, it would provide the basis of a very powerful defense of the approach used in this paper to resolve asset pricing puzzles.

Natural Expectations

According to the authors, "The premise of our approach . . . is that economic agents tend to make forecasts based on statistical or mental models that are reasonable given the data available to them, but that are 'too
simple' to fully capture the long-term dynamics of many economic time
series." These simple models lead agents to overestimate the persistence of shocks when the true process is hump-shaped.

   To consider the statistical issues involved, suppose you want to forecast a time series, Δd_t. Also suppose that for unspecified reasons you
consider only *univariate* models, say autoregressive moving average
(ARMA(p, q)) specifications of the form

$$\alpha(L)\Delta d_t = \beta(L)\varepsilon_t.$$

Here $\alpha(L)$ and $\beta(L)$ are polynomial operators in the lag operator of order
p and q, while ε_t is uncorrelated with lagged values of Δd_t or ε_{t-s}, $s \geq 1$.
The authors are interested in Δd_t processes that exhibit hump-shaped
dynamics; that is, processes that exhibit positive autocorrelation in the
short run, but partially revert to the mean in the long run. Their measure of the persistence in Δd_t is

$$\Gamma = \frac{1 + \beta(1)}{1 - \alpha(1)}.$$

   Recall that the spectral density of Δd_t at frequency zero is

$$S_w(0) = \Gamma^2 \sigma_\varepsilon^2.$$

This object is notoriously difficult to estimate with precision in small
samples (see, for example, Christiano, Eichenbaum, and Vigfusson
2006). It follows that it should be hard to estimate Γ with much precision.

   Suppose we take as a given that agents care about Γ per se. The statistical motivation in the paper for natural expectations focuses on the
difficulty of getting p and q right based on a particular statistical metric
like the AIC (Akaike Information Criterion) or BIC (Bayesian Information Criterion). These are criteria for choosing models that are good for
one step ahead forecasting exercises. So it is not surprising that models
based on such criteria could be very bad for long-horizon forecasts or
estimating Γ. But if the latter play an important role in agents' decision
problems, why would they use AIC-like criteria?

   More importantly, in the model, agents must forecast Δd_{t+s}, $s \geq 1$, to
solve an *economic* problem as opposed to a purely statistical one. In gen-

eral there is no reason to suppose they would separate their forecasting and control problems. Fuster et al. just take this separation property as a given in the sense that agents ignore both model and parameter uncertainty. By assumption, agents in the model first choose an ARMA(p, q) model for Δd_t. Next, they estimate the parameters of their preferred statistical model. Finally, they solve their economic optimization problem, taking the ARIMA specification and point estimates as true. This procedure seems very hard to defend. In general we would expect agents to take both model and parameter uncertainty into account when making their plans. Indeed, the more uncertainty there is about the data generating process, the more skeptical we ought to be about the authors' separation assumption.

Statistical Uncertainty

The measure of d_t, which Fuster et al. use in their asset pricing application is the log of real capital income.[3] By assumption the true data generating process for d_t is an ARIMA(40, 1, 0), which they estimate using data over the period 1947Q1–2010Q4. The implied point estimate of Γ for Δd_t is 0.43. Fuster, Laibson, and Mendel (2010) conduct a similar exercise using data on the log of per capita real GDP, which they assume is an ARIMA(0, 1, 12). The implied point estimate of Γ for Δd_t is 1.3. For both measures of d_t, Fuster et al. argue that if agents use a parsimonious ARIMA process to fit the data, they will overestimate the persistence of the process.

A key feature of the data is that there is a great deal of statistical uncertainty about the true value of Γ. To quantify this uncertainty I take as a given the authors' estimated ARIMA processes for the two measures of d_t, and generate 10,000 artificial time series, each of length 250. I then estimate the relevant ARIMA process for d_t using each time series and compute quantiles for the persistence statistic. Table 1 summarizes my results.

The key result here is that even if agents knew the true ARIMA for d_t, there would be a great deal of uncertainty about Γ.

Of course, agents do not know the true ARMA(p, q) process for Δd_t. The authors stress that agents might use "simple" univariate tests like AIC to determine p and q. But if agents proceeded this way, the most important thing that they would learn from the data is that there is an enormous amount of uncertainty about the values of p, q, and Γ. To make this point concrete, I suppose that the true data generating pro-

Table 1
Statistical Uncertainty

Real per Capita GDP	
Quantile (%)	Γ
2.5	0.50
50	1.3
97.5	2.04

Real Capital Income	
Quantile (%)	Γ
2.5	0.25
50	0.43
97.5	0.73

cess for d_t is the estimated ARIMA(40, 1, 0) for the log of capital income. I then simulated 100 synthetic time series of size 250. For each synthetic time series, I estimated an ARIMA(j, 1, 0), $j = 1, \ldots 40$, and calculated the preferred representation using the AIC. Figure 1 summarizes the cumulative distribution function for the preferred specification. It is evident that from the perspective of agents using the AIC criterion, there is a great deal of uncertainty about the true value of p. Of course, this uncertainty maps into enormous uncertainty about the response of Δd_t to a shock.

Viewed as a whole, the previous results make clear that the agents living in the authors' model face enormous uncertainty about features of the data that would seem to be critical to them as decision makers. In the face of such uncertainty why would we assume that agents condition their decisions on a particular statistical model?

The Key Mechanism in the Paper

Before providing a possible defense for the authors' assumptions it's useful to provide some intuition for the key mechanism in their model. The authors consider a small open endowment economy with two assets. The first asset is foreign debt, b_t, which can be held at a constant interest rate R,

$$\beta R = 1.$$

Here β is agents' common discount rate. The second asset is a domestic equity tree, which generates a dividend, d_t, governed by

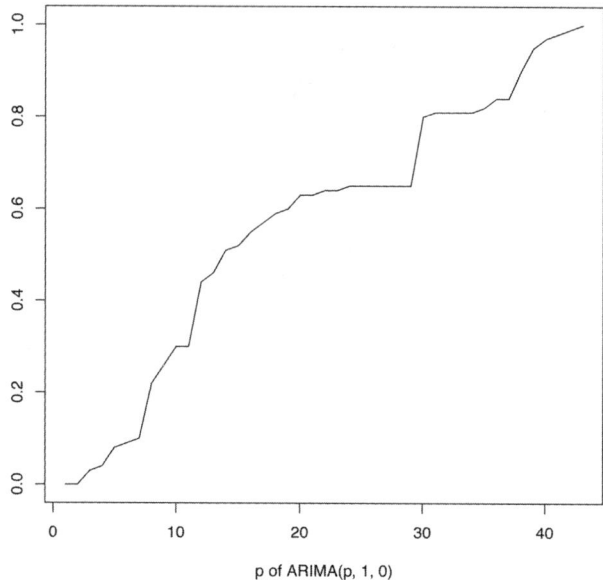

Fig. 1. Cumulative distribution function of AIC preference

$$\Delta d_t = \rho_1 \Delta d_{t-1} + \ldots + \rho_n \Delta d_{t-n} + \varepsilon_{dt},$$

where n is a nonnegative integer. The equity tree must be held by a representative domestic agent who has an exponential utility function with habit formation governed by the parameter $\gamma \in (0, 1)$.

Since the domestic agent can borrow and lend at a constant interest rate, we have the first-order condition

$$u'(c_t, c_{t-1}) = E_t u'(c_{t+1}, c_t).$$

If $\gamma = 0$, we obtain

$$u'(c_t) = E_t u'(c_{t+1}).$$

Since agents do not have rational expectations, $E_t(\cdot)$ does not correspond to the conditional expectations operator defined in terms of the true data generating process. So with natural expectations, the model does not predict martingale-like behavior for consumption even when $\gamma = 0$.

In this environment consumption is a weighted average of lagged consumption and the (risk-neutral) annuity value of perceived future dividends, x_t, down-shifted by a constant φ that involves a correction for risk aversion.

$$c_t = \frac{\gamma}{R} c_{t-1} + \left(1 - \frac{\gamma}{R}\right) x_t - \varphi.$$

The equilibrium price of the Lucas tree is given by,

$$p_t = \sum_{s=0}^{\infty} \frac{E_t d_{t+s}}{R^s} - \frac{R\alpha Var_t(\Delta c_{t+1})}{[1 - (\gamma/R)](R-1)^2}.$$

Note that when $\gamma = 0$, agents *plan* to respond to an innovation in d_t by raising consumption on a one-time basis. The larger is the present value of the change in d_t, the change in consumption, and the response of p_t.

Taking as a given the true data generating process, the order of p that agents use when estimating the law of motion for Δd_t is critical in determining inferences about persistence, the change in the present value of d_t induced by a shock to Δd_t, the change in consumption and $Var_t(\Delta c_{t+1})$. The lower is p, the higher is agents' point estimate of Γ. So the larger will be the initial change in consumption and the perceived riskiness of the Lucas tree.

To understand the last result, suppose that agents act as if Δd_t is governed by the AR(40, 0) model that Fuster et al. estimate from the data. Suppose that we simulate a time series of length 10,000 and estimate an ARMA(p, 0), $p < 0$ using the simulated data. In this way we calculate an approximation to the probability limit of the coefficients of the misspecified ARMA(p, 0) model. Figure 2 displays the impulse response function for d_t implied by different values of p. Note that persistence and the implied expected change in the present value of d_t induced by a shock is *decreasing* in p.

Not surprisingly, when agents use values of $p < 40$, they increase consumption by more than they would if they used the true value of p. The actual present value of the response of consumption must be the same across different values of p because agents' intertemporal budget constraint must hold. The way this happens is that over time, working through the lens of their incorrect statistical model, agents infer incorrectly that there is a sequence of negative shocks to earnings. So they decrease consumption relative to its peak value. It follows that even when $\gamma = 1$ and $\beta R = 1$, consumption will not be a martingale. More generally, a classic Hansen and Singleton (1982) type analysis would correctly reject the representative household rational expectations model of asset pricing. The underlying failure of the model is not heterogeneity among agents or financial frictions. It is simply the failure of the rational expectations assumption.

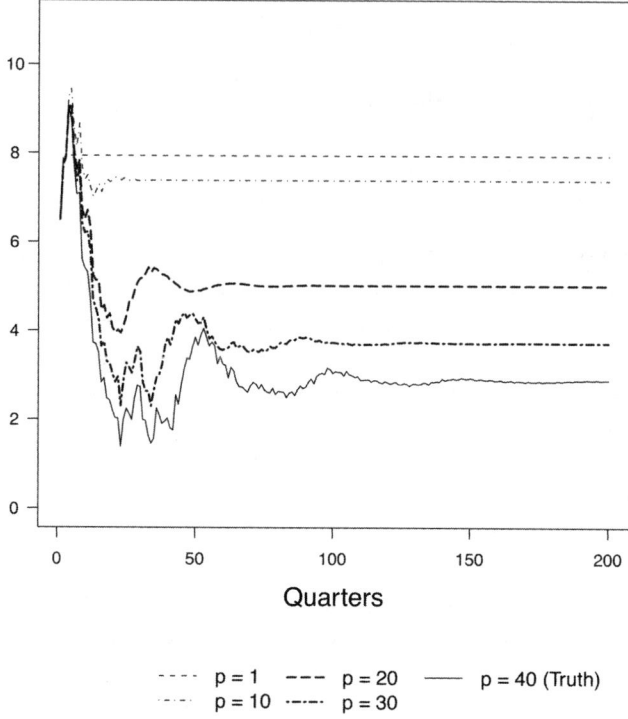

Quarters

- - - - p = 1   - - - p = 20   ——— p = 40 (Truth)
- ·- · p = 10   ·-·-· p = 30

Fig. 2.   Response of income in levels

Hopefully the previous discussion makes clear the intuition for why a "wrong" value for p affects the volatility of consumption. The same logic makes clear that agents ought to worry about model uncertainty; that is, they would pay a positive amount to know the true ARMA model for Δd_t. If this amount is large, I do not see how the authors can justify abstracting from the issue of how agents would act if they acknowledged model and parameter uncertainty. Absent some justification for the separation assumption, it is hard to have much confidence in the asset pricing implications of the model.

Cochrane (1989) to the Rescue?

Cochrane (1989) shows that for an interesting class of problems, feasible first-order mistakes in the choice variables of a single agent problem have second-order utility consequences. Moreover, these deviations can have a dramatic impact on the time series implications of consumption allocation models and the behavior of asset prices. Is that what's going on in this paper? If so, we have a possible rationale for the authors' assumption that agents do not worry about model mispecification. Indeed, the paper could be viewed as an interesting example of the Cochrane principle with the extra, important refinement that we can draw on the psychology literature to motivate the particular "small" mistake that agents are making.

To illustrate this point, consider the following modified version of one of Cochrane's examples. Consider a representative household with exogenous income given by

$$(1 - \rho L)d_t = \bar{y} + \rho_1(1 - \rho L)d_{t-1} + \ldots + (1 - \rho L)\rho_n d_{t-n} + \sigma\varepsilon_t.$$

The parameter ρ can be arbitrarily close to 1 so that we that we can mimic the time series behavior of ARIMA(p, 1, 0) processes well. The household maximizes the criterion

$$U = \frac{-1}{2} \sum_{t=0}^{\infty} \beta^t (c_t - \bar{c})^2,$$

where $\bar{c}$ is a nonnegative constant. The household can borrow and lend at the constant interest rate

$$R = 1 + r, \beta = \frac{1}{1 + r},$$

where r is a nonnegative constant. The household's budget constraint is given by

$$k_{t+1} = (1 + r)k_t + d_t - c_t.$$

Here k_t is beginning of period t accumulated capital or nonhuman wealth, and plays the role of bonds in Fuster et al.

Cochrane (1989) considers the case where $\rho_1 = \rho_2 = \ldots \rho_n = 0$. In this case, d_t is an AR(1) and optimal consumption evolves as

$$c_t^* = rk_t^* + m^*(d_t - Ed)$$

$$k_{t+1}^* = (1 - m^*)(d_t - Ed)$$

$$m^* = \frac{r}{1 + r - \rho}.$$

Here Ed denotes the uconditional expectation of d.

Motivated by Flavin's (1981) findings, Cochrane supposes that the agent's decision rule for consumption is given by

$$c_t^+ = rk_t^+ + m^+(d_t - Ed)$$

$$k_{t+1}^+ = (1 - m^+)(d_t - Ed)$$

$$m^+ > m^*.$$

By construction, the alternative decision rules, incorporating different values of m^+, respect the agent's budget constraint. Cochrane chooses m^+ to account for Flavin's (1980) influential estimate of the excess-sensitivity of consumption to current income. By construction, the model "solves" the excess-sensitivity puzzle.

Cochrane emphasizes that this solution is only interesting if the required deviation from the benchmark value of m^* is small in the sense that an agent would not pay much to go from m^+ to m^*. In fact, Cochrane shows that the agent pays only a trivial amount (substantially less than $1 a year) to go from m^+ to m^*. He argues that a similar logic applies to various asset pricing puzzles.

We can perform a similar experiment to evaluate the deviation from rational expectations adopted by Fuster et al. Suppose that the law of motion for $(1 - \rho L)d_t$ is the $AR(40)$ corresponding to the specification for Δd_t used in the paper. Also assume that agents incorrectly think that $(1 - \rho L)d_t$ is governed by a low order AR processes. In addition, I use the Cochrane calibration, which makes relative risk aversion equal to 4 in an area around steady state. This value is the same as the one used by Fuster et al.

Panel A of figure 3 displays the impulse response function of consumption for various value of p. For reference, panel B of figure 3 shows the impulse response function of consumption if agents assume $p = 4$, but I simply impose different value of m^* as in Cochrane.[4] The key results from panel A are as follows. First, under rational expectations, consumption adjusts once and for all and that is the end of the story. The rise in consumption induced by a unit shock to income is about one-third. Second, consistent with Fuster et al., the more parsimonious is the AR process used by agents, the larger is the initial jump in consumption. For example, in the AR(2) case, the ratio of the rise in consumption to the innovation in earnings is about 1.2. As in Fuster et al., when $p <$ 40 agents are using a misspecified model and are overestimating the present value of the change in income. Thus, consumption has to drop from its peak level. Consumption asymptotes to a level lower than the long-run response if agents had been using the correct AR specification. This decline must occur to ensure that agents' budget constraints hold.

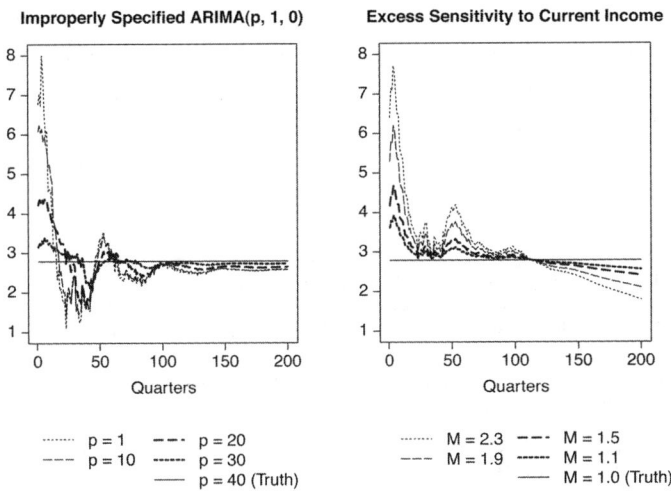

Fig. 3.   Impulse response of consumption

The key question is: how much would agents pay to know the truth? The answer is between 35 cents and $1.85 a quarter, depending on the AR that they mistakenly use. That's pretty small. Of course, lots of frictions could generate the kind of overshooting in consumption discussed earlier, including the psychological factors emphasized by Fuster et al. Panel B, which allows for different values of m^+, generates similar response patterns, with higher values m^+ corresponding roughly to lower values of p. Presumably different values of m^+ could be generated using various credit market imperfections.

Conclusion

This a very interesting paper that got me to think about lots of fascinating issues. It is clear that the authors' perturbation of the standard model helps them account for certain asset pricing puzzles. The key omission of the paper is a defense of the separation procedure that they invoke when modeling agents' behavior. That said, my calculations suggest that the authors might be able to come up with a potentially compelling defense of this procedure. Agents may just not be willing to pay very much to know the true data-generating mechanisms in their setup. My guess is that despite the fact that they are mistaken about the exact nature of the data-generating mechanism, agents' consumption levels are, on average, correct. By this I mean that their intertemporal budget constraint holds. To the extent that this defense of the separation procedure holds, it would be one more application of Lucas' (1987) point that once you get the levels right, the fluctuations do not seem to matter all that much.

Endnotes

I thank Ben Johannsen for superb research assistance in preparing this comment. For acknowledgments, sources of research support, and disclosure of the author's material financial relationships, if any, please see http://www.nber.org/chapters/c12405.ack.
   1. See, for example, Acemoglu and Ozdaglar (2011) for a review of recent research on belief and opinion dynamics in social networks.
   2. For recent reviews of this literature see Hansen and Sargent (2010) and Epstein and Schneider (2010).
   3. See footnote 30 of the paper for data definitions.
   4. I solve this version of the model by multiplying the coefficient on current d_t by a factor greater than its optimal value (one).

References

Acemoglu, Daron, and Asuman Ozdaglar. 2011. "Opinion Dynamics and Learning in Social Networks." *Dynamic Games and Applications* 1 (1): 3–49.
Christiano, Lawrence, Martin Eichenbaum, and Robert Vigfusson. 2006. "Assessing Structural VARs." In *NBER Macroeconomics Annual 2006*, vol. 21, edited by Daron Acemoglu, Kenneth Rogoff and Michael Woodford. Chicago: University of Chicago Press.
Cochrane, John. 1989. "The Sensitivity of Tests of the Intertemporal Allocation of Consumption to Near-Rational Alternatives." *American Economic Review* 79 (June): 319–37.
Epstein, Larry, and Martin Schneider. 2010. "Ambiguity and Asset Markets." *Annual Review of Financial Economics* 2 (1): 315–46.
Flavin, M. A. 1981. "The Adjustment of Consumption to Changing Expectations About Future Income." *Journal of Political Economy* 89 (5): 974-1009.
Fuster, Andrea, David Laibson, and Brock Mendel. 2010. "Natural Expectations and Economic Fluctuations." *Journal of Economic Perspectives* 24 (4): 67–84.
Hansen, L. P., and T. J. Sargent. 2010. "Wanting Robustness in Macroeconomics." In *Handbook of Monetary Economics*, vol. 3, edited by B. M. Friedman and M. Woodford. North Holland: Elsevier.
Hansen, L. P., and K. J. Singleton. 1982. "Generalized Instrumental Variables Estimation of Nonlinear Rational Expectations Models." *Econometrica* 50 (5): 1269–86.
Lucas, Robert E., Jr. 1987. *Models of Business Cycles*. New York: Basil Blackwell.
Muth, J. F. 1961. "Rational Expectations and the Theory of Price Movements." *Econometrica* 29 (3): 315–35.

Comment

George W. Evans, *University of Oregon and University of St. Andrews*

Introduction

Expectations clearly play a central role in modern macroeconomics. Households and firms are assumed to be dynamic optimizers, making decisions about work, consumption, savings, production, and investment, based in part on current economic conditions, but also to a great extent on the future state of the economy. Thus, in particular, household saving and portfolio decisions depend on expected future interest rates, inflation, and taxes and on the likely future trajectory of equity dividends and prices. Because of the key role of expectations in economics and finance, theories of expectations have been central to modern economic theory. Since the rational expectations (RE) revolution of the 1970s—associated with John Muth, Robert Lucas, and Thomas Sargent—the benchmark theory has been that expectations are formed rationally, in the sense that they are consistent with the true model and yield forecast errors that are orthogonal to agents' information sets.

In their paper in this volume, Andreas Fuster, Benjamin Hebert, and David Laibson present an asset-pricing model in which RE is replaced by natural expectations (NE). Under NE, agents misspecify the time-series model in a "natural" way: they chose a parsimonious model of dividends that omits longer lags. This captures short-run dynamics but misses long-run mean reversion. An earlier paper, Fuster, Laibson, and Mendel (2010), made similar arguments about other macroeconomic time series.[1] Taken together, the two papers suggest the even bolder possibility of NE as a general stylized description of expectation formation.

In the current paper, Fuster et al. insert an NE dividend forecasting equation into a Lucas-type consumption-based asset-pricing model with constant absolute risk aversion (CARA) preferences and habit persistence. Using this setup, Fuster et al. can replicate a number of stylized facts and puzzles about asset price data and consumption. These include the findings of excess volatility of stock prices, that excess returns are negatively predicted by lagged excess returns, price to earnings ratios, and consumption growth, and the existence of a large equity premium.

Outline of Their Argument

Fuster et al. consider a variation of the Lucas-type "tree" model of asset prices. In keeping with Lucas (1978) there is an endowment economy with a single risky asset, trees, which provide an exogenous stochastic dividend of the perishable, homogeneous consumption good. The principal variation is that Fuster et al. consider an open economy version in which agents can borrow or lend internationally at a fixed interest rate R. In addition, exponential (CARA) preferences with habits are used. Finally, Δd_t, the first difference in dividends, is assumed to follow to follow a stationary AR(p) process for some $p > 0$.

The exponential preferences give a type of mean-variance setup, and Fuster et al. show that the asset price p_t satisfies

$$p_t = \sum_{s=1}^{\infty} R^{-s}E_t d_{t+1} - \frac{R\alpha \times Var_t \Delta c_{t+1}}{(1 - R^{-1}\gamma)(R - 1)^2}.$$

Fuster et al. also show how to obtain closed-form expressions for p_t and for consumption, c_t, given beliefs about the AR(p) process for Δd_t. Here R is the inverse of the discount factor, α is the CARA measure of risk aversion, and γ is the habit-persistence parameter.

The key assumptions of the Fuster et al. model concern the stochastic process *actually* followed by dividends and the *perceived* process followed by dividends. The true dividend process is assumed to be a high-order stationary AR(p) for the first difference in dividends d_t; that is, $\Delta d_t = \sum_{i=1}^{p} \rho_i \Delta d_{t-i} + \varepsilon_t$, or

$$\Delta d_t = (1 - \Phi(L))^{-1}\varepsilon_t,$$

where ε_t is white noise and $\Phi(L) = \sum_{i=1}^{p} \rho_i L^i$. Furthermore, $\Phi(L)$ is assumed to be such that there is a hump-shaped impulse response function for dividend levels $\partial d_{t+j}/\partial \varepsilon_t$. Put differently, d_t is assumed to have a unit root with dynamics that lead to long-run mean reversion.

Evidence for this is given in Fuster et al.'s figure 2, which presents $\partial d_{t+j}/\partial\varepsilon_t$ based on empirical estimates of $\Phi(L)$ for $AR(p)$ processes with alternative values of p. (In the empirical work, Fuster et al. use earnings rather than dividends.) The long-run level of persistence is given by

$$\lim_{j\to\infty} \partial d_{t+j}/\partial\varepsilon_t = (1 - \Phi(1))^{-1},$$

and for $p \geq 15$ we have $0 < (1 - \Phi(1))^{-1} < 1$. Thus there is *mean reversion* in the sense that an innovation ε_t has a reduced permanent impact. Fuster et al. assume that large values of p (e.g., $p = 40$) correspond to the truth.

In contrast, for $p \leq 10$ estimates of long-run persistence are $(1 - \Phi(1))^{-1} > 1$. That is, based on low-order $AR(p)$ estimates, one would come to the conclusion that one should *extrapolate* innovations in dividends—that the long-run effects are larger than the impact effect. Fuster et al. assume that low-order $AR(p)$ estimates correspond to the *perceived* dividend process; that is, to the view held by economic agents.

The essence of Fuster et al.'s approach is thus that the beliefs of agents differ from the truth and do so in a particular way. Agents use simpler low-order time-series models that lead them to accentuate the importance of short-run trends and to neglect longer-run corrections in which dividends revert toward an underlying trend. This central feature leads to the empirical implications noted before.

What is the rationale for the discrepancy they assume between truth and perception? Fuster et al. give two types of argument—statistical/ econometric and psychological. The statistical argument is that econometricians have often argued that in forecasting there is an advantage in using parsimonious models in preference to more complex models. Furthermore, standard statistical procedures for model selection based on Akaike Information Criterion (AIC) and, especially, Bayesian Information Criterion (BIC) often select low-order models. The psychological argument is that agents, for a variety of reasons, prefer to use simple, parsimonious models in preference to complex models when trying to understand the world and make decisions.

Fuster et al. are usually careful not to be too dogmatic on this point. In essence they say: there is some evidence, as seen in their table 1 and figure 2, that a higher-order $AR(p)$ process of Δd_t might well be correct, while agents might plausibly believe in a low-order process. Their paper then explores the full implications of this assumption.

Links to the Macro Learning Literature

If the truth is that p is large, but agents believe that p is small, then clearly agents do not have RE. There is a now extensive macro literature, which started around 1980, in which RE is replaced, for example, by adaptive or econometric learning (see Sargent 1993 and Evans and Honkapohja 2001, 2009).

A major argument for the adaptive learning approach is what might be called the *cognitive consistency principle*.[2] According to this principle, agents should be assumed to have the same level of rationality as the economic modeler or policymaker (in contrast to both old-style adaptive expectations and to RE). On the adaptive learning approach agents are assumed to make forecasts in the same way that econometricians do—formulating models, estimating their parameters, and updating estimated coefficients over time as new data become available. When parameters are updated using a form of least-squares, this is known as least-squares (LS) learning.

The early macro learning literature focused on whether or not LS learning would converge over time to RE in *self-referential* models, in which the variables being forecasted are affected by the forecasts. Conditions were worked out that determined whether or not REE (RE equilibria) were indeed stable under LS learning. Stability under learning could then be used as a selection criteria in models with multiple REE, since in some cases only a subset of REE were stable under learning.

More recently, another major strand has been to show how learning can generate transitory or persistent "learning dynamics"; that is, dynamics different from RE. Much of the recent macro learning literature has emphasized learning dynamics induced by one or more of the following factors: (a) misspecified forecasting models (misspecified "perceived laws of motion" or PLMs); (b) discounted LS learning (downweighting past data due to concern about unknown structural change); and (c) dynamic predictor selection (selecting between alternative PLMs based on past performance) or Bayesian model averaging. Applications of the approach that emphasize learning dynamics include: the rise and fall of inflation in the United States, hyperinflation, business cycles, output and inflation inertia, optimal monetary and fiscal policy, and asset price anomalies.

One useful concept from the recent macro learning literature has been that of a restricted perceptions equilibrium (RPE), in which agents make the best forecast they can, given their misspecified PLM.[3] A special case of interest has been models that are underparameterized, either in terms of variables or lag lengths. The argument here has been precisely that econometricians recognize the value of parsimoniously specified models, and thus the cognitive consistency principle dictates that we should examine the implications of underparameterization. One can, for example, work out stability conditions for an RPE when agents use LS learning to update coefficients of a particular underparameterized model.

Thus the Fuster et al. approach fits well with the recent macro learning literature. The principal contribution of this paper, in this context, is that it posits a particular, plausible type of misspecification by agents, which can arguably explain several puzzling features of asset prices, and which may also be of more general applicability.

Discussion

I certainly find plausible Fuster et al.'s key assumption that economic agents underparameterize their forecasting models. This assumption is consistent with the cognitive consistency principle, given that many applied econometricians place value on parsimony and recognize the likelihood of misspecification. This hypothesis also fits well with the observation that many economists believe there is long-run mean reversion that is nonetheless difficult to detect.[4] That is, the misspecification that Fuster et al. assume is particularly plausible.

Other aspects of the Fuster et al. model are also attractive: the closed-form solutions under CARA preferences, for the class of perceived dividend processes examined, is likely to be more generally useful, and the simultaneous fit of a range of stylized facts is impressive.

It is therefore hard not to like this paper: the model is both simple and powerful. However, of course the model has some weaknesses, several of which are noticeable from the macro learning viewpoint. This in turn suggests a number of natural extensions.

Criticisms

In my critical discussion I will focus on three main issues. The first concerns the information set available to agents when making forecasts. By assumption, Δd_t is an exogenous univariate process, which leads Fuster et al. to examine alternative univariate forecasting models. However, within macroeconomics the norm is to consider multivariate forecasting models, and this issue is pertinent to the question of long-run persistence and to the plausibility of the form of underparameterization assumed. For example, in the early discussion of long-run GDP persistence, Campbell and Mankiw (1987) focused on univariate techniques, and found persistence levels greater than one. However, both the unemployment rate and the consumption-output ratio Granger cause output growth, and lower levels of persistence, with mean reversion, are found in multivariate models (e.g., see Evans 1989 and Evans and Reichlin 1994). In the current context Timmermann (1994), for example, has argued that stock prices Granger cause dividends. Thus a simple bivariate forecasting model might lead to different persistence results. The issue is whether simple—that is, low-order vector autoregressions— might show long-run mean reversion more clearly, in which case this feature of the data would be less plausibly missed by economic agents. Of course, many agents might still in practice use "natural" low-order univariate models, but a heterogeneous expectations model might then be more realistic.

My second concern is the fixed parameter assumption of Fuster et al. Suppose first that we agree that agents plausibly underparameterize Δd_t as an AR(1). From the learning viewpoint this leads to the corresponding RPE as the appropriate equilibrium to which the system would, if stable, converge. However, the cognitive consistency principle suggests that agents would not know the parameters of this process a priori, but, like real-world econometricians, would estimate the parameters and update their estimates over time. Furthermore, if agents are concerned about potential structural change, they might discount older data, leading to persistent learning dynamics around the RPE. This particular issue could easily be addressed by simulations in which fixed parameter natural expectations were replaced by discounted LS learning with the same AR(1) PLM.

Related to both of the previous two points, if long-run estimates of persistence are crucial for good decision making in their portfolio choices, one might expect agents to focus on this issue in their choice of forecasting models. They might estimate mean reversion directly and allow for uncertainty concerning its value in their decisions. Alternatively, they might adopt decision-making rules that are robust to errors in this dimension, along the lines of Hansen and Sargent (2007).

The third issue, which is probably most central from the learning perspective, is that the Fuster et al. model is not self-referential. Agents simply forecast dividends, which is treated as an exogenous process, and do not have a forecasting model for stock prices. Some learning models emphasize short-horizon decision making, in which the demand for stocks depends on short-horizon expected returns, and possibly also on the estimated conditional variance of returns. See, for example, Brock and Hommes (1998); Lansing (2010); Adam, Marcet, and Nicolini (2010); and Branch and Evans (2011). Indeed, one way to formulate the most basic risk-neutral model of stock prices is to assume that prices are determined by the sum of expected dividend and expected stock price in the coming period. These models are self-referential in the sense that asset prices today depend on the expected price tomorrow, so that the evolution of the variable being forecasted depends on the expectations themselves.

Self-referential models, because of this feedback, give a much greater role to expectations, and this makes more likely asset-price bubbles: self-fulfilling or nearly self-fulfilling asset price movements with complex dynamics in which prices can become detached from fundamentals for extended periods. My own view is that this dynamic plays a central role in asset prices.

Example: A Simple Model of Bubbles

An example of the scope for dramatic learning dynamics in self-referential asset price models is given in my work with William Branch, presented in Branch and Evans (2011). We use a simple mean-variance linear asset pricing model. The setup can come from an overlapping generations model in which agents have two period planning horizons, CARA preferences, and a choice between a risky stock and a risk-free asset. The central equation is

$$p_t = \beta E_t^*(p_{t+1} + d_{t+1}) - \beta a \sigma_t^2 z_{st},$$

where z_{st} is the iid random supply of the risky asset, E_t^* denotes the subjective expectations of agents, and σ_t^2 is their estimate of the conditional variance of returns. We assume the dividend process is known and that agents therefore need estimates of the price process to make their decisions.

With iid dividend and supply shocks, the REE for p_t is a constant + white noise. Under learning, agents forecast p_t as an AR(1) using discounted LS and they estimate σ_t^2 using a simple recursive algorithm. Because agents discount past data, prices under learning will occasionally break free from their fundamentals and exhibit bubbles and crashes. This results from the self-referential feature of the model.

An illustrative simulation is shown in figure 1 (see Branch and Evans

68   Evans

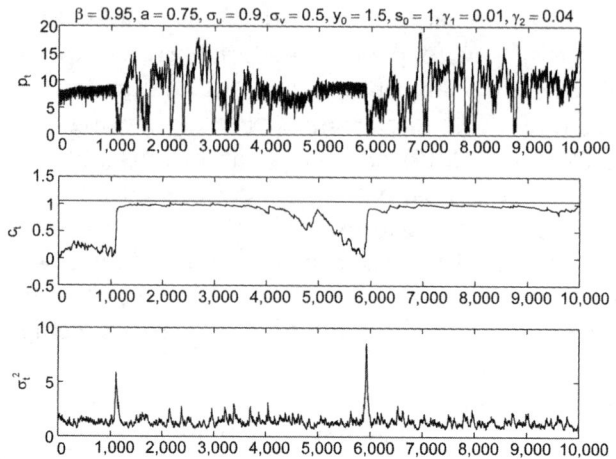

Fig. 1. Asset price dynamics in the Branch and Evans (2011) model

2011 for analysis and for other simulations). The figure shows the realized price p_t under learning and also the time series of estimates of two
key learning parameters, the AR(1) coefficient c_t and the estimate of the
conditional variance σ_t^2. The figure shows the price process initially
very close to the REE, which is a constant plus white noise in our setup.
However, under learning, asset prices occasionally break free into a
bubble regime in which stock prices are believed to follow a pure random walk ($c = 1$). In this regime p_t is particularly sensitive to changes in
the estimate of risk σ_t^2.

In summary, self-referential learning models have great scope for
generating some of the more extreme partially self-fulfilling movements of stock prices often described as bubbles and crashes. Intuitively, the reason for this is that the stock price p_t depends on expected
price $E_t^* p_{t+1}$ with a coefficient $\beta < 1$ that is close to one.

Other Types of Learning Dynamics

In various settings learning dynamics have also been shown in self-
referential models to lead to: (a) inertia of inflation and output, as in
Orphanides and Williams (2007) and Milani (2007); (b) overshooting
and nonmonotone impulse response functions (e.g., Eusepi and Preston
2011 and Evans, Honkapohja, and Mitra 2009); and (c) regime-switching
and parameter drift (e.g., Sargent 1999, Cogley and Sargent 2005, and

Branch and Evans 2007). For numerous examples and references, see Evans and Honkapohja (2011).

With this in mind, consider again the question of whether it is plausible that agents believe Δd_t is a specific constant coefficient AR(p) process with known parameters. Parameter drift and regime switching appear to be standard features of the data, as emphasized by Sims and Zha (2006), Cogley and Sargent (2005), and Sargent, Williams, and Zha (2006). The cognitive consistency principle suggests that agents should therefore allow for the possibility of structural change in their parameter estimation and through model selection, model averaging, or robust decision making.

In the Fuster et al. setup, under RE the risk premium is very small. In the late 1990s some people argued ("Dow 30,000") that the rise of the stock market was due to a recognition that the market risk premium was too high. An implication of Fuster et al. is that this view is fundamentally correct. Is it not, however, more plausible to believe that the risk premium reflects the uncertainty that economists and agents share?

Conclusions

Although I have indicated a number of reservations, overall I find the Fuster et al. story very attractive. The setup is conceptually simple, and it is based on the plausible premise that agents underparameterize their forecasting model. This is in line with standard econometric advice to estimate parsimonious models, as well as evidence from psychology that people are inclined to make decisions based on simple heuristics. The Fuster et al. model is disciplined and delivers a number of important empirical implications that appear to be in line with the data.

I would prefer to extend the model to include additional insights from the adaptive learning literature, but even as it stands the Fuster et al. model provides an impressive but simple benchmark model of asset-price behavior, which is sure to receive considerable attention.

Endnotes

For acknowledgments, sources of research support, and disclosure of the authors' material financial relationships, if any, please see http://www.nber.org/chapters/c12406 .ack.

1. Actually, in Fuster et al. (2010) the term "natural expectations" is used to denote an average between RE and what is called NE in the current paper.

2. See Evans and Honkapohja (2009, 2011).

3. Closely related concepts are those of "self-confirming equilibria" and "consistent expectations equilibria."

4. Estimating long-run persistence $(1 - \Phi(1))^{-1}$ is equivalent to estimating the spectrum of d_t at zero, and is understood to be subject to great uncertainty.

References

Adam, Klaus, Albert Marcet, and Juan Pablo Nicolini. 2010. "Learning and Stock Market Volatility." Working Paper.

Branch, William A., and George W. Evans. 2007. "Model Uncertainty and Endogenous Volatility." *Review of Economic Dynamics* 10:207–37.

———. 2011. "Learning about Risk and Returns: A Simple Model of Bubbles and Crashes." *American Economic Journal: Macroeconomics* 3:159–91.

Brock, William A., and Cars H. Hommes. 1998. "Heterogenous Beliefs and Routes to Chaos in a Simple Asset Pricing Model." *Journal of Economic Dynamics and Control* 22:1235–74.

Campbell, John Y., and N. Gregory Mankiw. 1987. *Quarterly Journal of Economics* 102: 857–80.

Cogley, Timothy, and Thomas J. Sargent. 2005. "The Conquest of US Inflation: Learning and Robustness to Model Uncertainty." *Review of Economic Dynamics* 8:528–63.

Eusepi, Stefano, and Bruce Preston. 2011. "Expectations, Learning and Business Cycle Fluctuations." *American Economic Review* 101:2844–72.

Evans, George W. 1989. "Output and Unemployment Dynamics in the United States: 1950–1985." *Journal of Applied Econometrics* 4:213–37.

Evans, George W., and Seppo Honkapohja. 2001. *Learning and Expectations in Macroeconomics.* Princeton, NJ: Princeton University Press.

———. 2009. "Learning and Macroeconomics." *Annual Review of Economics* 1:421–51.

———. 2011. "Learning As a Rational Foundation for Macroeconomics and Finance." In *Rethinking Expectations: The Way Forward for Macroeconomics,* Roman Frydman and Edmund S. Phelps (eds.), Princeton, NJ: Princeton University Press, forthcoming.

Evans, George W., Seppo Honkapohja, and Kaushik Mitra. 2009. "Anticipated Fiscal Policy and Learning." *Journal of Monetary Economics* 56:930–53.

Evans, George W., and Lucrezia Reichlin. 1994. "Information, Forecasts and Measurement of the Business Cycle." *Journal of Monetary Economics* 33:233–54.

Fuster, A., D. Laibson, and B. Mendel. 2010. "Natural Expectations and Macroeconomic Fluctuations." *Journal of Economic Perspectives* 24:67–84.

Hansen, Lars P., and Thomas J. Sargent. 2007. *Robustness.* Princeton, NJ: Princeton University Press.

Lansing, Kevin. 2010. "Rational and Near-Rational Bubbles without Drift." *Economic Journal* 120:1149–74.

Lucas, Robert E. 1978. "Asset Prices in an Exchange Economy." *Econometrica* 46: 1429–45.

Milani, Fabio. 2007. "Expectations, Learning and Macroeconomic Persistence." *Journal of Monetary Economics* 54: 2065–82.

Orphanides, Athanasios, and John C. Williams. 2007. "Robust Monetary Policy with Imperfect Knowledge." *Journal of Monetary Economics* 54:1406–35.

Sargent, Thomas J. 1993. *Bounded Rationality in Macroeconomics.* Oxford: Oxford University Press.

———. 1999. *The Conquest of American Inflation*. Princeton, NJ: Princeton University Press.

Sargent, Thomas J., Noah Williams, and Tao Zha. 2006. "Shocks and Government Beliefs: The Rise and Fall of American Inflation." *American Economic Review* 96:1193–224.

Sims, Christopher, and Tao Zha. 2006. "Were There Regime Switches in US Monetary Policy?" *American Economic Review* 96:54–81.

Timmermann, Allan. 1994. "Can Agents Learn to Form Rational Expectations? Some Results on Convergence and Stability of Learning in the UK Stock Market." *Economic Journal* 104:777–97.

Discussion

Robert Hall opened the discussion by questioning whether the authors should target a high equity premium for their model given that the equity premium over the last fifty years has dropped to 1.6 percentage points. Hall also asked why the agents in the model would not try to approximate the income process with an ARIMA process with moderate p and q values, as Box and Jenkins (1970) would suggest for processes with lengthy AR representations. Andreas Fuster responded that the authors used some moderate p/q specifications, but these specifications did not greatly improve on the performance of simpler models.

Hall also highlighted the role of valuation ratios in investor decision making, but noted that agents in the model do not use any valuation measures for forming expectations. Finally, Hall emphasized the importance of thinking about the environment in which investment decisions take place, where intermediaries have strong incentives to aggressively market financial products and advice to investors who may be less informed.

Darrell Duffie suggested that a model with delayed adjustment of investors' expectations would generate features similar to the authors' model. Delayed adjustment of expectations might be optimal given an attention or information cost and would match data on the low frequency of portfolio adjustment. Moreover, delayed adjustment of expectations would generate higher risk premia for short-dated securities versus longer-dated securities consistent with empirical evidence on returns documented in Van Binsbergen and Koijen (2009).

Following on the discussion by Martin Eichenbaum, Olivier Blanchard noted that, because investors' decisions do not affect the income process, the welfare costs of natural expectations may be underestimated. Blanchard also asked whether the bias in estimating a lower-order AR model (when the true model is a higher-order AR process) would necessarily go in one direction or the other. Fuster responded that the direction of bias is sample-specific. In theory, lower p models might have a downward or upward bias relative to the true higher p process.

Xavier Gabaix commented that the authors could cite results in behavioral finance to support their model of expectations formation. Gabaix noted that growth stocks command a premium to value stocks because investors tend to overestimate the persistence of earnings growth. On the welfare effects of natural expectations, Gabaix argued that providing the rational expectations agents access to a larger set of financial assets would magnify welfare effects by allowing these agents greater opportunities to exploit their informational advantage. Gabaix also responded to Eichenbaum's discussion that agents who do not know the true model might act more conservatively, citing evidence that people often ignore low probability events and respond to complexity by resorting to simple rules.

Reiterating Hall's comment, Albert Marcet asked about why agents do not use multivariate forecasting to estimate the income process. In particular, Marcet suggested that the use of the lagged price-dividend ratio may improve forecasts as a valuation measure. Marcet also disagreed with Gabaix's view that the introduction of additional assets would result in large gains for the agents with rational expectations. Marcet noted that the RE agents may still be constrained by incomplete asset markets or uncertainty.

Luigi Zingales asked about whether the long-term mean reversion observed in the dividend process is specific to the United States and whether this mean-reversion reflects a lack of disaster episodes. Like Gabaix, he suggested testing the model using returns for individual stocks given disaster episodes for companies in the form of bankruptcy.

James Kahn noted that Eichenbaum's welfare cost calculation did not include habit formation. He suggested that welfare costs may be larger if optimism leads to larger purchases, such as durable goods, and increase the disutility of the subsequent mean reversion in income.

Lars Hansen expressed concern that the authors' conclusions rely on the mean-reverting behavior of an AR process for income that may be overfit and urged the authors to try to incorporate this uncertainty in their calculations. Responding to Gabaix, he emphasized that a robustness approach does not preclude simple rules but simply recognizes the importance of considering the utility consequences of selecting different models.

Frederic Mishkin agreed with Eichenbaum about the need to consider whether the marginal rational expectations investor could use leveraged positions to exploit any asset mispricing and whether this trading would affect prices. He encouraged the authors to further develop their extensions, with rational expectations agents trading with natural expectations agents.

Daron Acemoglu sought clarification on interpreting the welfare analysis by Eichenbaum. He noted that the model is not purely general equilibrium since the real interest rate is fixed but asset prices are determined endogenously. The Eichenbaum welfare calculation may underestimate the welfare effect given that the rational expectations agents would benefit from the prices set by the natural expectations agents. Acemoglu also proposed an alternative approach where agents hold heterogeneous priors over simpler models and then ask how strong these priors would have to be so that the data in the sample fails to reject their prior. Finally, Acemoglu pointed out that the authors' assumption of a fixed interest rate may have important consequences. In particular, if their model of expectations formation is used to explain bubble episodes, the rise in desired consumption would require high interest rates. However, available evidence suggests that bubble episodes are accompanied by lower real interest rates.

Eichenbaum responded to questions about the welfare calculation brought up during the discussion. He emphasized that he did not consider the effect of the introduction of rational expectations traders on the margin in his calculations. Acemoglu responded that these agents would benefit from the fact that prices were set by agents with natural expectations even if their actions had no effect on prices.

Benjamin Hebert addressed questions about how introducing rational expectations agents would affect their results. He noted that RE agents would not make unbounded profits since they still faced risk, but RE investors benefit from both the equity premium and timing the market in their trading. These agents follow a buy and hold strategy, and future work will consider how a sufficiently large mass of RE investors would affect prices.

David Laibson agreed with Hall's comment that the authors examined only a particular way in which investors make mistakes. He emphasized that their objective was to characterize a fairly large set of ways in which individuals make mistakes in forecasting and generate testable predictions. Responding to Hansen and Evans, Laibson emphasized the inherent difficulty for investors to systematically address issues of model selection, robustness, and uncertainty. He acknowledged that the authors' assumption is that agents are overconfident and fail to fully address robustness concerns. Laibson closed the discussion by addressing the use of a fixed interest rate in their model. He noted that their results were unchanged with an endogenous interest rate because natural expectations agents perceive income to follow (nearly) a random walk. Therefore, the endogenous real interest rate is nearly constant.

2

House Price Booms and the Current Account

Klaus Adam, *Mannheim University and CEPR*
Pei Kuang, *University of Frankfurt*
Albert Marcet, *London School of Economics, CEP, and CEPR*

I. Introduction

We present a stylized open economy asset pricing model with rationally investing households that can quantitatively replicate the house price dynamics in the G7 economies over the years 2001–2008, as well as the associated dynamics of the current account.

In our model, boom and bust dynamics in house prices are triggered by macrofundamentals—for example, changes in real interest rates or housing preferences—but, as in the data, the response to these changes in fundamentals can vary across countries. Also similar to the data, price booms in our model are associated with an expansion of the housing stock, a deterioration of the current account, and a consumption boom, while the subsequent house price declines are accompanied by current account improvements and subdued consumption.

To study the relationship between house price movements, housing construction, consumption, and international borrowing, we generalize the closed economy asset pricing models developed previously in Adam and Marcet (2010, 2011) and Adam, Marcet, and Nicolini (2010) along three dimensions. First, we consider a setting with two assets, namely a domestically traded risky asset—the housing stock—and an internationally traded riskless bond. Second, we newly incorporate a borrowing constraint that limits household leverage and the overall amount of borrowing, following Kiyotaki and Moore (1997). Third, we consider a production economy with endogenous asset supply by explicitly incorporating a construction sector. Despite these extensions our model is relatively parsimonious.

The quantitative success of the model crucially rests on the assumption that we allow for households that are uncertain about how house prices relate to economic fundamentals. Our households are thus at par with academic economists who appear to be equally uncertain about the right model governing asset prices. We incorporate this feature by putting to work the concept of "internal rationality," as developed previously in Adam and Marcet (2010, 2011). Internally rational investors are utility maximizers in the standard sense and entertain fully specified and dynamically consistent beliefs about all payoff-relevant variables that are external to them (including competitive market prices). Internally rational agents, however, do not fully understand how market prices are formed, so that their subjective probability distribution about prices may not be exactly equal to the true equilibrium distribution. Agents nevertheless have a very good understanding of how to predict prices. First, their beliefs about prices are near-rational in the sense that they are assumed to be close to the rational expectations equilibrium (REE) beliefs typically attributed to agents in the literature. Second, the model that agents entertain about price behavior is validated by actual data, in the sense that it would be accepted by a standard testing procedure using actual data. Third, agents' house price model is validated by the outcome of the asset pricing model itself, in the sense that it would be rejected by an econometric test only as frequently as a model yielding rational expectations (RE).

Given agents' subjective uncertainty about price, optimal behavior implies that they update beliefs about house price behavior by applying Bayes' rule to market outcomes. Agents' price beliefs thus become a state variable and (Bayesian) learning gives rise to a dynamic feedback between price beliefs and actual price outcomes. As we show, this generates a considerable amount of additional propagation and can fuel boom and bust dynamics in house prices; that is, price dynamics that temporarily delink asset prices from their fundamental value. This is of interest because the momentum in house price changes that can be observed in the data has proven difficult to explain with the help of rational expectations models (see Glaeser and Gyourko 2006). Therefore, Glaeser, Gyourko, and Saiz (2008) previously suggested that models of learning can help resolve this empirical puzzle.

Learning about price dynamics turns out to be important for explaining the persistent rise and fall in house prices occurring over the years 2001–2008 in the G7. Our model thereby suggests that the strong fall in real interest rates after the year 2000 contributed significantly to the subsequent housing boom in some of the G7 economies. In line with the empirical evidence, however, the model predicts that these movements are not necessarily synchronized across countries. While some G7 countries experienced house price booms (United States, United Kingdom, Canada, Italy, France), they did so to very different degrees, and other countries (Japan, Germany) even displayed stagnant house prices over this period. The model successfully replicates this heterogeneity because the predicted house price evolution is highly dependent on agents' price beliefs at the time of the interest rate reduction, which in turn depend on the behavior of house prices in the respective economies prior to the fall in the real rate.

Our learning model is also compatible with observed house price expectations. Piazzesi and Schneider (2009) use the Michigan Survey of Consumers to document that the share of agents believing prices to increase further comoves positively with the house price level over the last housing boom. Specifically, the share of optimistic agents reached its peak precisely at the time when house prices peaked. This fact is consistent with the learning we propose and is difficult to reconcile with rational expectations.

The paper also suggests important policy lessons. Since the world interest rate is an exogenous parameter in the model, we can study the effects of alternative interest rate scenarios. For the US economy the model predicts that the recent US house price boom would have been largely avoided, and the current account deficit would have been considerably smaller, if interest rates had fallen by less at the beginning of the 2000s. Although such a link between real interest rates and house price booms is frequently discussed in the press,[1] to the best of our knowledge we present the first formal model in which a sizable *and* persistent house price boom can arise from a persistent reduction in the level of real interest rates.[2]

The paper is structured as follows. The next section discusses the related literature on house price fluctuations and current account dynamics. Section III presents stylized facts we seek to explain about the behavior of house prices, the current account, and private consumption in the G7. Section IV introduces a stylized open economy model, derives the household optimality conditions and the equations determining the equilibrium outcomes for a general set of subjective price beliefs. In Section V we show that the model has difficulties in replicating salient features of the data under RE. Section VI introduces subjective price beliefs that are close to the REE beliefs (in distribution) and learning about house price behavior. In Section VII we show how the learning model can qualitatively account for the observed dynamics in house prices, current accounts, and consumption in the G7. Sections VIII and IX then explore the quantitative model performance. Finally, Section X shows that learning agents who are confronted with the model-generated house price outcomes would reject their model of house price behavior approximately only as often as a model yielding rational expectations. A conclusion briefly summarizes.

II.   Related Literature

Relatively few papers study house price dynamics within dynamic equilibrium models before the recent recession. Important exceptions are Iacoviello (2005), who develops a monetary business cycle model with housing and collateral constraints, and Lustig and van Nieuwerburgh (2005), who study the role of house prices and housing collateral for the pricing of stocks.

Some recent papers use models of learning to explain observed house price data. Burnside, Eichenbaum, and Rebelo (2011), for example, present a model in which a temporary house price boom emerges from infectious optimism that eventually dissipates once investors become increasingly certain about fundamentals. Laibson and Mollerstrom (2010) present a model in which aggregate wealth fluctuates because agents learn about the expected future productivity of capital goods. Positive news about future productivity is shown to generate an increase in asset prices, a consumption boom, and a current account deficit. The small volatility of macroeconomic fundamentals, however, poses a problem for such news driven explanations of asset price fluctuations.

Other papers also account for some of the empirical features that we describe. Matsuyama (1990) provides a theoretical analysis of the income effect of government spending, housing subsidies, and sector-specific productivity change on residential investment and the current account. He shows that anticipated government spending shocks lead to a decline in house prices and residential investment, but that the effect on the current account depends on whether housing and nondurable consumption are substitutes or complements. Punzi (2006) evaluates the quantitative impact of the housing market on the current account using a two-sector, two-country dynamic stochastic general equilibrium (DSGE) model with heterogenous agents and a housing collateral constraint. In her setup, housing preference shocks generate a negative correlation between house prices and the current account.

Gete (2010) seeks to explain current account and housing price dynamics through cross-country heterogeneity in the evolution of housing demand. If the desire to smooth consumption across housing services and nondurable consumption goods is strong or if households' preferences feature low intratemporal substitution elasticity, then an increase in housing demand can give rise to a house price increase and a current account deficit.

III. Stylized Facts

A. *US House Prices and the Current Account 1996–2008*

A variety of house price measures indicate that house prices in the United States increased considerably over the years 1996–2006. Figure 1 depicts indices of the real house price (RHP), the price-to-income (PIR) ratio, and the price-to-rent (PRR) ratio normalizing indices to a value of 100 in the year 1996.[3] Prices increased—depending on the preferred house price measure—between 24% and 58% in the subsequent 10 years. While house prices started increasing well before the year 2000, all house price measures indicate that over 70% of the total increase takes place after the year 2000.

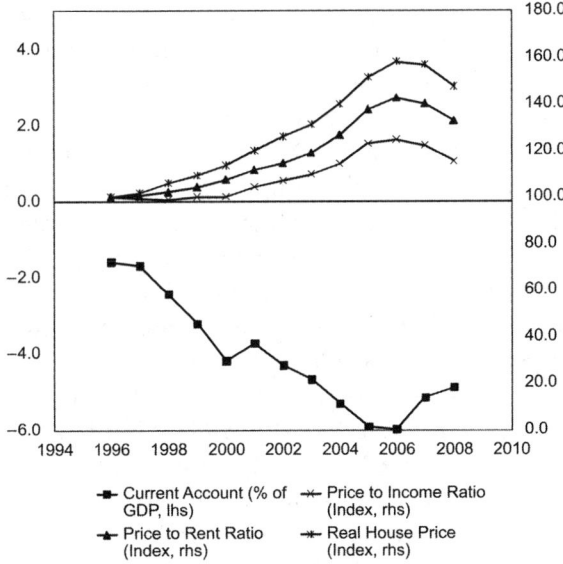

Fig. 1. United States: House price measures and the current account

Figure 1 also depicts the US current account deficit (in % of GDP).[4] The current account and the house price are strongly negatively associated over time, with the deficit widening considerably throughout the period 1996–2006, except for a slight and temporary improvement in the recession year 2001. Once house prices started to revert direction in the years 2007 and 2008, however, the US current account deficit also started to narrow, a development that accelerated in the year 2009 (see the current account data in table 1).

Table 1 reports the annual change in the value of the US housing stock (at market prices), together with the size of the current account deficit.[5] The bottom row in the table reveals that in the period 1996–2005, any one-dollar increase in the value of the US housing stock was on average associated with a 0.26 increase in international borrowing in the form of a current account deficit. This relationship is remarkably stable over these years (the standard deviation is just 0.04), but changes after the year 2006 when current account deficits improve only mildly, despite the domestic housing value either increasing less strongly (in 2006) or decreasing substantially (after 2007).

B. US: Real Rates, Consumption, and Construction

The house price and current account developments in the United States highlighted in the previous section were accompanied by a number of other broad macroeconomic trends that we now describe. We thereby focus on three variables, namely the behavior of real interest rates, private consumption, and construction activity

The acceleration of the US house price increase and the widening of current account deficits after the years 2000/2001 coincided with a considerable fall in ex ante real interest rates. Figure 2 illustrates this fact by depicting the one-year adjustable mortgage rate, subtracting from it the median expected one year ahead Consumer Price Index (CPI) inflation rate from the survey of professional forecasters.[6] The figure shows that ex ante real interest rates considerably dropped around the beginning of the year 2001 and stayed low for an extended period of time, before rising again around the year 2006. Overall, real interest rates display considerably less persistence than real house prices. While real interest rates completed a full cycle over the years 1996 to 2006, house prices steadily increased throughout this period. It thus appears far from immediate to establish a close link between house prices and real interest rates in the data.

To capture the interest rate evolution in a stylized way, we consider

Table 1
US Housing Value Appreciation and the Current Account

Year	1996	1997	1998	1999	2000	2001	2002	2003	2004	2005	2006	2007	2008	2009
Value change US house stock (vs. previous year, trn dollars)	+.4	+.5	+.9	+1.0	+1.7	+1.4	+1.3	+1.7	+2.6	+3.5	+1.0	-1.7	-3.8	-.8
US CA deficit (bn dollars)	114	129	205	292	410	392	452	516	625	741	798	717	670	380
CA deficit/change in house value	.27	.24	.22	.28	.25	.28	.34	.30	.23	.21	.84	-.41	-.18	-.45

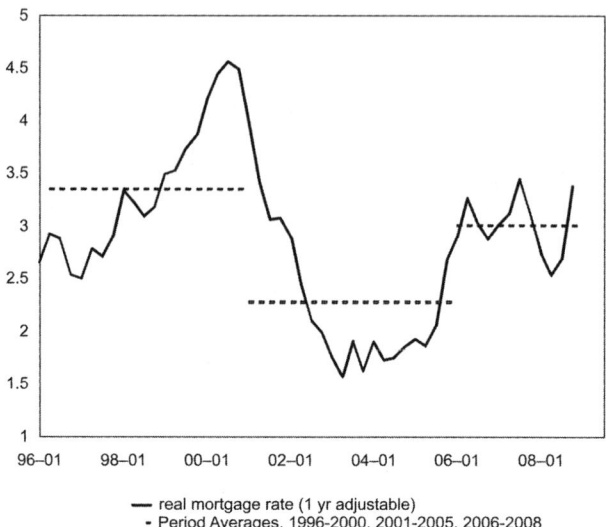

Fig. 2. United States: Ex ante real mortgage rate

three subperiods: a period with relatively high real rates over the years 1996–2000, a period with relatively low real rates over the years 2001–2005, and a period of moderately high rates in the years 2006–2008. The horizontal lines in figure 2 indicate the average interest rate for each of these subperiods.

Figure 3 depicts real private consumption growth together with various measures of house price growth.[7] Private consumption expanded over the years 1996–2006 by more than 3% each year, but came down after house prices reverted direction in 2007 and 2008. As has been documented before, there is thus a positive association between house price and consumption growth in the data.

The number of new houses built in the United States also strongly expanded over the period 1996–2006. Figure 4 reports the number of new housing units completed in the United States together with various house price measures.[8] The figure shows that the level of house prices and the number of housing completions are strongly positively correlated.

C. Cross-Sectional Evidence from G7 Economies

The facts documented for the US economy in the previous section appear in similar form in the cross-section of G7 economies.[9]

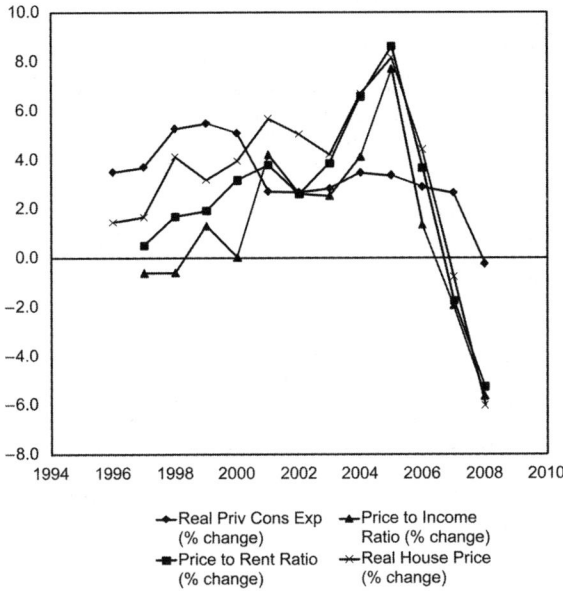

Fig. 3. United States: House price changes and consumption growth

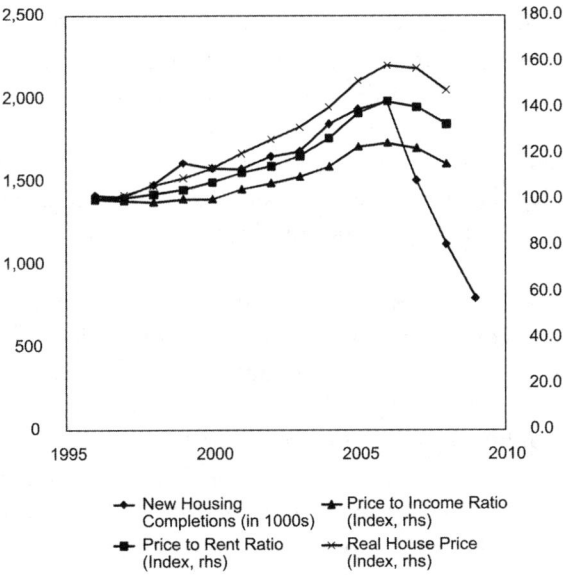

Fig. 4. United States: House prices and new housing completions

Table 2
Cross-Sectional Correlations in the G7

House Price Change 2001–2007	Current Account Surplus (2001–2007, Cum. Sum in % of GDP)	Real Priv. Cons. Increase (2001–2007, Cum. Sum in %)
Real house price	−.55	.72
Price-rent ratio	−.42	.75
Price-income ratio	−.52	.61

Table 3
Cross-Sectional Correlations in the G7

House Price Change 2007–2008	Change in Current Account Surplus 2008 vs. 2007 (in % of GDP)
Real house	−.75
Price-rent ratio	−.90
Price-income ratio	−.83

Table 2 shows that over the period 2001–2007, house price increases and current account surpluses are negatively correlated in the cross-section of G7 countries.[10] Countries with larger house price booms thus tended to also have larger current account deficits. This holds independently of the considered house price measure (RHP, PIR, PRR). Furthermore, house price increases are strongly positively correlated with real private consumption growth over the same period, showing that countries with larger house price booms also tended to have larger consumption booms. Finally, as shown in table 3, the house price reversals in 2007–2008 are similarly strongly negatively correlated with changes in the current account surplus. These cross-sectional relationships are consistent with the correlation over time that can observed for US data.

Although the G7 evidence confirms the comovements between house price, current account, and consumption dynamics documented for the United States, there exists a considerable amount of cross-sectional heterogeneity across the G7 economies. Figure 5 illustrates this fact by depicting the real house price indices for the G7 economies, normalizing the house price indices to 100 for the year 2000.[11] It is clear that house prices show high volatility and high persistence in all countries. Table 4 documents the latter fact by reporting the average serial correlation of housing prices over time across the G7 countries.

Importantly, however, the large low frequency movements in house

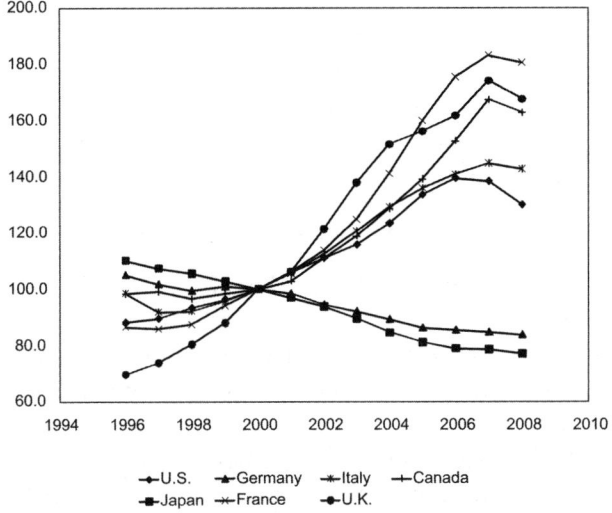

Fig. 5. Real house prices in the G7 (indices, normalized to 100 in year 2000)

Table 4
Autocorrelation of G7 House Prices

House prices measure	G7 average autocorrelation 1996–2008
Real house prices	.98
Price-to-rent ratio	.97
Price-to-income	.97

prices are not synchronized across countries. While four countries experienced sustained and even larger house price increases after 2000 than the United States, Japan and Germany witnessed real price decreases.

IV.   An Open Economy Model with Housing

This section presents a parsimonious open economy model with endogenous housing supply in which households can internationally borrow for consumption and investment purposes. Household borrowing is thereby subject to a collateral-based borrowing constraint, as in Kiyotaki and Moore (1997).

Preferences and Beliefs. We consider an economy populated by a unit mass of utility maximizing households. Households are identical in terms of preferences and beliefs—a fact that is not known to agents[12]— with the representative household maximizing

$$E_0^P \sum_{t=0}^{\infty} \delta^t (\xi_t h_t + c_t), \tag{1}$$

where $c_t \geq 0$ denotes consumption of goods, $h_t \geq 0$ consumption of housing services, $\delta \in (0, 1)$ the time discount factor, and $\xi_t > 0$ a housing preference shock. We assume that the preference shock evolves according to

$$\ln \xi_t = \ln \xi_{t-1} + \ln \varepsilon_t, \tag{2}$$

with ε_t being an i.i.d. innovation satisfying $E[\ln \varepsilon_t] = 0$ and $E[(\ln \varepsilon_t)^2] = \sigma_\varepsilon^2$. The preference shock ξ_t captures changes in the population's preferences for housing services relative to consumption. As we argue following, the assumed unit root specification is broadly consistent with the available data.

The household's expectation in (1) is computed using a (potentially subjective) probability measure P, which is defined over the space of payoff-relevant outcomes Ω. The measure P assigns probabilities to all subsets of Ω in a sigma-algebra B, so that agents entertain a standard probability space (P, B, Ω). Importantly, the set Ω includes all sequences of payoff-relevant variables that agents take as given. This includes fundamental shocks, but also competitive market prices. Agents' choices in a given period t are then functions of the realization of these payoff-relevant variables up to t. While the measure P itself is time-invariant (i.e., dynamically consistent), it will often imply that rational agents are learning about the house price process. This is the case, for example, if P is generated by a model that agents entertain about the stochastic process of house prices and by some prior beliefs about unknown parameters describing this process. Further details about the underlying probability space are given in Section IV, subsection A.

Budget Constraint and Collateral Constraint. We let $H_t \geq 0$ denote the stock of houses owned by the household in period t. The housing stock yields housing services h_t according to

$$h_t = G(H_t) \tag{3}$$

for some twice continuously differentiable and (weakly) concave function $G(\cdot)$, satisfying the conditions $\lim_{H \to 0} G'(H) = \infty$ and $\lim_{H \to \bar{H}} G'(H) = -\infty$ for some $\bar{H} \leq \infty$. We impose this latter condition for technical convenience: it insures the existence of an optimal house holding plan for all beliefs about house prices, satisfying the restriction that house prices cannot become negative. The previous assumptions imply that there is a bliss point H^B such that $G'(H^B) = 0$; with the additional assumption that this bliss point is unique we have $G'(H) \geq 0$ for $H < H^B$ and $G'(H) \leq 0$ for $H > H^B$. For reasons that will become apparent later, the housing stock may exceed this bliss point in equilibrium.

Using the consumption good as numeraire and letting q_t denote the price of houses, the agent's flow budget constraint is

$$c_t + (H_t - (1 - d)H_{t-1})q_t + Rb_{t-1} + k_t = y_t + b_t + \pi_t + k_{t-1}p_t, \qquad (4)$$

where $y_t \geq 0$ denotes an exogenous income process, b_t the household's new loans, R the gross real interest rate on maturing loans b_{t-1}, $d \in 0, 1)$, the rate at which the housing stock depreciates, π_t profits from the ownership of (housing development) firms, and $k_t \geq 0$ capital sold to competitive housing developers who use this capital as an input for the production of new houses. This capital stock fully depreciates in one period. To capture time lags in housing production and for simplicity we assume that the price p_t remunerating k_{t-1} is a competitive forward price that is fixed in period $t - 1$.

For notational simplicity we do not introduce a competitive market for housing services h_t. While the analysis would remain unchanged with such a market, it would imply that the competitive market for housing services is given by ξ_t. For this reason we interpret ξ_t as the rental price for housing in the remaining part of the paper. And to show that our unit root assumption for $\log \xi_t$ is indeed reasonable, table 5 reports the Dickey-Fuller test statistics for a unit root model with drift based on the log of the rental rate for housing in the respective countries.[13] For the considered sample, the 10% critical value for this statistic is -2.614, which is far from any of the reported test statistics. This suggests that our stochastic specification for ξ_t is indeed reasonable.

We assume that consumers' borrowing is subject to a collateral constraint of the form

$$b_t \leq \theta \frac{E_t^P q_{t+1}}{R} H_t \qquad (5)$$

as in Kiyotaki and Moore (1997). The parameter $\theta \in 0, 1 - d]$ captures the share of houses owned by the household today that can serve as

Table 5
Dickey-Fuller Test for Assumed ξ_t Process

	United States	Japan	Germany	France	United Kingdom	Canada
t-statistic	$-.921$	$-.848$	$-.383$	$-.131$	$.696$	$-.162$

collateral to lenders; this parameter is assumed fixed. A value of $\theta < 1$ thereby incorporates the effects of physical depreciation of houses, as well as the possibility that seizing the collateral in case of default is costly for lenders.

The borrowing constraint (5) is key to understanding the model-implied relation between house prices and current account dynamics. In a situation where actual and expected prices tend to grow, the borrowing constraint will be relatively loose. Agents can thus increase international borrowing when house prices grow, thereby establishing a connection between house price booms and current account deficits.[14]

We assume that there is a sufficiently wealthy risk-neutral international lender that holds the same beliefs $\mathcal{P}$ as domestic agents. The international lender has a time discount rate R^{-1}, which we assume to satisfy $R^{-1} \in (\delta, 1)$. The latter implies that the international lender is more patient than domestic households. In addition to simplifying the analysis, it captures the presence of China and other emerging economies as large and patient international lenders in the global economy. We also assume that the market for collateralized loans is internationally fully integrated. With these assumptions, the world equilibrium interest rate for collateralized loans is given by R.[15]

Housing Supply. We now turn to the determinants of housing supply. There exists a competitive housing development sector consisting of a unit mass of housing development firms. The representative firm operates a decreasing returns to scale technology for constructing new houses. The amount of new housing produced at t is given by

$$(\alpha\delta)^{-1}k_{t-1}^{\alpha},$$

with $k_{t-1} \geq 0$ denoting the amount of development capital used by housing developers and $\alpha \in (0, 1)$. To capture time lags in housing construction we assume that firms choose the level of input k_{t-1} in period $t - 1$; that is, one period in advance.

Firms in the housing sector are owned by the consumer in the small open economy, who receive profits as lump sum transfers. Since firms do not have a true intertemporal maximization problem (there is no state variable in the firms' problem), we can assume that they maximize expected profits from housing construction by choosing[16]

$$\max_{k_{t-1} \geq 0} E_{t-1}^{\mathcal{P}}\left(\frac{1}{\alpha\delta} k_{t-1}^{\alpha} q_t - p_t k_{t-1}\right),$$

where p_t is the price of period t inputs purchased from households in period $t - 1$ in a competitive forward market. The profit-maximizing input choice is given by

$$k_{t-1}^* = \left(\frac{E_{t-1}^P q_t}{\delta p_t} \right)^{1/(1-\alpha)}$$

and determines a supply function for new houses of the form

$$S(E_{t-1}^P q_t, p_t) = \frac{1}{\alpha \delta} \left(\frac{E_{t-1}^P q_t}{\delta p_t} \right)^{\alpha/(1-\alpha)}, \tag{6}$$

with $\alpha/(1 - \alpha)$ denoting the elasticity of housing supply with respect to the expected selling price $E_{t-1}^P q_t$. The housing stock then evolves according to

$$H_t = (1 - d)H_{t-1} + S(E_{t-1}^P q_t, p_t) \tag{7}$$

and developers' realized profits in period t are given by

$$\pi_t = \frac{1}{\alpha \delta} \left(\frac{E_{t-1}^P q_t}{\delta p_t} \right)^{\alpha/(1-\alpha)} q_t - p_t \left(\frac{E_{t-1}^P q_t}{\delta p_t} \right)^{\alpha/(1-\alpha)}. \tag{8}$$

A. The Underlying Probability Space

We now describe details of the underlying probability space $(\mathcal{P}, \mathcal{B}, \Omega)$. The probability space is entirely standard from the viewpoint of probability theory, but will be extended (or more general) when compared to the approach taken in the RE literature. Specifically, we define the state space of outcomes as

$$\Omega \equiv \Omega_p \times \Omega_q \times \Omega_\xi \times \Omega_y \times \Omega_\pi,$$

where $\Omega_X = \prod_{t=0}^{\infty} R_+$ is the space of possible infinite sequences for the variable $X \in \{p, q, \xi, y, \pi\}$. We thus do not restrict attention to the history of "fundamental" or exogenous variables (ξ, y), instead including all sequences of payoff-relevant variables that agents take as given in their decision problem. This includes prices and profits, in addition to the fundamental variables.

The set of all possible histories up to period t for some variable X is then denoted by Ω_X^t, and its typical element $X^t \in \Omega_X^t$, except for p where Ω_p^t denotes histories up to $t + 1$. Furthermore, we let $\Omega^t = \Omega_p^t \times \Omega_q^t \times \Omega_\xi^t \times \Omega_y^t \times \Omega_\pi^t$ denote the set of histories of all exogenous variables up to period t, and $\omega^t \in \Omega^t$ its typical element. Variable B is the sigma-algebra of all Borel subsets of Ω and P a measure on this sigma-algebra. The probability space (P, B, Ω) is assumed common to all agents, including firms, domestic consumers, and foreign agents.

The previous setup implies that agents can condition their decisions on the history of all observed realizations; that is, consumers choose for each t

$$(c_t, h_t, H_t, b_t, k_t) : \Omega^t \to R^5. \tag{9}$$

Conditioning on all observed realizations will be optimal whenever agents do not know how a given history of fundamentals $(y, \xi)^t$ maps into outcomes for prices and profits. This differs from a RE setting where prices (p_t, q_t) and profits π_t are known functions of the history of fundamentals, implying that conditioning also on the history of prices and profits would simply be redundant.

Agents express their uncertainty about the joint distribution of prices and fundamentals using the probability measure P. In the spirit of studying small deviations from rational expectations, we will specify in the following a probability measure P that is close—but not exactly equal—to the rational expectations equilibrium beliefs.

B. Household Optimality Conditions

We now derive the conditions characterizing optimal household behavior. We thereby proceed by assuming that a maximum for the household problem exists.[17] First-order conditions are then necessary and sufficient for household optimality because the objective function is concave and the constraints are linear in the households' choices.

Households maximize the objective (1) subject to the constraints (3), (4), and (5). Taking explicitly into account the nonnegativity constraints for c_t and k_t, the Lagrangian of the household problem is given by

$$\max_{\{c_t, H_t, b_t, k_t\}} E_0^P \sum_{t=0}^{\infty} \delta^t \left(\begin{array}{l} \xi_t G(H_t) + c_t - \lambda_t [c_t + (H_t - (1-d)H_{t-1})q_t + b_{t-1}R + k_t \\ -y_t - b_t - \pi_t - k_{t-1}p_t] + \gamma_t(\theta E_t^P q_{t+1} H_t - R b_t) + \mu_t c_t + \kappa_t k_t \end{array} \right),$$

where H_{-1}, k_{-1}, and b_{-1} are given initial conditions and the prices $\{q_t, p_t\}$, R are given.

The household's first-order conditions (FOCs) are

$$c_t : \lambda_t = 1 + \mu_t \text{ with } \mu_t \geq 0 \,\&\, c_t \mu_t = 0 \tag{10}$$

$$H_t : \xi_t G'(H_t) - \lambda_t q_t + \delta(1-d) E_t^P \lambda_{t+1} q_{t+1} + \gamma_t \theta E_t^P q_{t+1} = 0 \tag{11}$$

$$b_t : \lambda_t = \delta R E_t^P \lambda_{t+1} + \gamma_t R \text{ with } \gamma_t \geq 0$$

$$\&\, (\theta E_t^P q_{t+1} H_t - R b_t) \gamma_t = 0 \tag{12}$$

$$k_t : \lambda_t = \delta p_{t+1} E_t^P \lambda_{t+1} + \kappa_t \text{ with } \kappa_t \geq 0 \,\&\, k_t \kappa_t = 0 \tag{13}$$

for all $t \geq 0$. Equation (10) implies that $\lambda_t \geq 1$.

We now describe the evolution of the equilibrium variables. In the main text we thereby focus on the case where the nonnegativity constraint for c_t is not binding for all $t \leq T + 1$, where T denotes the sample size.[18] Since $R < 1/\delta$, the optimal solution then implies that the consumer will optimally borrow as much as possible, so that the collateral constraint is binding in each period $t \leq T$. Then, provided the fluctuations in house prices and house price expectations are not too large, the nonnegativity constraint for consumption will indeed not be violated.[19] In this case, $\mu_t = 0$ for all $t = 0, ..., T$ so that the FOC (10) is satisfied for $\lambda_t = 1$ and the FOC (12) holds for

$$\gamma_t = \frac{1}{R} - \delta > 0$$

for all $t = 0, ..., T$. Using these results and equation (11) one obtains

$$q_t = \rho E_t^P q_{t+1} + \xi_t G'(H_t) \tag{14}$$

where

$$\rho \equiv \delta(1 - d - \theta) + \frac{\theta}{R} < 1. \tag{15}$$

Given q_t and $E_t^P q_{t+1}$, equation (14) determines the optimal amount of houses demanded by the household. Since $G'(\cdot)$ continuously varies between $+\infty$ and $-\infty$, this equation always has a solution for the optimal housing stock $H_t > 0$, for any given pair $(q_t, E_t^P q_{t+1})$.

Importantly, for $q_t < \rho E_t^P q_{t+1}$, equation (14) implies $G'(H_t) < 0$, so that housing demand exceeds the bliss point level H^B. If houses are expected to appreciate sufficiently strongly, it can become individually optimal to purchase housing above the bliss point since housing investment generates capital gains and relaxes the household's borrowing constraint.

When the collateral constraint is binding in the first $T + 1$ periods, the optimal level of borrowing follows from the binding collateral constraint and is given by

$$b_t R = \theta E_t^\mathcal{P} q_{t+1} H_t. \tag{16}$$

The capital offered by the consumer to housing developers is only restricted to satisfy

$$(1 - \delta p_{t+1}) k_t = 0,$$

so that either $p_t = \delta^{-1}$ or $k_t = 0$. If the nonnegativity constraint on k is nonbinding, the agent is indifferent between consuming today and increasing by one unit the capital sold to firms in exchange for δ^{-1} units of consumption tomorrow. Since firms' production function implies that firms always have a positive demand for k, market clearing occurs at

$$p_t = \delta^{-1}, \tag{17}$$

with k_t being determined by firms' demand function.

Finally, consumption can be obtained residually from the flow budget

$$c_t = y_t + b_t + \pi_t - \left(H_t - (1 - d)H_{t-1}\right) q_t - b_{t-1} R - k_t + k_{t-1} \delta^{-1}, \tag{18}$$

where we imposed (17).

C. Equilibrium Dynamics for General Beliefs $\mathcal{P}$

For arbitrary and given beliefs $\mathcal{P}$, the equilibrium evolution of the house price q_t and the housing stock H_t must satisfy equations (14) and (7), rewritten here as

$$q_t = \rho E_t^\mathcal{P} q_{t+1} + \xi_t G'(H_t) \tag{19}$$

$$H_{t+1} = (1 - d)H_t + S(E_t^\mathcal{P} q_{t+1}, \delta^{-1}). \tag{20}$$

These equations can be solved for the process $\{q_t, H_t\}_{t=0}^\infty$. Borrowing then follows from equation (16), housing supply from (6), profits from (8), and equilibrium consumption from (18).

V.   Rational Expectations Equilibrium (REE)

We now assume rational expectations ($E_t^\mathcal{P}[\cdot] = E_t[\cdot]$) and determine the REE for the case where the nonnegativity constraint on consumption is never binding. We first find the deterministic steady state, then analyze the effects of preference and income shocks, and finally discuss the effects of changes in international real interest rates. As will become clear from the following discussion, under RE the model has great difficulties in replicating the observed house price dynamics.

A. Deterministic Steady State

We start out by determining the deterministic steady state; that is, the REE in which $\xi_t = \xi$ and $y_t = y$ for all t. Letting variables without time subscripts denote steady outcomes, equations (19) and (20) imply

$$q^{ss} = \frac{\xi G'(H^{ss})}{1-\rho} \tag{21}$$

$$H^{ss} = \frac{1}{\alpha\delta d}(q^{ss})^{\alpha/(1-\alpha)}, \tag{22}$$

which jointly determine a unique steady state value for q^{ss} and H^{ss}.[20] Steady state capital, borrowing, and consumption are given by

$$k^{ss} = (q^{ss})^{1/(1-\alpha)}$$

$$b^{ss} = \theta\frac{q^{ss}H^{ss}}{R}$$

$$c^{ss} = y + \theta\left(\frac{1}{R}-1\right)q^{ss}H^{ss} - (q^{ss})^{1/(1-\alpha)}.$$

B. Stochastic Equilibrium: Linear Approximation

We now analyze the effects of shocks to housing preferences ξ_t and household income y_t. In the interest of deriving closed form approximate solutions, we first consider solutions to equations (19) and (20) when the function $G(\cdot)$ is linearized around its steady state. This simplifies the analysis because it allows using results previously derived in Adam, Marcet, and Nicolini (2010) to describe the model behavior under learning. We consider a concave function $G(\cdot)$ separately in the following.

Substituting $G'(H_t)$ by $G'(H^{ss})$ in equation (19) implies that the REE house price to rent ratio is (approximately) given by

$$\frac{q_t^{RE}}{\xi_t} = \frac{G'(H^{ss})}{1-\rho}, \tag{23}$$

so that log house price growth evolves according to

$$\ln \frac{q_t^{RE}}{q_{t-1}^{RE}} = \ln 1 + \ln \varepsilon_t. \tag{24}$$

For the linear approximation we thus have $E_t q_{t+1}^{RE} = q_t^{RE}$ and $p_t = \delta^{-1}$, so that the housing stock approximately evolves according to:[21]

$$H_{t+1}^{RE} = (1-d)H_t^{RE} + \frac{1}{\alpha\delta}(q_t^{RE})^{\alpha/(1-\alpha)}.$$

The previous findings show that preference and income shocks both fail to affect the price-to-rent ratio (23) and that the real house price follows a unit root in this approximate REE. With rational expectations, preference and income shocks thus cannot explain the large swings in the price-to-rent ratio and are unlikely to explain the persistent boom and bust patterns in real house prices observed in the data.

C.   Stochastic Equilibrium: Linear-Quadratic Approximation

While the linear approximation considered in the previous section is convenient, assuming linearity of $G(\cdot)$ violates our basic assumptions required to guarantee existence of an equilibrium. We therefore consider a model with a concave $G(\cdot)$ in all subsequent computations, but use the linear approximation from the previous section for intuitive explanations. The appendix shows that with a linear-quadratic approximation to $G(\cdot)$, the REE dynamics evolve according to

$$\hat{q}_t = a^{RE}\hat{\xi}_t + b^{RE}\hat{H}_t$$

$$\hat{H}_{t+1} = c^{RE}\hat{H}_t + d^{RE}\hat{\xi}_t,$$

where hatted variables denote deviations from the steady state and $(a^{RE}, b^{RE}, c^{RE}, d^{RE})$ are given coefficients satisfying $a^{RE} > 0$, $b^{RE} < 0$, $0 < c^{RE} < 1$, and $d^{RE} > 0$.

Importantly, preference shocks still cannot explain the observed house price dynamics. A positive innovation to the rental price ξ_t increases the rental price on impact, but leads to a reduction of the equilibrium price in the subsequent period.[22] The model will thus have difficulties with generating a persistent increase of the house price. Furthermore, the previous equation implies that the stock of housing and the price-to-rent ratio move in opposite directions. This is intuitive, since the price-to-rent ratio q_t/ξ_t is equal to the discounted sum of future G' and a higher housing stock H reduces the value of G'. This feature of the rational expectations model is also hard to reconcile with the data, where the price-to-rent ratio and the stock of houses display strong positive comovement.

D.   Calibration, House Prices, and Real Interest Rates

We now analyze the effects of unexpected changes in the real interest rate for the REE house price. As equation (23) shows, a reduction in real interest rates generates an increase in the real house price and in the price-to-rent ratio. As we document later, however, it is unlikely that changes in real interest rates can properly account for the observed house price dynamics.

To analyze the effects of real interest rate changes we assume that the economy starts from a steady state position in the year 2000. We then subject it to the stylized changes in the real interest rate indicated by the dashed line in figure 2. Specifically, we consider a persistent and unexpected decrease in the real rate in the year 2001, followed by an equally unexpected real rate increase in the year 2006.[23] The effects of anticipated real rate changes will be discussed separately later.

The remaining model parameters are calibrated as follows. We set $\theta =$ 0.26, which is the 1996–2005 average of the annual value change change in the US housing stock over the current account deficit (see table 1). For the annual discount factor we choose $\delta = 0.96$, so that the discount factor is slightly below the real interest rate path that we feed into the model.[24] We set the annual house depreciation rate equal to $d = 3\%$.

To illustrate the effects of interest rate changes we abstract from uncertainty about preference shocks: we set $\xi_t = \xi$ and normalize $\xi G'(H)$ such that the initial steady state real house price in the year 2000 (prior to any change in the real interest rate) is equal to 100. Finally, for reasons that will become clear later on, we choose a value for the constant second derivative G'' so that there is a small amount of curvature; that is, we set $-G''H^{ss}/G' = 0.007$. None of the results shown below prove particularly sensitive to the assumed parameter values.

The resulting REE real house price dynamics from unexpected changes in the interest rate are illustrated by the upper line in figure 6.[25] The figure reveals that RE imply that house price changes occur simultaneously with unanticipated changes in real interest rates.[26] For the US economy, however, one cannot find a close simultaneous association between changes in the real mortgage rates and house prices changes. Mortgage rates, for example, stayed approximately constant between the beginning of 2003 until the end of 2005 (see figure 2) while house prices increased strongly over these two years. Likewise, real mortgage rates were roughly constant over the years 2006–2008, while house prices decreased considerably over these years. Due to this close association with interest rates, house prices under RE do not exhibit the persistence that can be observed for house price fluctuations in the data.

Furthermore, the amplitude of the fluctuations generated by interest rate shocks tends to be small compared to the data. The RE model justifies a 4% appreciation between 2000 and 2005, while the United States experienced a tenfold increase over this period. From a RE viewpoint, it thus appears difficult to account for the observed house price dynamics using changes in real interest rates as a driving force.

Even greater difficulties arise if one assumes instead that agents fully anticipate future changes in real interest rates, instead of assuming that any given change is considered permanent. If agents anticipate the 2006 real interest rate increase, then house prices evolve according to the lower line shown in figure 6. The initial house price increase in 2001 is then even smaller and followed by a gradual decrease, due to the anticipated real rate increase (and house price decrease) in the year 2006. In the data, however, house prices increased strongly after the year 2001.

We can conclude that under RE it is difficult to account for the US house price dynamics using the observed interest rate dynamics. Rather than predicting house price increases over the years 2001–2006, RE predicts that house prices move together with interest rates, that fluctuations are fairly small, and that house price persistence is relatively low.

VI. Specifying Near Rational Beliefs

Under the rational expectations hypothesis, agents are assumed to know that the joint distribution over exogenous shocks and market prices has a singularity and where exactly this singularity is located.[27] Yet even expert economists rarely agree on the correct economic model linking fundamentals to prices. For this reason it appears of interest to consider agents that face similar doubts and to relax the assumption that agents know the correct model of price behavior.

We shall assume that agents express uncertainty about the true price process by formulating a perceived joint distribution $\mathcal{P}$ over prices and fundamentals. This joint distribution $\mathcal{P}$ does not necessarily have to incorporate a singularity linking house prices to the history of fundamentals. In the following we construct a specific measure $\mathcal{P}$ deviating from RE beliefs along exactly this dimension. Subsection A of Section VI then shows how one can impose further restrictions that insure that the model outcomes generated by $\mathcal{P}$ are indeed close to the beliefs entertained by agents. And subsection B of Section VI shows that our specification for $\mathcal{P}$ is consistent with the behavior of house prices in the data.

We define the probability space $(\mathcal{B}, \Omega)$ as in subsection A of Section IV. And to simplify the analysis we assume that agents have correct beliefs about all variables except for house prices; that is, agents hold rational expectations about the exogenous processes $\{y_t, \xi_t\}_{t=0}^{\infty}$ and about $\{p_t = \delta^{-1}\}_{t=0}^{\infty}$.[28] We relax, however, the assumption that agents believe that average house price growth is equal to zero at all times, as is implied by the approximate REE outcome (24). Instead, we consider agents who believe that the process for house price growth evolves according to

$$\ln \frac{q_t}{q_{t-1}} = \ln \beta_t + \ln v_t, \qquad (25)$$

where β_t denotes a time-varying persistent component and v_t a transitory component. This relaxation of beliefs relative to the REE outcome (24) is motivated by the empirical evidence on house price behavior, which displays periods of persistently increasing prices ($\ln \beta_t > 0$ for a number of periods) and periods of persistently falling prices ($\ln \beta_t < 0$ for a number of periods).

For simplicity, we shall assume that the persistent component follows a random walk[29]

$$\ln \beta_t = \ln \beta_{t-1} + \ln \eta_t, \qquad (26)$$

and that the innovations are given by

$$\begin{pmatrix} \ln v_t \\ \ln \eta_t \end{pmatrix} \sim iiN\left(\begin{pmatrix} 0 \\ 0 \end{pmatrix}, \begin{pmatrix} \sigma_v^2 & 0 \\ 0 & \sigma_\eta^2 \end{pmatrix} \right). \qquad (27)$$

Agents' prior beliefs about the persistent component at time zero is assumed normal with

$$\ln \beta_0 \sim N(\ln m_0, \sigma_0^2) \qquad (28)$$

and σ_0^2 denoting the steady state (Kalman filter) uncertainty; that is,

$$\sigma_0^2 = \frac{-\sigma_\eta^2 + \sqrt{(\sigma_\eta^2)^2 + 4\sigma_v^2\sigma_\eta^2}}{2}.$$

The prior beliefs (28), together with the process (25) through (27), completely specify agents' beliefs $\mathcal{P}$ about house price behavior.

The present setting gives rise to a learning problem because agents observe the realized house price growth rates q_t/q_{t-1}, but do not separately observe the persistent component β_t and the transitory component v_t. This requires that agents optimally update their beliefs about β_t in the light of new house price growth observations.

We complete the overall description of $\mathcal{P}$ by assuming that agents know how to map a history of prices into profits. In other words, agents know that profits in t are given by a function $\pi(E_{t-1}^P q_t, q_t)$ equal to the right-hand side of equation (8) for $p_t = \delta^{-1}$.

A. Insuring Near Rationality of Beliefs

In this section we impose further restrictions on the beliefs $\mathcal{P}$ of agents to insure that these beliefs are close (in distribution) to the outcomes generated by the model. We thereby proceed as follows. First, we show how to impose restrictions on $\mathcal{P}$ so that these beliefs approach (in distribution) the beliefs entertained by agents in the linearized REE (24) for any given finite amount of time.[30] Second, as agents' beliefs converge to the REE beliefs, model outcomes equally converge to the REE outcomes (in distribution) because equilibrium prices and quantities are continous functions of agents' beliefs. Since beliefs and model outcomes both converge (in distribution) to the linearized REE outcome (24), agents' beliefs will be approximately validated by the model behavior.

To insure that the beliefs $\mathcal{P}$ are close (in distribution) to the REE beliefs, we proceed as follows. First, we center initial beliefs so as to be consistent with the average growth rate of prices in the REE (24); that is, we choose $m_0 = 1$. Agents thus initially believe that there is no growth in real house prices on average. Second, we consider the case where the innovation variance of the persistent house price component vanishes (i.e., $\sigma_\eta^2 \to 0$). As a result of this second assumption, prior uncertainty σ_0 about initial price growth also vanishes ($\sigma_0^2 \to 0$). Agents' prior beliefs thus become increasingly concentrated at the point $\beta_t = 1$. Formally, as $\sigma_0^2 \to 0$ agents' beliefs about prices converge to the REE beliefs (24) in distribution (or "in law").[31]

This shows that for sufficiently small values of σ_η^2, house price beliefs are indeed close to the model implied beliefs. In our empirical application, we shall consider small but positive values for σ_η^2. Section X then shows that agents would hardly be able to reject their belief specification for the empirically calibrated value of σ_η^2.

B. Agents' Beliefs and House Price Behavior in the Data

This section shows that the belief specification (25) and (26) is also consistent with the behavior of actual house prices in the data. Specifically, we derive testable implications from our belief specification and evaluate to what extent these are consistent with the behavior of the G7 house price data.

The belief equations (25) and (26) imply that $\ln q_t/q_{t-1}$ has a unit root and that $\Delta \ln q_t/q_{t-1}$ is an MA(1) process of the form

$$\Delta \ln \frac{q_t}{q_{t-1}} = \ln \eta_t + \ln v_t - \ln v_{t-1}. \tag{29}$$

Conditional on all the shocks being normally distributed, the fact that $\Delta \ln q_t/q_{t-1}$ is an MA(1) process exhausts the empirical implications of the agents' model (25) through (27).[32]

One might be tempted to test (29) using an augmented Dickey-Fuller (ADF) test with a number of lags to capture the fact that $\Delta \ln q_t/q_{t-1}$ is serially correlated under the null hypothesis. This approach is problematic, however, because σ_η^2 is small relative to σ_v^2, so that the autoregressive coefficients decay only very slowly with the lag length. This would require including a very large number of lags to have a valid ADF test, thereby greatly reducing the degrees of freedom and the power of the test.

A more attractive approach is based on the observation that equation (29) implies

$$cov\left(\Delta \ln \frac{q_t}{q_{t-1}}, \ln \frac{q_{t-i}}{q_{t-i-1}} \right) = 0 \qquad \text{for all } i = 2, 3, \ldots$$

so that one can run the regression

$$\Delta \ln \frac{q_t}{q_{t-1}} = \sum_{i=2}^{N} \alpha_i \ln \frac{q_{t-i}}{q_{t-i-1}} + e_t \tag{30}$$

and test the joint hypothesis that $\alpha_i = 0$ for $i = 2, \ldots, N$. Under the null hypothesis this test is valid for any number of lags N. In addition, the hypothesis that $\alpha_i = 0$ for all $i > 1$ is sufficient for $\Delta \ln q_t/q_{t-1}$ to be MA(1). The test thus exhausts the empirical implications of the model (25) through (27).

Table 6
Testing the Belief Specification Against the Data

	United States	Japan	Germany	France	Italy	United Kingdom	Canada
W statistic	3.6771	4.2934	4.1107	3.6825	5.8853	3.6530	3.7493

The appendix explains how we construct a test statistic W to test for the null hypothesis $\alpha_i = 0$ $(i = 2, \ldots, N)$ and that this statistic has an χ^2 asymptotic distribution in the case with stationary regressors. Under the agents' model, however, the regressors contain a small nonstationary component, so that we use Monte-Carlo simulations to find the confidence intervals.

Table 6 reports the test statistic for $N = 4$, using data for the years 1970–2008 for each country. The 10% critical value for W is equal to 6.4.[33] The results in table 6 thus show that agents would accept their model of house price behavior (25) and (26) in the light of the G7 house price data.[34]

C. Internal Rationality and Discounted Sums

It appears to be a commonly held view among academic economists that rational behavior leaves no room for independent beliefs about prices once beliefs about fundamentals are specified. Individual rationality, so the argument goes, implies that agents know how to formulate prices as discounted sums of future fundamentals. Yet, as discussed in Adam and Marcet (2010), this view is generally incorrect and, as explained later, it also fails to apply for the model studied in the present paper.

Agents with the belief system $\mathcal{P}$ described in the previous section fail to hold enough knowledge to be able to formulate beliefs about prices as a function of their beliefs about fundamentals only. This is the case despite all agents being rational. This can be most easily demonstrated for the case where the nonnegativity constraint on consumption is never binding, so that equation (14) holds each period. Forward iteration on this equation then yields a discounted sum formulation for the house price

$$q_t = E_t^{\mathcal{P}} \sum_{j=0}^{\infty} \rho^j \xi_{t+j} G'(H_{t+j}), \qquad (31)$$

which holds under internal rationality. Importantly, this discounted sum involves beliefs about future housing decisions (H_{t+j}), in addition to beliefs about future fundamentals (ξ_{t+j}). The agent's optimal plan for future H_{t+j}, however, is a function of the agent's beliefs about future house prices, so that beliefs about future prices still enter the discounted sum (31). Moreover, since the belief system $\mathcal{P}$ fails to incorporate a singularity linking the future house price to the history of fundamentals, one cannot replace beliefs about future house prices by beliefs about fundamentals only. The agent's price beliefs are thus required to determine the discounted sum (31), while the agent's beliefs about fundamentals are insufficient.

VII. Equilibrium Dynamics with Learning

We now explore the equilibrium dynamics in an economy in which agents hold the near-REE beliefs $\mathcal{P}$ specified in the previous section. We first derive the evolution of the conditional house price growth expectations m_t implied by the probability measure $\mathcal{P}$, then discuss the resulting price dynamics.

A. Belief Updating

Bayesian updating of beliefs implies that agents' posterior beliefs about β_t at time t are given by

$$\ln \beta_t \sim N(\ln m_t, \sigma_0^2),$$

where $\ln m_t$ evolves recursively according to

$$\ln m_t = \ln m_{t-1} + g \left(\ln \frac{q_t}{q_{t-1}} - \ln m_{t-1} \right), \tag{32}$$

with the "gain" parameter given by

$$g = \frac{\sigma_0^2}{\sigma_v^2} > 0.$$

Agents' conditional expectations of house price growth are then given by

$$E_t^{\mathcal{P}} \frac{q_{t+1}}{q_t} = m_t e^{(1/2)(\sigma_0^2 + \sigma_\eta^2 + \sigma_v^2)} \approx m_t,$$

with m_t evolving according to equation (32). Furthermore, to avoid simultaneity between price expectations and price outcomes, it is convenient to assume that information on prices is introduced with a delay in m_t, so that we actually use

$$\ln m_t = \ln m_{t-1} + g\left(\ln \frac{q_{t-1}}{q_{t-2}} - \ln m_{t-1}\right). \tag{33}$$

A microfounded belief system justifying this delay is provided in proposition 2 in Adam and Marcet (2010).

B. Qualitative Behavior of Equilibrium Prices under Learning

This section discusses the qualitative behavior of equilibrium house prices under learning. To simplify the discussion we consider the approximate solution when linearizing G around its steady state value, so that G' is constant. The asset pricing equation (19) then implies that the equilibrium asset price under learning is (approximately) given by

$$q_t = \frac{\xi_t G'(H^{ss})}{1 - \rho m_t}, \tag{34}$$

so that realized log house price growth is

$$\ln \frac{q_t}{q_{t-1}} = \ln \frac{1 - \rho m_{t-1}}{1 - \rho m_t} + \ln \varepsilon_t. \tag{35}$$

For the case with vanishing prior uncertainty ($\sigma_\eta^2, \sigma_0^2 \to 0$), the gain g is small so that m_t changes only slowly from period to period. Beliefs then remain close to $m_t = 1$ for all t in the sample and the aforementioned price is well defined because $\rho < 1$.

The key feature of house prices under learning is that there is feedback between expectations of price growth and actual price growth. Equation (34) shows that higher expected growth m_t leads to higher price and thus higher realized price growth, which in turn increases the expectations tomorrow via the belief updating rule (32). Therefore, the model has the potential to generate price booms that are fueled by the interaction between expectations and realized prices.

This can formally be shown by combining (35) and (33) to obtain a nonlinear second-order difference equation governing the behavior of m_t. The dynamics of this difference equation are very similar to those described in section 4.2.1 of Adam, Marcet, and Nicolini (2010) for stock prices. They show that price changes display momentum locally around the REE value; that is, once prices start growing (falling), there is a tendency for prices to continue growing (falling), as well as there being mean reversion in the longer run.

Within the linearized system, house price increases will come to an end when realized house price growth falls short of the expected price growth. Equation (35) shows that this occurs whenever the *increase* in price growth optimism becomes too weak to sustain the high *level* of price growth expectations. For example, if m_t is very high, but stays constant from one period to the next ($m_t = m_{t-1}$), then equation (35) implies that realized price growth is equal to 1 on average (i.e., falls short of expectations).

More generally, the upward price dynamics can come to an end for a number of additional reasons. For example, if there is an increase in real interest rates that causes house prices to increase less than initially expected, or if a negative shock to housing preferences materializes. Finally, the endogenous model dynamics will make it difficult for sustained price increases to continue forever, especially in the more general case with a concave G function. Upward price dynamics and the associated expansion of the housing stock then lead to a fall in G' and thereby to a fall in the asset price.

Once price growth realizations fall short of agents' expectations, this sets in motion a sequence of downward belief revisions. Following the initial disappointment, there will be a decrease in price growth expectations, thereby a further fall in realized house price growth; that is, a sequence of downward belief revisions and a price bust. The model thus has the potential to generate a house price boom, which eventually will lead to a bust.

C. The Qualitative Response to Interest Rates Changes

We now explore the effects of an unanticipated decrease in real interest rates in period t.[35] Equation (35) implies that realized house price growth in period t increases as a result of a reduction in real interest rates.[36] The price increase is thereby stronger for an economy in which agents in period t are more optimistic about future price growth (in which m_t is higher).

After a fall in real interest rates, the initial increase in realized price growth will feed into future beliefs about price growth via the belief updating equation (33). Due to the presence of momentum this leads to a sequence of further increases in realized price growth.

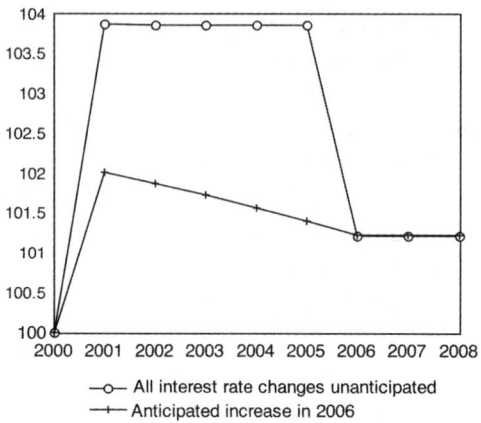

Fig. 6. RE real house price dynamics (stylized real rate from figure 2)

Key to explaining the real house price data shown in figure 6, however, is the fact that interest rates are not the only determinant of
whether or not a price boom occurs. If the house price in a given country has been increasing already before the reduction in interest rates,
then the interest rate reduction will make it more likely that the house
price boom will continue in this country. Conversely, in a country where
house prices have been decreasing, the interest rate reduction may only
ameliorate the decrease in house prices. Therefore, the model is consistent with the observation that house price booms are not synchronized
across countries, even though interest rates behave in a similar way.

A house price boom also relaxes the collateral constraint and leads to
an increase in total borrowing, which is given by

$$b_t = \frac{\theta q_t m_t}{R} H_t.$$

House price increases are thus associated with increased international
borrowing; that is, a current account deficit. Provided investment in
new houses is not too elastic, the house price boom will also be associated with a consumption boom.

Finally, from equation (6) it follows that an increase in expected house
price growth leads to an increase in the production of new houses,
thereby qualitatively matching the observation about new housing
supply displayed in figure 4. Admittedly, the model cannot reproduce
the asymmetric and sharp decline in new housing construction after the

year 2006. Given the simplicity of the model, however, this should be hardly surprising.

Qualitatively, the previous findings show that the model has the potential to explain a housing boom that is associated with a current account deficit, a consumption increase, and an increase in the production of new housing units. The next sections explore the ability of the learning model to quantitatively account for the real house price and current account dynamics in the United States and the remaining G7 economies.

VIII.   The US Experience: 2001–2008

We now calibrate the learning model to the US economy and show that it can quantitatively replicate the real house price and current account developments for the US economy over the years 2001–2008. The performance for the remaining G7 economies is analyzed in the next section.

We use as data inputs the history of real house prices over the years 1996–2000 and the stylized path for real interest rates of the years 2001–2008, as captured by the dashed line in figure 2.[37] Except for the stylized information about the real interest rate, the predictions we show following do not use any data after the year 2000.

As in Section V, subsection D, we choose $\theta = 0.26$, $\delta = 0.96$, and $d = 3\%$. The gain parameter g in the belief updating equation (33) and second derivative G'' are chosen to minimize the distance between the model-implied prediction for the real house price and the data (we will be more precise about this step in Section IX). This leads to an annual gain of $g = 0.06$, which implies that agents believe that, on average, 94% of any observed annual house price increase is transitory in nature.

We set the initial price growth expectations in 1996 as if the model had been in REE for a very long time (i.e., we choose $m_{1996} = 1$). We then use the belief updating equation (33) from the model and the real house price growth observation from the US data for the years 1996 to 2000 to impute house price beliefs for the year 2000 (m_{2000}). We then use m_{2000} and the real interest rate $R_{1996-2000}$ to compute the equilibrium real house price for the year 2000. We thereby normalize the equilibrium real house price in the year 2000 to 100 by choosing the value of $\xi G'(H)$ correspondingly.[38] We then use the model to predict the real house price for the years 2001–2008, using as inputs only the interest rate decrease for the years 2001–2005 and the increase for the years 2006–2008.

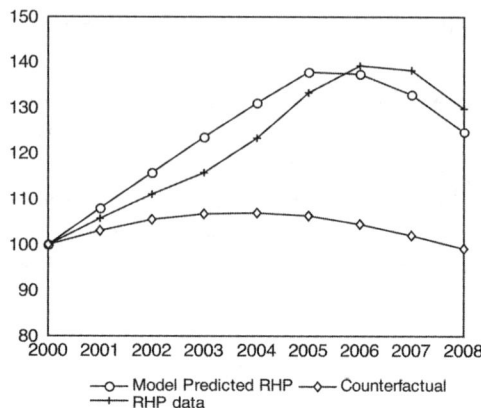

Fig. 7. US real house prices: Model predictions, data and counterfactual

Figure 7 reports the model-predicted outcome jointly with the US real house price series for the years 2000–2008. The model shows that the decrease in real interest rates in the year 2001 gives rise to an initial increase in the real house price. Since realized price increases feed positively into future beliefs via the updating equation, the initial increase will be followed by further upward price movements, giving rise to a house price boom. The increase comes to an end in the year 2006 when interest rates move up again, causing the house price to slowly revert direction, in line with the data. The resulting downward revision in beliefs then sets in motion a sequence of price reductions.

Figure 7 also depicts the model-predicted counterfactual house price path that would be obtained if real interest rates in the years 2001–2008 remained at their pre-2001 average.[39] House prices would then have increased only very mildly. A small increase would have occurred nevertheless, simply because of the positive price momentum that existed already prior to the year 2000. The model is thus consistent with the view that the US housing price boom was mostly caused by interest rates being too low for too long.

The current account dynamics implied by the housing boom in figure 7 depend partly on the long-run housing supply elasticity $(\alpha/(1 - \alpha))$, because housing can be used as collateral in international borrowing. For their preferred specification, Topel and Rosen (1988) estimate a long-run housing supply elasticity of 3 for the United States. Since there is considerable uncertainty about this parameter, we allow

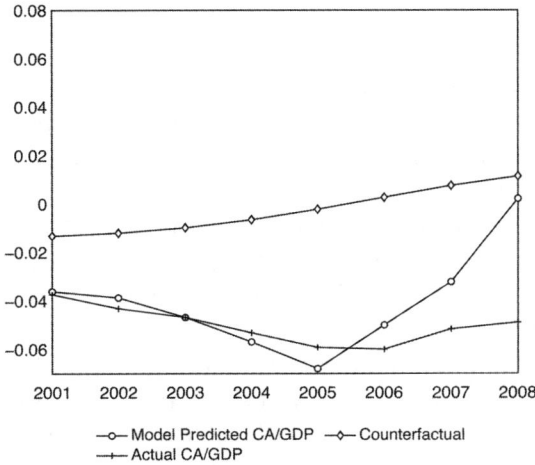

Fig. 8.   US current account deficit ratio: Model predicted and data

for values between 1 and 5, and choose the long-run elasticity that best fits the data, we will be more precise about the fitting procedure below.[40] The model then prefers a relative elastic supply with $\alpha/(1 - \alpha) = 5$. Figure 8 depicts the current account ratio in the data and the one implied by the model. The model predicts well the deterioration of the US current account over the years 2001 to 2005, but overpredicts the improvements following the house price collapse after 2005. Overall, the quantitative performance of the model is surprisingly good, given that it abstracts from so many other factors known to be relevant for the current account (e.g., public borrowing).

Figure 8 also depicts the counterfactual reaction of the current account if real interest rate had stayed at their 1996–2000 average. The model predicts that a large part of the current account deficits would have been eliminated, had interest rates not decreased after the year 2000. This is the result of a lower volume of collateral and a lower collateral value in the absence of a price and construction boom.

IX.   Other G7 Economies: 2001–2008

We now evaluate the ability of the learning model to explain the real house price and current dynamics over the years 2001–2008 in the remaining G7 economies and we describe in detail the calibration procedure for the parameters g, G'', α, y.

A.   Real House Price Dynamics

We tie our hands by using the same model parameters for all G7 countries.[41] We also subject each of the G7 economies to the same stylized interest rate path as the US economy, which amounts to interpreting the US real mortgage rate as a proxy for international real interest rates. Clearly, this approach biases results against us, as we could instead choose to parameterize the model for each country to achieve a better fit with the data. As we show following, the model nevertheless performs surprisingly well.

It is important to note that countries differ because of the method for finding initial beliefs m_{2000}, so that the different country-specific house price histories over the years 1996–2000 lead to different imputed beliefs in the year 2000.

In order to obtain the parameters g, G'', α we proceed as follows. We first obtain (g, G'') by minimizing the square deviations between model and actual data. More precisely, letting boldface letters denote actual data, we choose (g, G'') to minimize

$$\sum_{i=1}^{6} \sum_{t=2000}^{2008} (q_t^i - \mathbf{q}_t^i)^2,$$

where q_t^i is the model implied house price in country i and period t for a given value of parameters. We exclude the United Kingdom from this computation, as our experience is that for the value of g that is chosen by this procedure, the United Kingdom generates an explosive path for prices. Proceeding in this way we obtain the values $g = 0.06$ and $G'' = 0$, as mentioned in the previous section. The best match with the data is thus achieved for a linear G function. Yet, to keep our analysis within a well-specified model, we impose a minimal amount of curvature by setting $\xi G''/G' = -0.007$.[42] Next, we determine separately the optimal value for g for the United Kingdom, which turns out to be $g = 0.046$.

The outcome from simulating the economy with these parameters is depicted in figure 9. It shows that our model predicts strong house price increases for France, Italy, and the United Kingdom, in line with the empirical evidence. The model predicts considerably weaker price increases for Germany and Japan than for the countries just mentioned, albeit it fails to replicate the observed fall in house prices. Since real house prices in Germany and Japan have been falling prior to the year 2000, the presence of momentum in house price changes implies that

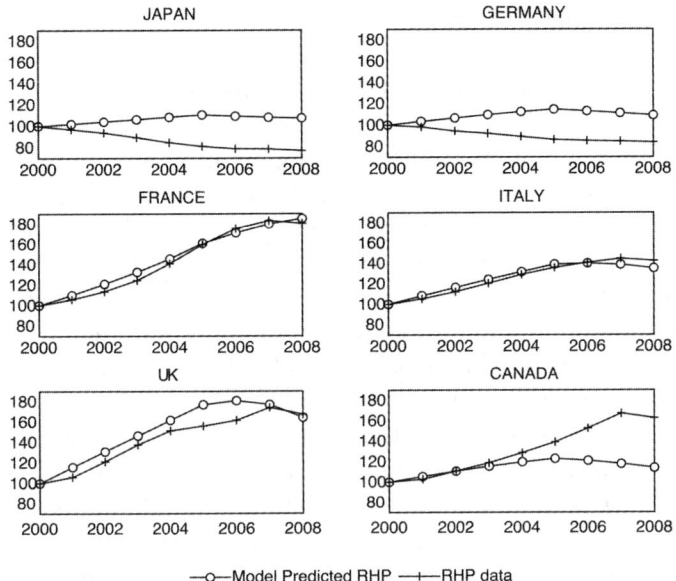

Fig. 9. Other G7 economies: Model predicted real house prices and real house price data.

Table 7
Yearly Cross-Sectional Correlation between Model-Predicted and Actual Real House Price for the G7

Year	2001	2002	2003	2004	2005	2006	2007	2008
House price	.84	.91	.92	.90	.86	.83	.79	.76

agents' price growth expectations tend to decrease further. Yet the interest rate reduction turns this negative momentum into some slight positive momentum. For Canada the model predicts a house price boom, but underpredicts its size, especially at the end of the sample period.

Table 7 reports for each year the cross-country correlation between the model-predicted real house price and the real house price in the data. The table shows that this correlation is very high throughout. The model thus accounts surprisingly well for the asynchronous low frequency movements in house prices, despite the fact that we subject all economies to the same interest rate shocks and use a very parsimonious parameterization.

B. Current Account Dynamics

We now evaluate the ability of the learning model to explain the current account dynamics for the remaining G7 economies. Using the values of (g, G'') determined in the previous section, we choose the value of the long-run housing supply elasticity $\alpha/(1 - \alpha)$ that best fits the observed current account dynamics across countries and periods. We thereby use an analogous objective function, as in the case when matching the house price dynamics. We restrict the search to supply elasticities in the interval $\alpha/1 - \alpha \in 1, 5]$ to be consistent with the findings in Topel and Sherwin (1988), as discussed in Section VII. Our procedure then chooses the highest admissible value in this interval.

The model is clearly not well suited to explain the level of the current account in all countries. Since the discount factor of domestic households falls short of R^{-1}, all countries will want to be borrowers on average, while some countries (e.g., Germany and Japan) are known to have persistent surpluses and also to have accumulated positive net foreign asset positions. Given this, we explore the ability of the model to explain the cyclical movements across time and the overall improvement or worsening of the current account during the studied period.

Table 8 reports the annual correlation across countries, between the model-implied current account to GDP ratio and the actual current account to GDP ratio, where output y in the model is chosen to be time-invariant and equal to ten times the steady state housing output. As is apparent from the table, the model is able to capture a sizable part of the current account fluctuations across countries.

As a further check, we determine the model-implied correlation (across countries) between the total accumulated current account deficit over the period 2000–2007 and house price growth over the same period. In the model, this correlation equals to −0.98. In the data this correlation is of the same sign but achieves a lower value of around −.5, depending on the precise measure for house prices used (see table 2). The fact that the correlation is much higher in the model than

Table 8
Yearly Cross-Sectional Correlation between Model-Predicted and Actual Current Account GDP Ration for the G7

Year	2001	2002	2003	2004	2005	2006	2007	2008
CA/GDP ratio	.47	.57	.53	.60	.61	.57	.49	.30

in the data arguably reflects the fact that other model-omitted factors have influenced the current account behavior in the data. Introducing such additional factors into the model would most likely reduce the model-implied correlation.

X. Testing the Model Consistency of Beliefs

This section discusses whether agents in our calibrated model could easily detect that they are using a wrong model to forecast house prices. While outcomes and beliefs are close to each other (in distribution) when σ_η^2 is sufficiently small, it remains to check that this is indeed the case for the values of σ_η^2 implied by the calibrated gain parameter $g = 0.06$.

We address this issue by assuming that agents apply an econometric test to the data generated by their model (25) and (26) of price behavior.[43] Specifically, we compute the probability that agents would reject their model of house price behavior using the W test-statistic proposed in Section VI, subsection B, which is based on the regression (30). We thereby assume that agents run this test using data for the years 2000–2008 and compute the probability that the model will be rejected when ζ follows a unit root with the estimated standard deviation of $\sigma_\varepsilon = 0.0115$, which is obtained from data on rental prices. We use 50,000 replications of the model under learning with the calibrated parameter values. Table 9 reports the probability of rejecting the agents' beliefs when testing at the 1%, 5%, and 10% significance level, respectively. The test uses data generated by the model and confidence intervals for the W statistic obtained from the Monte-Carlo simulation for a sample length of 8 model periods (corresponding to the years 2001–2008).

Table 9 shows that the probability of rejecting the model is fairly close to the actual confidence level. Clearly, under rational expectations, the rejection probabilities would exactly equal the corresponding confidence levels. The table thus shows that our learning agents reject their forecasting model with very similar likelihood as agents holding rational expectations who also test their forecasting model.

Table 9
Testing Belief Specification with W Statistic on Data Generated by the Learning Model

Confidence level	1%	5%	10%
Probability of rejecting	.0106	.573	.1251

XI. Conclusions

A simple model of learning can quantitatively account for the G7 house price developments over the recent housing boom and bust period. The model also explains a sizable portion of the cross-sectional dispersion of the G7 current accounts and the correlation between the current account and house prices over time.

The model predicts that a persistent fall in the level of the real interest rate can fuel a persistent and long-lasting increase in real house prices. Whether or not such a boom materializes depends crucially on the degree to which agents expect future capital gains already—that is, on the past price dynamics and shocks hitting the economy.

The model suggests that house price booms can give rise to important welfare distortions because they lead to an overextension of the housing stock. It thus appears of interest to explore to what extent policy instruments (e.g., adjustments in the permissible leverage ratio or real interest rates) can usefully prevent an excessive build-up of the housing stock. The welfare effects of a house price boom thereby depend not only on the size and duration of the house price increase, but also on the underlying elasticity of housing supply.

Appendix

Nonnegativity Constraints on Consumption

We now determine the behavior of the model when the nonnegativity constraints on consumption are binding.

Since $\delta R < 1$, it is immediate that c_0 is high and b_0 is against the borrowing limit as long as the limit is tight enough.

In the main text we supposed that the collateral constraint is binding in all periods. As we show now, this could lead to a violation of the nonnegativity constraint on consumption whenever income y_t is not high enough. Consider, for example, a case when $E_j^P q_{j+1} H_j$ has large fluctuations, it is very high at $j = t$ and very low at $j = t + 1$. If borrowing is at the collateral limit in both periods, then this implies a large decrease in debt at $t + 1$. And if income y_{t+1} is not high enough, this would require negative consumption in $t + 1$. The optimal solution then cannot have the feature that the collateral constraint is binding periods t and $t + 1$ simultaneously.

In such a situation one can determine the optimal solution as follows.

Conjecture that the nonnegativity constraint on consumption is binding only in period $t + 1$ but not binding in period t, so that we have $\gamma_t = 0$. From the nonbinding zero limit in t we have $\lambda_t = 1$ and from (12) we obtain $\lambda_{t+1} > 1$, as $\delta R < 1$, so that indeed $c_{t+1} = 0$. The binding borrowing constraint at $t + 1$ then determines b_{t+1}. Using this and the fact that $c_{t+1} = 0$, one obtains b_t from the budget constraint at $t + 1$. The value for c_t then follows from the budget constraint at t. Moreover, since $\gamma_{t+1} > 0$ we can have (12) holding and $\lambda_{t+2} = 1$ so that $\mu_{t+2} = 0$ and $c_{t+2} > 0$, so that from $t + 2$ onwards we are back in the case analyzed in the main text where consumption is positive and the collateral constraint is binding.

If the previous solution would still imply negative consumption in t, then one would have to extend the approach to a setting where consumption is zero for more than one period, say between periods $t + 1, \ldots,$ $t + n$. In this case we would have that the collateral constraint being nonbinding for n periods (i.e., for periods $t, \ldots, t + n - 1$) and one could work backwards to derive a candidate solution in the same manner as described earlier. Again, after period $t + n$ one would be back in the setting analyzed in the main text.

Therefore, if $E_j^P q_{j+1} H_j$ is anticipated to be very low in the next period, today's borrowing limit is not binding. All that is required to have an equilibrium where the borrowing limit is always binding is that fluctuations in $E_j^P q_{j+1} H_j$ are not large and that the parameter θ is sufficiently low.

Details for the Linear-Quadratic Approximation

The main text derives equilibrium quantities under the linear approximation to G. We now extend the analysis to a quadratic approximation of $G(\cdot)$. Besides increasing the order of the approximation, this is of interest because it introduces an interaction between housing prices and the level of housing construction. Considering concavity in $G(\cdot)$ is also useful because it makes it less likely that explosive paths for prices will arise under learning: as house prices and new construction increases, the marginal value of housing services $G'(H_t)$ decreases, which exerts a dampening effect on the upward prices dynamics under learning.

We show following that the unique locally nonexplosive RE solution then takes the form

$$\hat{q}_t = a^{RE}\hat{\xi}_t + b^{RE}\hat{H}_t$$

$$\hat{H}_{t+1} = c^{RE}\hat{H}_t + d^{RE}\hat{\xi}_t,$$

where hatted variables denote deviations from the steady state and $(a^{RE}, b^{RE}, c^{RE}, d^{RE})$ are given coefficients satisfying $a^{RE} > 0$, $b^{RE} < 0$, $0 < c^{RE} < 1$, and $d^{RE} > 0$.

We now derive a first-order accurate approximation to the RE solution of the equation system

$$q_t = \left(\frac{\theta}{R} + (1 - d - \theta)\delta \right) E_t^p q_{t+1} + \xi_t G'(H_t) \tag{36}$$

$$H_{t+1} = (1 - d)H_t + S(E_t^p q_{t+1}, \delta^{-1}). \tag{37}$$

We linearize these equations around some steady state (q, H, ξ); that is, around a point solving the above system of equation for $q_t = q$, $H_t = H$, and $\xi_t = \xi$ for all t. Letting hatted variables again denote deviations from steady state values, a first-order approximation to (36) delivers

$$\hat{q}_t = \rho E_t^p \hat{q}_{t+1} + G'\hat{\xi}_t + \xi G''\hat{H}_t, \tag{38}$$

where, as in the text, $\rho = [(\theta/R) + (1 - d - \theta)\delta]$ and with all derivatives evaluated at the steady state. A linearization of (37) delivers

$$\hat{H}_{t+1} = (1 - d)\hat{H}_t + S'E_t^p q_{t+1}. \tag{39}$$

We now conjecture a perceived law of motion (PLM) of the form

$$\hat{q}_t = a\hat{\xi}_t + b\hat{H}_t.$$

With RE and using the law of motion for ζ_t we have

$$E_t \hat{q}_{t+1} = a\hat{\xi}_t + bE_t \hat{H}_{t+1}. \tag{40}$$

Substituting into (39) delivers

$$\hat{H}_{t+1} = (1 - d)\hat{H}_t + S'(a\hat{\xi}_t + bE_t \hat{H}_{t+1}).$$

Taking the expectations E_t of this equation delivers

$$E_t \hat{H}_{t+1} = \frac{(1 - d)}{(1 - S'b)} \hat{H}_t + \frac{S'a}{(1 - S'b)} \hat{\xi}_t, \tag{41}$$

so that (40) implies

$$E_t \hat{q}_{t+1} = a\hat{\xi}_t + \frac{(1 - d)b}{(1 - S'b)} \hat{H}_t + \frac{S'ab}{(1 - S'b)} \hat{\xi}_t. \tag{42}$$

Substituting this into (38) delivers the actual law of motion (ALM)

$$\hat{q}_t = \left(\rho a + \rho \frac{S'ab}{(1 - S'b)} + G' \right) \hat{\xi}_t + \left(\rho \frac{(1 - d)b}{(1 - S'b)} + \xi G'' \right) \hat{H}_t.$$

Equation coefficients in the ALM and PLM delivers two conditions for a^{RE} and b^{RE} given by

$$a^{RE} = \rho a^{RE} + \rho \frac{S'a^{RE}b^{RE}}{1 - S'b^{RE}} + G'$$

$$b^{RE} = \rho \frac{(1-d)b^{RE}}{1 - S'b^{RE}} + \xi G''.$$

The second equation depends only on b^{RE} but is quadratic, the first is linear in a^{RE}, conditional on b^{RE}

$$0 = S'(b^{RE})^2 + (-1 + \rho(1-d) - S'\xi G'')b^{RE} + \xi G'',$$

which has two solutions

$$b_1^* = \frac{(1 - \rho(1-d) + S'\xi G'') + \sqrt{(-1 + \rho(1-d) - S'\xi G'')^2 - 4S'\xi G''}}{2S'}$$

$$b_2^* = \frac{(1 - \rho(1-d) + S'\xi G'') - \sqrt{(-1 + \rho(1-d) - S'\xi G'')^2 - 4S'\xi G''}}{2S'}.$$

The corresponding solution for a is

$$a_i^* = \frac{G'}{1 - [\rho/(1 - S'b_i^*)]}. \tag{43}$$

From (39) and (42) it follows that the dynamics for $\hat{H}_t$ are given by

$$\hat{H}_{t+1} = (1-d)\hat{H}_t + S'E_t^p q_{t+1}$$

$$= (1-d)\hat{H}_t + S'\left(a_i^* \hat{\xi}_t + \frac{(1-d)b_i^*}{(1 - S'b_i^*)} \hat{H}_t + \frac{S'a_i^* b_i^*}{(1 - S'b_i^*)} \hat{\xi}_t \right)$$

$$= \frac{1-d}{1 - S'b_i^*} \hat{H}_t + \frac{S'a_i^*}{1 - S'b_i^*} \hat{\xi}_t. \tag{44}$$

Since $1 > d > 0$, we have that $S'b_i^* < 0$ is a sufficient condition for the dynamics for $\hat{H}_t$ to be locally nonexplosive. It is easy to show that the solution (a_2^*, b_2^*) is nonexplosive, while (a_1^*, b_1^*) implies locally explosive dynamics. Therefore, $(a^{RE}, b^{RE}) = (a_2^*, b_2^*)$ and $b^{RE} < 0$. The values for (c^{RE}, d^{RE}) follow from equation (44). As we show in the next section, there exists no other locally nonexplosive RE equilibrium.

Local Uniqueness of the RE Solution

We now show that there exists no other locally nonexplosive RE solution than the one derived in the previous section. We bring the linearized equation (39) and (38) in vector notation:

$$
\begin{pmatrix} 1 & -S' \\ 0 & \rho \end{pmatrix}
\begin{pmatrix} \hat{H}_{t+1} \\ E_t^p \hat{q}_{t+1} \end{pmatrix}
=
\begin{pmatrix} 1-d & 0 \\ -\xi G'' & 1 \end{pmatrix}
\begin{pmatrix} \hat{H}_t \\ \hat{q}_t \end{pmatrix}
+
\begin{pmatrix} 0 \\ -G' \end{pmatrix} \xi_t.
$$

Inverting the matrix on the left, which is always invertible, we get

$$
\begin{pmatrix} \hat{H}_{t+1} \\ E_t^p \hat{q}_{t+1} \end{pmatrix}
=
\begin{pmatrix} 1 - \dfrac{\xi}{\rho} G''S' - d & \dfrac{1}{\rho} S' \\ -\dfrac{\xi}{\rho} G'' & \dfrac{1}{\rho} \end{pmatrix}
\begin{pmatrix} \hat{H}_t \\ \hat{q}_t \end{pmatrix}
+
\begin{pmatrix} -\dfrac{1}{\rho} G'S' \\ -\dfrac{1}{\rho} G' \end{pmatrix}
\begin{pmatrix} 0 \\ -G' \end{pmatrix} \xi_t,
$$

which is a system with one predetermined and one "jump" variable. It has a locally unique REE if the first matrix on the right-hand side has one explosive and one stable eigenvalue. The eigenvalues are

$$
\lambda_1 = \frac{1}{2\rho}(\rho - d\rho - \xi G''S' + 1 + \sqrt{(\rho - d\rho - \xi G''S' + 1)^2 + 4\rho(d-1)})
$$

$$
\lambda_2 = \frac{1}{2\rho}(\rho - d\rho - \xi G''S' + 1 - \sqrt{(\rho - d\rho - \xi G''S' + 1)^2 + 4\rho(d-1)}).
$$

It is straightforward to show that λ_1 is unstable ($\lambda_1 > 1$) while λ_2 is a stable eigenvalue ($-1 < \lambda_2 < 1$).

Test of Agents' Model

This appendix shows how to design a test statistic for equation (30). Following standard practice in the unit-root literature, the statistic is such that it would be efficient within a certain class of estimators in the stationary case. Consider a version of equation (30)

$$
\Delta \ln \frac{q_t}{q_{t-1}} = \alpha' x_t + e_t, \tag{45}
$$

where x_t is stationary and ergodic, orthogonal to e_t, and $\Delta \ln(q_t/q_{t-1})$ is MA(1). Let α_T^{OLS} be the ordinary least squares (OLS) estimator with a sample of T observations. We define the test statistic

$$
W_T \equiv \alpha_T^{OLS'} \left[(X'X)^{-1} S_{w,T} (X'X)^{-1} \right]^{-1} \alpha_T^{OLS}
$$

where
$$X = [x_1, ..., x_T]'$$

$$S_{w,T} = \sum_{t=1}^{T}\left(\Delta\log\frac{q_t}{q_{t-1}}\right)^2 x_t x_t' + \frac{T}{T-1}\sum_{t=2}^{T}\left(\Delta\log\frac{q_t}{q_{t-1}}\right)\left(\Delta\log\frac{q_{t-1}}{q_{t-2}}\right)x_t x_{t-1}'$$

$$+ \frac{T}{T-1}\sum_{t=1}^{T-1}\left(\Delta\log\frac{q_t}{q_{t-1}}\right)\left(\Delta\log\frac{q_{t+1}}{q_t}\right)x_t x_{t+1}'.$$

Clearly, $(1/T)S_{w,T}$ is a consistent estimator of the spectral density evaluated at frequency zero when e_t is MA(1) and independent of x_t.

Using standard results it can be shown that under the null hypothesis $(\alpha = 0)$ we have

$$W_T \to \chi_3^2 \text{ in distribution as } T \to \infty.$$

Clearly, this asymptotic result cannot be applied to testing equation (30), since the regressors in (30) are nonstationary. We therefore derive correct confidence intervals for W_T by Monte-Carlo simulation for a given sample size T and given parameter values (the confidence intervals turn out not to be very different from those of an χ^2 distribution). The set of parameters consists only of the variances σ_η^2 and σ_v^2, so that it is easy to test for the sensitivity of the confidence intervals. We find that the main results would be nonaltered for a wide range of values for these variances.

Endnotes

We thank Lars Hansen, Michael Woodford, and Daron Acemoglu for useful comments. All errors are our own. Marcet acknowleges funding from Ministerio de Educación y Ciencia and Generalitat de Catalunya. Contacts: adam@uni-mannheim.de, a.marcet@lse.ac.uk, and pei.kuang@hof.uni-frankfurt.de. For acknowledgments, sources of research support, and disclosure of the authors' material financial relationships, if any, please see http://www.nber.org/chapters/c12408.ack.

1. For example, *The Economist* (August 23, 2007), "Does America Need a Recession?", Economic Focus.

2. Himmelberg, Mayer, and Sinai (2005) show that with low real interest rates a further reduction in rates can give rise to a large house price increase under rational expectations. It fails, however, to give rise to a persistent sequence of house price increases.

3. The data is taken from the Organization of Economic Cooperation and Development (OECD) Economic Outlook No. 87, 2010, Annex Tables 59 and 60. The real house price index is the nominal house price index deflated by CPI price index.

4. The data is from the OECD Economic Outlook No. 87, 2010, Annex Table 51.

5. The change in housing value is computed using the Federal Reserve Board Flow of Funds Statistics, Table B.100, Release 2010-12-9. The current account numbers are taken from the National Income and Product Accounts (NIPA) tables, as downloaded through the FRB St. Louis FRED database.

6. The mortgage rate is the "1-year adjustable rate mortgage average in the United States" from Freddie Mac (SeriesID: MORTGAGE1US).

7. The real private consumption growth data is from the OECD Economic Outlook No.87, 2010, Annex Table 3. The house price series employ the same data as used for figure 1.

8. The housing units data is from the US Census Bureau, using the series "new privately owned housing units completed." The house price series are the same as the ones shown in figure 1.

9. Data limitations prevent us from discussing the behavior of new housing construction or the relationship between value changes of the housing stock and the current account for all G7 countries.

10. Aizenman and Jinjarak (2009) also provide evidence on the strong positive association between current account deficits and the appreciation of real estate prices across a number of countries.

11. The figure looks very similar when depicting instead the the price-to-rent ratio or the price-to-income ratio.

12. As explained in Adam and Marcet (2011), common knowledge of agents' preferences and beliefs might place additional restrictions on the house price beliefs that rational agents can entertain, so we need to assume absence of common knowledge.

13. The data is from the OECD, using a sample spanning the years 1970–2008. Italy is excluded because the rental data is only available from 1996 onwards. The regression used in the Dickey Fuller test is based on the model $\log \xi_t = \alpha + \rho \log \xi_{t-1} + \varepsilon_t$, and the null hypothesis $\alpha = 0, \rho = 1$ is tested against the alternative $\alpha \neq 0$ and $\rho < 1$. The reported statistic is the estimate for $\rho - 1$ divided by its estimated standard deviation.

14. Using current houses prices instead of expected future prices in the borrowing constraint (5) would make virtually no difference for our purposes, as actual and expected prices tend to move together in the learning model we consider.

15. It is easy to rule out interest rates below R as then domestic and foreign agents both wish to borrow, implying that the loan market cannot clear. For interest rates above R the foreign lender wishes to borrow up to its borrowing constraint. If the foreign agent is sufficiently wealthy, this would lead to a violation of the nonnegativity constraint on domestic consumption. It thus has to be the case that the interest rate equals R. Provided the foreign lender is sufficiently wealthy, lending to domestic agents will imply nonnegative consumption for the foreign lender.

16. As should become from Section IV, subsection A, one should use a slightly different belief system for firms than used for consumers because profits are a choice variable for firms, while consumers take profits as given. Since this does not affect the expectations showing up in the subsequent firm optimality conditions, we ignore this issue in the text.

17. Existence of a maximum can be insured, for example, by imposing that the utility from consumption (c_t) is bounded at some very high level. See Appendix A.1 in Adam and Marcet (2011) for how this can be achieved in a related model.

18. A full characterization of optimal outcomes is found in the appendix. Since zero consumption does not accord well with the data, this approach appears justified.

19. Although a large drop in the expected future house price may imply that loans have to be repaid to an extent that consumption would have to become negative, we consider values of the shocks for which this does not occur for the $T + 1$ periods in our simulations.

20. Existence and uniqueness follow from the following considerations. Equation (21) defines q as a continuous and (weakly) decreasing function of H, which approaches $+\infty$ as $H \to 0$ and $-\infty$ as $H \to \bar{H}$. From (22) we have that q is a strictly increasing function of H. As a result, there exists a unique intersection.

21. The subsequent equation reveals that sufficiently small housing perference shocks will indeed imply that H_t stays in the neighborhood of H with high likelihood, as initially assumed.

22. The former follows from $a^{RE} > 0$, and the latter from $d^{RE} > 0$ and $b^{RE} < 0$.

23. The initial real interest rate is set equal to the average ex ante gross real mortgage rate over the periods 1996–2000 (i.e., $R_{96-00} = 1.0335$). In the year 2001 we then consider an expected and permanent fall in the real interest rate that lasts for five years to a value

of R_{01-05} = 1.0228, which is equal to the average ex ante US real mortgage rate for this period. Thereafter, we consider an unexpected and permanent upward shift in real rates to R_{06-08} = 1.0301, which is again taken from the data.

24. This is required to insure optimality of the binding collateral constraint.

25. Since $\zeta_t = \zeta$, the price-to-rent ratio is simply proportional to the real house price series.

26. The intuition for this outcome should become clear from the linear-approximate solution derived in Section V, subsection B.

27. This holds true even in a Bayesian Rational Expectations Equilibrium in which agents learn about fundamentals (see Adam and Marcet 2011 for details).

28. Since the process for y_t and ζ_t are exogenous to the model, it is straightforward to relax this assumption for these variables.

29. The fact that β_t is nonstationary is not important for our results. The model outcomes are almost the same when specifying instead a stationary process

$$\ln \beta_t = (1 - \rho) + \rho \ln \beta_{t-1} + \ln \eta_t$$

and choosing some value $\rho < 1$ that is sufficiently close to one.

30. Convergence can only occur for an arbitrarily large but finite horizon because of the unit root present in agents' beliefs.

31. Again, this holds only for any arbitrarily large but finite horizon.

32. This is the case because one can recover v_t and η_t from the MA process and then find β_t.

33. The 10% critial value reported in the text assumes a gain parameter of $g = 0.06$, which is the value that we estimate for our model later on. The critical value, however, changes very little over a wide range of values for g.

34. An alternative test is based on using lags of the price over rent ratio on the right side of the regression (30), which leads to very similar findings. Rent prices, however, are not available for Italy prior to 1996 in our OECD data set.

35. Technically, the change in the real interest rate is a probability zero event under the postulated beliefs.

36. The interest rate enters in the definition of ρ (see equation [15]).

37. Specifically, for the years 1996–2000 we set real interest rates equal to the average ex ante gross real mortgage rate (i.e., R_{96-00} = 1.0335). To capture the real interest rate decrease following in years 2001–2005, we set real interest to R_{01-05} = 1.0228, which is again the average ex ante US real mortgage rate for this period in the data. Finally, we capture the upward shift in real rates in the years 2006–2008 by setting R_{06-08} = 1.0301, which is again taken from the data.

38. We keep $\xi G'(H)$ fixed at this calibrated value in all subsequent model periods. The value for $\xi G'(H)$ only normalizes the house price level, but has no impact on the dynamics.

39. Gross ex ante real interest rates are then assumed to stay constant at their 1996–2000 average, which is R_{96-00} = 1.0335.

40. To obtain a model-implied current account to GDP ratio, one also has to take a stand on the exogenous income process. We choose a time-invariant income (i.e., $y_t = y$) so as to match the data.

41. This is true, except for the value of $\xi G'$, which is chosen in each country to normalize the model-implied real house prices in the year 2000 to 100.

42. The performance of the model deteriorates only slightly, but concavity is required to have an independent role for price beliefs, as explained in Section VI, subsection C.

43. A similar approach has been used in models of learning; see Bray and Savin (1986) for an early reference.

References

Adam, K., and A. Marcet. 2010. "Booms and Busts in Asset Prices." London School of Economics Unpublished manuscript.

————. 2011. "Internal Rationality, Imperfect Market Knowledge and Asset Prices." *Journal of Economic Theory* 146:1224–52.

Adam, K., A. Marcet, and J. P. Nicolini. 2010. "Learning and Stock Market Volatility." Mannheim University mimeo.

Aizenmann, J., and Y. Jinjarak. 2009. "Current Account Patterns and National Real Estate Markets." *Journal of Urban Economics* 66:75–89.

Bray, M., and N. Savin. 1986. "Rational Expectations, Equilibria, Learning, and Model Specification." *Econometrica* 54:1129–60.

Burnside, C., M. Eichenbaum, and S. Rebelo. 2011. "Understanding Booms and Busts in Housing Markets." Northwestern University mimeo.

Gete, P. 2010. "Housing Markets and Current Account Dynamics." Georgetown University mimeo.

Glaeser, E., and J. Gyourko. 2006. "Housing Dynamics." NBER Working Paper no. 12787. Cambridge, MA: National Bureau of Economic Research, December.

Glaeser, E., J. Gyourko, and A. Saiz. 2008. "Housing Supply and Housing Bubbles." Harvard University mimeo.

Himmelberg, C., C. Mayer, and T. Sinai. 2005. "Assessing High House Prices: Bubbles, Fundamentals, and Misperceptions." *Journal of Economic Perspectives* 19 (4): 67–92.

Iacoviello, M. 2005. "House Prices, Borrowing Constraints and Monetary Policy in the Business Cycle." *American Economic Review* 95:739–64.

Kiyotaki, N., and J. Moore. 1997. "Credit Cycles." *Journal of Political Economy* 105:211–48.

Laibson, D., and J. Mollerstrom. 2010. "Capital Flows, Consumption Booms and Asset Bubbles: A Behavioural Alternative to the Savings Glut Hypothesis." *Economic Journal,* forthcoming.

Lustig, H., and S. V. Nieuwerburgh. 2005. "Housing Collateral, Consumption Insurance, and Risk Premia: An Empirical Perspective." *Journal of Finance* 60:1167–219.

Matsuyama, K. 1990. "Residential Investment and the Current Account." *Journal of International Economics* 28:137–53.

Piazzesi, M., and M. Schneider. 2009. "Momentum Traders in the Housing Market: Survey Evidence and a Search Model." *American Economic Review, Papers and Proceedings* 99:406–11.

Punzi, M. T. 2006. "Housing Market and Current Account Imbalances in the International Economy." University of Alicante mimeo.

Topel, R., and S. Rosen. 1988. "Housing Investment in the United States." *Journal of Political Economy* 96:718–40.

Comment

Edward L. Glaeser, Harvard University and NBER

Introduction

The housing boom and bust that occurred between 1996 and 2009 is an empirical event that shattered older theories of the housing market and left a gaping need for a richer model of housing dynamics. Simple theories that link housing prices with interest rates or other credit market variables cannot explain the magnitude of the boom or bust with standard assumptions about rationality (Glaeser, Gottlieb, and Gyourko 2010). If we assume enough irrationality of the right kind, then the most extreme cycle will not reject our theory, but such a freewheeling model does not really generate any testable hypotheses either. The goal is to find that solid, middle place with enough freedom to actually explain what happened, but enough clearly refutable predictions so that the model can be properly tested.

"House Price Booms and the Current Account," by Klaus Adam, Pei Kuang, and Albert Marcet, attempts to find that high ground. Their open economy model enables the interest rate to be formed endogenously, which is quite preferable to most housing models, but their largest contribution is their modeling of beliefs. They assume a belief structure that is "near rational," still tethered to conventional assumptions about rationality but with enough flexibility to generate more extreme price swings. While I am unsure as to whether their precise formulation of near-rationality will become standard, this basic approach seems correct—a reasonable balance of psychological realism and traditional modeling parsimony.

The model is able to generate the large price swings that we have recently experienced. It can also generate the one-year serial autocorrelation in price movements that is such a strong feature of the data

(Case and Shiller 1989). To achieve this with a relatively simple model is a significant step forward, but to make further progress, their model needs to be subjected to a tougher range of empirical tests.

The Empirical Problems

While explaining the magnitude of price convulsions is not the only empirical challenge facing housing theorists, it is certainly the most extreme. Between 2001 and 2005, the Case–Shiller Index (20-city repeat sales increase) experienced a 46% increase in real terms. Between 2006 and 2009, the index fell by over one-third. The more nationally representative Federal Housing Finance Agency (FHFA) repeat sales index showed a less extreme boom-bust cycle, but even that index experienced a 53% real price gain between 1996 and 2006 and a substantial decline since then.

The recent housing convulsion is an extreme event, but it is symptomatic of a more general tendency of housing prices to exhibit high levels of variance. Glaeser and Gyourko (2006) write down a simple dynamic housing model and find that the variance of price movements over time and space is about far too high in many markets to be explained by "fundamentals" such as local income changes. This high level of variance is frequently identified with housing cycles, and America and the world have certainly experienced many earlier booms and busts. New York City during the 1920s was such an example, and the Japanese boom-bust cycle over 20 years ago is another.

Beyond high volatility of prices, a second empirical puzzle is the strong positive serial correlation of price changes at shorter time horizons, such as one year (Case and Shiller 1989). Predictability of housing price movements is not itself a challenge to conventional theory, since houses deliver far more than just financial returns, but the extent of this predictability is hard to explain. Glaeser and Gyourko (2006) report a one-year coefficient of price changes on lagged price changes of .71. This extremely high figure is hard to match with any obvious "fundamental" cause.

But while housing prices are positively serially correlated in the short run, they mean revert significantly in the longer run (Cutler, Poterba, and Summers 1991). Glaeser and Gyourko (2006) estimate a five-year coefficient of price changes on lagged price changes of –.32. This coefficient is somewhat easier to reconcile with benchmark models, if building new housing takes time and if fundamentals mean revert over time, as they appear to do.

While construction also shows significant volatility—positive serial correlation of prices at one-year horizons and mean reversion at five-year horizons—these facts are probably best seen as a natural consequence of the price movements rather than as independent puzzles. As long as prices are quite volatile, we should expect construction to also change substantially over time. Given standard housing supply elasticities (which are often estimated to be above one), the construction boom of 2003–2006 was, if anything, somewhat smaller than the price movements would suggest, at least for the nation as a whole, which may be explained by heterogeneity in housing supply elasticities across space.

The final empirical challenge may be hardest—explaining why some areas experienced housing price explosions, while others did not. Glaeser, Gyourko, and Saiz (2008) present evidence that price fluctuations were less extreme in areas with more elastic housing supply. Economic theory certainly predicts that any demand shock—whether caused by rational or irrational forces—should impact price less and quantity more in places where supply is more elastic.

But while supply elasticity appears to impact how bubbles play themselves out, there is plenty of variation that is not explained by supply elasticity. Both Phoenix and Dallas appear to have fairly elastic supplies of housing. Dallas experienced little price appreciation during the boom—it built a vast number of new homes. Phoenix managed to see both huge increases in construction and huge increases in prices. Indeed, a lasting puzzle from the boom is why home buyers in areas like Phoenix and Las Vegas (where land is relatively abundant, permitting is relatively easy, and prices have historically stayed extremely close to construction costs) were willing, for a very short time, to pay so much for housing.

The cross-national variation is also quite interesting. Many other nations experienced price booms similar to the United States, but others did not. Germany and Japan, for example, had extremely stable housing prices. Some speculate that the memory of their earlier boom-bust cycle dampened excessive optimism, but we really have little ability to explain the appearance of housing price convulsions across time and space.

The Adam, Kuang, and Marcet Framework

Adam, Kuang, and Marcet begin their paper by empirically documenting the negative time series relationship between the current account surplus and housing prices over the 1996–2006 period. This evidence motivates paying close attention to credit markets in their theoretical work, and surely these played some significant role in facilitating the housing price convulsion.

They also show that real interest rates were relatively low during the 2000–2005 period when prices were going up. Their choice of measure for the real rate, the one-year adjustable mortgage rate adjusted by inflation expectations provided by expert survey respondents, presents a more volatile series than more standard measures, such as the ten-year rate adjusted for similarly survey-based inflation expectations. Their choice is not necessarily wrong, but it does present more rate volatility.

More interest rate volatility makes it potentially easier for credit market variables to explain the housing market price shifts, but only if the rate shifts line up with the price shifts. The low rates of the 2000–2005 period seems to go well with the rising prices during that period, but prices were also rising between 1996 and 2000 when their measure of real rates were high. Over a longer time horizon that includes the 1980s, the correlation between real rates and housing is quite modest. Glaeser, Gyourko, and Gottlieb (2010) find that a 100 basis point swing in real rates is typically associated with a 7% swing in housing prices, and that coefficient falls when we include even the most basic of controls, such as a time trend.

But any analysis of the connection between interest rates and housing prices is compromised by the endogeneity of real rates. This endogeneity is typically ignored by housing economists, while Adam, Kuang, and Marcet quite thoughtfully connect interest rates to broader movements in the current account. This is potentially important because rates may certainly reflect demand for housing credit, as well as the supply of credit. One reason why the measured relationship between interest rates and housing prices is relatively modest is that high housing demand may push interest rates up.

This reverse causality is particularly likely when using measured mortgage rates, which may reflect assessment of default risks, instead of ten-year treasury bond rates, which is more standard in the literature. If assessed default risk is low during boom periods, this could create a spurious negative correlation between prices and interest rates. The Adam, Kuang, and Marcet model, however, does treat the real interest rate as an exogenous variable, determined by an international lender. Perhaps, given the more than 15 trillion dollar size of the American mortgage market, it would be sensible for future work to allow some feedback where housing borrowing impacts the real rate.

Their core model assumes a representative consumer that receives shocks to the demand for housing. This representative consumer approach is standard in macroeconomics, but is somewhat less common in urban economics, where housing prices typically reflect the value associated with one place versus another. Consumers may be identical, but housing is not. If Adam, Kuang, and Marcet were more interested in explaining the heterogeneous experiences of the boom, then they should probably move to a dynamic Rosen-Roback spatial equilibrium model, perhaps along the lines of Glaeser and Gyourko (2006).

Their homogeneous place, homogeneous consumer model does enable them to incorporate important aspects of the housing, such as collateral constraints. The borrowing constraint is itself realistic and important, although one can question their decision to allow future prices to influence the constraint. Their assumption means that higher rates of expected price growth make it easier to borrow. I suspect that this is actually true—banks discounted default risk during the boom because they expected plenty of price appreciation—but the assumption is somewhat nonstandard in the housing literature. It would be more normal to assume that current prices alone influence the constraint. At this point, I think their assumption is best seen as shorthand for a more complex model of the banking structure that could be fleshed out in further work.

Adam, Kuang, and Marcet deserve considerable credit for incorporating housing supply into the model. Often supply is treated as exogenous, or even more problematically, rents are treated as exogenous and prices are derived as a function of the expected rent series. Yet the ability to deliver new homes is certainly important in mediating price changes, which is exactly what Glaeser, Gyourko, and Saiz (2008) find.

Their specific assumptions about housing supply are well in line with the literature. Their iso-elastic functional form assumption, for example, is not unusual. Perhaps the most important departure from realism is the assumption of a common national supply elasticity. Actual supply elasticities differ significantly from place to place. Building in greater Houston is just very different from building in greater San Francisco and that would matter as they attempt to think more seriously about differences within the United States.

Using this model, they calculate a deterministic steady state and then use linear, and linear quadratic, approximations to calculate the impact of shocks in a stochastic environment. Their appendix makes it clear that the somewhat more general linear quadratic assumption does not change the primary implications of their simulation.

The key result of the simulation is the interest rate changes that we see in the data are too small to generate large increases in housing prices when expectations are rational. If buyers do not anticipate that low rates will become high again, then the observed interest rate change predicts a price jump of approximately 4%. If buyers anticipate the real rate increase experienced in 2006, then the price jump is only 2%.

Moreover, the timing of the price jump is quite unlike the price growth that America actually experienced. Their model predicts that prices will immediately jump and then either stay at the higher level, if no real rate increase is anticipated, or gradually fall, if a rate increase is expected. In reality, prices rose steadily over this period.

Their conclusion is exactly the same as reached by Glaeser, Gyourko, and Gottlieb (2010) using a very different methodology: the observed change in real rates is far too small to explain the observed price boom. Their calculation is that the predicted price increase is about 10% of the actual price growth. We have a slightly higher number, but one that is still very far below the actual price growth. Their work supports the view that if credit markets matter, they must matter because of some interaction between credit availability and less than perfectly rational consumers.

Near Rationality and Price Movements

The primary contribution of this paper lies in its modeling of near rationality. The authors wisely attempt to balance more psychological realism and the modeling degrees of freedom that come with it against the advantages of staying near rationality. Limited departures from rationality are attractive both because they keep closer ties with the standard economics and because they impose more discipline on new models.

Adam, Kuang, and Mercet specifically assume that individuals forecast price growth by assuming that the log of price growth is the sum of a transitory component and a permanent component. In each period, there are two shocks to price growth—one becomes permanent and the other immediately fades away. Home buyers then attempt to forecast the model with the available data. Specifically, they assume that the expected value of price growth between periods t and $t + 1$ is equal to a weighted average of their expectation of growth between periods $t - 1$ and t and the actual price growth between $t - 2$ and $t - 1$. They use the one period lag of price growth to avoid simultaneity.

Adam, Kuang, and Marcet work to build the case that this is not profound irrationality, but something quite near actual rationality. If information is sufficiently limited, this is not a completely insane learning rule. Beliefs can converge to the rational expectations beliefs if the variance of the shocks to the growth rate converge to zero.

While there are ways in which this model resembles a standard learning model, no one should think that this is not a fairly large leap from standard rationality. Assuming that beliefs about price growth evolve so that future price growth is a weighted sum of lagged beliefs and lagged growth is very different than what I would typically think is using all of the available data to forecast a price. They micro-found their learning model by assuming that agents believe that growth rates follow a particular stochastic process, which is a permanent and transitory component that is not particularly linked to the forces that actually drive price changes. Individual readers can decide whether they share the authors' belief that this is "near rationality."

Their assumptions produce results that resemble the old adaptive expectations models that were discarded decades ago, but perhaps those models were discarded too rapidly. There is something very appealing about complete rationality, especially from a modeling perspective. There is only one way to get things exactly right and an uncountable number of ways to get things wrong, which makes assuming any particular error prone prediction assumption seem somewhat arbitrary. Yet adaptive expectations seem as reasonable as any other erroneous way of thinking, and survey evidence on home buyers suggests that there is some truth to the assumption. The key test is whether this model does well at explaining the data.

The first, particularly attractive, feature of the model comes out of the theory even before simulations—price changes are positively serially correlated. Price growth during one period creates the expectation of further price growth and that pushes price up further during the next period. Around the rational expectations equilibrium, the implied coefficient when the logarithm of price changes is regressed on the lagged logarithm of price changes equals their g parameter, which is the ratio of variance of the expected log of the growth rate in prices divided by the variance of the shocks to the log growth rate times the parameter ρ, which if housing depreciates very slowly, is a weighted average of the market discount factor and the private discount factor, as such is some number less than but close to one. As we do not currently know much about the variance of these beliefs about price growth rates, theory does not predict much about how big the serial correlation in price growth is going to be, but it certainly can be quite large. Adaptive expectations deliver that result.

Their simulations then show that a positive shock to real interest rates pushes prices up immediately and then that has feedback effects on future price growth. One period of fundamentals drives growth in the next period, which then fuels further growth. Eventually, growth comes in below expectations and the bubble starts unwinding.

They then use this model to make sense of the international experience. In the United States, the interest rate shock produces a boom-bust cycle that is in line with what America actually experienced. They obtain similar results for France, Italy, and the United Kingdom. Some countries have different predicted price experiences because of different levels of pre-2000 price changes. Those places, like Germany and Japan, that had less price growth before 2000 are predicted to have less of a boom and that is what the data says. They predict too little of a boom for Canada.

The next place to take the model is to more rigorous testing. The general implication that there will be positives serial correlation will surely be borne out in the data. But the model does seem to predict that past interest rate shocks should also have large effects, at least if the pattern of preshock price movements is right. I am more skeptical that this will be borne out in the data.

More generally, it would be good to have a version of the model that is more focused on subnational data, since there is so much more ability to run tests at a subnational level. Elasticity differences are significant, but so will be the track record of preshock price movements. These will provide added opportunities to test their model, or some similar adaptive expectations-based model.

One way to think about their model is that the adaptive expectations framework creates a multiplier effect, where exogenous shocks create a far larger price increase than would be predicted by a more standard model. This logic should work for other shocks beyond real rates. As such, a natural test of the model would be to look at price responses to other local demand shocks, such as oil price movements for Texas and so forth.

Conclusion

This paper is an important contribution to the growing literature about housing price fluctuations. They make two important contributions.

First, they show that the changes in real rates cannot explain the magnitude of the boom given standard assumptions about rationality, which supports Glaeser, Gottlieb, and Gyourko's (2010) quite similar claim. Second, they show that one model of near rationality can generate price dynamics that look far more realistic.

The first result helps eliminate past theories of housing price change that assume extreme levels of buyer knowledge. The second result points toward the future, where hopefully richer models that respect the limits of human cognition will give us a better ability to understand and predict large housing price movements. I like their model and think that it is an important contribution to the literature. Only future work can tell us whether it is the right framework for incorporating near rationality into housing and other asset models.

Endnote

For acknowledgments, sources of research support, and disclosure of the author's material financial relationships, if any, please see http://www.nber.org/chapters/c12409.ack.

References

Adam, Klaus, Pei Kuang, and Albert Marcet. 2011. "House Price Booms and the Current Account." In *NBER Macroeconomics Annual 2011*, edited by Daron Acemoglu and Michael Woodford. Chicago: University of Chicago Press.

Case, Karl E., and Robert J. Shiller. 1989. "The Efficiency of the Market for Single-Family Homes." *American Economic Review* 79 (1): 125–37.

Cutler, David M., James M. Poterba, and Lawrence H. Summers. 1991. "Speculative Dynamics." *Review of Economic Studies* 58 (3): 529–46.

Glaeser, Edward L., Joshua D. Gottlieb, and Joseph Gyourko. 2010. "Can Cheap Credit Explain the Housing Boom?" NBER Working Paper Series no. 16230. Cambridge, MA: National Bureau of Economic Research, July.

Glaeser, Edward L., and Joseph Gyourko. 2006. "Housing Dynamics." NBER Working Paper Series no. 12787. Cambridge, MA: National Bureau of Economic Research, December.

Glaeser, Edward L., Joseph Gyourko, and Albert Saiz. 2008. "Symposium: Mortgages and the Housing Crash: Housing Supply and Housing Bubbles." *Journal of Urban Economics* 64 (2): 198–217.

Comment

Lars Peter Hansen, *University of Chicago and NBER*

Introduction

Adam, Kuang, and Marcet propose and analyze an interesting model of house price dynamics. It is pitched as an open economy model and used to study the relationship between aggregate debt and house prices. The model suggests a linkage between the current account and the value of the housing stock. The authors present some figures that motivate their analysis, with the financial crisis an important component of their data summaries. Their modeling of asset valuation follows Kiyotaki and Moore (1997) by exploring the role of collateral and follows Adam and Marcet (2011) (and related unpublished work) by exploring a particular way to relax an assumption of rational expectations. My comments focus primarily on a simplified version of their model, which I use to suggest ways to make this line of research more empirically ambitious. I also remark on the potential role of nonlinearities in the model specification for altering the implications.

Housing As an Asset

The paper adopts a simple valuation model as a device to model housing values. Consumers have preferences of the form:

$$E\left[\sum_{t=0}^{\infty} \delta^t(\xi_t h_t + c_t)\right],$$

where δ is a discount factor, ζ_t is a preference shock process and evolves as:

$$\log \xi_t = d + \log \xi_{t-1} + \log \varepsilon_t, \tag{1}$$

and c_t is consumption. Preferences are linear in consumption. Strictly speaking their specification has $d = 0$, and thus the marginal rate of substitution between housing services and consumption is expected to increase over time at a rate given by one half the variance of log ε_t. It seems likely that adding a drift to this specification would not alter the analysis in an important way, and in what follows I include it.

To complete the preference specification, Adam et al. (2011) introduce the possibly nonlinear transformation:

$$h_t = G(H_t),$$

where H_t is the stock of housing. There are two possible interpretations of resulting preference specification. One interpretation is that h_t is the service flow from housing, in which case ζ_t is the implied rental rate as the authors write in their paper. This is not the only possible interpretation, however. Since consumers rent H_t not h_t, we may take $\xi_t G'(H_t)$ as the implied rental rate for housing where the service flow is assumed to be equal to the stock. This measure of the rental rate is distinct from ζ_t. While the authors think of G as a nonlinear transformation from housing stock to services, G might just as well represent curvature in preferences. This discussion is only interesting when G is nonlinear, and in this paper the nonlinearity of G seems not to play much of a role in the analysis. With the exception of the reported outcome of a Dickey-Fuller test for a unit root, time series on rental rates are used rather informally. Formally incorporating time series data on rental rates simultaneously with housing prices would direct the analysis toward a more serious discussion of whether G represents "preferences" or "technology." In some of my subsequent discussion I will consider other reasons to use rental rates in an econometric analysis.

Adam, Kuang, and Marcet follow prior research by Kiyotaki and Moore (1997) and others in which a financing constraint is introduced:

$$b_t \leq \theta \frac{E_t q_{t+1}}{R} H_t = \theta \frac{E_t q_{t+1}}{q_t R} V_t, \qquad (2)$$

where R is the interest rate assumed to be constant and given externally to the model, q_t the price of a homogeneous unit of housing, and $V_t = q_t H_t$ is the value of the housing stock. Prospective limits to the amount of borrowing induces a collateral value to the housing stock. Increases in the value of a house enlarges the amount of permissible debt, and this adds to the value to home owning beyond the direct consumption of housing services.

The asset-pricing formula for the stock of housing must account for its value as a source of collateral. Adam et al. follow previous literature by imposing an incentive for borrowing. The gross rate of interest R, assumed to be constant and determined outside the model, is less than $1/\delta$. As a result, the borrowing constraint binds and a house gains additional value by allowing for additional borrowing. The motivation for the inequality relating the subjective rate of discount to the interest rate is the time series data on the current account for the United States. With these simplifying assumptions on R, the relevant discount factor for housing is:

$$\rho = \delta(1 - d) + \theta\left(\frac{1}{R} - \delta\right),$$

where d is the depreciation rate. The second term captures the collateral value of the house. This term increases the discount factor ρ and thus adds to the value of house.

The model in Adam et al. focuses on rental rates induced by random preference shocks as the source of fluctuations in housing values. Is this really the most important source of variation in housing values? Recent dynamic stochastic equilibrium models feature other sources of fluctuations. For instance, temporal variation in θ has been used to capture changes in borrowing environments. See, for instance, Jermann and Quadrini (2011). Of course, such an approach leads naturally to the question of what might induce such fluctuations. Interest rates are typically not constant in such models, and interest rate fluctuations are of particular interest for understanding fluctuations in housing prices. More generally, stochastic discount factor variation induced by risk averse investors, and perhaps amplified by market imperfections, could be critical to understanding the behavior of expected returns, including returns to investing in the housing market.[1] The lack of interest variability and the absence of time variation in risk prices closes down two important channels for asset price determination. As we will see, the linearized version of the equation that determines housing prices becomes a version of the present-value model that LeRoy and Porter (1981) and Shiller (1981) challenged empirically in their study of stock prices. In the macro/finance literature, part of this puzzling finding has been attributed to time-variation in risk premia induced by changes in risk prices or exposures. I suspect these additional channels for variation in asset values are important for understanding housing values. Adam et al. explore an alternative channel that is also interesting: distorted expectations. I will have more to say about that channel later. To the authors' credit, they consider the impact of changing real interest rates in experiments in which investors presume before and after the change that interest rates will remain constant. The overall model may be linear enough that the calculations have more general validity as an interesting approximation. Nevertheless, a more complete attempt at shock accounting for housing-market would be a useful complement to the current results in this paper.

Model Solution

I now expand on a pedagogically useful simplification of the model when G is linear and borrowing constraints are known to bind. Of course this simplification misses some potentially interesting nonlinearities, but it gives us a valuable starting point. The model solution proceeds as follows.

1. Solve for the housing price q_t as a function of the preference shock (rental rate).

2. Use the housing price solution to infer the housing stock H_t from supply considerations.

3. Use the binding financing constraint to infer the aggregate debt b_t.

Absent this linearity of the transformation G, we are compelled to solve for (q_t, H_t) simultaneously (combine steps 1 and 2). Absent a binding borrowing constraint, all three steps must be done simultaneously. While the authors have the more ambitious model as their target, the actual analysis does not drift far away from the simplified version.

The basic housing price formula is:

$$q_t = \sum_{j=0}^{\infty} \rho^j E[\xi_{t+j} G'(H_{t+j})|\mathcal{F}_t].$$

When $G'(H) = g$ this formula simplifies to:

$$q_t = \left(\frac{g}{1-\lambda}\right)\xi_t$$

where

$$\lambda = \rho \exp\left(g + \frac{\sigma_\varepsilon^2}{2}\right).$$

While the distinction between ρ and λ plays no role in this paper, equality could be induced by setting $g = -(\sigma_\varepsilon^2/2)$ in contrast to the $g = 0$ specification posed in this paper. The variance adjustment does not show up in the first-order approximation in the shock exposure, consistent with some of the calculations that follow, so I will also ignore the variance adjustment in this section; but I will include g when I consider a more general specification of the process ζ. Recall that in the house-price formula, ρ includes both the usual discount and depreciation rate adjustments intertwined with an adjustment for the collateral value of housing.

I generalize the specification for ζ by representing its growth rate as an infinite-order moving average:

$$\log \xi_{t+1} - \log \xi_t = d + \eta\psi(L)\varepsilon_{t+1}$$

where $\psi(L)$ is an infinite-order row vector of polynomials in the the lag operator, L, and ε is a possibly multivariate i.i.d. shock process with mean zero and covariance I. For future reference, the "z-transform" of the moving-average coefficients is:

$$\psi(z) = \sum_{j=0}^{\infty} \psi_j(z)^j, \quad \sum_{j=0}^{\infty} |\psi_j|^2 < \infty,$$

which defines a function of the complex variable z that is well-defined as a power series for $|z| < 1$. The parameter η scales the shock exposure and is used as a way to compute an approximate solution.

Construct the deterministic counterpart as:

$$\log \xi_{t+1}^0 - \log \xi_t^0 = d,$$

and a "first derivative" component with respect to η as:

$$\log \xi_{t+1}^1 - \log \xi_t^1 = \psi(L)\varepsilon_{t+1}.$$

Of course, this is really not an approximation but a decomposition, because the first-order adjustment leads to an exact representation.

As is standard in the asset pricing literature with growth, it is convenient to work with the counterpart to the logarithm of a dividend-price ratio:

$$v_t = \log q_t - \log \xi_t.$$

Compute $v_t^0 = \bar{v}$ by solving for the deterministic $\eta = 0$ value:

$$\bar{v} = \frac{g}{1-\lambda},$$

where $\lambda = \rho\exp(d)$. The derivative process for v satisfies the difference equation:

$$v_t^1 = \lambda E(v_{t+1}^1 \mid \mathcal{F}_t) + \lambda E(\log \xi_{t+1}^1 - \log \xi_t^1 \mid \mathcal{F}_t).$$

I solve this model using the same tools as in Hansen and Sargent (1980), Whiteman (1983), and others, by converting moving-average coefficients into power series of a complex variable z that converges for $|z| < 1$. This allows me to represent the solution in terms of a function of a complex variable. I guess a solution represented as an infinite-order moving average of current and past shocks:

$$v_t^1 = \upsilon(L)w_t.$$

Then the function

$$\upsilon(z) = \lambda\left[\frac{\upsilon(z) - \upsilon(0)}{z}\right] + \lambda\left[\frac{\psi(z) - \psi(0)}{z}\right] \tag{3}$$

for $|z| < 1$. The terms in square brackets are the z-transforms of the moving-average coefficients for the one-step-ahead forecasts. Rearranging terms of (3):

$$(z - \lambda)\upsilon(z) = -\lambda\upsilon(0) + \lambda[\psi(z) - \psi(0)].$$

By evaluating this equation at $z = \lambda$,

$$\upsilon(0) = \psi(\lambda) - \psi(0).$$

Therefore,

$$\upsilon(z) = \frac{\psi(z) - \psi(\lambda)}{z - \lambda}.$$

This formula gives the (first-order approximate) solution for the logarithm of the ratio of the price of the stock of housing to the rental rate. It shows how the stochastic dynamics of the exogenously specified process ζ get transmitted into the stochastic dynamics for the housing price. The formula for υ looks problematic because of the division by $z - \lambda$ suggesting that the function might be poorly behaved near $z = \lambda$. Notice that $\psi(z) - \psi(\lambda)$ is also zero at $\lambda = z$, so in fact there is an implicit cancellation that can be done and behavior near $\lambda = z$ is not unusual. This formula depicts the restrictions embedded in the present-value formula and essentially reproduces a result in Hansen and Sargent (1980).

To understand the empirical challenge implied by a time series on housing prices, it is also of interest to "invert" this mapping. For this computation I take as a given the housing price dynamics and infer what rental rate processes are consistent with these dynamics. Suppose:

$$\log q_t^1 - \log q_{t-1}^1 = \phi(L)w_t$$

where

$$\phi(z) = (1 - z)\upsilon(z) + \psi(z) = \frac{\psi(z) - \lambda\psi(z) + z\psi(\lambda) - \psi(\lambda)}{z - \lambda}. \tag{4}$$

I take (4) and solve for the function, $\psi(z)$, used to represent the linear dynamics for ζ:

$$\psi(z) = \frac{1 - z}{1 - \lambda}\psi(\lambda) + \frac{z - \lambda}{1 - \lambda}\phi(z).$$

This equation does not pin the $\psi(\lambda)$, where

$$\psi(\lambda) = \sum_{j=0}^{\infty} \psi_j \lambda^j$$

is the discounted response of the housing services to a shock. Given $\psi(\lambda)$ and $\phi(z)$ we can infer a unique $\psi(z)$. What do I make of this? To the extent there is an empirical challenge posed by a rational expectations version of this model, it relies on explicit restrictions on the process ζ used model rental rates. The resulting empirical challenge may very much be similar in nature to the stock-price excess volatility puzzle analyzed initially by LeRoy and Porter (1981) and Shiller (1981). The puzzle they analyze is sensitive to the stochastic properties of stock prices and dividends, and not just stock prices alone.

While Adam et al. use some information on rental rates in their discussion, they posit a model in which $\psi(z)$ is constant. It follows that ϕ is equal to this same constant, as implied by (4). Thus the linearized rational expectations version of the model implies that growth rates in housing prices are not predictable. While this latter finding becomes a platform to explore the consequences of modifying the rational expectations assumption, a good complementary exercise is to consider alternative models of rental rates that might have some empirical validity. Such an analysis would provide a better and more general statement of the empirical shortcomings of the rational expectations version of their model.

A Digression on Rational Expectations Econometrics

Adam et al. model investors as using house prices to forecast future rental rates. Before discussing their approach, let me review previous literature related to relational expectations econometrics. My digression is meant to add clarity about the role of the restrictions across rental rates and housing prices for empirical analysis and to help place the approach to expectations taken in Adam et al. in the context of an earlier literature.

Formula:

$$v(z) = \frac{\psi(z) - \psi(\lambda)}{z - \lambda} \tag{5}$$

derived previously captures the cross-equation restrictions embedded in the assumption of rational expectations. The function ψ that governs rental rate dynamics, together with the discount factor λ, determine the dynamics for housing prices relative to rental rates. To apply this formula, I am compelled to say something about the information that is available to economic agents. This is reflected in part in the specification of number of shocks, but also by how much information is revealed by these shocks that is useful in forecasting future rental rates.

A feature of this linearized model is that we can allow economic agents to observe more than an econometrician. This linearized model is a special case of what Hansen and Sargent (1991) call an exact linear rational expectations model. Suppose that the econometrician observes both rental rates and housing prices. Include $\log \xi_t - \log \xi_{t-1}$ and $\log q_t - \log \xi_t$ as the first two components of the vector y_t observed by the econometrician. Other variables observed by economics agents may be included in this vector. Suppose that

$$y_t = \sum_{j=0}^{\infty} \Psi_j \varepsilon_{t-j} + \mu \sum_{j=0}^{\infty} \text{trace} \Psi_j (\Psi_j)' < \infty$$

where ε is an i.i.d. sequence of shock vectors with mean zero and covariance matrix I. In addition, suppose that the dimension of ε agrees with the dimension of y, and that the matrix function $\Psi(z)$ is nonsingular for $|z| < 1$. This nonsingularity restriction guarantees that linear combinations of current past value of y_t generate the same information as linear combinations of current and past values of ε_t. On the other hand, linear combinations of current and past values of ε_t may generate more information germane for forecasting future values of ξ_t than linear combinations of current and past value of ε_t. Consistent with our assumption about what economic agents know, current and past values y_t are in the information set of economic agents, but economic agents might observe more.

Building on an insight in Shiller (1972) and applying the Law of Iterated Expectations, restrictions (5) continue to apply to the econometrician's specification of information, where I now let $\psi(z)$ be the first row of $\Psi(z)$ and $\upsilon(z)$ be the second row of $\Psi(z)$. In other words, the cross-equation restrictions are robust to an econometrician specifying too little information provided that the econometrician uses house prices (or in fact the ratio of house prices to rental rates) in the analysis. In some rational expectations models an important component of information for economic agents is determined endogenously (see Lucas 1972 for an initial example). In my discussion, however, house prices are being used by an econometrician, even though within the economic model itself agents have other information to forecast future rental rates. While prices *within the model* do not reveal new information to the agents, *outside the model* prices reveal information to an econometrician.

Distorted Beliefs

Adam et al. push back on rational expectations to generate interesting low frequency movements in house prices. As I argued, the rational expectations version of the model has no scope for prices to reveal new information, although it may provide a useful summary statistic about future beliefs when growth rates in the rental process are predictable. Adam et al. entertain the notion that economic agents use prices to help them make forecasts and this can provide an intriguing way to modify the rational expectations assumption.

They suppose that economic agents form beliefs based on:

$$E[\log q_{t+1} - \log q_t \mid \mathcal{F}_t] = \log m_t$$

$$\log m_{t+1} - \log m_t = \gamma(\log q_t - \log q_{t-1} - \log m_t),$$

where $0 < \gamma < 1$. In the limiting case in which $\gamma = 0$, $\log m_t$ is invariant over time, but smaller values of γ allow for deviations that depend on past price movements. This allows for temporal dependence in the growth rate of house prices, even when it will be absent in the rational expectations counterpart economy.

To the extent that such a specification is successful, how do we rule out low frequency movements in rental rates? A more general claim might be that even with a more flexible rental rate specification constrained to be empirically plausible, one cannot generate the necessary price movements. As I mentioned previously, this empirical claim is not formally addressed in the paper. Nevertheless, we may have other good reasons to explore deviations from rational expectations. Since the Adam et al. model of the housing market has similar aims to models with speculative bubbles, there should be scope for making some interesting comparisons to such models.

In defense of their approach, Adam et al. argue:

[E]ven expert economists rarely agree on the correct economic model linking fundamentals to prices. Therefore, it appears of interest to relax the assumption that agents know the correct model of prices and to consider instead agents who do not know exactly how prices behave. We assume that agents express their uncertainty about the true process by formulating a perceived joint distribution over prices and fundamentals.

While I like very much this motivation, the paper falls short of explaining how we jump to the last sentence. Other work on uncertainty aversion, robustness, and belief fragility put more structure on this problem. For example, see Hansen (2007) and Hansen and Sargent (2010). In this literature the expression of uncertainty and concerns about model misspecification have important implications for asset pricing, as reflected in a fluctuating uncertainty premia. Such fluctuations could be an additional source of asset pricing dynamics.

Potential Nonlinearities

My discussion has focused on a simplified version of the model and has abstracted from some potentially important sources of nonlinearities that could be explored. While the model specification given in Adam et al. allows for some nonlinearities, the actual calculations from the model do not seem to move far from a linear specification.

I have already discussed the transformation:

$$h_t = G(H_t),$$

where G can be nonlinear. I prefer to think of this as a way to put curvature in the utility function for housing services.

A second source of nonlinearity that could be intriguing to explore is the potential for endogenous regimes whereby the financing constraint only binds some of time. These fluctuations could be induced by interest rate variation or time series variation in θ, a parameter that plays an essential role in determining the collateral value of a house. Such generalizations result in a model that is harder to solve and would likely render perturbation type methods of solution inappropriate. Allowing for endogenous changes in the financing regimes could, however, allow for the study of much longer time series. Time series data could be analyzed that included episodes in which financing was severely limited, along with episodes in which such restrictions are much less important. Conceptually minor (but not computationally minor) changes in the model could lead to a rich extension of the current analysis.

Conclusions

In summary, my comments suggest some important next steps for this line of research.

• Introduce empirically plausible persistence into the growth rate specification for the preference shock process. This will allow for a richer discussion of the empirical implications of the model and a more revealing comparison to rational expectations models. Such an analysis will be all the more valuable if it is accompanied by an extensive exploration of the information embedded in rental rates on houses.

• Engage in a quantitative analysis of multiple shocks within the context of an extended version of this model. In addition to the preference shock considered here, stochastic fluctuations in the exogenous input to collateral value of housing, and an explicit stochastic analysis of interest rates, could be part of a comparison of the roles shocks play in accounting for the time series evidence.

• Modify the model to accommodate interesting fluctuations in stochastic discount factors and hence fluctuations in risk or uncertainty prices, perhaps motivated by investors' struggles with potential model misspecification.

The paper provides much food for thought.

Endnotes

In preparing this discussion, I benefitted from comments and suggestions by Rui Cui and Grace Tsiang. For acknowledgments, sources of research support, and disclosure of the author's material financial relationships, if any, please see http://www.nber.org/chapters/c12410.ack.

1. See Hansen and Renault (2010) for several examples of stochastic discount factor models explored in the macro/asset pricing literature.

References

Adam, Klaus, Pei Kuang, and Albert Marcet. 2011. "House Price Booms and the Current Account." In *NBER Macroeconomics Annual 2011*, edited by Daron Acemoglu and Michael Woodford. Chicago: University of Chicago Press.

Adam, Klaus, and Albert Marcet. 2011. "Internal Rationality, Imperfect Market Knowledge and Asset Prices." *Journal of Economic Theory* 146 (3): 1224–52.

Hansen, Lars Peter. 2007. "Beliefs, Doubts and Learning: Valuing Macroeconomic Risk." *American Economic Review* 97 (2): 1–30.

Hansen, Lars Peter, and Eric Renault. 2010. "Pricing Kernels." In *Encyclopedia of Quantitative Finance*. Hoboken, NJ: John Wiley and Sons, Ltd.

Hansen, Lars Peter, and Thomas J. Sargent. 1980. "Formulating and Estimating Dynamic Linear Rational Expectations Models." *Journal of Economic Dynamics and Control* 2 (1): 7–46.

———. 1991. "Exact Linear Rational Expectations Models." In *Rational Expectations Econometrics*, Underground Classics in Economics, 45–76. Boulder, CO: Westview Press.

———. 2010. "Fragile Beliefs and the Price of Uncertainty." *Quantitative Economics* 1 (1): 1–38.

Jermann, Urban, and Vincenzo Quadrini. 2011. "Macroeconomic Effects of Financial Shocks." *American Economic Review*, forthcoming.

Kiyotaki, Nobuhiro, and John Moore. 1997. "Credit Cycles." *Journal of Political Economy* 105 (2): 211–48.

LeRoy, Stephen F., and Richard D. Porter. 1981. "The Present-Value Relation: Tests Based on Implied Variance Bounds." *Econometrica* 49 (3): 555–74.

Lucas, Robert E. 1972. "Expectations and the Neutrality of Money." *Journal of Economic Theory* 4 (2): 103–24.

Shiller, Robert J. 1972. "Rational Expectations and the Term Structure of Interest Rates." PhD diss., Massachusetts Institute of Technology.

———. 1981. "Do Stock Prices Move Too Much to be Justified by Subsequent Changes in Dividends?" *The American Economic Review* 71 (3): 421–36.

Whiteman, Charles H. 1983. *Linear Rational Expectations Models: A User's Guide*. Minneapolis: University of Minnesota Press.

Discussion

Robert Gordon opened the discussion by noting that the authors' presentation mainly focused on the housing boom rather than the current account. He questioned the authors' focus on a negative correlation between housing prices and the current account. Gordon proposed that a boom in housing would worsen the current account by increasing residential investment and decreasing national saving by loosening capital constraints. Klaus Adam responded that since supply of houses is inelastic, investment would be unchanged in their model, but that saving would decrease by the channel that Gordon specified.

Gordon also remarked that the authors used financial constraints in the model without mentioning financial institutions. He thought that differences in the institutions that regulate and implement financing constraints may help to explain the different behavior of housing prices across countries in the recent past.

Finally, Gordon was skeptical about the connection asserted between the real interest rate and house prices. He noted that the authors were using a short sample of only 10 years to document this relationship. He asserted that the relationship is less clear over a longer period. Adam replied by noting that financial constraints were more stringent in earlier times. The model might imply a weaker relationship between real interest rates and housing prices under a more stringent regulatory regime.

Xavier Gabaix compared the model to Kindleberger's model of manias, bubbles, and crashes. Kindleberger assumed an initial "displacement," a perfectly rational initial reason why prices go up, after which agents extrapolate this initial increase in prices into the future. Eventually, the behavior given these beliefs should violate budget constraints, which triggers a crash. Gabaix remarked that the initial increase in prices in the authors' model was due to the decrease in the interest rate. He wondered why the authors were only focusing on house prices as opposed to all asset prices. He also noted that the magnitude of the housing price increase was not only due to the magnitude of the initial interest rate drop but also due to the initial level of the interest rates. If an asset price is inversely proportional to the interest rate then the change in the interest rate affects the price by more the lower the initial value of the interest rate. He thought that it would be interesting to look at historical data and see what other bubbles the model can predict. Adam agreed that the agents have to hold wrong expectations to get a bubble. He asserted that the expectations data provide a justification for their mechanism. He noted that Marcet's and his earlier papers, where the authors consider stock market prices, provide some evidence that expectations move up jointly with asset prices.

David Laibson pointed out that the agents in the model believe that there will be a lot of long-run volatility in asset prices. Thus, it is puzzling that banks were willing to give so many mortgages at zero or 5% down and that other institutions were willing to write credit default swaps insuring derivatives on these mortgages.

James Kahn addressed the evidence of heterogeneous behavior of house prices across countries.

He noted that the authors presented a figure with an increase in the prices in five countries and a decrease in prices in two countries. He claimed that the countries with declining house prices are disproportionally represented in this sample. He asserted that with a bigger sample, it would be harder to justify the thesis of heterogeneous behavior of prices across countries in the recent past.

James Poterba followed up on Hansen's comment about learning from the rental market. The agents looking to buy a house can learn from rental prices. The issue is what agents learn from the rental market and how the agents translate this information to the housing market. Poterba proposed to extend the model with taste shocks between renting and owning a house. This type of shock would affect both the owner-occupied market and the rental market. Even if it is difficult to infer information about the shock from the owner-occupied market data, it could still be possible to infer additional information from rental market data. Next, Poterba suggested that the reason for looking at cross-country differences is the possibility of getting variation in the tax treatment of housing. He claimed that there is virtually no country that taxes the implicit rental value of housing. However, there are substantial differences across countries in the tax rules that are applied to the capital gains on houses. There are also differences in other aspects of tax rules, for example, the tax treatment of mortgage interest that might change the user cost specification for housing units. He added that even in the United States, there were some changes in the tax treatment of capital gains on housing that took place around 1997 that tend to reduce the tax burden on owner-occupied houses.

Daron Acemoglu insisted that it is important to justify a particular departure from the rational expectations assumption. He stressed that he did not see such a justification in this paper. He thought that a model where only a fraction of agents have misspecified beliefs would be more reasonable. However, he warned that it would probably be difficult to solve.

Acemoglu wanted the authors to specify a metric for the departure from rational expectations and suggested that the authors conduct a sensitivity analysis with respect to the value of this metric. Michael Woodford also thought that the question of the degree to which the departure from the rational expectations should be thought of as small is a central issue. According to his summary of their argument, the authors say that the model is similar to a model with rational expectations in the sense that they could nest a model with rational expectations within their specification, and they estimate the value of their beta parameter that best fits the data. He proposed that an alternative metric for asking if agents have beliefs that are close to rational expectations would be to ask instead how similar agents' beliefs are to the data-generating process. Adam responded by noting that if the beliefs converge to the rational expectations beliefs then, due to the continuity of the model outcomes with respect to the beliefs, the outcomes will converge to the rational expectations equilibrium outcomes. He noted that with a unit root component for very large horizons, beliefs and model outcomes will diverge. However, they will converge in the limit for any finite horizon.

Woodford also reinforced Hansen's point about the extent to which one should regard agents as having fairly dogmatic beliefs. However, one can ask to what extent behavior would be different if one allowed the priors to be more diffuse than the specific prior that the authors assumed.

Darrell Duffie reinforced the point made by Hansen that the collateral constraint on borrowing is constant over time in the model. He provided an example from the US mortgage market: as the collateral constraint was relaxed, low income, subprime borrowers stayed constrained and levered even more, in contrast with high income borrowers who were at their interior maxima and did not lever more.

Mark Bils thought that the negative correlation between the current account and housing prices that the authors present in figure 1 of the paper was striking. However, he stressed that this is a short horizon for making such an inference. He added that the mechanism that drives this correlation is more about the production of housing. He observed that the current account deficit increased by 5% as a share of GDP since 1996. He wondered what fraction of this increase can be explained by the model.

Klaus Adam responded to some points that Hansen raised in his discussion. First, he noted that it is difficult to solve the model with occasionally binding constraints. Second, he stated that it is possible to get uncertainty premia if the agents in the model are risk averse with respect to consumption.

Albert Marcet started by commenting on why they did not include various complications into the model. He stated that the objective of the paper was to show that a small deviation from rational expectations can deliver new results. He acknowledged that they could not match many features, because they chose to use the simplest model that suited their objective. Next, he commented on Hansen's point about the linear nature of the model. He agreed that it would be interesting to explore nonlinearities and mentioned that they have an appendix where they explore some of these effects. Next he addressed the issue of the plausibility of the assumed deviation from rational expectations. First, he noted that economists are comfortable using many different utility functions to model behavior. He argued that economists should enjoy a similar degree to freedom in modeling expectations formation. He stressed that their model includes a system of beliefs that offers testable predictions.

3

Risk Topography

Markus K. Brunnermeier, *Princeton University and NBER*
Gary Gorton, *Yale University and NBER*
Arvind Krishnamurthy, *Northwestern University and NBER*

I belong to those theoreticians who know by direct observation what it means to make a measurement. Methinks it were better if there were more of them.

—Erwin Schrödinger (quoted in Walter Moore, *Schrödinger: Life and Thought,* 1989, 58–59)

I. Introduction

The financial crisis of 2007–2008 dramatically revealed that it is time to rethink the measurement of economic activity. In particular, because of derivative securities, off-balance sheet vehicles, and other financial innovations, traditional measures of aggregate risk, such as leverage, are inadequate. It is imperative that we build an economy-wide risk topography, and submaps of different financial sectors of the economy. Measuring only cash instruments and income and balance sheet items is not sufficient for understanding the economy; instead we should measure risks, and think in terms of risks, in addition to quantities.

The situation today, and during the crisis, is not so different from the 1930s when Simon Kuznets, Arthur Burns, Wesley Mitchell, and their colleagues developed the first official measures of economic activity for the overall US economy, the National Income and Product Accounts (NIPA), and business cycle chronology. This occurred in the midst of and just after the Great Depression. Referring to the Great Depression, Richard Froyen (2009) put it this way:

One reads with dismay of Presidents Hoover and then Roosevelt designing policies to combat the Great Depression of the 1930s on the basis of such sketchy data as stock prices indices, freight car loadings, and incomplete indices of industrial production. The fact was that comprehensive measures of national income and output did not exist at the time. The Depression, and with it the growing role of government in the economy, emphasized the need for such measures and led to the development of a comprehensive set of national income accounts (Froyen 2009, 13).[1]

During the financial crisis of 2007–2008 policymakers faced a similar problem. Relevant information about the financial sector and its linkages to the real economy was missing. Very basic measures were inadequate. For example, a measure such as "leverage" has little meaning in a world with derivatives and off-balance sheet vehicles. "Liquidity" was not clearly defined, let alone appropriately measured. Existing measures did not account for the shadow banking system, the size of the repo market, or the extent of different financial institutions' exposure to residential mortgages and credit derivatives.

Measurement is the root of science, and is also the basis of macroprudential regulation and of firms' risk management systems. Recognizing these measurement problems, the Dodd-Frank Wall Street Reform and Consumer Protection Act (Pub. L. 111-203, H.R. 4173) includes a provision for the establishment of the Office of Financial Research (OFR), a new division within the Treasury. The OFR is tasked with providing research and information to the newly created Financial Stability Oversight Council. The OFR has subpoena power to require financial institutions to produce data that the OFR requests. One possible role for the OFR would be to implement new measurement systems. Similarly, in Europe, the European Systemic Risk Board (ESRB) was established to oversee the build-up of systemic risk.

In this paper we outline a system of measuring risks and liquidity in the financial sector and producing a risk topography for the economy. We see two tangible benefits to implementing these ideas.

First, such a measurement system would improve significantly on the standard accounting paradigms in capturing the risks that are most relevant for systemic risk assessment by regulators and financial market participants. The basic idea behind the measurement metrics is to elicit from financial firms their sensitivity to a number of prespecified factors and scenarios on a regular basis. Essentially, firms report their "deltas" with respect to the specified factors; that is, the dollar gain or loss that occurs when the specified factor changes by a specified amount. In addition, they report their liquidity deltas: the increase or decrease in their liquidity as defined by a liquidity index, the Liquidity Mismatch Index (LMI).[2] For example, we ask what the capital gain or capital loss is to your firm if house prices fall by 5%, 10%, 15%, and 20%, and what if they rise by the same increments. By deviating from standard accounting paradigms for measurement and moving closer to risk-management scenarios, these metrics reflect derivatives, liquidity, and other important features of a modern financial system. For example, an important point we develop in Section III is that the liquidity/capital delta measures are more informative than accounting measures of leverage. Standard measures of leverage may be meaningless in a world of derivatives, while the liquidity/capital deltas will better measure the "fragility" of the financial sector.

The data can reveal risk and liquidity pockets in the economy. Currently, the absence of information about the risk exposures of the financial system mean that firms can be in "crowded trades" without knowing it. That is, their risk exposures may be viewed as small for their firm, but may be large if all other firms have a similar exposure. Data on risk pockets can trigger better private risk management as well as enhance regulatory risk assessment. The data can also detect trends in liquidity or risk imbalances in the economy. For example, the data may show the financial sector's reliance on the repo market grew over the 2000 to 2007 period and resulted in a significant liquidity imbalance for dealer banks. We discuss these types of uses of collected data in Section V.

Second, current macroeconomic models, which for the most part do not incorporate a financial sector, would have the essential data to guide such an endeavor. Theorists do not need data, but their thinking and their models are strongly influenced by what is measurable.

Solow (1970) is explicit that the stylized facts that were the outcome of the work of Kuznets and others were at the root of conceptualizing the neoclassical growth model, which is the current workhorse macro model. Burns and Mitchell's (1946) measurement of business cycles and Kuznets' work allowed Kaldor (1961) to state six "stylized facts" about the macroeconomy, which were instrumental in subsequent business cycle and growth research. The intellectual history is recounted by Lucas (1977) and Kydland and Prescott (1990). It seems clear that systematically collecting the relevant financial sector data will have an impact on the set of macro models that are developed.

Such macro modeling is essential for understanding systemic risk and financial crises. While the triggers for crises are varied, the amplification mechanisms that play out in crises exhibit common patterns. These patterns may be direct due to contractual links or indirect through equilibrium feedbacks on asset prices and liquidity. The important question in assessing systemic risk is to ask, for example, if the commercial banking sector takes a $500bn loss next year, how will this spill over to other asset markets and players, and what will be the resulting system-wide or aggregate general equilibrium dislocations? Developing a data set on the actions and exposures of different parts of the financial sector in varying economic conditions can allow a researcher to develop quantitative models of common amplification mechanisms. For example, a key response indicator of the spillover effects is the liquidity mismatch index (LMI). We expect that firms with a very negative LMI will be forced to fire-sell assets and hence amplify the crisis and lead to excessive spillover effects. On the other hand, firms with positive (or moderately negative) LMI can ride out adverse effects and not cause any externalities. We discuss the use of data in modeling of systemic risk in Section VI.

Like the construction of the National Income and Product Accounts, it will take a significant effort and time to build this risk topography, although financial firms already currently produce much of the data that we suggest gathering.[3] We take advantage of the data and knowledge of the private sector internal risk models. Truth-telling can be ensured by cross-checking the various internal models across all market participants.

There would be substantial benefits to making such measurements publicly available, just as with other government-collected data (e.g., National Accounts, Bank Call Reports, Federal Reserve Flow of Funds, etc.). The responses can be aggregated, suitably anonymized, and then made public. An important principle is that the data be made publicly available to all (in a form that protects some proprietary responses).

Related Literature. Three strands of literature are related to the ideas in this paper: the first is on measurement, the second concerns stress testing. On measurement, in the United States the current systems include the bank Call Reports of Condition and Income and the Federal Reserve Flow of Funds data. Both of these data sets were explicitly developed to aid regulators to monitor banks. The Call Reports were mandated by the National Bank Act (1863) (Sec. 5211) and have continued (and been expanded) to this day. In essence, these reports contain fairly detailed balance sheet and income statement information of regulated banks, but fail to capture other financial institutions and risk sensitivity measures. Similar to the Call Reports, we emphasize eliciting the same scenarios repeatedly and regularly to develop a risk map. Over time, such data will become a large library of information that can be used to build and fine-tune models. Secondly, we emphasize that the data elicited (suitably anonymized) be made public so that academics, regulators, and industry participants will be in a position to build their own models of systemic risk.

The Flow of Funds data was designed by Morris Copeland (1947, 1952) to characterize money flows in the economy. Notably, at first, economists did not see how to use the Flow of Funds; see, for example, Dawson (1958) and Taylor (1958).

Central banks currently recognize that existing measurement systems are not up to the task and have begun to think about revisions and additions. See, for example, Eichner, Kohn, and Palumbo (2010) and European Central Bank (2010). Compared with these proposals and ideas, we suggest to fundamentally change the nature of the information that is collected by deviating from the accounting paradigm and operating under a measurement paradigm closer to risk management scenarios. We want to collect data that will, over time, be useful for developing macroeconomic models of crises. We argue that this requires data on risk. In addition, we emphasize that measuring "liquidity" is central to understanding crisis.

The second related literature concerns bank stress testing. Bank stress testing is an evaluation of the impact of a particular scenario or event on a firm, the scenario usually being a movement in financial variables. Stress testing is an adjunct to statistical models, such as value-at-risk models. There are many papers that provide a general introduction to stress testing. Examples include Blaschke et al. (2001); Jones, Hilbers, and Slack (2004); Cihák (2007); and Drehmann (2008). Collections of articles that discuss stress testing include Quagliariello (2009). International organizations have developed stress testing procedures: the Bank for International Settlements (BIS 2009), the Committee on the Global Financial System (2005), and the International Monetary Fund, which started the Financial Sector Assessment Program in May 1999. Other articles include Haldane, Hall, and Pezzini (2007) and Hoggarth and Whitley (2003). Hirtle, Schuermann, and Stiroh (2009) discuss the US Supervisory Capital Assessment Program (SCAP)—these were the stress tests applied to the largest US bank holding companies from February to May 2009 (see Board of Governors of the Federal Reserve System 2009a, 2009b). The data that we would like to collect are akin to that collected in the stress tests.

The third strand of literature is macroeconomic and banking theory, which guides our thinking concerning what data to collect. This strand is discussed in Section II.

Following Section II the paper proceeds as follows. In Section III we present simple examples to illustrate the data issues that arise in practice, and to motivate our approach to measurement. In Section IV we more formally present our approach of eliciting risk and liquidity deltas. In Section V we first discuss certain simple risk indicators for fundamental risks and liquidity risk. Section VI discusses the use of the data for macro modeling of amplification effects within the financial sector and the economy as a whole. Section VII concludes.

II. Guidance from Existing Theoretical Research

What data should be collected in order to better understand the vulnerability of the economy to systemic risk? Existing research in macroeconomics and finance can guide us in answering this question. Macro models with financial frictions focus on leverage and the dynamics of net worth/capital, limiting the leverage ratio, while models in finance highlight in addition the important role of liquidity.

The most influential macroeconomic models of financial market frictions are the works of Bernanke, Gertler, and Gilchrist (BGG) (1996) and Kiyotaki and Moore (KM) (1997). Technically, these models only feature a corporate sector that is subject to financial frictions rather than a financial sector subject to such frictions, but as Brunnermeier and Sannikov (2010) show, it is possible to rework these models so that the results are driven by frictions in the financial sector. We henceforth discuss these models in such terms and dispense with this qualification.

The BGG model emphasizes that the "net worth" of the financial sector is an important state variable in driving macroeconomic phenomena. Net worth is commonly thought of as the equity capital of the financial sector. Thus, in this model, when banks take losses that deplete their equity, they increase the rates charged on loans and/or cut back on lending, thus causing a credit crunch. The Kiyotaki-Moore model adds an important ingredient to this analysis. Agents in the model have collateral that they pledge to raise funds from lenders. Since the market value of agents' collateral is partly dependent on their financial health, it affects leverage in the system, which in turn affect the value of capital. With high leverage, losses deplete capital more dramatically and feedback to further reducing the market value of collateral, and so on.

The roles of net worth and leverage in these models are suggestive, but the challenge is to determine what these correspond to in reality. Most notably, as we will show with some simple examples in the next section, reliance on cash measures to capture net worth or leverage misses the effects of derivatives.

Work in the finance tradition emphasizes in addition the importance of "liquidity" for understanding financial crisis. Diamond and Dybvig (1983) is the canonical model in this literature. In this model, it is not just borrowing or leverage of the financial sector that is salient, but rather the proportion of debt that is comprised of short-term demandable deposits. More broadly, the literature describes that when the financial sector holds illiquid assets financed by short-term debt, the possibility of "counterparty run" behavior emerges that can precipitate a crisis. This literature also describes a feedback mechanism between capital problems and liquidity problems. See, for example, Allen and Gale (2004). When the financial sector runs into liquidity problems, triggered by runs by lenders, the sector sells assets whose prices then reflect an illiquidity discount. The lower asset prices lead to losses that deplete capital, further compromising liquidity. Brunnermeier and Pedersen (2009) model the interaction between funding liquidity and market liquidity for modern collateralized (wholesale) funding markets. Importantly, they model liquidity spirals and "collateral runs." An adverse shock heightens volatility, leading to higher margins/haircuts. This lowers funding liquidity and forces institutions to fire-sell their assets, thus depressing market liquidity of assets and increasing volatility further.

In sum, the existing micro-founded literature points to net worth/leverage of the financial sector, and liquidity exposure, often expressed as maturity mismatch, as key state variables that drive systemic crises.

III.   Measurement Challenges—Four Examples

In this section we present some extremely simple examples to illustrate the measurement issues and to emphasize the weaknesses of traditional measures of leverage and maturity mismatch.

Even though leverage is well-defined in simple stylized models, it is an ill-defined measure in practice in current financial markets. Given derivatives and off-balance sheet vehicles, the standard leverage measure (on-balance sheet debt/equity) is at best noisy, and more likely useless, as a measure of the fragility of the financial sector.

Liquidity refers to many related concepts. Following the banking literature, liquidity mismatch in banks emerges when the market liquidity of assets is less than the funding liquidity on the liability side of banks' balance sheets. However, insurance of demandable deposits since 1934 make the textbook Diamond-Dybvig bank runs unlikely. On the other hand, it is widely understood that "collateral run" phenomena have been important in the asset-backed markets and the shadow banking sector in the 2007–2009 crisis (see Gorton and Metrick 2010). As another example, when a major financial institution—AIG is a good example here—is downgraded, its derivative counterparties will require that the institution post a large amount of collateral. This is a liquidity drain for the institution that is conceptually similar to the run by a number of short-term lenders.

The measurement issues that arise in practice are best presented in a series of very simple examples. The examples are simplified in the extreme and so they are clearly not realistic, nor are they intended to be. All values should be thought of as market values.

Benchmark: Consider a firm with $20 of equity and $80 of five-year debt with a coupon rate of 4.5%. The firm makes loans to two different firms, each for $50 for one year at an interest rate of 5%.

This example is a benchmark; it is a plain vanilla firm that resembles a traditional bank, though it does not take deposits. Call Report-type data would record the income and balance sheet items from this bank, and in this example that might suffice. The debt-to-assets ratio for this firm is 80%.

There are, however, some measurement issues even in this case. For example, the loans are one-year loans, but the debt is five-year debt. This bank is potentially facing a large loss if at the end of the year the term structure of interest rates were to change, resulting in a lower competitive rate for loans. For example, if the loans can only be made at 3% in one year's time, then this bank is facing a loss. Simple concepts like duration would capture this, but nothing that is currently reported would measure this interest rate sensitivity. Our measurement ideas involve asking what happens to firm value if, for example, the one-year loan rate in one year's time moves up by 100 basis points (bps), by 500 bps, down by 100 bps, or down by 500 bps, and so on?

Liquidity Mismatch: Consider a firm with $20 of equity and $80 of debt as above, but now half the debt is overnight repo financing at 1% and the other half is five-year debt *at 4.5%. The firm buys one Agency mortgage-backed security (MBS) for $50 (which is financed via repo at a zero haircut) and loans $50 to a firm for one year at an interest rate of 5%.*

This example complicates the benchmark case by making the bank sensitive to funding risk, in addition to interest rate risk. What if the firm cannot renew the repo financing, and is forced to liquidate some of its assets? Standard measures, such as leverage, will not pick up this funding risk. That is, they will treat the overnight debt and the five-year debt symmetrically. One could construct a leverage measure that focused on the maturity mismatch in this example—such as a short-term leverage measure—but this too may prove inadequate. For example, suppose that instead of the Agency MBS, the bank owned $50 of private-label MBS, which is less liquid than the Agency MBS. Now this bank has more of a liquidity mismatch, stemming from the asset side. Thus it is clear that a liquidity measure needs to incorporate information from both the asset side of the balance sheet and the liability side (market liquidity and funding liquidity).

For this firm the Liquidity Mismatch Index (LMI), which roughly reflects the market liquidity on the asset side (price impact if sold at fire-sale prices) minus the funding liquidity on the liability side (effective maturity structure), we construct would be negative. Because the repo is overnight the firm is exposed to funding risk. In the next section, we discuss a liquidity index that measures funding and market liquidity risk. In this specific example, there is an MBS worth $50, which has a liquidity weight of, say, $\lambda_{ABS} = 0.9$, so the asset liquidity is $45. (Cash or Treasuries have a liquidity weight of one.) On the liability side, the MBS bond is funded by repo of $50 with $\lambda_{Repo} = 1$, so the Liability Index is −$50, which gives a net liquidity index of $−5. What happens if repo haircuts suddenly increase to 20%? Then in renewing the repo financing, the firm can raise less money against the MBS. The asset is less liquid in that borrowing against it raises less cash—say, now $\lambda_{ABS} = 0.8$. Then the Liability Index goes to $−10.

There is currently no measuring system (accounting or regulatory) that detects the sensitivity of a firm to change in market and funding liquidity conditions. The Liquidity Mismatch Index is designed to understand such potential stresses. In this example, one could further ask what would happen if the securitization secondary market were to become less liquid. That is, we could ask the firm to report its LMI if the liquidity weight on MBS was $\lambda_{ABS} = 0.5$, for example.

Rehypothecation: The bank lends $100 to a hedge fund for three days and receives a bond with a market value of $100 as collateral (a reverse repo). The bank then uses the bond as collateral to borrow $100 in the overnight repo market. (Whatever else the bank is doing we ignore for purposes of the example.)

The bank has a liquidity mismatch since the repo is overnight, but the reverse repo is for three days. If the repo does not roll over, then the bank must sell the bond or find some other funding. This sensitivity would be captured by our Liquidity Mismatch Index, discussed following. The liquidity weight on the three-day reverse repo loan is lower than on the overnight repo, entering negatively in the firm's liquidity index.

The Liquidity Mismatch Index is designed to capture the sensitivities to these kinds of issues, which were particularly important in the recent crisis, but which, again, are not captured by any current reporting system.

Synthetic Leverage: Consider a firm with $20 of equity and $80 of debt; half the debt is overnight repo financing at 1% and the other half is five-year debt at 4.5%. The firm buys $100 of US Treasury securities and writes protection (using credit default swaps [CDS]) on a diversified portfolio of 100 investment-grade US corporates, each with a notional amount of $10; so there is a total notional of $1,000. The weighted-average premium received on the CDS is 5%.

This firm is sensitive to movements in the term structure of interest rates, and also to funding risk, as in the previous examples. But now it is also quite significantly exposed to a macro risk that could cause failures of investment-grade firms. The risk is not idiosyncratic because the CDS portfolio is diversified, but if there were a recession in which three or four firms failed there would be losses on this portfolio. If we ask what would happen if four investment-grade US firms in their portfolio failed, with 50% recovery, the answer would be that the firm would be bankrupt because a loss of $(50\%)(4)(10) = 20$, which is the amount of equity in the firm. Thus, the CDS creates "leverage" in this firm, which any standard measure will miss.

Note that the CDS position would be marked-to-market for accounting purposes. Thus, the marks would contain expectations about future defaults of the firms in the portfolio (and risk premia). However, we want to detect what would happen in specific events (e.g., four firms fail), rather than the probability weighted market price.

Also, note that this firm has another complication. Derivatives trade under the International Swaps and Derivatives Association master agreement. This agreement usually has a Credit Support Annex (CSA), a legal document, which sets forth the conditions under which each party must post collateral. Suppose that in this example the CSA has collateral-posting requirements based on the market value of the CDS position. If the marks widen—that is, when it is more likely that a firm or firms in the portfolio will default—this firm will have to post collateral to the counterparty. It has a Treasury bond, which could be posted. The LMI calculation takes into account the CSA provisions. To see the issue note that if half the Treasury holdings are posted, then this falls out of the LMI. In the extreme, imagine that the entire Treasury holding is posted. Then the only remaining asset the firm has is the CDS portfolio. Measuring the liquidity index of this firm in the event that four firms fail will capture the liquidity risk of this firm.

As another example of a liquidity event triggered by derivatives, consider the effect of a ratings downgrade. The CSA typically prescribes that if the bank is downgraded during the term of the derivative contract, it will have to post more collateral, which again uses liquidity. Moreover, if the firm had written many derivative contracts—that is, the CDS as in the example, plus interest rate derivatives—the need for liquidity will apply to all derivative contracts. Thus, the downgrade is potentially a significant liquidity risk that arises when firms use derivatives.

Cross Scenarios: Consider a firm with $20 of equity and $80 of debt; half the debt is overnight repo financing at 1% and the other half is five-year debt at 4.5%. The firm buys a Spanish residential mortgage-backed security (MBS), denominated in Euros, for the equivalent of $50 and lends the other $50 to a US firm. The firm does not hedge its Euro exposure.

This firm is sensitive to house prices in Spain and to the Dollar/Euro exchange rate (as well as other risks). The bank may be fine if (1) Spanish house prices go down, but the exchange rate stays the same; or (2) the Euro weakens against the dollar, but house prices do not decline. But, if Spanish house prices decline and the Euro weakens against the dollar, then the bank may be in trouble.

This possible stress scenario would not be revealed by anything the firm would report to regulators or in Securities and Exchange Commission (SEC) filings, under the current system. The example would be a bit more complicated if the firm did hedge the exchange rate risk. Since the firm receives Euros on the MBS, but pays dollars on its debt (and equity dividends), it enters into a swap to receive dollars in exchange for

Euros. But, this transaction is with a counterparty, which might weaken in some states of the world, introducing counterparty risk. Also, as seen earlier, the firm might have to post collateral.

These examples are intended to illustrate the difficulties of measuring risks based on accounting measures. Many more such examples, increasingly complicated, can be produced. The point is that measurement systems based solely on accounting-type measures are inadequate.

IV. Measurement Metrics

In this section we explain our ideas using simple notation. We then introduce the Liquidity Mismatch Index, and discuss reporting. Finally, we say a bit more about what the exact scenarios could be.

A. Basic Set-up

There are two dates. Date 0 is the ex ante date at which each firm makes risk and liquidity decisions by choosing cash assets and cash liabilities, as well as derivative positions and off-balance sheet positions. Derivative positions may have a market value of 0 at date 0, but are sensitive to the risk factors. At date 1 a state $\omega \in \Omega$ is realized, some of which may be a systemic crisis, depending on what decisions firms have made. Firm i chooses assets A^i and liabilities L^i. The assets are a mix of cash, repo lending to other firms, derivative exposure, and outright asset purchases. Liabilities include short-term debt, long-term debt, secured debt, equity, and so forth.

The equity value of a firm i is given by $E^i_\omega = A^i_\omega - L^i_\omega$, where A^i_ω is the asset value in state ω and L^i_ω is the value of the total liabilities in state ω. The equity value E^i measures how close firm i is to insolvency and can feed into how the firm is likely to behave given considerations such as capital constraints, the risk of bankruptcy, managerial compensation contracts, and so on. In addition to the total value of assets and liabilities as well as the equity value, we are interested in the liquidity position of each firm.

For reporting purposes, the regulator specifies ω and elicits ΔA^i_ω, that is, the change in asset value as a result of state ω. This will be a dollar amount gained or lost in that scenario. The firm simply calculates the effect of the state on their current position; that is, the dollar gain or loss due to the current position being affected by changing to the specified state. The firm *does not* take into account what their response would be to a change to that state. The response of the system as a whole can, in principle, be calculated using a macro model, discussed in the following.

B.   *The Liquidity Mismatch Index (LMI)*

Each asset and liability is assigned a liquidity weight λ_ω^j for each state of the world. We index assets with positive j, while liabilities j takes on a negative value. Super-liquid monetary assets such as bank reserves and Treasuries of "flight to quality sovereigns" to have a λ_ω^{money} of one across all states. For something like an MBS, we can imagine measuring λ_ω^{MBS} as one minus the repo haircut on that MBS in state ω. Alternatively, λ_ω^{MBS} could measure the price discount that firm i has to accept if it immediately wanted to convert the asset into cash. The key point is that λ_ω^j measures the *immediate cash-equivalent value* of asset j across states. Aggregating liquidity across the asset side, one obtains firm i's asset liquidity $\Lambda_\omega^{A,i}$ for the different states in the economy. We also measure the liquidity of the liabilities, funding liquidity, as $\lambda_\omega^{j<0} < 0$. Overnight debt has liquidity of -1 in all states, while longer-term debt has $-1 < \lambda_\omega^{LT} < 0$. Common equity is $\lambda_\omega^{equity} = 0$ for all states ω. Note that assets that are held on margin contain a short-term debt component. If margins can be reset from 10% to 50% on a daily basis, 40% is essentially overnight debt. Aggregating all liability positions gives the total funding liquidity of firm i, $\Lambda_\omega^{L,i}$. Overall, firm i's liquidity position is: $\Lambda_\omega^i \equiv \Lambda_\omega^{A,i} - \Lambda_\omega^{L,i}$. Further, this can be aggregated across all firms (or across particular sectors) to determine the economy's liquidity state in state ω at time t.

As shown earlier, the regulator specifies the ω and the firm reports $\Delta\Lambda_\omega^i$, the change in liquidity due to being in that state or scenario. Also as previously shown, the firm simply calculates this delta. It does not try to take into account its response to a change to that state of the world. The firm also reports its current liquidity index, which we denote as Λ_0^i.

The liquidity weights are not zero or one. Determination of the liquidity weights is an empirical question. One way to determine these weights would be to set the base case weights based on spreads to LIBOR (the London Interbank Offered Rate). However the base case is determined, different liquidity scenarios correspond to different specifications of weights, shocking one or more at a time. Brunnermeier, Gorton, and Krishnamurthy (2011) discuss further details of the construction of the liquidity weights and the LMI.

C. Reporting

The dimensions of the Ω state space that describes a firms' asset, liability, and liquidity positions can be huge. We focus on states s within an S-dimensional factor space, a subspace of Ω. Factors consist of certain prices (risk factors) or liquidity/funding conditions (liquidity factors). For example, a risk factor might be a change in real estate prices, while a liquidity factor could be a change in haircuts or margins, or the shutdown of a given market. Individual market participants take these as a given, but they are endogenously determined in the financial system. The selection of factors is discussed in more detail in Section IV.

For the specified factors, firms report a "value-liquidity" vector that consists of their calculated equity delta and liquidity mismatch delta for each specified factor/state. For example, if there is only one risk factor (e.g., with N real estate price levels) and one liquidity factor (e.g., with M overall haircut levels), then the state space can be characterized by an $N \times M$-matrix. Firms have to report their estimated value-liquidity indices in the first row and first column. From this one can derive the partial sensitivities of each firm along each single factor. In addition, firms will be asked to report their value and liquidity indices for some prespecified cross scenarios, in the nth column, mth row.

In addition to repeating the elicitation of data for the same set of scenarios every reporting date, we also look for special, one-off stress scenarios, as described in the following.

D. Factor Scenarios

The "s-states" just described are stress scenarios. The choice of scenarios is critical to the assessment of systemic risk. There are two considerations driving the choice. First, the propagation and patterns of a crisis are similar across events. Crises invariably involve capital and liquidity problems in important parts of the financial sector. Shocks interact with these capital and liquidity problems and lead to adverse general equilibrium feedback loops. By collecting data on a core set of factors that are held constant over time, the data can shed light on the common propagation patterns that underlie all financial crises.

Second, history suggests that the trigger for crises varies from event to event. Thus, at any time the regulator needs to choose factors that are informed by prevailing economic conditions. For example, the regulator may choose to focus on the effects of an Internet stock price shock in the late 1990s, but such a shock may not have been relevant in 2007, where subprime mortgages were a more significant concern.

Third, in most cases, particular cross-scenarios are of special interest; for example, a scenario involving a simultaneous change in house prices, unemployment, and liquidity. This is the thinking behind the successful bank stress tests (SCAP). One approach to institutionalizing the cross-scenario stresses is as follows. In each quarter, we ask each firm to submit a suggested cross-scenario that the firm deems to be the "worst-case" for itself. The regulator then examines these suggested cross-scenarios across firms to see if many firms have a similar worst case. If so, then that cross-scenario will be part of next quarters' survey.

Notably, scenarios can include events that have never happened before, that is, events that are not in recorded experience. Broadly, stress scenarios fall into four groups. The first three are specified changes in market risks, idiosyncratic risks, and in liquidity factors. The scenarios in the first three categories are orthogonal stress scenarios. These correspond to partial derivatives of value and liquidity indices with respect to the factor. The last group asks for more complicated cross scenarios; for example, what if house prices fall 20% and repo haircuts rise to 10%. We provide examples of scenarios.

Examples of market risk scenarios include specifications of changes in:

• Interest rates (yields) on major government bonds (e.g., United States, United Kingdom, Germany, Japan, China), bond rates for different maturities; also swap rates in LIBOR, FIBOR (Frankfurt), PIBOR (Paris), HIBOR (Hong Kong), and so forth, at different maturities.

• Credit spreads: Changes in major credit derivative indices (CDX, CMBX, LCDX) at different maturities.

• Exchange rates of major currencies.

• Stock prices, measured by major indices.

• Commodity prices, measured by sector and aggregate indices.

• Commercial real estate prices, for example, the NCREIF (National Council of Real Estate Investment Fiduciaries) property index.

• Residential house prices, for example, Case-Shiller index.

A liquidity risk scenario corresponds to a shock to liquidity as follows:

• Firms are unable to access the market to raise new cash for one month, three months, and six months.

• Repo haircuts on some asset classes rise.

• The syndicated loan market, or the securitization market, shuts down for some period.

Idiosyncratic risk refers to scenarios specific to the reporting firm. Such scenarios include:

• Default by the largest (second largest, third largest) of the firm's counterparties.

• Default by largest supplier of bank lines.

• Default by a major clearing bank, or clearing system.

• Reputational event, which prevents new security issuance for six months (one year).

• Inability to issue new securities for one month, three months, six months.

• Inability to clear for three days, ten days.

• Rating downgrade of the senior unsecured debt of the company by three notches, six notches.

These idiosyncratic scenarios can shed some light on the network-linkage effects that play an important role in crises. For example, we envision that the first item on counterparty exposures will be measured for the largest financial firms. However, we should stress that our measures are not designed to inform a regulator on the dynamics during a crisis. That is, it seems clear from recent experience that it would be useful for regulators to know in real-time the counterparty exposures to the default of AIG or the default on Lehman bonds. With such information, the regulator can make decisions on how or when to intervene during a crisis. For this, regulators would need data that is much more detailed (e.g., individual position data) than what we are suggesting here (e.g., see Duffie 2010). Our coarser measures, on the other hand, shed light on the risk build-up and possibility of systemic risk in advance of a crisis. From this standpoint, what is important is to measure the extent of, say, real estate risk held by major financial institutions, including, for example, Lehman and AIG. These firms are in a market equilibrium with other financial firms, so that real-estate losses can be expected to affect other firms; whether the loss transmission is through a direct default, or through a firm unwinding a large risk position, lowering prices (and thus inflicting losses on other firms) is more detail than we think is necessary to understand systemic risk.

E. Discussion

If the goal is to provide information on a broad class of risk exposures, then elicited information should include events or scenarios that have never happened before; that is, events that are not in recorded experience. The bulk of the elicited information should remain constant over time to develop a panel data set, as with the Call Reports.

Elicited information will involve the use of models by firms. We view this as a desirable feature. Furthermore, they constantly evolve as innovation occurs. But we recognize that there will be problems. First, these models are not homogeneous across firms, so the elicited information will have different degrees of accuracy. Also, these models will evolve over time so that the accuracy of the responses will change over time (presumably it will improve). Second, some verification of models and outputs will have to be performed by bank regulators (who, in any case, will have to become more sophisticated). Cross-checks will need to be developed in order to verify the integrity of reported data. This could be done by horizontal comparison across similar firms. Also, adding-up constraints and zero-sum conditions should be applied wherever possible in order to make it difficult for market participants to misreport their exposures. See the next section on risk and liquidity aggregates for adding-up conditions.

One of the important aspects of the current crisis was that the amount of information supplied to regulators varied widely across different types of firms. Our view is that all firms significantly engaged in financial activities should report scenario responses. However, the amount supplied should vary by size. Larger firms should supply more data, smaller firms less data.

V. Firm and Regulatory Risk Management

This section first discusses model-free indicators of systemic risk that can be constructed from the value and liquidity deltas. Secondly, such data can be useful for regulatory risk assessments as well as to provide data that may enable firms to improve their own risk management. We discuss several applications of the risk measures. In the next section, we turn to a more significant and more challenging macroeconomic step: in order to fully understand systemic risk one has to model the *endogenous response* of various market participants to adverse shocks and analyze the general equilibrium.

Risk Aggregates. The "delta" of asset value, A^i, with respect to a particular risk factor $\Delta^{i,A}$, is a measure of risk exposure that naturally aggregates over firms. That is, the sum

$$\sum_i^I \Delta^{i,A}.$$

is the total exposure of all measured firms to, say, real estate risk. We would expect that some firms are long exposure and others are short exposure. If we measured all important parts of the economy, the sum should equal the physical supply of risk. For risks in positive net supply such as real estate, we can arrive at what the sum should be considering how much real estate exists in the economy. For risks in zero-net supply such as pure derivatives, the sum should be zero. In both cases, the risk measures have the feature that they can be aggregated into something meaningful. Even at less aggregated levels—say, sectoral—the risk aggregates are likely to be informative. They will reveal pockets of risk concentration and can serve to diagnose systemic risk.

Liquidity Aggregates. The LMI measures can also be aggregated. An interbank loan that is a liquid asset for firm i is a drain on liquidity for the borrower, firm j (i.e., negative liquidity weight). Aggregating across firm i and firm j the interbank loan will net out. Consider the net LMI for firm i,

$$\Lambda^i = \Lambda^{A,i} - \Lambda^{L,i}.$$

Again consider the sum,

$$\sum_i^I \Lambda^i.$$

Summed across all sectors, the liquidity aggregate equals the supply of liquid assets: the Λ-weighted sum across all relevant liquid assets. The aggregate measures are analogous to Barnett's (1980) divisia indices for monetary aggregates. Barnett devised indices to weight different components of the money supply based on their usefulness as a transaction medium. The LMI index is similar but is based on both assets and liabilities, and has weights that reflect the financial liquidity of the asset and liability.

The aggregates are most interesting in describing the liquidity position of particular sectors. We may expect to find, for example, that the banking sector always carries a negative liquidity position, while the corporate sector or household sector carries a long liquidity position. The extent of liquidity transformation done by the banking sector may also be informative for diagnosing systemic risk. For example, in the period from 2000 to 2008, it is likely that the aggregate LMI grew substantially. However, for systemic risk purposes, what would have been most interesting is a diagnosis that the aggregate growth reflected a growing mismatch between the banking sector and the other sectors in the economy.

Intermediation chains. The LMI index can be constructed with either symmetric weights or asymmetric weights. We have discussed the index in the case where the weight of a loan from firm i (asset for that firm) is equal to the negative of the weight of that loan to firm j (liability for that firm). However, it may be interesting to construct asymmetric weights, so that the asset weight is set equal to, for example, 90% of the liability weight on the same transaction. With asymmetric weights, the LMI aggregate will decrease as liquidity chains grow. For example, it is widely thought that financial fragility is created by the long chains of assets and liabilities that underlie the securitization model (i.e., household mortgage, packaged into MBS, further packaged into collateralized debt obligation [CDO], and then serving as collateral for a repo, which may be rehypothecated many times). The aggregate LMI can measure this fragility.

Liquidity risk. A second dimension of liquidity that our measures shed light on is liquidity risk. The LMI can be aggregated in the different macro stress-events. For example, the LMI for a given bank in the event that housing prices fall by 10% tells us how much the liquidity of that bank will suffer with a housing shock. This liquidity risk measure can be aggregated, at sectoral levels and across the economy, to diagnose the liquidity risk of the economy.

Mutually inconsistent plans. The data on risk and liquidity exposures can reduce systemic risk by allowing the private sector to improve its own risk management. Consider the problem of mutually inconsistent plans, which is a recurring theme in many financial crises. As Grossman (1988) argues, in the 1987 market crash, firms were following dynamic trading strategies to insure them against market downturns. These strategies involved firms selling stocks as prices fell, replicating a synthetic put option. In the crash, it became apparent that such strategies were mutually inconsistent: if everyone follows a portfolio insurance strategy, markets will not clear. Perhaps more relevant, in a bank panic, withdrawals—failure to roll over repo—can cause the very dangerous deleveraging that was the fear motivating the run in the first place.

To go back to the model, suppose that firm i (and all other firms), carrying out its risk management, planned that in the event certain prices fell, so that the firm's liquidity and solvency were reduced, it would sell some of its assets to reduce risk and at the same time cut back on interbank repo lending to preserve liquidity. The regulator elicits information on all firms and makes such information public. The firms then recognize that their plans are mutually inconsistent. As a result, all firms adjust their positions to reduce risk exposure and enhance liquidity.

In addition to simply making public the exposure data, we can imagine that a regulator will additionally provide guidance for private risk management. It could reveal the results of its own analysis that private plans are mutually inconsistent. Or, it could survey firms on how they would behave in the low price scenario and then make public the result of this survey. Such a survey may be similar to the senior loan officer's survey of the Fed or the new Fed survey of dealer credit terms (see Eichner and Natalucci 2010).

Systemically important institutions. New banking regulations require greater oversight and higher capital requirements for systemically important institutions. One cut at judging who is systemically important is to rank institutions by size of assets. However, this type of ranking suffers from all of the shortcomings of relying on balance sheet entries for asset holdings, which we have discussed earlier. Economically, it is more meaningful to judge firms in terms of their magnitude of their (aggregate) risk exposures and liquidity exposures. Thus, our data at the firm level can provide guidance on which institutions should be judged systemically.

Regulatory Capital Requirements. Notions of "risk-based" capital need some metric for measuring "risk." The approach outlined here naturally leads to the idea that regulatory capital be based on measures of risk that correspond to the deltas and LMI that we discussed earlier.

VI. Macroeconomic Modeling of Systemic Risk

The measures we have discussed in the previous section allow us to answer the following type of question: If real estate prices decline by 20% over the next year, how much capital and liquidity will the commercial banking sector lose? On one hand, it is possible that the banking sector is well capitalized to handle such losses and the event is not systemic. On the other hand, it is possible that the losses trigger a credit crunch, fire-sales of assets, and so forth, so that the losses are amplified into a systemic crisis.

We define *systemic risk* as the risk that shocks affect the financial sector and trigger an endogenous adverse feedback significantly amplifying these shocks, causing further deterioration in the financial sector, and leading to significant output losses.

Systemic risk is inherently endogenous. There are endogenous feedbacks that can lead to a small shock having a large effect. This key point is often obscured (or absent) in policy discussions. To diagnose systemic risk, the data on shock-deltas must be viewed through the lens of a model. That is, it is not enough to measure the losses that may arise from a 20% fall in real estate prices. Measurement does not show how the impact of such a response can endogenously lead to a crisis. The important step for systemic risk assessment is to compute the general equilibrium response of the economy to such a shock. What behavioral response can we expect of different parts of the financial sector to the losses? What is the resulting general equilibrium? And when does that equilibrium feature a significant amplification mechanism?

To provide another example, the measures of the previous section describe how a firm's LMI will fall in some state, described by the vector of asset/liability λ's for that state. However, the λ's themselves are endogenous. That is, the liquidity of assets depends on the behavior of agents. If many key liquidity providers are insolvent in some state, then the asset market λ's will fall in that state, and such a fall in λ's may further compromise the financial sector, and so on. To understand systemic risk, one needs to compute a general equilibrium in which liquidity is treated endogenously.

As should be clear, this is a macroeconomic model building exercise and is a fertile area for both academic and policy research. This section describes how the data we have suggested collecting may be useful to further this research. To be clear, we do not propose here a specific model of systemic risk – such models do exist in the literature, and there are probably more that will be developed. Rather, we wish to illustrate how the data can be useful for macro modeling.

A. Modeling Behavioral Responses

Any macroeconomic model of systemic risk needs to posit a relation between a firm's decisions (lending, trading, etc.) and the firm-specific

variables such as the deltas we have discussed as well as macroeconomic state variables that may affect the investment opportunities
faced by the firm. For example, moral hazard considerations may imply
that as the capital of a bank falls, it reduces its lending and investments
and moreover increases the premium it requires to take on risky investments. The LMI is another key response indicator. Models may predict
that firms with very negative LMI will be forced to fire-sell their asset and cause negative spillover effects to others—even to market participants they have no direct contractual relationship with. Firms with
positive (or moderately negative) LMI might hold on to their positions
and hence limit the negative impact on others.

The data as outlined can help model agents' behavioral responses to
a shock. Let us suppose that the deltas are collected over time to form
a long panel data set.

Consider, for example, the measured Δ^i for real estate risk for firm i.
The Δ^i comes from firm i's choices over the amount of MBS to own, both
through derivatives and through direct holdings, as well as the amount
of real estate lending the firm has undertaken. The time series of these
Δ^i's is a time series of portfolio choices of the firm in different economic
environments. These choices are influenced by the expected return and
risk profile (both fundamental and liquidity-driven) of MBS. They are
influenced by the overall macroeconomic environment. They are also
influenced by the current capital and liquidity of the firm.

Likewise, consider the measured liquidity delta of the firm. This liquidity delta is influenced by whether MBS is owned directly or through
derivatives, and whether it is funded using short-term debt, long-term
debt, or equity. It is influenced by the collateral arrangements in the derivatives taken on by the firm. Again, the liquidity choices can be thought
of as portfolio choices of the firm in varying economic conditions.

A macroeconomic model makes choices that result in a behavioral
function $f^i(\cdot)$:

$$\Delta_{i,t} = f^i(\text{own firm characteristics}_{t-1}, \text{aggregate } \Delta's_{t-1}, \text{macroeconomic state}_{t-1}).$$

Here, firm characteristics may include capital and liquidity, in addition
to typical measures of organizational function (size, industry, etc.). The
macroeconomic state may measure expected returns, volatility, and so
forth. We have suggestively included a separate role for the aggregate
Δs to highlight interdependences within the financial sector.

Since, as we have just discussed, the time series data reflects these
choices in varying economy conditions, they will be useful in disciplin-

ing models of systemic risk. We view this as an important part of our approach, since a panel data set allows us to verify various future models using the whole history of data from the beginning of the data collection onwards.

B. Financial Aggregates

In much of the existing literature, the only financial measure that a macro-finance model aims to match is the credit spread (e.g., the Commercial Paper-Treasury Bill spread). The large gap between theory and measurement is striking and needs to be closed.

The data we would like to collect can form the "financial aggregates" that macro-finance models should aim to match. For example, suppose we used the data to construct aggregated risk-deltas across the financial sector, and formed a time series of these variables. Likewise, we aggregate the LMIs and liquidity-deltas across the financial sector to measure the liquidity and liquidity risk of the sector. The behavior of these variables would be akin to that of "leverage" in stylized models, in that high deltas may tell us something about the susceptibility of the financial sector to a meltdown.

In the spirit of Kaldor (1961), potential stylized facts concerning the interaction between the financial sector and macro could be:

1. The risk-deltas tend to display a high coherence with more traditional measures of economic activity, such as output or hours worked. That is, the risk-deltas of different sectors (e.g., housing, credit, commodities) tend to be positively correlated with output.

2. The risk-deltas in financial firms rises from trough to peak, and falls from peak to trough.

3. Risk becomes more concentrated over the cycle. This does not necessarily mean that, on average, risk in individual firms becomes concentrated in certain risk sectors.

4. Real estate-related risk is the main type of risk for 1 and 2.

5. The liquidity aggregate is countercyclical, declining as output rises.

6. The liquidity aggregate is positively related to commercial and industrial loans.

7. Liquidity risk is procyclical.

8. Risk-deltas and liquidity are negatively related to the Commercial Paper-Treasury Bill spread.

These conjectured stylized facts are suggestive of the types of moments that would need to be matched, in addition to moments relating to the real economy.

C. Medium and Large Crises

To model systemic risk, ideally we would like data that includes periods of extreme financial crises with large real economic fallouts, such as the current Great Recession. Fortunately or unfortunately, these extreme events are rare. However, there are numerous medium-size crises that occur more frequently. For example, recent experience has included the 1987 stock market crash and the 1994 mortgage market crisis, as well as the 1998 hedge fund crisis. These crises all reflected significant shocks to financial intermediaries. The shocks were amplified and spilled over across asset markets, but either because the shocks were small or because of significant government intervention, the crises involved negligible real effects.

If one assumes that the amplification mechanisms present in the medium-sized crises are also present in larger crises, collecting data on these crises can be extremely useful. Models can be built to match behavior in medium-sized crises, and these same models can be used in counterfactual exercises to gauge the effects of large shocks. The obvious caveat here is that such an exercise has to mechanically take nonlinear effects into account. We would like to stress that any model of the 1987 crash, for example, will likely already include significant nonlinearities.

Finally, it is worth highlighting the commonality with and differences to extreme event analysis in general. Extreme value theory and other methods covering rare events rely critically on certain statistical assumptions. The probability distribution of outcomes deep in the tails is typically assumed. In comparison, macroeconomic modeling involves assumptions about structural parameters that govern behavior both in medium events and in tail events. Such modeling is less subject to the Lucas critique. In addition, models of financial market frictions often describe behavior in terms of constraints, rather than beliefs or preferences. If constraints are tighter in extreme events, then it seems plausible that the models may better approximate behavior during such events so that a modeling exercise may perform better than a statistical exercise. However, like statistical models, modeling assumptions for extreme events or behavior in extreme events are unavoidable due to limited data.

VII.   Final Comments

The financial crisis is a strong reminder that measurement is at the root of science. The measurement systems that we currently have are outmoded, leaving regulators, academics, and risk managers in a dangerous position. Assessing systemic risk requires viewing data on the financial sector through the lens of a macroeconomic model. However, macroeconomics in particular frames questions and builds models based on available data, and we have so far lacked the data to construct macro-finance models.

In order to track systemic risk in the economy, there needs to be an overhaul of the reporting done by financial firms. While not perfect, our suggestions can be implemented, as the SCAP stress tests demonstrated. Based on our discussions with risk managers at major banks, most of the data can be produced by these firms already. Nevertheless, we recognize that there will have to be a lot of work to determine reporting standards (especially with respect to foreign subsidiaries, branches, etc., and with respect to different currencies). The reported numbers will change over time as the underlying models change even if the underlying risks remain the same. Presumably, over time models will get better, so reported numbers will become more accurate. This is true of any measurement system. There is no alternative. The OFR has already been mandated, so the first step with regard to infrastructure for measurement has already occurred.

Ours is not the only set of ideas for what new data collections systems should look like. In terms of what the Office of Financial Research (OFR) and the Federal Reserve System should collect, some have proposed that financial firms should submit *all* position data and *all* transaction data. There are several troubling problems with this proposal. First, the regulators would then have to develop summary measures themselves, independently of the firms from which they collected the data. Meaningful measures would be some kind of summary statistics of the data. We have suggested such summary statistics. But moreover, our ideas rely on the firms' own models. Without this the regulators would have to invent their own models, which not only seems like reinventing the wheel, but reasonably seems like they would not be as good as firms' models. There is no reason for everyone to have to calculate the National Income and Product Accounts themselves. Another problem would be that the data that would be made available publicly would be the regulators' summary statistics, rather than the underlying data.

Throughout the earlier discussion we have mentioned several principles that seem important for any data project. We summarize them here.

• There is no substitute for better data. Without the proper measurement, science, macroeconomics, and risk management cannot make progress.

• Science is based on replication, reusing, and criticizing published work. This requires that scientific data be publicly available.

• Not all data should be collected, but a subset. Measurement must be intelligent and based on theory in designing summary statistics.

Endnotes

We thank Robert Berry, Slim Bentami, Darrell Duffie, Richard Evans, Mike Gibson, William Gonska, Vinit Joshi, Anil Kashyap, Sasa Pilipovic, Cheryl Ratheun, Martin Schmalz, Hyun Shin, Paul Walker, Marc Weinberg, and participants at the NBER Summer Institute (Capital Markets and the Economy), NBER Systemic Risk Initiative, IMF, CMU Accounting Conference, Banco de Chile, 2011 AEA meetings, and the 16th International Financial Risk Institute Annual Roundtable for their comments. For acknowledgments, sources of research support, and disclosure of the authors' material financial relationships, if any, please see http://www.nber.org/chapters/c12412.ack.

1. This quotation is also cited by Landefeld, Seskin, and Fraumeni (2008).

2. We focus on measuring these two dimensions—capital gain/loss and change in liquidity—because the theoretical literature on financial crises has centered on capital and liquidity as the most significant factors underlying the behavior of financial firms during crises.

3. The bank stress tests that took place during the financial crisis (the Supervisory Capital Assessment Program; see Board of Governors of the Federal Reserve 2009a, 2009b) also show that (large) financial firms are (at least embryonically) in a position to produce the numbers that we propose.

References

Allen, Franklin, and Douglas Gale. 2004. "Financial Intermediaries and Markets." *Econometrica* 72:1023–61.
Bank for International Settlements (BIS). 2009. "Principles for Sound Stress Testing Practices and Supervision." Basel Committee on Banking Supervision.
Barnett, William A. 1980. "Economic Monetary Aggregates: An Application of Aggregation and Index Number Theory." *Journal of Econometrics* 14:11–48.

Bernanke, Ben, Mark Gertler, and Simon Gilchrist. 1996. "The Financial Accelerator and the Flight to Quality." *Review of Economics and Statistics* 78:1–15.

Blaschke, Winfrid, Matthew T. Jones, Giovanni Majnoni, and Soledad Martinez Peria. 2001. "Stress Testing of Financial Systems: An Overview of Issues, Methodologies, and FSAP Experiences." IMF Working Paper No. 01/88. Washington, DC: International Monetary Fund.

Board of Governors of the Federal Reserve System. 2009a. "The Supervisory Capital Assessment Program: Design and Implementation." White paper.

———. 2009b. "The Supervisory Capital Assessment Program: Overview of Results." White paper.

Brunnermeier, Markus, Gary Gorton, and Arvind Krishnamurthy. 2011. "Liquidity Mismatch Measurement." Working Paper, Northwestern University.

Brunnermeier, Markus, and Lasse Pedersen. 2009. "Market Liquidity and Funding Liquidity." *Review of Financial Studies* 22 (60): 2201–38.

Brunnermeier, Markus, and Yuliy Sannikov. 2010. "A Macroeconomic Model with a Financial Sector." Working Paper, Princeton University.

Burns, Arthur F., and Wesley C. Mitchell. 1946. *Measuring Business Cycles*. New York: National Bureau of Economic Research.

Cihák, Martin. 2007. "Introduction to Applied Stress Testing." IMF Working Paper WP/07/59. Washington, DC: International Monetary Fund.

Committee on the Global Financial System. 2005. *Stress Testing at Major Financial Institutions: Survey Results and Practice*. Report issued by the Bank for International Settlements.

Copeland, Morris. 1947. "Tracing Money Flows through the United States Economy." *American Economic Review, Papers and Proceedings* 37:31–49.

———. 1952. *A Study of Money Flows in the United States*. New York: National Bureau of Economic Research.

Dawson, John. 1958. "A Cyclical Model for Postwar U.S. Financial Markets." *American Economic Review* 48:145–57.

Diamond, Douglas, and Phillip Dybvig. 1983. "Bank Runs, Deposit Insurance, and Liquidity." *Journal of Political Economy* 91:401–19.

Drehmann, Mathias. 2008. "Stress Tests: Objectives, Challenges and Modeling Choices." Riksbank *Economic Review* (June):60–92.

Duffie, Darrell. 2010. "Systemic Risk Exposures: A 10-by-10-by-10 Approach." Working Paper, Stanford University, Graduate School of Business.

Eichner, Matthew, Donald Kohn, and Michael Palumbo. 2010. "Financial Statistics for the United States and the Crisis: What Did They Get Right, What Did They Miss, and How Should They Change?" Board of Governors of the Federal Reserve System, Finance and Economics Discussion Series, No. 2010-20.

Eichner, Matthew, and Fabio Natalucci. 2010. "Capturing the Evolution of Dealer Credit Terms Related to Securities Financing and OTC Derivatives: Some Initial Results from the New Senior Credit Officer Opinion Survey on Dealer Financing Terms." Board of Governors of the Federal Reserve System, Finance and Economics Discussion Series, No. 2010-47.

European Central Bank. 2010. *Central Bank Statistics: What Did the Financial Crisis Change?* Frankfurt: European Central Bank.

Froyen, Richard. 2009. *Macroeconomics: Theories and Policies*. Englewood Cliffs, NJ: Prentice Hall.

Gorton, Gary, and Andrew Metrick. 2010. "Securitized Banking and the Run on Repo." *Journal of Financial Economics*, forthcoming.

Grossman, S. J. 1988. "An Analysis of the Implications for Stock and Futures Price

Volatility of Program Trading and Dynamic Hedging Strategies." *Journal of Business* 61 (3): 275–98.

Haldane, Andrew, Simon Hall, and Silvia Pezzini. 2007. "A New Approach to Assessing Risks to Financial Stability." Bank of England, Financial Stability Paper No. 2.

Hirtle, Beverly, Til Schuermann, and Kevin Stiroh. 2009. "Macroprudential Supervision of Financial Institutions: Lessons from the SCAP." Federal Reserve Bank of New York, Staff Report no. 409.

Hoggarth, G., and J. Whitley. 2003. "Assessing the Strength of UK Banks through Macroeconomic Stress Tests." Bank of England *Financial Stability Review* (June).

Kaldor, Nicholas. 1961. "Capital Accumulation and Economic Growth." In *The Theory of Capital*, edited by F. A. Lutz and D. C. Hague, 177–222. New York: St. Martins Press.

Kiyotaki, Nobuhiro, and John Moore. 1997. "Credit Cycles." *Journal of Political Economy* 105:211–48.

Kydland, Finn, and Edward Prescott. 1990. "Business Cycles: Real Facts and a Monetary Myth." *Quarterly Review of the Federal Reserve Bank of Minneapolis* (Spring):3–18.

Jones, Matthew, Paul Hilbers, and Graham Slack. 2004. "Stress Testing Financial Systems: What to Do When the Governor Calls." IMF Working Paper No. 04/127. Washington, DC: International Monetary Fund.

Landefeld, J. Steven, Eugene P. Seskin, and Barbara M. Fraumeni. 2008. "Taking the Pulse of the Economy: Measuring GDP." *Journal of Economic Perspectives* 22 (2): 193–216.

Lucas, Robert. 1977. "Understanding Business Cycles." In *Stabilization of the Domestic and International Economy*, edited by Karl Brunner and Allan Meltzer, 7–29. Carnegie-Rochester Conference Series on Public Policy 5. Amsterdam: North-Holland.

Quagliariello, Mario. 2009. *Stress Testing the Banking System: Methodologies and Applications*. New York: Cambridge University Press.

Solow, Robert. 1970. *Growth Theory: An Exposition*. New York: Oxford University Press.

Taylor, Stephen. 1958. "An Analytic Summary of the Flow-of-Funds Accounts." *American Economic Review, Papers and Proceedings* 48:158–70.

Comment

Darrell Duffie, *Stanford University and NBER*

Systemic risk is the risk that the financial sector will suffer a significant loss of effectiveness. The key financial-sector services at risk are the intermediation of credit, capital, and risk, as well as the operation of various types of payments and settlements systems. It is now widely understood that the performance of the general economy depends significantly on the resilience and efficiency of the financial sector. In the event that financial firms or utilities that collectively provide a significant amount of these services become impaired through a loss of capital or liquidity, or suffer operational failures, one anticipates a commensurate deterioration in the ability of ultimate borrowers to obtain financing from ultimate lenders and in the ability of demanders and providers of risk bearing to execute efficient risk transfers.

Beyond the direct macroeconomic impact of a reduction in the effectiveness of the financial system, a mere increase in perceived systemic risk can lead producers, consumers, and financial market participants to take precautions such as reducing leverage and conserving liquidity. These defensive actions can decelerate the general economy, with effects that are magnified by a self-reinforcing "spiral" of asset price declines, further delevering, and further weakness in the financial sector.

The authors of "Risk Topography," Brunnermeier, Gorton, and Krishnamurthy, have suggested a general framework, including some novel tools, for monitoring systemic risk. My objective here is to re-emphasize some of the points made in their contribution, taking a slightly different perspective, and to suggest the importance of monitoring the entity-to-entity flows of risks through the financial system. Monitoring link-based systemic-risk information is an important supplement to monitoring the resilience of individual financial institutions because some of the key mechanisms associated with the propagation of financial risk are associated with counterparty exposures and with defensive bilateral actions. Furthermore, an understanding of network-based risks can contribute to an understanding of the changing nature of risk concentrations across various types of assets and entities, can identify new systemically important financial institutions, and can trigger deeper supervisory attention of specific firms and markets.

In addition to the roles of regulated and central banks, the financial system depends on the services of asset managers (including hedge funds, mutual funds, sovereign wealth funds, and private-equity firms); brokers and dealers of securities, derivatives, and other assets; and special-purpose issuers of structured credit products such as collateralized debt obligations. For basic operational functionality, the financial system also depends on a range of financial utilities, the most critical of which are asset custodians, exchanges, and various providers of payment and clearing services such as FedWire, CLS Bank, central clearing parties (CCPs) for securities and derivatives, and tri-party repo agents. Connecting these various nodes of the financial system is a complex web of contractual links, the most relevant of which here are loans, master swap agreements, repurchase agreements, clearing agreements, prime-brokerage contracts, and securities lending contracts. These contracts are the main channels by which credit and risks of various types flow through the financial system and beyond.

The financial system is among the most intricate of inventions. Compounding the complexity of its institutional structure, many of the system's most important actors have significant discretion and incentives. The most destructive potential effects of these incentives from a systemic-risk viewpoint are socially excessive leverage at "risk-on" times and, at times of financial stress, a tendency to quickly delever, conserve liquidity, and run from weak counterparties. These destructive effects can be mitigated through improvements in market-wide infrastructure and institutional arrangements, such as clearing and judicious systemic-risk disclosures, and through regulatory capital and liquidity buffers.

In order to measure systemic risk, regulators routinely monitor the ability of individual financial firms to withstand specified financial shocks without failure or a need to quickly delever. Weaknesses uncovered at regulated firms can be mitigated through micro-prudential adjustments in capital and liquidity requirements.

Risk Topography, by Brunnermeier, Gorton, and Krishnamurthy (2011), provides a firm conceptual foundation for systemic risk monitoring, emphasizing the use of stress tests, by which one measures the gains or losses of market value associated with various types of macroeconomic and asset-price shocks. The authors' most innovative proposal is the monitoring of a Liquidity Mismatch Index (LMI) for important financial institutions. For this purpose, the liquidity weight $L(i)$ of the institution's i-th asset or liability is defined as the fraction of its contribution $V(i)$ to market value (which is negative for liabilities) that may be converted to cash on short notice. For example, an unencumbered bond that can be financed at a haircut of 10% has a liquidity weight of 0.90. An overnight liability has a liquidity weight of 1.The Liquidity Mismatch Index is $V(1)L(1) + \ldots + V(n)L(n)$. A low LMI implies a high exposure to loss of liquidity. An adverse change in liquidity mismatch is thus a concern. The authors propose various stress tests for the LMI in order to judge the vulnerability of the institution's liquidity to various potential changes, including changes in market prices and changes in the liquidity of various types of assets.

In my view, the LMI is an excellent new approach to monitoring levels and changes in liquidity. Some additional work will be needed to incorporate the illiquidity associated with certain types of financial relationships, such as over-the-counter (OTC) derivatives and prime brokerage, whose impact on liquidity is not directly related to their market valuations, as discussed in Duffie (2010a).

For example, the devastating loss in liquidity that can be caused by a prime-brokerage run is illustrated by the dramatic loss in liquidity suffered by Morgan Stanley during the days following the failure of Lehman Brothers. This loss in liquidity was largely associated with the reduced access of Morgan Stanley to financing associated with the ability to pledge the assets of its prime-brokerage clients. Of the $85 billion dollar reduction in Morgan Stanley's liquidity pool over the period September 15–22, $56 billion was due to prime brokerage liquidity loss, according to a supervisory communication from Morgan Stanley to the Federal Reserve that was disclosed under a Freedom of Information Act request. When "PB" clients left in droves, Morgan Stanley was forced to seek central-bank support. Rule 15c3 of the Securities and Exchange Act of 1934 places some limits on the ability of a US dealer to finance itself on the back of its clients' assets. The London-based businesses of these and other dealers, however, operate with few limits on the use of client assets. (This regulatory gap should be fixed.)

Going beyond the specific approaches suggested in Brunnermeier, Gorton, and Krishnamurthy (2011), I would emphasize the importance of monitoring flows of gains and losses in market value and liquidity from entity to entity that are caused by financial shocks of various specified types. This would ease the detection of points of concentration of systemic stress across asset markets and among market participants. Further, the results of such link-based information may uncover new systemically important entities, enabling them to receive additional regulatory attention.

Among the most important flows of risk through the system are exposures to counterparty default. These can propagate financial stress through domino-style failures and incite runs on weak counterparties. Rapid defensive withdrawals of collateral and access to credit, or increases in proportional margin requirements ("haircuts"), are destabilizing. Monitoring should focus on total counterparty exposures, inclusive of loans and other debt instruments, equity investments, OTC derivatives, securities lending, and repo. Exposures should be measured before and after collateral. The amounts and types of collateral subject to disposal in fire sales should be quantified. General capital and liquidity requirements are blunt instruments for mitigating risks associated with counterparty default exposure because they do not treat the propagation of shocks. Regulations should therefore also focus on minimum levels of collateral or margin and, where amenable, central clearing.

Ongoing public disclosure of the sensitivity of the financial system to various sources of stress enables general market participants to reduce their exposures to increasing sources of risk before they become dangerously elevated. These exposure reductions may be direct responses to the disclosure or be indirectly induced by the endogenous repricing of the associated risks caused by disclosure. Systemic risk information should generally be provided publicly in only aggregated form in order to preserve socially efficient individual investment incentives and to mitigate runs on individual firms.

I disagree with former Federal Reserve Chairman Greenspan's remark that "regulators, and for that matter everyone else, can never get more than a glimpse at the internal workings of the simplest of modern financial systems."[1] I envision significant improvements in effective systemic risk monitoring.

A 10-by-10-by-10 Approach to Monitoring Systemic Risk

As a complement to other forms of systemic risk information, I have proposed in Duffie (2010b) a "10-by-10-by-10" approach to monitoring systemic risk. By this approach, each of, say, "10" systemically important firms would report, for each of "10" systemic stress scenarios, its own gain or loss, and its gain or loss relative to each of its "10" largest counterparties for that particular stress. The gains and losses would be measured in terms of changes in market values and also in terms of cash flows over a short period such as 30 days. For each of the stresses, the identities of the largest 10 counterparties associated with the particular stress would also be reported.

Most of the stresses would be extreme-but-plausible specified changes in the prices or performance of large asset classes. I believe this approach benefits from relevance, ease of interpretation, comparability across reporting firms, and limited scope for measurement error or interpretation by reporting firms in comparison with probabilistic measures such as "Value at Risk" or generally described macroeconomic scenarios. Macroeconomic stress scenarios can be converted by a regulator to stipulated changes in the prices or performance of balance-sheet instruments.

One of the 10 stresses should be counterparty default, implying that the 10 associated counterparties for this stress are those presenting the greatest default exposures to the reporting firm, inclusive of loans, derivatives, repo, equities, and other contractual exposures.

The headline number "10" is a placeholder that signals my view that this form of monitoring should be tightly focused, at least until implemented and refined. This monitoring should be globally adopted, allowing inclusivity and comparability across reporting institutions in various major jurisdictions.

Despite significant progress in financial regulations since the crisis of 2007–2009, some large dealer banks likely remain vulnerable to sudden runs by their prime-brokerage clients, short-term creditors, and derivatives counterparties. The systemic risk associated with runs on major securities dealers by their clearing banks is now being lowered by operational reforms in the tri-party repo market. These reforms are reducing the daylight exposures of the two major clearing banks, JP Morgan Chase and BONY-Mellon, to participants in tri-party repos.

The latest approach to "resolving" systemically important financial institutions has not, in my view, substantially lowered the adverse systemic spillovers associated with their failures. Fortunately, the likelihood of financial distress is being reduced by significant ongoing improvements in regulatory capital and liquidity requirements. I would be more comfortable with the Basel III reforms if the liquidity coverage requirements were more realistic regarding the vulnerability of certain large banks to losses of liquidity associated with runs by OTC derivatives counterparties and prime-brokerage clients.

Putting aside the risks to these large institutions themselves, the flows of risk and liquidity through the major dealer banks are generally indicative of the nature of financial risks in the system as whole. These banks have bird's-eye views of the financial system; a systemic-risk regulator can benefit from the information available from the same vantage points. This is a motive for the 10-by-10-by-10 approach to systemic risk monitoring.

Concluding Remarks

I anticipate substantial progress in understanding and lowering systemic risk within the financial system. I am not persuaded by the notion that regulators cannot hope to "keep up" with banks in the face of complexity, financial innovation, and compensation differences between the public and private sector. Much progress has been made recently, and there remains a significant amount of low hanging fruit yet to be tasted. High capital and liquidity standards are by far the most important bulwark against systemic risk, but I see the potential for significant additional reductions in systemic risk from better infrastructure, especially in the form of new approaches to systemic monitoring. The authors of Risk Topography offer a sophisticated and useful contribution toward this objective.

Endnotes

This comment was prepared for publication in the *NBER Macroeconomics Annual 2011*. For nonacademic relationships that may present a conflict of interest, please see www.stanford.edu/~duffie/. For acknowledgments, sources of research support, and disclosure of the author's material financial relationships, if any, please see http://www.nber.org/chapters/c12413.ack.
    1. See Greenspan (2011).

References

Brunnermeier, Markus, Gary Gorton, and Arvind Krishnamurthy. 2011. "Risk Topography." In *NBER Macroeconomics Annual 2011*, edited by Daron Acemoglu and Michael Woodford. Chicago: University of Chicago Press.
Duffie, Darrell. 2010a. *How Big Banks Fail and What to Do About It*. Princeton, NJ: Princeton University Press.
———. 2010b. "Systemic Risk Monitoring—A 10-by-10-by-10 Approach."

Graduate School of Business, Stanford University, November. In *Systemic Risk and Macro Modeling*, Markus K. Brunnermeier and Arvind Krishnamurthy, editors. Chicago: University of Chicago Press, forthcoming.

Greenspan, Alan. 2011. "Dodd-Frank Fails to Meet Test of Our Times." *Financial Times*, March 29.

http://www.federalreserve.gov/newsevents/testimony/tarullo20100212a.htm.

Comment

Hyun Song Shin, *Princeton University and NBER*

The proposals in this paper are path-breaking, but one of their many advantages is that the proposals are also practical. Most systemic financial institutions that are to bear the brunt of the reporting requirements already collect the necessary information. Estimating the sensitivity (the "delta") to key risk factors (such as commercial and residential property prices, interest rates, credit spreads, and so on) are the staple of the risk management functions of large banks and other financial institutions.

However, private sector risk management practices failed comprehensively in the run-up to the recent global financial crisis, and so one natural concern might be that the proposals in the current paper would also similarly fall short. The answer to this concern is that although the measurement exercise bears a superficial resemblance to existing private sector risk management practices, the information will be put to a very different use, pursuing very different objectives and based on a very different philosophy.

Take the paper's proposal to construct the Liquidity Mismatch Index (LMI). The index will build on the discrepancy measure for individual financial intermediary assets and liabilities in realizable value, but the objective is to aggregate the information across firms to come up with an overall picture of the extent of maturity transformation in the financial system, and how such maturity transformation interweaves with other vulnerabilities.

The perspective here is very different from the thinking in a private sector institution. There, the objective is to lay off one's risks to others by hedging and to remain agile and flexible so that the institution can "cut and run"—that is, flee from exposures—when risks begin to materialize. Although cutting and running and "letting the devil take the hindmost" is a feasible strategy for an individual institution, the system as a whole cannot do it. There is a limit to how much risk can be shed when viewed in the aggregate. A thought experiment due to Hellwig (1995) expresses the limits well.

[C]onsider an institution that finances itself by issuing fixed-interest securities with a maturity of n months and that invests in fixed-interest rate securities with a maturity of $n + 1$ months. On the face of it, maturity transformation is small, and interest risk exposure is minimal. Suppose, however that we have 479 such institutions. These institutions may be transforming a one-month deposit into a forty year fixed interest rate mortgage, with significant interest rate risk exposure of the system as a whole. The interest rate risk exposure of the system as a whole is not visible to the individual institution unless it knows that it is but an element of a cascade and that credit risks in the cascade are correlated. (p. 730)

Cutting and running is not only a theoretical possibility. It happens in practice, especially among the most sophisticated institutions with the best risk management systems. Figure 1 plots the two weighted average measures of Value-at-Risk for the (initially five, then down to two) Wall Street investment banks from 2001 to 2010, taken from Adrian and Shin (2008), updated to include the crisis period.

Value-at-Risk (VaR) is a quantile measure that gives the approximate worst case loss in the sense that the realized loss being larger than the Value-at-Risk is smaller than some fixed, small probability set by the

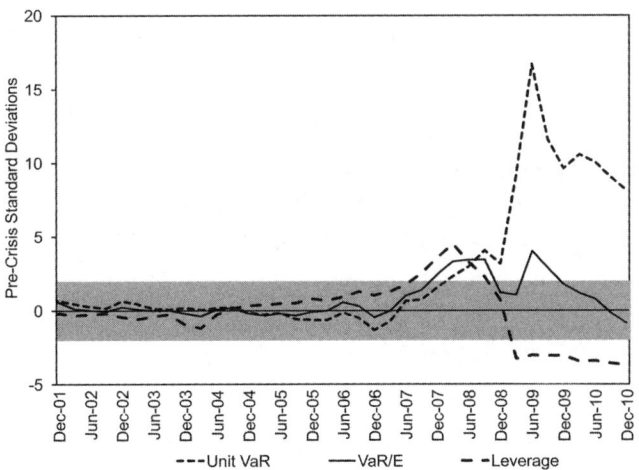

Fig. 1. Value-at-Risk and leverage for Wall Street investment banks
Source: Adrian and Shin (2008, updated 2011).

risk manager. The dotted line (unit VaR) is the Value-at-Risk per dollar of assets, while the solid line is the VaR normalized by equity. All series are measured in units of precrisis standard deviations.

The unit VaR series shoots up at the height of the crisis, reflecting the increase in measured risks such as the VIX index, credit and CDS (credit default swap) spreads, and so on. But the increased measured risks are met by the shedding of those risks, as can be seen by the sharp decline in leverage (the dashed line). VaR/Equity actually *drops* even as unit VaR explodes at the height of the crisis. Importantly, the decline in leverage is achieved not by the raising of new equity, but by the shedding of assets (Adrian and Shin 2008).

The shedding of assets by an intermediary means contraction of lending to the customers of the intermediary. The prudent shedding of risks by the lenders to Bear Stearns or Lehman Brothers will feel like a *run* from the point of view of Bear Stearns or Lehman Brothers. It is this fallacy of composition that is the weakness of existing private sector risk management practices. A close cousin of private sector risk management practices is the *microprudential* approach to financial regulation that builds on such private sector "best practice."[1] The strength of the proposal by Brunnermeier, Gorton, and Krishnamurthy is that their approach starts with an explicitly system-wide perspective.

However, it would be important not to underestimate the difficulty of the task the authors have set themselves. In line with the changed focus toward system-wide risks, much of the weight will be borne by the model that is imposed on the data. The exercise will only be as useful as the model that underpins the aggregation of the inputs.

To see the size of the task, consider how the authors propose to use the disclosed inputs. The individual deltas and liquidity mismatch will be aggregated taking account of intermediation chains and weeding out mutually inconsistent plans to solve the mapping from the *measured* risks to the true *realized* risks. That is, the mapping envisaged is of the form:

$$\Delta_{1,t} = f^1(\Delta's_{t-1}, \theta_{1,t-1}, x_{t-1})$$

$$\vdots \tag{1}$$

$$\Delta_{n,t} = f^n(\Delta's_{t-1}, \theta_{n,t-1}, x_{t-1}),$$

where $\Delta_{i,t}$ is the profile of deltas of firm i at date t, s_{t-1} are shocks to the deltas, $\theta_{i,t-1}$ are firm i's characteristics, and x_{t-1} is the macro state. The objective is to derive the true deltas $\{\Delta_{i,t}\}$ from the individual measured deltas inside the brackets on the right-hand side of (1).

Getting the right mapping $f(\cdot)$ in (1) will determine the success or otherwise of such an exercise. This will be a new venture. Existing private sector risk management exercises do not rest of calculating (1), since their objective does not extend to incorporating system-wide externalities.

The challenge in constructing (and updating) the correct model that underpins the function $f(\cdot)$ will be formidable. Theoretical modeling will need to be employed much more than is customary in regulatory settings. The reason is that a purely empirical exercise relying on historical data will fail to capture the pent-up risks in the system.

Take the example from the period before the global financial crisis. Figures 2 and 3 plot the CDS spreads of Bear Stearns and Lehman Brothers, with figure 2 giving the long perspective and illustrating how the spreads increase sharply with the onset of the crisis. However, what is remarkable is how tranquil the CDS measure is before the crisis. There is barely a ripple in the series in the period 2004–2006 when the vulnerability was building up fastest. Figure 3, which plots the CDS series for the precrisis period of January 2004 to January 2007 shows that CDS spreads were actually *falling* over the period when the worst excesses were building up in the financial system.

The challenge for the proposals in Brunnermeier, Gorton, and Krishnamurthy is to come up with a theoretical construct—the theory that

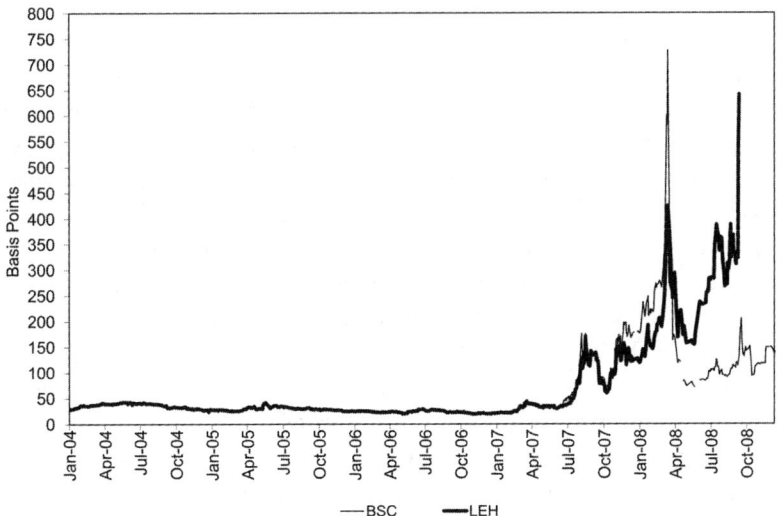

Fig. 2. CDS spreads of Bear Stearns and Lehman Brothers (2004–2008)

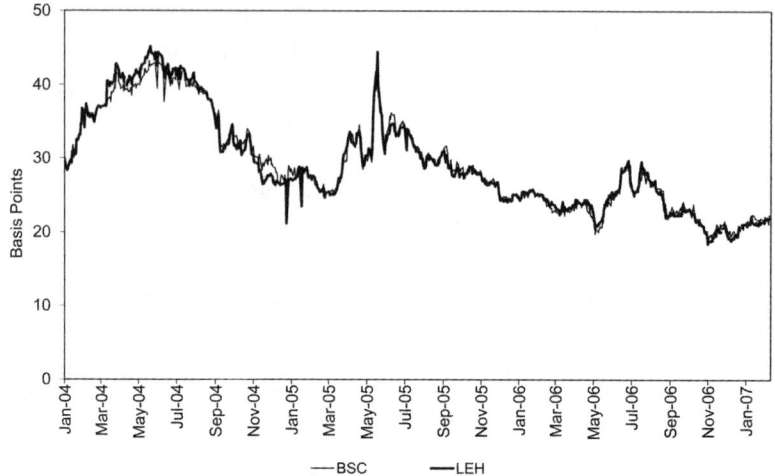

Fig. 3. CDS spreads of Bear Stearns and Lehman Brothers (2004–2006)

underpins the mapping in (1)—that will be able to flag the impending problems while they are building up rather than waiting for the signs of trouble to materialize. As the former BIS (Bank of International Settlements) head Andrew Crockett (2000) has put it,

The received wisdom is that risk increases in recessions and falls in booms. In contrast, it may be more helpful to think of risk as *increasing* during upswings, as financial imbalances build up, and *materialising* in recessions.

The authors are skeptical that balance sheet aggregates such as the liabilities of financial intermediaries will be able to capture the overall risks to the system due to the neglect of off-balance sheet exposures such as over-the-counter derivatives. However, it would be important to maintain the system-wide perspective rather than slipping back into the thinking of individual financial institutions. For individual banks and intermediaries, the off-balance sheet exposures are as important as the on-balance sheet ones, but from the perspective of the system as a whole, the off-balance sheet items would be of interest only due to their contributions to aggregate risks. If the bet between two institutions is zero-sum, then the net impact of this exposure will be less than if they held long positions in the same risky asset. To this extent, balance sheet aggregates may capture a good part of the overall risks to the system, and tracking such aggregates may be a good first step.

Another way to express this principle is to note that the behavior of individual institutions is the result of solving constrained optimization problems of the form:

$$\text{Maximize expect profit subject to acceptable risks} \qquad (2)$$

When the environment is tranquil, more exposure can be taken on without breaching the risk constraint. The solution to the optimization problem in tranquil times will result in larger balance sheets as a consequence. As with any nontrivial constraint in an optimization problem, the risk constraint binds all the time. In tranquil times, the constraint binding means that the notional exposures have to be that much larger. Tracking aggregate notional exposures, which is what is involved when measuring balance sheet aggregates, will therefore be a useful first step in gauging the potentially highly nonlinear crisis dynamics around the corner.

Endnotes

For acknowledgments, sources of research support, and disclosure of the author's material financial relationships, if any, please see http://www.nber.org/chapters/c12414.ack.

1. Morris and Shin (2008) discuss the various dimensions of the fallacy of composition in financial regulation.

References

Adrian, Tobias, and Hyun Song Shin. 2008. "Procyclical Leverage and Value-at-Risk." FRBNY Staff Report 338. http://www.newyorkfed.org/research/staff_reports/sr338.html.

Crockett, Andrew. 2000. "Marrying the Micro- and Macro-Prudential Dimensions of Financial Stability." Bank for International Settlements. http://www.bis.org/review/rr000921b.pdf.

Hellwig, Martin. 1995. "Systemic Aspects of Risk Management in Banking and Finance." *Schweizerische Zeitschrift für Volkswirtschaft und Statistik* 131 (4/2): 723–37.

Morris, Stephen, and Hyun Song Shin. 2008. "Financial Regulation in a System Context." *Brookings Papers on Economic Activity* (Fall):229–74.

Discussion

Robert Hall began the discussion by addressing data collection issues. He thought that it was wrong to limit the discussion of gathering data to only the data that will later be made public. He categorized data into four levels. First, there is all data: every position of every financial institution. Only a limited number of people have access to all the data and there is a huge security issue associated with storing this data. Second, there is data for regulators and the Office of Financial Research economists. This is similar to the data that people working in the Bureau of Labor Statistics or the Census utilize. Third, there is data that can be used by outside researchers under confidentiality agreements. Finally, there is public data that has to be aggregated carefully. He added that it is also useful to age the data and make it public. He doubted that an investment bank, for example, cares a lot about disclosing its data with a three-year lag. Markus Brunnermeier agreed that the data dissemination problem is quite important and has to be addressed. He also remarked that it is very important for economists to use the data to differentiate among different macro models with financial sectors. Once economists have better macro models with a financial sector, it will help to gather better data.

Hall made a comment on the great variety of risk factors. He asserted that historically there was only one risk factor: real estate. He claimed there is only one asset class upon which the whole leverage apparatus of the US financial system is built. He mentioned that there has never been a crisis in the financial system based on any other source of asset price decline except for real estate, concluding that the focus should be entirely on real estate. Daron Acemoglu responded by saying that there was no Swiss real estate bubble, but Swiss banks were in trouble. So, real estate of different countries presents an example of more than just one risk factor. Brunnermeier agreed that real estate is a critical source of risk. However, he believed that there are other sources of risk that should be considered.

Acemoglu commented on the systematic aspect of risk raised by both Darrell Duffie and Hyun Song Shin. He posited that there are two sources of systematic risk. First, there can be extreme events when all or the majority of firms experience a shock. Second, there are situations when some firms are hit by a shock and it spreads and creates cascade effects. There are two issues associated with studying the latter source of systematic risk. First, one needs to understand the network structure. Second, it is important to describe the behavior of agents. Acemoglu remarked that, to the first-order approximation, almost all of the local interactions structures that are observed in the data will be stable. He thought that the reason for nonlinear behavior of the system is that during certain times, agents will take precipitous actions leading the system to a state where some firms start failing. He asserted that to capture the nonlinearities one cannot just use data but must also model behavior. Specifically, one has to understand what shocks and risk factors make agents withdraw liquidity that initiates an avalanche of failures. Brunnermeier agreed with Acemoglu that the systematic risk is about the feedbacks and behavior. He thought that it was important to distinguish between domino effects and general equilibrium price movements. He pointed out that they were trying to capture the latter effect in this paper. He repeated that the deltas that they defined in the paper are the measure of the choice of a risk exposure by a firm. He noted that it is important to compute these deltas not only with respect to a firm's value but also with respect to the liquidity mismatch index that describes the firm's sensitivity to changes in market and funding liquidity. He stressed that one can use leverage instead of the liquidity mismatch index; however, as the paper shows through a series of examples, leverage is an outdated concept. After one understands firms' behavior, one can feed this into a general equilibrium model to see the equilibrium outcome. Brunnermeier highlighted that there are two types of information related to the effects just described. First, the information about the build up of a crisis—information about liquidity mismatch. Second, the information about network structure. He noted that the latter type of information can help understand which agents will be impaired once the crisis hits, while the former type of information, which the authors are focusing on, could potentially help to detect the build up of a crisis. He acknowledged that both types of information are equally important.

Eichenbaum said that if one wants to take Acemoglu's proposal seriously, then the number of details that one has to understand to create an effective regulation is daunting. He noted that if one considers real estate as the main source of risk then one has to increase mortgage requirements. An alternative approach would be to acknowledge that the financial system is too complex and try to make it simpler. He gave the example of Canada, which has a less complicated financial system and has suffered smaller losses than the United States in the current crisis. He concluded by noting that the more sophisticated data has to be, the harder it is to collect.

Jeremy Stein agreed with Acemoglu's discussion points and provided an example: all of the quantitative equity funds experienced 30 to 40 standard deviations events over a couple of days in August 2007. He claimed that these funds are the best case for measurement. It was possible to find out what equities they held and one could elicit from them any stress test scenario. However, he pointed out that one would never have gotten from them that under a 30 to 40 standard deviations event, they would liquidate everything. He stressed that it is important to determine tipping points when investors start pulling out in such a way that the funds liquidate everything, exposing other firms. He added that understanding agents' behavior may be desirable from an academic point of view but would not necessarily prevent a future financial crisis.

Brunnermeier thought that the liquidation of assets by the equity funds was a good example of a micro-crisis that can be analyzed. He noted that it was not itself a systematic event, though it triggered a systemic event. He thought that mechanisms exist that could be gleaned from smaller crises and extrapolated for a bigger crisis.

Xavier Gabaix reiterated that the authors want to not just elicit how much a firm would lose in terms of money in a particular event but also how much a firm would sell. He insisted that it is important to elicit information about that behavior under very low probability events and not only what is considered extreme now.

Laibson stated that if this project had been in place in 2005, the same financial crisis would have occurred. He noted that Alan Greenspan in 2005 argued repeatedly that there could not be a national decline in housing prices. His extreme event might have been a 5% to 10% decline in the national housing index. Banks were considering a 5% to

10% decline in the national prices as extreme scenarios as well. Laibson warned that it is not enough to ask banks about extreme scenarios of 2, 3, or 4 standard deviations, but it is important to go deeper into the tails. He concluded that the knowledge of the behavior under the belief about the extreme events that agents held in 2005 would not help avoid the current crisis. However, the current knowledge about tail risks can help avoid the next crises.

Gorton closed by emphasizing the opportunity to shape the work of the Office of Financial Research.

4

A Fistful of Dollars: Lobbying and the Financial Crisis

Deniz Igan, *Research Department, International Monetary Fund*
Prachi Mishra, *Research Department, International Monetary Fund*
Thierry Tressel, *Research Department, International Monetary Fund*

I. Introduction

On December 31, 2007, the *Wall Street Journal* reported that Ameriquest Mortgage and Countrywide Financial, two of the largest mortgage lenders in the United States, spent respectively $20.5 million and $8.7 million in political donations, campaign contributions, and lobbying activities from 2002 through 2006.[1] The sought outcome, according to the article, was the defeat of anti-predatory lending legislation that could have mitigated reckless lending practices and the consequent rise in delinquencies. Such anecdotal evidence suggests that the political influence of the financial industry contributed to the 2007 mortgage crisis, which, in the fall of 2008, generalized in the worst bout of financial instability since the Great Depression.[2] In spite of the importance of these claims, formal analysis of the political economy factors underlying the crisis has so far remained scant.

This paper asks whether lobbying lenders behaved differently from nonlobbying lenders in the 2000–2007 period and how they performed in 2008. To the best of our knowledge, this is the first study that examines empirically the relationship between lobbying by financial institutions and mortgage lending in the United States. We construct a unique data set combining information on mortgage lending activities and lobbying at the federal level. By going through individual lobbying reports, we identify all federal bills targeted by the financial industry lobbying, and focus on the lobbying specifically aimed at rules and regulations of consumer protection in mortgage lending, underwriting standards, and securities laws (henceforth, the "specific issues").[3]

First, we analyze the relationship between lobbying and ex ante characteristics of loans originated. We focus on three measures of mortgage lending: loan-to-income ratio (which we consider as a proxy for lending standards), proportion of loans sold (negatively correlated with the quality of loans originated), and mortgage loan growth rates (positively correlated with risk-taking).[4] Controlling for unobserved lender and area characteristics as well as changes over time in the macroeconomic and local lender and borrower conditions, we find that lenders that lobbied more intensively (a) originated mortgages with higher loan-to-income ratios (LIR); (b) securitized a faster growing proportion of loans originated; and (c) had faster growing mortgage loan portfolios.

Next, we analyze measures of ex post performance of lobbying lenders. In particular, we explore whether, at the Metropolitan Statistical Area (MSA) level, delinquency rates—an indicator of loan performance—were linked to the expansion of lobbying lenders' mortgage lending. We find that faster relative growth of mortgage loans by lobbying lenders during 2000–2006 was associated with higher delinquency rates in 2008. We also carry out an event study during key episodes of the financial crisis to assess whether the stocks of lobbying lenders performed differently from those of other financial institutions. We find that lobbying lenders experienced negative abnormal stock returns at the time of the failures of Bear Stearns and Lehman Brothers, but positive abnormal returns around the announcement of the bailout program. Finally, we examine the determinants of how bailout funds were distributed and find that being a lobbying lender was associated with a higher probability of being a recipient of these funds.

We perform a number of tests to establish robustness of the results. First, we control for lender, MSA, and time fixed effects as well as various lender-MSA-time-varying controls. Second, we conduct falsification tests by exploiting information about lobbying on financial issues that are *unrelated* to mortgage lending and securitization. Next, we adopt a difference-in-difference strategy to test whether the characteristics of mortgage loans originated by lobbying lenders responded differently to the introduction of anti-predatory lending laws at the state level, than those originated by other lenders. Finally, we adopt an instrumental variable strategy using as instrument the distance between the headquarters of the financial institution and Washington, DC, which is exogenous and proxies for the cost of lobbying. (See Section V for details.) While these results are robust to a number of controls and alternative estimation strategies, we are cautious not to interpret them as a causal link between lobbying activities and mortgage lending. Reverse causality remains a concern: lenders that choose to lobby more intensively may be the risky type to begin with.

Our findings indicate that lobbying was associated ex ante with more risk-taking and ex post with worse performance. This is consistent with some lenders being more likely to benefit from lax regulation: these lenders lobbied more aggressively; the ensuing lax regulatory environment allowed them to engage in riskier lending; and such lending exposed them, directly or indirectly, to worse outcomes during the crisis. Interestingly, the market anticipated lobbying lenders to benefit more from the bailout, and they indeed did, perhaps because they were hit harder by the crisis and/or because they had closer connections to policymakers.

Why are some lenders more likely to benefit from lax regulation? These lenders, for example, may be specialized in catering to riskier borrowers, or they may be overoptimistic and may have honestly underestimated the likelihood of an adverse shock. Then, these lenders may have lobbied to signal their private information to the policymaker and prevent tighter regulation that would otherwise have restricted profitable lending opportunities. If lobbying lenders are specialized or overoptimistic, their motive for lobbying is consistent with information-based theories. Alternatively, some lenders may have distorted incentives and might have lobbied to create a regulatory environment that allows them to exploit short-term gains at the cost of long-term profits. An extreme view could be that certain lenders engaged in specialized rent-seeking and lobbied to increase their chances of preferential treatment, for example, a lower probability of scrutiny by bank supervisors or even a higher probability of being bailed out in the event of a financial crisis.[5] If lobbying lenders are short-termist or lobby to increase their chances of preferential treatment, the motive for lobbying involves moral hazard elements and seems to fit better with theories of rent-seeking.

Overall, our findings suggest that the political influence of the financial industry played a role in the accumulation of risks, and hence, contributed to the financial crisis.[6] However, it is hard to distinguish whether it was information-revealing or rent-seeking that drove lobbying by the financial industry. There is evidence suggesting that lobbying was not motivated solely by information dissemination. Still, the findings fall short of firmly establishing the existence of rent-seeking motives.

The rest of the paper is organized as follows. Section II discusses the related literature. Section III provides some background for the empirical specifications. Section IV describes the data set, Section V presents the results, and Section VI concludes.

II. Related Literature

Lobbying is broadly defined as a legal activity aiming at changing existing rules or policies or procuring individual benefits. Private benefits could materialize in the form of preferential access to credit, bailout guarantees, privileged access to licenses, or procurement contracts (Fisman 2001; Johnson and Mitton 2003; and Faccio and Parsley 2009). Building upon the private-interest theories of regulation (Stigler 1971), research on lobbying has developed into two broad strands: studies that focus on the relationship between lobbying activities and specific *policies* (see, for instance, Grossman and Helpman 1994, Goldberg and Maggi 1999, and Ludema, Mayda, and Mishra 2010, for the case of trade policy; Facchini, Mayda, and Mishra 2011 for the case of immigration policy; Kroszner and Stratmann 1998 and Kroszner and Strahan 1999 for financial services) and those that aim to explore the consequences of lobbying on firm-specific economic *outcomes* (see, for example, Bertrand et al. 2004 and Claessens, Feijen, and Laeven 2008). Issues specific to banking and finance have been studied by, among others, Khwaja and Mian (2005), who find that in Pakistan politically-connected firms obtain exclusive loans from public banks and have much higher default rates; Raddatz and Braun (2010), who present evidence suggesting that politicians provide for beneficial regulation in exchange for a nonexecutive position at a bank in the future, consistent with a capture-type private interest story; and Faccio (2006), who shows that political connections increase firm value. Our study, focusing on lobbying and lending behavior, fits more closely in the second strand.

Our paper is also related to the emerging literature on the current crisis. While this literature has characterized the relaxation of lending standards and its link to increasing defaults in mortgage markets, evidence on the role of political economy factors remain scarce.[7] For example, Mian, Sufi, and Trebbi (2010b) focus on the consequences of financial crisis, showing that constituent and special interests theories explain voting on key bills in 2008. Similarly, Mian, Sufi, and Trebbi (2010a) also analyze voting patterns on a few key bills prior to the crisis. In contrast to these papers, we conduct our analysis at the lender-level and study the role of political economy factors in shaping lending behavior during the credit boom and the impact on loan outcomes during the crisis.

III. Background

Certain firm characteristics may drive both the decision to lobby and lending behavior. Examples of such characteristics include screening technology, underwriting and securitization techniques, specialization of the lender, or the capacity to acquire private information regarding future states of the world. Given such characteristics, certain lenders would make riskier loans, and also have more to gain from a relaxation of the regulatory rules that limit risk-taking. In order to ensure that the regulatory environment remains/becomes lax, these lenders would lobby more intensively against tighter rules and regulations so that they can continue/start making risky loans. Consider a simple example where lender i has a comparative advantage due to a lower cost of securitizing loans. In that case, any regulation that reduces restrictions on securitization activities may generate higher gains for lender i compared to other lenders with higher costs. Hence, the benefits from lobbying for such regulations would be higher for lender i. Lender i would therefore lobby more than other lenders at time t, even if other lenders may free-ride and also benefit (but to a lesser extent) from lax regulations because of higher gains that accrue to him from lobbying.[8] If lobbying efforts are successful and the rules are not tightened, this would allow lender i to engage in riskier lending in period $t + 1$ and in subsequent periods. Although the new rules would apply to all lenders, lender i has a comparative advantage, which enables him to take more risks under these rules compared to other lenders. Moreover, given their risky portfolios, lender i would be more likely to experience worse loan outcomes and experience higher losses, if hit by adverse shocks.

For example, Citigroup lobbied intensively against H.R. 1051, Predatory Lending Consumer Protection Act of 2001 (spending a total of $3 million over January–June 2002 on this and other issues related to mortgage and securities markets), which aimed to put tighter restrictions on lenders (see appendix for more details on the bill: http://www.nber.org/data-appendix/c12416/appendix.pdf), and this was never signed into law. Indeed, during 1999–2006, 93% of all the bills promoting tighter regulation were never signed into law. Importantly, two key pieces of legislation to promote lax lending in mortgage markets—American Homeownership and Economic Opportunity Act of 2000, and American Dream Downpayment Act of 2003—were in fact signed into law.

The lax regulatory environment that emerged allowed certain lenders to engage in riskier lending during 2000–2007, and end up with worse outcomes during the crisis. To illustrate with an example, the *Wall Street Journal* on December 31, 2007 reported

Data from federal and state campaign-finance records, Internal Revenue Service filings, and the National Institute on Money in State Politics show that from 2002 through 2006, Ameriquest, its executives and their spouses and business associates donated at least $20.5 million to state and federal political groups. . . . Ameriquest became a player in the business of lending to low-income homeowners. The company persuaded many homeowners to take cash out of their houses by refinancing them for larger amounts than their existing mortgages. . . . Home loans made by Ameriquest and other subprime lenders are defaulting now in large numbers.

This mechanism implies that one would observe lobbying in period t to be associated with riskier lending behavior in period $t + 1$. The empirical specifications discussed in the following are based on this mechanism.

Once the financial crisis hit and the government was forced to intervene, the factors that determined who would be bailed out included, for example, how badly the financial institution was hurt, how systematically important it was, how healthy the balance sheets were, and perhaps how well connected the institution was to the politicians. For instance, the *Wall Street Journal* on January 23, 2009 reported

Troubled OneUnited Bank in Boston didn't look much like a candidate for aid from the Treasury Department's bank bailout fund last fall. . . . Nonetheless, in December OneUnited got a $12 million injection from the Treasury's Troubled Asset Relief Program, or TARP. One apparent factor: the intercession of Rep. Barney Frank, the powerful head of the House Financial Services Committee. . . . Some powerful politicians have used their leverage to try to direct federal millions toward banks in their home states. "It's totally arbitrary," says South Carolina Gov. Mark Sanford. "If you've got the right lobbyist and the right representative connected to Washington or the right ties to Washington, you get the golden tap on the shoulder."

The channels highlighted in such anecdotes suggest that one is likely to observe an empirical association between lobbying and ex post performance as well as the likelihood of bailout in 2008. This motivates our empirical analysis of outcomes during the crisis.

IV. Data Description

A. Mortgage Lending

Mortgage lenders are required to provide detailed information on the applications they receive and the loans they originate under the Home Mortgage Disclosure Act (HMDA). Enacted by Congress in 1975, HMDA data covers a broad set of depository and nondepository financial institutions. Comparisons of the total amount of loan originations in the HMDA and industry sources indicate that around 90% of the mortgage lending activity is covered in this database. Our coverage of HMDA data is from 1999 to 2007 to match the lobbying database. We collapse the data to MSA-lender level with 378 MSAs and almost 9,000 lenders. Then, we construct our variables of interest: loan-to-income ratio at origination, loan securitization rates, mortgage loan growth rate, and the extent of activity by lobbying lenders at the MSA level.

B. Lobbying

Lobbyists in the United States—often organized in special interest groups—can legally influence the policy formation process through two main channels. First, they can offer campaign finance contributions, in particular through political action committees (PACs). These activities have received a fair amount of attention in the literature.[9] Second, they are allowed to carry out lobbying activities in the executive and legislative branches of the federal government. These lobbying activities, albeit accounting for the bulk of politically-targeted expenditures, have in contrast received scant attention in the literature. Individual companies and organizations have been required to provide a substantial amount of information on their lobbying activities, starting with the introduction of the Lobbying Disclosure Act of 1995. Since 1996, all lobbyists (intermediaries who lobby on behalf of companies and organizations) have to file semiannual reports to the Secretary of the Senate's Office of Public Records (SOPR), listing the name of each client (firm), the total income they have received from each of them, and specific lobbying issues. In parallel, all firms with in-house lobbying departments are required to file similar reports stating the *total* dollar amount they have spent (either in-house or in payments to external lobbyists). Legislation requires the disclosure not only of the dollar amounts actually received/spent, but also of the issues for which lobbying is carried out. Thus, unlike PAC contributions, lobbying expenditures of companies can be associated with very specific targeted policy areas. Such detailed information is reported by roughly 9,000 companies, around 600 of which are in the finance, insurance, and real estate (FIRE) industry.

C.   Other Data

We supplement the information from the lobbying and HMDA databases with MSA-level and state-level data on economic and social indicators such as income, unemployment, population, and house price appreciation.[10] We also obtain data on delinquent loans from LoanPerformance, a private data company. The stock price return is computed using data from Compustat. The information on the enactment of antipredatory lending laws is from Bostic et al. (2008).[11] Finally, the data on the 2008 bailout program is based on original records provided by the Treasury through the Office of Financial Stability.[12]

D.   Construction of the Data Set

1.   Matching Lobbying Firms to Lenders

The matching of the lobbying and HMDA databases is a tedious task. We use an algorithm that finds common words in lender names to narrow down the potential matches in HMDA of lenders in the lobbying database and then go through these one by one to determine the right match. We examine meticulously the corporate structure of the firms in the lobbying database and those that may be a match to an HMDA lender based on our algorithm (see the appendix for more details). We create four lobbying identifiers reflecting several types of matches: (a) exact matches; (b) matches to parent firm; (c) matches to affiliated firms; and (d) matches to subsidiaries. The lobbying variables used in the regressions combine these four variables.

   We also consider lobbying expenditures by associations. The list of member firms for each association in the lobbying database is compiled by going on each association's website. A portion of the associations' lobbying expenditures is assigned to each member firm based on the share of its own spending in the total of all members.

2.   Identifying Lobbying Activity Targeted to the Mortgage Market

Our analysis distinguishes between lobbying activities that are related to mortgage-market-specific issues from other lobbying activities. We first concentrate only on issues related to the five general issues of interest (accounting, banking, bankruptcy, housing, and financial institutions) and then gather information on the specific issues, which are typically acts proposed at the House or the Senate, that were listed by the lobbyists as the main issue for the lobbying activity.[13] Then, we go through these specific issues one by one and determine whether an issue can be directly linked to restrictions on mortgage market lending. For example, H.R. 1163 of 2003 (Predatory Mortgage Lending Practices Reduction Act) and H.R. 4471 of 2005 (Fair and Responsible Lending Act), regulating high-cost mortgages, are bills that we deem to be relevant to the mortgage market. On the other hand, H.R. 2201 of 2005 (Consumer Debt Prevention and Education Act) and the Sarbanes-Oxley Act of 2002, although in general related to financial services, do not include any provisions directly related to mortgage lending and are not classified as mortgage-market-specific issues.

After classifying all listed issues, we calculate lobbying expenditures on specific issues by splitting the total amount spent evenly across issues. To be more precise, we first divide the total lobbying expenditure by the number of *all* general issues and multiply by the number of general issues selected. Then, we divide this by the total number of specific issues listed under the five general issues and multiply by the number of specific issues of interest.[14] In order to illustrate the construction of the final lobbying variable, suppose firm A spends $300 and lobbies on three general issues (banking and housing, which are general issues of interest, and trade, which is not a general issue of interest); it lists two specific issues under banking and housing (H.R. 1163, which is a relevant specific issue, and H.R. 2201, which is not relevant). In this example, the final lobbying expenditure variable is calculated as $((300/3) \cdot (2/2) \cdot 1 = \$100$.

E.   *Summary Statistics*

As shown in table 1, between 1999 and 2006, interest groups have spent on average about $4.2 billion per political cycle on targeted political activity, which includes PAC campaign contributions and lob-

Table 1
Targeted Political Activity Campaign Contributions and Lobbying Expenditures (millions of dollars)

Election Cycle	1999–2000	2001–2002	2003–2004	2005–2006
Contributions from PACs	326	348	461	509
Overall lobbying expenditure	2,972	3,348	4,081	4,747
Of which expenditure by finance, insurance, and real estate industry (FIRE)	437	478	645	720
Share of FIRE in overall lobbying (in percent)	14.7	14.3	15.8	15.2
Total targeted political activity	3,298	3,696	4,542	5,256

Source: Center for Responsive Politics.

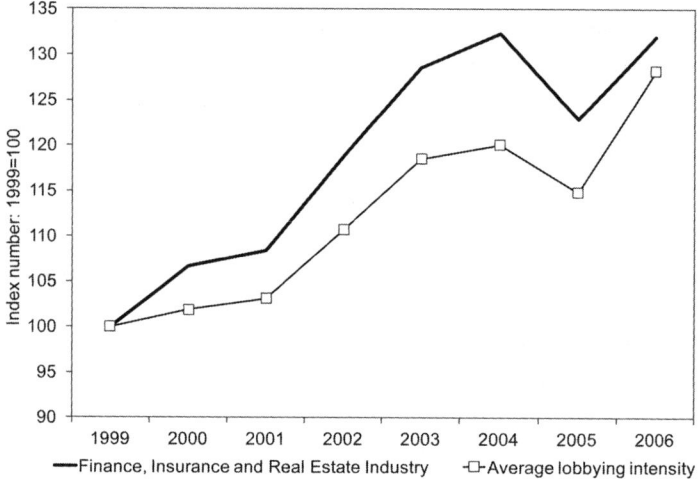

Fig. 1. Evolution of lobbying intensity (expenditures per firm) over time

bying expenditures. Lobbying expenditures represent by far the bulk of all interest groups' money spent on targeted political activity (close to 90%). Expenditures by FIRE companies constitute roughly 15% of overall lobbying expenditures in any election cycle. Approximately 10% of all firms that lobbied during this time period were associated with FIRE. Moreover, the lobbying intensity for FIRE increased at a much faster pace relative to the average lobbying intensity over 1999–2006 (figure 1). Similar inspection of the HMDA database reveals time trends indicating higher LIR and increased recourse to securitization (figure 2).

Our matching process ends up matching around 250 firms in the

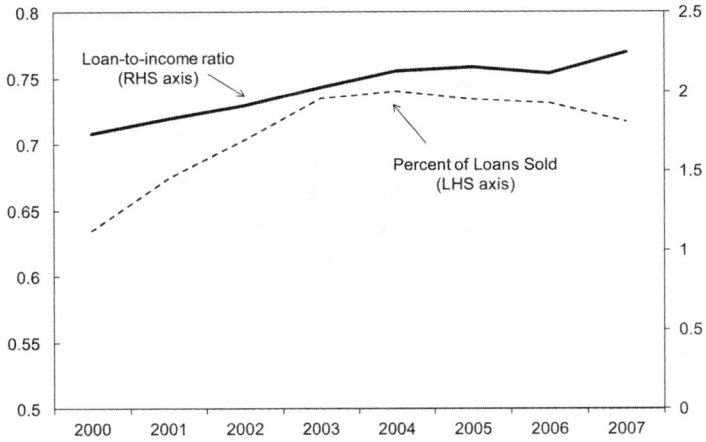

Fig. 2.   Lending standards and securitization

lobbying database to one or more lenders in the HMDA database, corresponding to roughly 40% of FIRE firms that lobby. In the final MSA-lender-year level data set, lenders that lobby on specific issues comprise around 11% of the observations. Lobbying was performed by the lender itself in 25% of these observations and by the parent financial institution, affiliated firms, and subsidiaries in 65, 23, and 5%, respectively. This suggests that it was mainly the parent firms, which are likely to be large, national financial institutions or holding groups, that lobbied on specific issues relevant for their subsidiaries. In terms of magnitudes, the matched lenders spent in total roughly half a billion dollars for lobbying on specific issues during 1999–2006. Lobbying expenditures by lenders' associations during the same period remained comparatively small (8% of total spent).

As shown in figure 3, lobbying lenders (a) tend to be larger either by assets or market share, (b) less likely to be HUD-regulated, (c) more likely to be subprime, and (d) cater to richer borrowers. In terms of measures of lending, they had (a) slightly higher LIRs, (b) lower tendency to securitize, and (c) faster growing loan portfolios. In addition, lobbying lenders were significantly more likely to be bailed out.[15] The most striking difference between the lobbying and nonlobbying lenders appears to be in terms of size. Lobbying lenders in terms of log assets tend to be 25% larger than nonlobbying lenders (figure 3). Translated to levels, this difference is even starker, where lobbying lenders are six

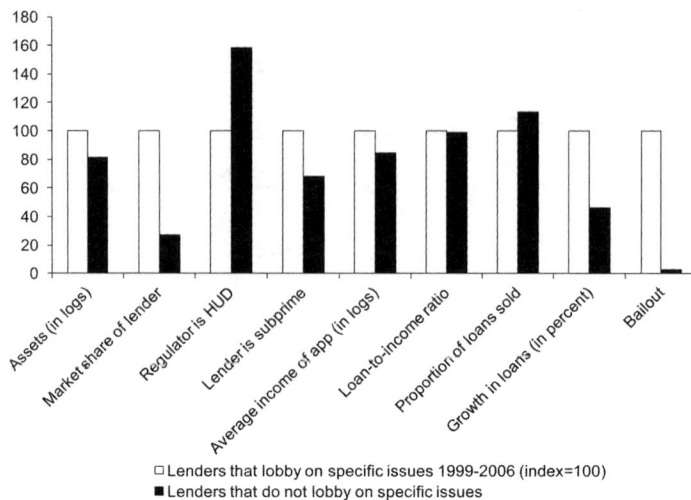

□ Lenders that lobby on specific issues 1999-2006 (index=100)
■ Lenders that do not lobby on specific issues

Fig. 3.   Difference between lobbying and nonlobbying lenders

times as large. In the following section, we examine these relationships rigorously. Summary statistics on the variables used in the empirical analysis are shown in table 2.

V.   Empirical Analysis

This section presents the empirical specifications and regression results, based on the mechanisms discussed in Section III. First, we analyze the relationship between lobbying and the ex ante characteristics of loans originated (the loan-to-income ratio; the proportion of loans sold; the growth rate of loans originated). Second, we explore the relationship between lobbying and ex post outcomes (delinquency rates; stock returns during the crisis; likelihood of being bailed out).

A.   Empirical Analysis of Loan-to-Income Ratio

We estimate the following panel equation:

$$y_{imt} = \alpha + \beta \cdot l_i + \lambda \cdot Z_{imt} + v_m + \pi_t + v_m^* \pi_t + \varepsilon_{imt} \qquad (1)$$

where y_{imt} is a measure of loan characteristics for lender i, in MSA m during year t. Variable l_i is a dummy for lenders that lobby the federal government on specific issues,[16] and Z_{imt} denotes a set of control variables at the lender-MSA level. Variables v_m and π_t denote a set of MSA

Table 2
Summary Statistics

	Observations	Mean	Median	Std. Deviation
		Lender-Level Variables		
Lenders that Lobby on Specific Issues				
Loan-to-income ratio	73,374	2.02	1.98	.70
Proportion of loans sold	73,374	.63	.80	.38
Growth in amount of loans originated (in percent)	56,504	3.80	.12	143.63
Market share of lender	73,374	.01	.00	.03
Average income of loan applicants (in logs)	73,374	7.65	7.49	2.38
Assets (in logs)	73,374	14.65	16.76	4.31
Dummy = 1 if regulator is HUD	73,374	.37	.00	.48
Dummy = 1 if lender is subprime	73,374	.30	.00	.46
Lobbying expenditures on specific issues (in logs)	73,374	6.68	9.96	5.37
Lenders that do not Lobby on Specific Issues				
Loan-to-income ratio	575,564	2.00	1.93	.95
Proportion of loans sold	575,564	.71	1.00	.41
Growth in amount of loans originated (in percent)	371,875	1.75	.07	38.13
Market share of lender	575,564	.00	.00	.01
Average income of loan applicants (in logs)	575,564	6.47	6.18	2.01
Assets (in logs)	575,564	11.89	1.34	3.31
Dummy = 1 if regulator is HUD	575,564	.59	1.00	.49
Dummy = 1 if lender is subprime	575,564	.21	.00	.41
		MSA-Level Variables		
Average income (in thousands)	648,938	31.72	3.61	7.29
GDP growth	648,938	.05	.05	.03
Self-employment rate	584,237	.04	.04	.03
Unemployment rate	648,084	.05	.05	.02
Population (in logs)	648,938	13.30	13.00	1.39
House price appreciation	646,366	.07	.05	.07
Number of competing lenders (in logs)	648,938	5.49	5.48	.47
Number of loan applications (in logs)	648,938	9.91	9.78	1.30
Delinquency rate in 2008	648,938	.17	.16	.05
Share of subprime loans in total loans	648,938	.10	.09	.04
Share of Hispanics in population	512,547	.21	.12	.26
Share of college graduates in population	512,547	.23	.22	.07

and year fixed effects, respectively, while $v_m^* \pi_t$ captures the effect of all MSA-time varying factors on loan characteristics, which are constant across lenders. The MSA fixed effects control for any time-invariant MSA level omitted variable, which could be correlated with lobbying and also affect loan characteristics. In addition, the interaction between MSA and year effects allows us to capture any time-varying MSA characteristics. Time effects control for global shocks, affecting all lenders and areas equally. The parameter of interest is β, which captures average differences in mortgage loan characteristics between lenders that lobby and lenders that do not lobby.[17]

Our main variable capturing ex ante characteristics is the loan-to-income ratio (LIR) averaged at the lender-MSA level. This measure is a simplified version of a commonly used indicator, debt-to-income ratio, to determine whether a borrower can afford a mortgage loan. Lenders usually require that mortgage payments cannot exceed a certain proportion of the applicant's income.[18] As the maximum proportion allowed increases, the burden of servicing the loan becomes harder and the default probability potentially increases. We compute the LIR as a proxy for such limits required by the lender and interpret increases in this ratio that are not explained by lender, location characteristics, or by time fixed effects as a loosening in lending standards.

Table 3 presents the regression results of the LIR of originated loans on a dummy variable for lenders lobbying on specific issues. The coefficient on this dummy variable is positive and statistically significant at the 1% level in all the specifications, establishing that mortgage loans originated by lenders lobbying on specific issues have higher LIR on average. This finding remains unaffected when controlling for observable MSA and lender-MSA characteristics (column [2]). Lender-MSA level control variables ensure that the estimated coefficient on the dummy for lobbying lenders does not reflect characteristics such as the size of the lender (proxied by log of assets), the market power of the lender in a particular MSA (proxied by its market share), or other factors proxying for observable and unobservable characteristics of a lender's pool of applicants such as (a) whether the lender focuses on community development mortgages or has a brokerage-type business model (proxied by a dummy for HUD-regulated lenders); (b) whether the lender specializes in subprime lending; and (c) the average income of applicants of loans originated by the lender in a particular MSA. Moreover, the size of the coefficient increases as control variables are added to the regression, suggesting that omitted variables at the MSA level and at the lender-MSA level may have resulted in attenuation bias.

Adding MSA, year, and MSA-year fixed effects does not affect the magnitude or the significance of the estimated coefficients (columns [4] and [5]). This set of fixed effects confirm that our results do not reflect unobserved, either time-invariant or time-varying MSA characteristics, or time effects common to all MSAs. Importantly, MSA-year interac-

Table 3
Lobbying and Loan-to-Income Ratio

	(1)	(2)	(3)	(4)	(5)	(6)
Dummy = 1 if lender lobbies on specific issues	.016*** [.005]	.144*** [.004]	.075*** [.004]	.138*** [.004]	.145*** [.004]	.142*** [.004]
Dummy = 1 if lender lobbies only on other issues						−.017*** [.005]
Number of observations	648,938	581,105	648,938	581,105	648,938	648,938
R^2	.00	.10	.14	.16	.18	.18
MSA fixed effects	No	No	Yes	Yes	Yes	Yes
Year fixed effects	No	No	Yes	Yes	Yes	Yes
MSA*year fixed effects	No	No	No	No	Yes	Yes
Additional controls	No	Yes	No	Yes	Yes	Yes

Notes: Dependent variable: Loan-to-income ratio at (lender, MSA, year) level. The regressions are run on the lender-MSA-year panel from 1999–2007. The dummy for lobbying on specific issues is equal to 1 if the lender lobbies for those issues in any year during 1999–2006. Lobbying on specific issues refers to lobbying on bills and regulations related to mortgage lending and securitization. Columns (2) and (4) include MSA-year-level controls for average income, GDP growth rate, self-employment rate, unemployment rate, population, house price appreciation, number of competing lenders, and number of loan applications, as well as lender-year-level controls for assets and dummies for HUD regulation and subprime, and MSA-lender-year-level controls for market share of lender and average income of loan applicants (calculated for each lender separately in each MSA using the loan applications and originations by the lender in a particular MSA in a given year). Columns (5) and (6) include only the MSA-lender-year-level and lender-year-level controls. Standard errors denoted in parentheses are clustered at the lender-MSA level.
* Significant at the 10% level.
** Significant at the 5% level.
*** Significant at the 1% level.

tions in column (5) guarantee that the estimated effect is not biased due to, for example, the average quality of the borrower pool at the MSA level. If the relationship between lobbying and loan characteristics reflected mainly a specialization of lenders, we should expect the estimated coefficient to become smaller and insignificant when we include controls for lender characteristics, such as whether it is regulated by the US Department of Housing and Urban Development (HUD) or is classified as a subprime lender by the HUD. We find, on the contrary, that the estimated coefficient becomes larger. This evidence casts some doubt that lender specialization could be the explanation for the difference in loan characteristics between lobbying lenders and other lenders.[19]

The magnitude of the difference in LIR between lobbying lenders and other lenders is not trivial. The estimated coefficient of 0.15 in column (5) implies that the average LIR of mortgages originated is about 0.15 points higher for lobbying lenders than for other lenders. This is about 8% of the average LIR of 1.97 in the complete sample.

The estimated relationship between LIR and the lobbying decision may reflect a *general* propensity to lobby, for example, in order to gain access to policymakers to get private benefits, rather than a desire to influence *specific* rules. Then, we would expect to obtain a similar result for lenders that lobby on financial sector issues that are *unrelated* to mortgage markets. To carry out this falsification exercise, we create a dummy variable for lenders lobbying on issues that are *not* related to mortgage lending and securitization, for example, consumer credit and security of personal information, financial services other than mortgage lending, and anti-money laundering (henceforth, the "other issues"). We repeat our preferred specification presented in column (5) of table 3 by adding the new dummy. Column (6) displays the results. We find that the dummy for lobbying on specific issues has a positive and significant coefficient, while the dummy for lobbying on *other* issues has a negative and significant sign. This suggests that the desire to influence specific rules was one of the drivers of lobbying efforts.

Second, we estimate the following panel equation:

$$y_{imt} = \alpha + \delta \cdot (\ln LOBAM)_{it-1} + s_i + v_m + \pi_t + v_m^* \pi_t + \lambda \cdot Z_{imt} + \varepsilon_{imt}, \quad (2)$$

where outcome variables are the same as in equation (1), $(\ln LOBAM)_{it-1}$ is the logarithm of the amount of lobbying expenditures by lender i during year $t-1$, and s_i denotes a set of lender fixed effects that capture the effect of all lender-specific time-invariant factors on loan characteristics.[20] Note that lender fixed effects account for any unobserved lender-specific omitted variable that does not vary over time. The preferred specification includes lender, MSA, year effects, and MSA-year interactions; lobbying expenses only change at the lender-year level, so we cannot include lender-year interactions. The advantage of using the level of lobbying expenditures is that the time variation in lobbying amounts allows us to introduce lender fixed effects, and therefore to identify the coefficient of interest on the *within* dimension, in contrast to equation (1), where the coefficient of the lobbying dummy reflects systematic differences *between* firms.

Table 4 reports regressions of LIR on lobbying expenditures. The coefficient on the lobbying amount is positive and significant at a 1% level

Table 4
Lobbying Expenditures and Loan-to-Income Ratio

	(1)	(2)	(3)	(4)	(5)
Lobbying expenditures on	.007***	.009***	.003***	.003***	.002***
specific issues (in logs), lagged	[.000]	[.000]	[.001]	[.001]	[.001]
Assets (in logs)					.006***
					[.000]
Market share of lender					3.017***
					[.090]
Average income of loan applicants					−.031***
(in logs)					[.001]
Number of observations	406,035	406,035	406,035	406,035	406,035
R^2	.00	.17	.10	.12	.12
MSA fixed effects	No	Yes	Yes	Yes	Yes
Year fixed effects	No	Yes	Yes	Yes	Yes
Lender fixed effects	No	No	Yes	Yes	Yes
MSA*year fixed effects	No	No	No	Yes	Yes

Notes: Dependent variable: Loan-to-income ratio at (lender, MSA, year) level. The regressions are run on the lender-MSA-year panel from 2000–2007. Lobbying on specific issues refers to lobbying on bills and regulations related to mortgage lending and securitization. Assets vary at the lender-year level only. Market share of lender and average income of loan applicants are calculated for each lender separately in each MSA using the loan applications and originations by the lender in a particular MSA in a given year. Standard errors denoted in parentheses are clustered at the lender-MSA level.
* Significant at the 10% level.
** Significant at the 5% level.
*** Significant at the 1% level.

for various sets of fixed effects and control variables. In specifications including lender fixed effects (columns [3] to [5]), the coefficient of interest therefore reflects a correlation over time between the LIR and the lobbying amounts for lobbying lenders only. Hence, any time-invariant lender-specific factors—such as a superior screening technology—affecting both the decision to lobby and lending standards are absorbed by the lender fixed effects. Another concern is that there may be shocks common to all lenders, which we address by introducing time dummies. Columns (2) to (5) show that the coefficient remains significant. Furthermore, Columns (4) and (5) include MSA-year interactions controlling for time-varying local conditions faced by lenders.[21] The range of estimated coefficient suggests that a one standard deviation rise in lobbying expenditures is associated with a 0.02 to 0.11 points rise in LIR. This constitutes 1 to 5% of the average LIR of 1.97 in the complete sample.[22]

B. *Difference-in-Difference Estimations Using State-Level Laws*

We make use of difference-in-difference estimations exploiting
across-state variation in lending laws to uncover whether the existence
of anti-predatory lending laws at the state level have differential effects on the mortgage lending behavior of lenders that lobby relative
to those that do not lobby.[23] The hypothesis is that lobbying lenders
were originating riskier loans than other lenders in the absence of anti-
predatory lending laws. Therefore, when a law comes into effect at the
state level they tighten their loan terms more than other lenders to meet
the minimum legal requirements. In one sense, this is a mirror image
of the relationship between lobbying and lending we explored in the
earlier subsections: when tighter federal regulations fail to pass or lax
federal regulation comes to effect, lobbying lenders increase LIR more;
here, when tighter state regulation comes into effect, we expect lobbying lenders to decrease LIR more.

We estimate the following difference-in-difference panel equation:

$$y_{imt} = \alpha + \beta.APL_{st} + \delta \cdot (\ln LOBAM)_{it-1} + \phi \cdot (\ln LOBAM)_{it-1} \cdot APL_{st}$$
$$+ \gamma \cdot X_{mt} + \lambda \cdot Z_{imt} + s_i + v_m + \pi_t + \varepsilon_{imt} \tag{3}$$

Variable APL_{st} is a dummy equal to 1 if there exists an anti-predatory
lending law in state s, where MSA m is located, at time t.[24] Variable X_{mt}
denotes a set of MSA-year varying controls.

As shown in table 5, the coefficient on the interaction term between
the dummy for an anti-predatory lending law and lobbying intensity
is negative and significant at the 1% level in columns (2) through (4).
This result is consistent with the hypothesis that lobbying lenders, at
the margin, raise their lending standards more than other lenders when
anti-predatory lending laws are in place. This implies that these laws
happened to be more binding for lobbying lenders and that, before the
law came into place, lobbying lenders were more likely to have engaged
in risky lending practices.

The result is robust to include lender, MSA and year fixed effects, and
when we control for MSA-time, lender-time, or lender-MSA-time level
observable characteristics. In addition, the overall effect of an anti-
predatory lending law being in place, evaluated at the average lobbying
expenditures in the sample, is $\beta + \phi \cdot (\overline{\ln LOBAM}) < 0$. This suggests that
LIR is lower in MSAs that belong to states with anti-predatory lending
laws in place.

Table 5
Lobbying and Loan-to-Income Ratio: Difference-in-Difference

	(1)	(2)	(3)	(4)
Dummy = 1 if anti-predatory lending law	.166***	.015***	.006	.006
in (MSA, year)	[.004]	[.005]	[.005]	[.005]
Lobbying expenditures on specific	.007***	.009***	.008***	.007***
issues (in logs), lagged	[.001]	[.001]	[.001]	[.001]
Lobbying expenditures on specific	−.001	−.007***	−.006***	−.005***
issues (in logs), lagged*Lending law	[.001]	[.002]	[.002]	[.001]
Number of observations	406,035	406,035	355,656	355,656
R^2	.01	.10	.10	.10
Lender fixed effects	No	No	Yes	Yes
MSA fixed effects	No	Yes	Yes	Yes
Year fixed effects	No	Yes	Yes	Yes
Additional controls	No	No	Yes	Yes

Notes: Dependent variable: Loan-to-income ratio at (lender, MSA, year) level. The regressions are run on the lender-MSA-year panel from 2000–2007. Information on the enactment of state-level anti-predatory lending laws is from Bostic et al. (2008). Lobbying on specific issues refers to lobbying on bills and regulations related to mortgage lending and securitization. Column (3) includes MSA-year-level controls for average income, GDP growth rate, self-employment rate, unemployment rate, population, house price appreciation, number of competing lenders, and number of loan applications. Column (4), in addition to these MSA-year-level controls, includes lender-year-level controls for assets and MSA-lender-year-level controls for market share of lender and average income of loan applicants (calculated for each lender separately in each MSA using the loan applications and originations by the lender in a particular MSA in a given year). Standard errors denoted in parentheses are clustered at the lender-MSA level.
* Significant at the 10% level.
** Significant at the 5% level.
*** Significant at the 1% level.

C.   *Evidence on Lobbying and Securitization and Mortgage Credit Growth*

In addition to LIR, we use as two other dependent variables that provide additional information on lending practices: (a) the proportion of mortgages securitized and (b) the annual growth rate in the amount of loans originated. Recourse to securitization has been shown to weaken monitoring incentives; hence, a higher proportion of securitized loans can be associated with lower credit standards (see Keys et al. 2010 for evidence that securitization leads to less monitoring and worse loan performance). Next, fast expansion of credit could be associated with lower lending standards for several reasons. First, if there are constraints on training and employing loan officers, increased number of applications will lead to less time and expertise allocated to each application to assess their quality (see Berger and Udell 2004). Second, in a booming economy, increasing collateral values will increase credit-worthiness of intrinsically bad borrowers and, when collateral values drop during the bust, these borrowers are more likely to default (see Kiyotaki and Moore 1997). Third, competitive pressures might force lenders to loosen lending standards and extend loans to marginal borrowers in order to preserve their market shares.

Table 6 (columns [1] and [2]) shows that the proportion of mortgage loans securitized is positively correlated with lobbying expenditures within lenders. Hence, securitization increased faster over time for lobbying lenders than for other lenders. The result is robust to the inclusion of lender, MSA and year fixed effects, and MSA-year interactions. Moreover, columns (3) and (4) show that lobbying is also positively correlated with the growth of mortgage lending. This result is significant

Table 6
Lobbying Expenditures, Proportion of Loans Sold, and Credit Growth Dependent variable: Alternative measures for loan-to-income ratio

Dependent variable at (lender, MSA, year) level →	Proportion of loans sold		Credit growth	
	(1)	(2)	(3)	(4)
Lobbying expenditures on specific issues (in logs), lagged	**.007*** [.000]**	**.007*** [.000]**	**.318** [.130]**	**.321*** [.118]**
Assets (in logs)		−.000** [.000]		−.113** [.047]
Market share of lender		.216*** [.026]		−27.736** [12.114]
Average income of loan applicants (in logs)		.002*** [.000]		.740*** [.079]
Number of observations	406,035	406,035	406,996	385,701
R^2	.01	.01	.00	.00
MSA fixed effects	Yes	Yes	Yes	Yes
Year fixed effects	Yes	Yes	Yes	Yes
Lender fixed effects	Yes	Yes	Yes	Yes
MSA*year fixed effects	Yes	Yes	Yes	Yes

Notes: The regressions are run on the lender-MSA-year panel from 2000–2007. Lobbying on specific issues refers to lobbying on bills and regulations related to mortgage lending and securitization. Assets vary at the lender-year level. Market share of lender and average income of loan applicants are calculated for each lender separately in each MSA using the loan applications and originations by the lender in a particular MSA in a given year. Standard errors denoted in parentheses are clustered at the lender-MSA level.
* Significant at the 10% level.
** Significant at the 5% level.
*** Significant at the 1% level.

at the 1% level, suggesting that lobbying lenders, through faster expansion of their mortgage loan portfolios, tend to lend more aggressively. In terms of magnitudes, a one standard deviation increase in lobbying expenditures is associated with an 11% increase in the proportion of loans securitized and a 3 percentage point rise in credit growth.

D. Mortgage Lending by Lobbying Lenders and Delinquency Rates

We relate delinquency rates in 2008 in a given area (recall from Section IV that our data on delinquency rates are at the MSA level) to the growth of lobbying lenders' market share during 2000–2006. Our explanatory variable measures the expansion of mortgage loans by lobbying lenders *relative to* the expansion of such loans by all lenders during the period of interest. Specifically, we estimate the following cross-sectional empirical model:

$$dr_{m,2008} = \alpha + \theta \cdot \overline{gmsh}_m + \mu \cdot X_m + \eta \cdot Z_m + \varepsilon_{m'} \tag{4}$$

where $dr_{m,2008}$ is the MSA level delinquency rate as of 2008, $\overline{gmsh}_m$ is the average annual growth rate of the total market share of lobbying lenders in the MSA over 2000–2006, X_m is a set of MSA characteristics, and Z_m is a set of mortgage loan characteristics and lender characteristics averaged at the MSA level. The coefficient of interest θ captures the partial correlation between delinquency rates and the growth rate of mortgage lending by lobbying lenders relative to nonlobbying competitors.

Regression results reported in table 7 show that delinquency rates in 2008 were significantly higher in MSAs in which mortgage lending by lobbying lenders has expanded relatively faster than mortgage lending by other lenders. This result is robust to the inclusion of various MSA-level characteristics, including characteristics of the mortgage market such as the share of subprime loans and the number of lenders (column [1]). These control variables ensure that the correlation does not reflect the fact that lobbying lenders may have expanded faster in areas that ex post suffered more from the decline in house prices, or that had a higher proportion of risky borrowers, or that were affected more by the economic downturn. The exclusion of states in which the housing boom-bust cycle was more severe (Arizona, California, Florida, and Nevada) ensures that mortgage market outcomes of these four states are not driving the results (column [2]). The estimated effect is economically significant: a one standard deviation increase in the relative growth of

Table 7
Lending by Lobbying Lenders and Delinquency Rates

	(1)	Excl. CA, FL, NV, and AZ (2)	(3)	IV: 2SLS (4)	IV: LIML (5)
Growth in market share of lenders lobbying on specific issues (average 2000–2006)	.718*** [.152]	.662*** [.147]	.734*** [.158]	2.052** [.816]	2.064** [.825]
Growth in market share of lenders lobbying on other issues (average 2000–2006)			−.022 [.059]		
F-test of excluded instruments				9.63	9.63
Observations	305	253	305	305	305
R^2	.53	.61	.53	.34	.33
Hansen's J stat (p value)				.744	.745

Notes: Dependent variable: Delinquency rate in 2008 at MSA level. The regressions are run on the MSA cross-section. Lobbying on specific issues refers to lobbying on bills and regulations related to mortgage lending and securitization. All regressions include controls for average income, GDP growth rate, self-employment rate, unemployment rate, population, number of competing lenders, number of loan applications, share of subprime loans, share of Hispanics, and share of college graduates (averages over 2000–2006 for each MSA). We also include house price appreciation, which is the cumulative change in house prices from 2000 to 2006. In columns (4) and (5), growth in market share of lenders lobbying on specific issues is instrumented by the initial market share of lenders lobbying on specific issues weighted by the distance of headquarters to DC (in logs) and the initial market share of lenders lobbying on unrelated issues weighted by the distance of headquarters to DC (in logs). Robust standard errors are in brackets.

* Significant at the 10% level.
** Significant at the 5% level.
*** Significant at the 1% level.

mortgage loans of lobbying lenders is associated with almost a 1.5 percentage point increase in the delinquency rate.

We perform two tests to address concerns that, even if we included many control variables, omitted factors could still be driving the correlation between delinquency rates and the expansion of lobbying lenders. First, as in the analysis of loan characteristics at origination, we make use of a falsification test to show that the expansion of mortgage lending by lobbying firms does not merely reflect lender characteristics that may be correlated with a general propensity to lobby. Indeed, we find no statistically significant relationship between delinquency rates and the relative expansion of mortgage lending by lenders that lobbied on *other* issues (column [3], table 7).

Second, we develop an instrumental variable strategy. As a first instrument, we consider the combined 1998 market share in the MSA of lenders who lobbied on specific issues, in which each lender's initial market share is weighted by the distance between each lender's headquarters and Washington, DC. This instrument is valid if (a) the initial presence of a lender in an MSA is predetermined and is not correlated with lending conditions that prevailed in this MSA in the following years; and (b) the distance between a lender's headquarters and Washington, DC—a proxy for certain costs of lobbying—is uncorrelated with lending conditions in any specific MSA. The correlation between this instrument and the endogenous variable is negative (first stage results are available upon request), potentially because a smaller initial market share coupled with low cost of lobbying results in faster subsequent growth of lobbying lenders in that area. We consider a second instrument defined in a similar way (initial market share weighted by the distance variable), but using instead the initial market share of lenders lobbying on *other* issues. The sign of the correlation between this instrument and the endogenous variable is positive possibly because, in MSAs in which these other lenders have a larger initial presence, lenders lobbying on specific issues may intensify their lobbying and lending activities and gain market share even more when these other lenders have a higher cost of lobbying and a high initial market share.

Regression results confirm the conclusions of our ordinary least squares (OLS) estimations (column [4], table 7). When instrumenting the variable of interest, the coefficient increases significantly, suggesting that there might be an attenuation bias in the OLS estimates. Moreover, the Hansen J test does not reject the validity of the instruments. Furthermore, to allay concerns of weak instrument bias, we also make

use of the Limited Information Maximum Likelihood (LIML) estimator known to be more robust to weak instrument bias and confirm the
two-stage least squares (2SLS) results (column [5], table 7). All in all, the
evidence is suggestive of a causal relationship between the expansion of
mortgage lending by lobbying institutions and subsequent delinquency
rates.

E.   Stock Price Returns during the Crisis

Following the methodology developed in recent studies assessing the
value of political connections (Fisman 2001; Faccio 2006; and Fisman
et al. 2006), we perform an event study around the major events of the
financial crisis and ask whether lenders that lobbied on specific issues
experienced abnormal stock market returns during the month the event
took place.[25] We consider the following empirical specification:

$$R_{ie} = \alpha + \beta \cdot l_i + \gamma \cdot X_i + \varepsilon_i, \tag{5}$$

where R_{ie} is the ex-dividend monthly return on firm i's stock over the
event period e, l_i is a dummy for financial institutions that lobby on
specific issues during 1999–2006, X_i is a set of control variables, and ε_i
is a residual.[26] We use the market- and risk-adjusted return defined as
the stock return adjusted for the predicted return based on the capital
asset pricing model (CAPM).[27] If lobbying was systematically related to
risk-taking and the quality of loans made, then we would expect lobbying lenders to have lower abnormal returns during negative events and
higher abnormal returns during positive events.

We consider three major events of the crisis, namely, the collapse of
two key investment banks (negative events) and the government's ultimate response to the turmoil in the financial system (a positive event).
The event dates are: (a) March 11–16, 2008 (JP Morgan acquired Bear
Stearns after Fed provides $30 billion in nonrecourse funding; Fed ex-
panded liquidity provision); (b) September 15–16, 2008 (Lehman Brothers filed for bankruptcy while AIG was bailed out); and (c) October, 14,
2008, when the bailout program was announced.

Regression results are reported in table 8. Our analysis indicates that
lenders that lobbied on specific issues experienced negative abnormal
returns during the collapse of key financial institutions, suggesting that
these lenders were significantly more exposed, directly or indirectly,
to bad mortgage loans. Finally, lobbying lenders experienced positive
abnormal returns during the announcement of the Troubled Asset Re-

Table 8
Lobbying and Abnormal Stock Returns

Market Event	Bear Stearns and Lehman Failures (1)	Lehman Failure (2)	Bailout Announcement (3)
Dummy = 1 if lender lobbies on specific issues	**−.207**** **[.090]**	**−.365**** **[.175]**	**.301***** **[.106]**
Dummy = 1 if regulator is HUD	−.044 [.106]	−.091 [.204]	−.18 [.143]
Dummy = 1 if lender is subprime	.210** [.096]	.373** [.185]	−.105 [.122]
Assets (in logs)	−.017 [.014]	−.033 [.026]	.018 [.018]
Mortgage loans originated/assets	.0000 [.000]	−.0001 [.000]	−.0003** [.000]
Number of observations	92	45	45
R^2	.14	.22	.37

Notes: Dependent variable: Market- and risk-adjusted return at lender level. Market- and risk-adjusted return is the stock price return over the month of the event, adjusted for the predicted return based on a CAPM where the market portfolio is proxied by the stock price index of financial institutions in the S&P500. Market events around which market- and risk-adjusted returns are analyzed are (1) March 11–16, 2008: JP Morgan acquired Bear Stearns after Fed provided $30 billion in nonrecourse funding; (2) September 15–16, 2008: Lehman Brothers filed for bankruptcy and the authorities stepped in to rescue AIG; and (3) October 14, 2008: Troubled Asset Relief Program (TARP) making $700 billion available for asset purchases was announced. The dummy for lobbying on specific issues is equal to 1 if the lender lobbies for those issues in any year during 1999–2006. Lobbying on specific issues refers to lobbying on bills and regulations related to mortgage lending and securitization. The HUD and subprime dummies are equal to one if the lender was HUD regulated or subprime respectively in any year during 1999–2007. Assets and mortgage loans to assets are for the year 2006. Event fixed effects are included in column (1). Robust standard errors are in brackets.
* Significant at the 10% level.
** Significant at the 5% level.
*** Significant at the 1% level.

lief Program (TARP), potentially implying that the market anticipated lobbying lenders to be more connected to the policymakers and have higher chances of benefiting from the bailout. Note that the estimated coefficient on the lobbying dummy does not merely reflect the effect of a specialization of the lender considered (as proxied by the subprime dummy or by total mortgage loans originated in proportion to total assets). We also control for the size and exposure to mortgages of the lender as a proxy for size, but find no significant effect on abnormal stock returns.

The coefficient of interest is statistically significant at conventional levels for all three events. Moreover, the estimated effects are very large. Lobbying financial institutions lost on average 21% during the 2008 events. The differential loss of value is even more impressive during the Lehman failure: a 37% additional loss of value when returns are adjusted for the market correlation. The results suggest that these financial institutions were significantly more exposed to bad mortgage loans than other financial institutions. However, these institutions gained 27% when TARP was announced.

F. Lobbying and Bailout

In this section, we examine whether the likelihood of getting bailed out in 2008 is correlated with lobbying in 2000–2006. We estimate the following regression specification:

$$\text{Bailout}_{i,2008} = \alpha + \beta \text{LOBBY}_{i,2000-06} + \mu \cdot X_i + \varepsilon_i, \qquad (6)$$

where $\text{Bailout}_{i,2008}$ is a dummy that is 1 if the lender got funds under TARP or the amount of TARP funds received by lender (in logs). $\text{LOBBY}_{i,2000-06}$ is either a dummy equal to 1 if the lender lobbied on specific issues in any year between 2000–2006 or the sum of lobbying expenditures during 2000–2006. The specification controls for a number of lender level characteristics, which include proxies for their size, proxies for specialization (whether they are regulated by HUD, or whether they are classified as subprime lenders by HUD), the average income level of the borrowers, and, importantly, the average LIR of the loans they originated over 1999–2006 as an additional control for the riskiness of their mortgage loan portfolio over this period.

The regression results are shown in table 9. We find that lenders who lobbied were more likely to be bailed out (columns [1] and [2]) and received larger amounts of TARP funds (columns [3] and [4]). Lastly, lenders that spent more on lobbying activities received a bigger piece of the cake (columns [5] and [6]). In terms of magnitude, lobbying lenders are 7% more likely to be bailed out (for comparison, less than 1% of the lenders in the data set were bailed out), yet a one standard deviation increase in lobbying expenditures is associated with a relatively small 0.4% increase in the TARP funds received. Another interesting finding is that larger lenders were more likely to be bailed out, as suggested by the positive and statistically significant coefficient on the two proxies for size—assets and market share. This is in line with the too-big-to-fail argument.[28]

Table 9
Lobbying and Bailout

Dependent Variable at (Lender) Level →	Dummy = 1 if the Lender got Funds under TARP		TARP Funds Received by Lender (in Logs)			
	(1)	(2)	(3)	(4)	(5)	(6)
Dummy = 1 if lender lobbies on specific issues	.073*** [.018]	.069*** [.018]	1.683*** [.404]	1.582*** [.405]		
Lobbying expenditures on specific issues (in logs), total over 2000–2006					.035*** [.010]	.032*** [.011]
Assets (in logs)		.001*** [.000]		.033*** [.007]		.031*** [.007]
Dummy = 1 if regulator is HUD		.003** [.001]		.062** [.030]		.054* [.029]
Dummy = 1 if lender is subprime		-.003 [.004]		-.083 [.084]		-.067 [.074]
Market share of lender		.079* [.042]		1.695* [.925]		1.720* [.920]
Average income of loan applicants (in logs)		.000 [.000]		.007 [.010]		.013 [.010]
Loan-to-income ratio (averaged over 1999–2006)		.001 [.001]		.022 [.025]		.028 [.025]
Observations	13,315	13,172	13,315	13,172	14,041	13,883
R^2	.03	.03	.03	.03	.02	.02

Notes: Dependent variable: Bailout probability/amount at lender level. The regressions are run on the lender cross-section. The dummy for lobbying on specific issues is equal to 1 if the lender lobbies for those issues in any year during 1999–2006. Lobbying on specific issues refers to lobbying on bills and regulations related to mortgage lending and securitization. In columns (1) and (2), the dependent variable is 1 if the lender or any of its affiliates were granted funds under the Troubled Asset Relief Program (TARP) and 0 otherwise. In columns (3) to (6), the dependent variable is the amount, in logs, of funds received by the lender under TARP. Large lenders are defined by the top quartile of lobbying lenders (in terms of assets). Columns (2), (4), and (6) include lender-level controls for assets and dummies for HUD regulation and subprime and market share of lender and average income of loan applicants (calculated for each lender separately in each MSA using the loan applications and originations by the lender in a particular MSA and then averaged across MSAs and years). Loan-to-income ratio, averaged for each lender across MSAs and over the years from 1999 to 2006, is also introduced as a right-hand-side variable to control for the riskiness of the mortgage loan portfolio over this period. Robust standard errors are in brackets.
* Significant at the 10% level.
** Significant at the 5% level.
*** Significant at the 1% level.

G. *Discussion of Results*

To summarize, lobbying was associated ex ante with more risk-taking at mortgage origination as measured by higher LIR, higher securitization rates, and faster mortgage credit expansion. Ex post, delinquency rates were higher in areas in which lobbying lenders expanded their mortgage lending more aggressively. Moreover, lobbying lenders had negative abnormal stock returns during the Bear Stearns rescue and the collapse of Lehman Brothers, but positive abnormal stock returns around the date the bailout package was announced. Finally, lobbying lenders were more likely to be bailed out than other lenders.

While these results should not be interpreted as establishing a causal link between lobbying and mortgage lending, taken together, they are consistent with the stories outlined in Section III. Certain lenders were more likely to benefit from lax regulation. These lenders lobbied more aggressively; the ensuing lax regulatory environment let them take more risks and exposed them to worse outcomes during the crisis. In addition, the evidence is consistent with the market anticipating that lobbying lenders would be more likely to benefit from the bailout and they indeed did.

There may be several characteristics that determine whether lenders are more likely to benefit from lax regulation. First, these lenders may be specialized, for example, in catering to borrowers with lower income levels or in areas with higher average property prices. They may lobby to signal their information on special lending opportunities, thereby preventing tighter regulation that would otherwise limit growth in their particular segments. In the empirical analysis, we include explicit controls, for example, whether the lender is subprime or is regulated by HUD, size of the lender (which may be another proxy for specialization if specialized lenders are smaller), and the average income level of borrowers, to capture certain kinds of specialization effects. The coefficient on lobbying variable remains significant, so the results are not much likely to be driven by lenders specialized along these dimensions (although they may still be driven by specialization along other dimensions).

Second, certain lenders may be overly optimistic and may have underestimated the likelihood of an adverse event affecting the mortgage market more than other financial intermediaries did.[29] Owing to a genuine and systematic underestimation of default probabilities, overly optimistic lenders might have lobbied to inform the policymaker of the "true" state of the world and prevent a tightening of lending laws. Then, they may have taken more risks ex ante and had higher exposures to bad loans ex post. Interestingly, we find that the difference in LIR of originated loans between lobbying lenders and other lenders was even larger during 2005–2007, implying that lobbying lenders relaxed their lending standards more during this period (see column [7] of table A4 in the appendix). It is not clear why lobbying lenders would have become even more overly optimistic during the years when signs of stress in the housing market were becoming visible. Moreover, one would expect that if lobbying lenders were genuinely expecting better prospects for mortgage loans, they would have securitized at a slower pace in order to keep these loans in their balance sheets rather than shift risks, contrary to what we find in the data.

Third, certain lenders may have a greater desire or ability to exploit high short-term gains associated with riskier lending strategies. These lenders lobby to prevent a tightening of lending laws that may reduce the benefits associated with short-termist strategies emphasizing short-term gains over long-term profit maximization. Short-termism can lead to moral hazard and result in more risk-taking ex ante and worse performance ex post.[30]

A more cynical alternative story could be that certain lenders lobby the policymaker to increase their chances of preferential treatment, for example, a lower probability of scrutiny by bank supervisors or a higher probability of being bailed out in the event of a financial crisis. This in turn could lead to moral hazard and induce lenders to originate loans that would appear riskier ex ante.[31] Assuming all else equal, these loans would have a higher probability of default ex post. On the one hand, lobbying on *any* issue should establish connectedness, increase chances of getting preferential treatment, and enhance incentives to take more risk. However, as discussed in table 3, lobbying on other issues was not significantly associated with risk-taking, which weakens the case for such motives for lobbying. On the other hand, there is evidence that large lenders were the ones lobbying more aggressively and ultimately getting bailed out with a higher probability. These suggest that lobbying might have been driven in part by too-big-to-fail concerns and, in turn, by expectations of preferential treatment.

It is empirically extremely difficult to pin down the most likely motivation for the financial industry's lobbying during our sample period. Ultimately, we do not know the exact activities on which lobbying expenditures are spent. If lobbying lenders are specialized or overly optimistic, their motive for lobbying appears to be consistent with information-based theories, which assert that lobbying firms have better information than the policymakers and partly reveal their information by endogenously choosing their lobbying effort (Potters and van Winden 1992; Lohmann 1995; Grossman and Helpman 2001). If lobbying lenders are short-termist or lobby to increase the chances of preferential treatment, their motive for lobbying seems to fit better with theories of rent-seeking, where lobbying firms compete for influence over a policy by strategically choosing their contribution to politicians (Bernheim and Whinston 1986; Grossman and Helpman 1994).

While we cannot firmly tell apart alternative theories of information dissemination and rent seeking, we can try to distinguish the channels through which lobbying was associated with lending: relaxation of rules or earning preferential treatment. Specifically, lenders differ in their capacity or willingness to take risks: some lenders are the risky type and are more likely to benefit from (a) relaxation of lending rules, and (b) discretion of regulators favoring them over others, for example, less supervision or perceived insurance against adverse outcomes. These risky lenders lobby more and they take more risk (a) if lobbying efforts are successful and the lending rules remain/become lax, and (b) if they are under less scrutiny or have insurance.

To what extent is ex ante risk-taking by lobbying lenders explained by changes in regulations, that benefits many lenders (free riding), or by anticipation/realization of firm-specific favors? We do a simple test that can help us quantify the relative magnitudes of these two channels. First, taking LIR in 1999 (after purging the MSA effects) as an indicator of initial risk bearing, we label the lenders in the top quartile as the risky type. Let $\Delta\text{LIR}_R^{L-NL}$ be the difference in the LIR during 2000–2007 (after purging the MSA and year effects) of the risky type between the lobbying and nonlobbying lenders. Since the lenders we are comparing are the same type and, hence, benefit the same way from the same rules, we do not expect to observe any difference in risk-taking due to the effect of lobbying on lending rules. Therefore, any difference can be attributed to expectation/realization of firm-specific benefits associated with lobbying.

Similarly, let $\Delta\text{LIR}_{NL}^{R-LR}$ be the difference in the LIR during 2000–2007 (after purging the MSA and year effects) of nonlobbying lenders between the risky and less-risky types. With relaxation of rules, nonlobbying risky lenders free-ride and increase their LIR while the less-risky types do not have the capacity to take as much risk. So, any difference can be attributed to free-riding.

In the end, we compare $\Delta\text{LIR}_R^{L-NL}$ and $\Delta\text{LIR}_{NL}^{R-LR}$ to evaluate the relative magnitudes of the two channels. We find that both differences are positive and statistically significant at the 1% level. Moreover, they are roughly the same magnitude with $\Delta\text{LIR}_R^{L-NL} = 0.14$ and $\Delta\text{LIR}_{NL}^{R-LR} = 0.16$ (7 and 8% of the sample average LIR, respectively). Consequently, the association we establish between lobbying and lending in our sample period appears to be driven equally by both channels: changes in rules and preferential treatment.

VI. Conclusion

This paper studies the relationship between lobbying by financial institutions and mortgage lending during 2000–2007. To the best of our knowledge, this is the first study documenting how lobbying may have contributed to the accumulation of risks leading the way to the current financial crisis. We carefully construct a database at the lender level combining information on loan characteristics and lobbying expenditures on laws and regulations related to mortgage lending and securitization. We show that lenders that lobby more intensively on these specific issues engaged in riskier lending practices ex ante, suffered from worse outcomes ex post, and benefited more from the bailout program.

While pinning down precisely the motivation for lobbying is difficult, our analysis suggests that the political influence of the financial industry contributed to the financial crisis by allowing risk accumulation. Therefore, it provides some support to the view that the prevention of future crises might require a closer monitoring of lobbying activities by the financial industry and weakening of their political influence. However, the precise policy response would depend on the true motivation for lobbying. Specialized rent-seeking for preferential treatment such as bailouts would require curtailing lobbying as a socially nonoptimal outcome. Distorted incentives due to short-termism linking risky lending and lobbying would require public intervention in the design of executive compensation. If, however, lenders lobbied mainly to inform the policymaker and promote innovation, lobbying would remain a socially beneficial channel to facilitate informed decision making.

Endnotes

We would like to thank the participants at the IMF Research Brown Bag Seminar, 2009 NBER Summer Institute, Center for Analytical Finance (Indian School of Business) 2009 Summer Research Conference in Finance, World Bank Macroeconomics Seminar, De Nederlandsche Bank 12th Annual Research Conference, Wharton/FIRS/JFI Workshop on the Financial Crisis, IMF 10th Jacques Polak Annual Research Conference, Toulouse School of Economics Conference on the Political Economy of the Financial Crisis, University of Maryland, and 2010 NBER Political Economy Program Meeting for useful discussions and suggestions. Sumit Aneja, Mattia Landoni, and Lisa Kolovich provided excellent research assistance. For acknowledgments, sources of research support, and disclosure of the authors' material financial relationships, if any, please see http://www.nber .org/chapters/c12416.ack. Deniz Igan: digan@imf.org; Prachi Mishra: pmishra@imf.org; Thierry Tressel: ttressel@imf.org. The views expressed here are those of the authors and do not necessarily represent those of the IMF or IMF policy. This paper was also issued as IMF Working Paper 09/287.

1. Simpson, Glenn, "Lender Lobbying Blitz Abetted Mortgage Mess," Wall Street Journal, December 31, 2008; available at http://online.wsj.com/public/article_print /SB119906606162358773.html. See also the Financial Times front page coverage of the Center for Public Integrity study linking subprime originators (a large share of which are now bankrupt) to lobbying efforts to prevent tighter regulations of the subprime market ("U.S. Banks Spent $370 Million to Fight Rules," May 06, 2009, available at http://www .ft.com/cfms/s/0/a299a06e-3a9f-11de-8a2d-00144feabdc0.html?nclick_check=1).

2. For a detailed account of the subprime mortgage crisis, see Gorton (2008a, 2008b) and Diamond and Rajan (2009).

3. A sample lobbying report, shown in the appendix table A2, filed by Bear Stearns and Co. to the Senate's Office of Public Records (SOPR) documents that the company lobbied to change regulations related to mortgage lending standards for the period January to June 2007.

4. Securitization may weaken monitoring incentives leading to lower-quality loans, hence increasing risk in the financial system. This is why increasing recourse to securitization may be a sign of riskier loan origination. For an analysis of the correlation between fast credit growth and risk, see Dell'Ariccia and Marquez (2006).

5. See Acemoglu (2009) for a similar argument on how the financial industry sets its own rules.

6. See Johnson (2009) for a similar view.

7. For instance, Mayer, Pence, and Sherlund (2009) show that no-documentation, no down-payment loans represented a large share of rapidly-growing subprime lending between 2001 and 2006. Mian and Sufi (2009) find that the expansion in subprime lending is highly correlated with the increase in securitization, a finding consistent with distorted incentives. Dell'Ariccia, Igan, and Laeven (2008) provide evidence that areas in which lenders relaxed loan standards more also experienced larger increases in subprime delinquency rates.

8. For example, among the top twenty lenders lobbying on specific issues, six were also among the top ten underwriters of collateralized debt obligations during 2005–2008 ("Vampire Squished," The Economist, April 24, 2010).

9. See, for instance, Snyder (1990); Goldberg and Maggi (1999); Gawande and Bandyopadhyay (2000).

10. Data sources include the Bureau of Economic Analysis (BEA), the Bureau of Labor Statistics (BLS), the Census Bureau, and the Office of Federal Housing Enterprise Oversight (OFHEO).

11. North Carolina was the first state to pass an anti-predatory lending law in 1999 and other states followed suit. By 2007, all but six states have some form of anti-predatory lending law in place.

12. The data can be downloaded from http://bailout.propublica.org/main/list /index.

13. "General issue area codes" are provided by the SOPR and listed in line 15 of the lobbying reports while the "specific lobbying issues" are listed in line 16. See appendix for more details on what the reports look like and a full list of general issues as well as that of specific issues selected for the analysis.

14. For robustness, we adopt an alternative splitting approach that distributes expenditures, using as weights the proportion of reports that mention the specific issues of interest. The results remain the same.

15. Sixteen of the twenty lenders that spent the most on lobbying between 2000 and 2006 received funds provided by the government under the TARP. In total, lenders that lobbied on specific issues received almost 60% of the funds allocated.

16. Recall from Section IV that lobbying activities are reported at the lender level and do not vary across MSAs.

17. Free-riding problems may bias the estimated coefficient if lenders also benefit from lobbying activities of others. However, the bias will be small if the externality is common to all other lenders, as the average effect of the externality will be absorbed by year fixed effects (or by MSA-year fixed effects if the externality to other lenders depends on the MSAs in which a lender is active).

18. See, for instance, Sirota (2003).

19. As noted in Section IV, subsection E, there is a stark difference in terms of size between lobbying and nonlobbying lenders. In order to allow for nonlinear effects of size that may stem from this difference, we introduce the square of log assets as an additional variable in the regressions. The results remain unaltered.

20. LOBAM is assumed to be equal to $1 when a lender does not lobby.

21. We conduct further robustness tests for: (a) clustering at MSA level; (b) exclusion of outliers; (c) alternative split of total expenditures into specific and nonspecific issues based on share of reports; (d) alternative measure of lobbying expenditures, scaled by the importance of the regulations for which the firm lobbies, giving more weight to lobbying for bills that appear more often in the lobbying reports; (e) using lobbying expenditures scaled by assets; and (f) taking into account lobbying expenditures by bankers' associations. The main result that more lobbying is associated with higher LIR remains unaltered (see table A4 in the Appendix). Another potential concern could be that there are lender-specific time trends that drive the propensity of a lender to take risk as well as to lobby. To address this concern, we augment equation (2) with $s_i \cdot t$ and the coefficient on lobbying remains positive and statistically significant at the 1% level.

22. For a 10% increase in LOBAM, the outcome variable changes by $dy_{imt} = \delta \cdot d \ln \text{LOBAM}_{imt-1} = \delta \cdot \ln(\text{LOBAM}_{imt-1}/\text{LOBAM}_{imt-2}) \approx \delta \cdot 0.1$.

23. Keys et al. (2009) use a similar identification strategy based on state lending laws in their analysis of securitization and monitoring incentives. A potential concern is that state lending legislation efforts may be affected by the financial industry's overall lobbying activities; however, lobbying at the *federal* level is less likely to influence any individual state's decision to pass a law. Moreover, what we are interested in is the differential response of lobbying versus nonlobbying lenders to the regulatory changes once a law comes into effect rather than the causal effect of the law.

24. In some cases, a single MSA contains areas in several states. Then we assume that the MSA has a law in place if any one of the states does.

25. There exists a key difference with the approach of these papers that quantify the value of political connections. They conduct the event study around periods of news under the assumption that these news a priori specifically affect politically connected firms only, while other firms should not be directly impacted, and confirm the initial hypothesis. In our case, however, all firms are a priori potentially affected by the market news, but we show that the effect of news on market value varies systematically across financial intermediaries according to lobbying behavior in a direction that is consistent with our hypothesis.

26. Monthly stock returns are computed from the end of the previous month to the end of the month considered.

27. The market- and risk-adjusted return is defined as: $Abnormal\_return_{ie} = R_{ie} - K_{it}$ where $K_{it} = a_i + b_i \cdot R_{mt}$, where a_i and b_i are firm-specific coefficients estimated over 2007–2008, and R_{mt} is the market return (proxied by the return on the stock market index of banks in the S&P500). The results presented in this section are robust if we consider (a) simple stock return or (b) the mean-adjusted return, defined as the stock return of firm i adjusted for its mean over 2007–2008.

28. The results shown in table 9 are estimated by OLS; they are also robust to using probit. These results should be interpreted with caution as unobserved lender-level characteristics could be driving our results.

29. For example, rating agencies and sponsors severely underestimated the probability of default and loss given default when assigning ratings to mortgage-backed securities (Calomiris 2009).

30. Short-termism in executive compensation is explored theoretically by, among others, Bolton, Scheinkman, and Xiong (2006), while empirical evidence on whether distorted incentives contribute to excessive risk-taking is mixed (Agarwal and Wang 2009; Cheng, Hong, and Scheinkman 2010; Fahlenbrach and Stulz 2009). In policy circles, flaws in compensation contracts have become a key issue since the crisis (see, for instance, a speech by the Fed Chairman Bernanke at http://www.federalreserve.gov/news events/speech/bernanke20091023a.htm).

31. See Tressel and Verdier (2011) for a model of regulatory forbearance of banks emphasizing this moral hazard channel.

References

Acemoglu, D. 2009. "The Crisis of 2008: Structural Lessons for and from Economics." Working paper, MIT.

Agarwal, S., and F. H. Wang. 2009. "Perverse Incentives at the Banks? Evidence from a Natural Experiment." Working paper, Federal Reserve Bank of Chicago.

Berger, A., and G. Udell. 2004. "The Institutional Memory Hypothesis and the Procyclicality of Bank Lending Behavior." *Journal of Financial Intermediation* 13:458–95.

Bernheim, B. D., and M. D. Whinston. 1986. "Menu Auctions, Resource Allocation, and Economic Influence." *Quarterly Journal of Economics* 101 (1): 1–31.

Bertrand, M., F. Kramarz, A. Schoar, and D. Thesmar. 2004. "Politically Connected CEOs and Corporate Outcomes: Evidence from France." Working paper, University of Chicago.

Bolton, P., J. Scheinkman, and W. Xiong. 2006. "Executive Compensation and Short-Termist Behaviour in Speculative Markets." *Review of Economic Studies* 73:577–610.

Bostic R., K. Engel, P. McCoy, A. Pennington-Cross, and S. Wachter. 2008. "State and Local Anti-Predatory Lending Laws: The Effect of Legal Enforcement Mechanisms." *Journal of Economics and Business* 60:47–66.

Braun, M., and C. Raddatz, 2010. "Banking on Politics: When Former High-ranking Politicians Become Bank Directors." *World Bank Economic Review,* Oxford University Press, vol. 24 (2): 234–79.

Calomiris, C. 2009. "The Subprime Turmoil: What's Old, What's New, and What's Next." *Journal of Structured Finance* 15 (1): 6–52.

Cheng, I.-H., H. Hong, and J. Scheinkman. 2010. "Yesterday's Heroes: Compensation and Creative Risk-Taking." NBER Working Paper no. 16176. Cambridge, MA: National Bureau of Economic Research, July.

Claessens, S., E. Feijen, and L. Laeven. 2008. "Political Connections and Preferential Access to Finance: The Role of Campaign Contributions." *Journal of Financial Economics* 88 (3): 554–80.

Dell'Ariccia, G., D. Igan, and L. Laeven. 2008. "Credit Booms and Lending Standards: Evidence from the Subprime Mortgage Market." Center for Economic and Policy Research (CEPR) Discussion Paper no. 6683.

Dell'Ariccia, G., and R. Marquez. 2006. "Lending Booms and Lending Standards." *Journal of Finance* 61 (5): 2511–46.

Diamond, D. W., and R. Rajan. 2009. "The Credit Crisis: Conjectures about Causes and Remedies." NBER Working Paper no. 14739. Cambridge, MA: National Bureau of Economic Research, February.

Facchini, G., A. M. Mayda, and P. Mishra. 2011. "Do Interest Groups Affect U.S. Immigration Policy?" *Journal of International Economics* 85(1): 114–28.

Faccio, M. 2006. "Politically Connected Firms." *American Economic Review* 96 (1): 369–86.

Faccio, M., and D. C. Parsley. 2009. "Sudden Deaths: Taking Stock of Geographic Ties." *Journal of Financial and Quantitative Analysis* 44:683–718.

Fahlenbrach, R., and R. M. Stulz. 2009. "Bank CEO Incentives and the Credit Crisis." NBER Working Paper no. 15212. Cambridge, MA: National Bureau of Economic Research, August.

Fisman, D., R. Fisman, J. Galef, and R. Khurana. 2006. "The Cheney Effect: Valuing Political Connections in America." Working paper, Columbia University.

Fisman, R. 2001. "Estimating the Value of Political Connections." *American Economic Review* 91:1095–102.

Gawande, K., and U. Bandyopadhyay. 2000. "Is Protection for Sale? Evidence on the Grossman-Helpman Theory of Endogenous Protection." *Review of Economics and Statistics* 82(1): 139–52.

Goldberg, P. K., and G. Maggi. 1999. "Protection for Sale: An Empirical Investigation." *American Economic Review* 89 (5): 1135–55.

Gorton, G. 2008a. "The Panic of 2007." Paper presented at the proceedings of the 2008 Jackson Hole Conference, "Maintaining Stability in a Changing Financial System," Federal Reserve Bank of Kansas City.

———. 2008b. "The Subprime Panic." NBER Working Paper no. 14398. Cambridge, MA: National Bureau of Economic Research, October.

Grossman, G. M., and E. Helpman. 1994. "Protection for Sale." *American Economic Review* 84:833–50.

———. 2001. *Special Interest Politics*. Cambridge, MA: MIT Press.

Harstad, B., and J. Svensson. 2008. "From Corruption to Lobbying and Economic Growth." Working paper, Kellogg School of Management.

Johnson, S. 2009. "The Quiet Coup." *The Atlantic*, May. http://www.theatlantic.com/doc/200905/imf-advice.

Johnson, S., and T. Mitton. 2003. "Cronyism and Capital Controls: Evidence from Malaysia." *Journal of Financial Economics* 67:351–82.

Keys, B. J., T. Mukherjee, A. Seru, and V. Vig. 2010. "Did Securitization Lead to Lax Screening? Evidence from Subprime Loans." *The Quarterly Journal of Economics* 125 (1): 307–62.

Khwaja, A., and A. Mian. 2005. "Do Lenders Favor Politically Connected Firms? Rent Provision in an Emerging Financial Market." *Quarterly Journal of Economics* 120 (4): 1371–411.

Kiyotaki, N., and J. Moore. 1997. "Credit Cycles." *Journal of Political Economy* 105:211–48.

Kroszner, R., and P. Strahan. 1999. "What Drives Deregulation? Economics and Politics of the Relaxation of Bank Branching Restrictions." *Quarterly Journal of Economics* 114 (4): 1437–67.

Kroszner, R., and T. Stratmann. 1998. "Interest-Group Competition of Congress: Theory and Evidence from Financial Services' Political Action Committees." *American Economic Review* 88 (5): 1163–87.

Lohmann, S. 1995. "Information, Access, and Contributions: A Signaling Model of Lobbying." *Public Choice* 85:267–84.

Ludema, R., A. M. Mayda, and P. Mishra. 2010. "Protection for Free: An Analysis of U.S. Tariff Exemptions." CEPR DP no. 7951, IMF Working Paper no. 10/211.

Mayer, C., K. Pence, and S. M. Sherlund. 2009. "The Rise in Mortgage Default." *Journal of Economic Perspectives* 23 (1): 27–50.

Mian, A., and A. Sufi. 2009. "The Consequences of Mortgage Credit Expansion: Evidence from the U.S. Mortgage Default Crisis." *Quarterly Journal of Economics* 124 (4): 1449–96.

Mian, Atif, Amir Sufi, and Francesco Trebbi. 2010a. "The Political Economy of the Subprime Mortgage Credit Expansion." NBER Working Paper no. 16107. Cambridge, MA: National Bureau of Economic Research, June.

———. 2010b. "The Political Economy of the U.S. Mortgage Default Crisis." *American Economic Review* 100 (5): 1967–98.

Potters, J., and F. Van Winden. 1992. "Lobbying and Asymmetric Information." *Public Choice* 74:269–92.

Sirota, D. 2003. *Essentials of Real Estate Finance*. Chicago: Dearborn Financial Publishing.

Snyder, J. M. 1990. "Campaign contributions as investments: The US House of Representatives 1908–1986." *Journal of Political Economy* 61:195–206.

Stigler, G. 1971. "The Theory of Economic Regulation." *Bell Journal of Economics and Management Science* II:3–21.

Tressel, T., and T. Verdier. 2011. "Financial Globalization and the Governance of Financial Intermediaries." *Journal of the European Economic Association* 9 (1): 130–75.

Comment

Jeremy C. Stein, *Harvard University and NBER*

This very interesting paper poses the following question in the first line of the abstract: "Has lobbying by financial institutions contributed to the financial crisis?" This is fundamentally a question about the causal effects of lobbying activity. The thrust of my comments in what follows is that the paper has some striking and extremely useful findings about a number of factors that are correlated with lobbying activity, but that it does not really deliver an answer to the causal question it starts with. This is, of course, not to say that the hypothesis is implausible, or incorrect. Like many other observers, I strongly suspect that lobbying, and political influence more broadly, can have a number of pernicious effects on legislative and economic outcomes, both in this case and in many others. And the circumstantial evidence in this paper is certainly consistent with this view. But there is little in the way of a smoking gun.

To clarify, note that there are several distinct questions that one could ask about lobbying activity in the current context. The first question is one about the determinants of lobbying: looking across banks, what factors explain their lobbying expenditures on issues relating to mortgage lending and securitization? Here, the paper uses the rich data set that the authors have assembled to provide a clear answer: at the level of individual financial institutions, lobbying is associated with a number of hallmarks of aggressive lending behavior, including lower credit quality, faster loan growth, and heavier use of securitization. It also tends to be carried out by much larger firms, consistent with there being economies of scale in lobbying, as well as free-riding effects.

A second question one might ask is whether lobbying works—whether the firms that spend money on lobbying see any tangible return on their investment in terms of legislative outcomes. This question is not taken up here, though recent work by Mian, Sufi, and Trebbi (2010) suggests that the answer is yes. They find that during the years of the subprime mortgage expansion, mortgage industry campaign contributions increasingly predicted the voting patterns of US representatives on housing-related legislation.

A third question is whether lobbying expenditures have a causal effect on various ex post outcomes, including loan delinquencies, and the likelihood of a given bank being bailed out. The paper offers some statistically significant correlations here, but it seems to me that any attempt at causal interpretation is problematic. There is an obvious tension at work: this is ultimately a paper that aims to address both the causes and consequences of lobbying—that is, one that seeks to put lobbying on both the left-hand side and the right-hand side of the regression. Absent a convincing instrument for lobbying, this is a hard trick to pull off. Moreover, the paper's success on the first task undermines its ability to take on the second. For if we learn that those banks that lobby have different characteristics than those that do not—and in particular that they were more aggressive in their lending behavior—we should not be surprised to find that they are also more likely to wind up with delinquent loans, or to be bailed out ex post. But this could all be driven by their different underlying lending strategies, not by the fact that they lobbied per se.

With respect to the determinants of lobbying behavior, the paper documents that either a dummy for lobbying, or total lobbying expenditures, is positively correlated with a bank's average loan-to-income ratio, as well as with its rate of credit growth, and the proportion of loans that it sells off.[1] A natural interpretation of these findings is that banks have heterogeneous business strategies, and some are innately predisposed to be more aggressive on a number of dimensions. For example, some banks may—by virtue of either their geographic location, their customer bases, or their organizational culture—naturally have a comparative advantage in lending to low credit-quality subprime-type borrowers. If so, these banks would have a greater economic interest in lobbying to expand or maintain subprime lending opportunities.

One might label this mechanism an "Angelo Mozilo effect," in honor of the former CEO of Countrywide, one of the most aggressive subprime lenders in the period leading up to the crisis. Mozilo, who was subsequently named by Condé Nast Portfolio as the second-worst CEO of all time, and who was charged by the Securities and Exchange Commission (SEC) with securities fraud and insider trading, was heavily involved in political influence; his now-notorious "Friends of Angelo" VIP lending program is one example of this effort to curry favor with influential political figures. Of course, it would be strange to say that Mozilo's attempts at political influence caused Countrywide to lend in the reckless manner it did. Rather, both were likely manifestations of some unobserved underlying set of determinants—Mozilo's personality, Countrywide's business model, and so forth.

This observation strongly colors how one interprets the remaining results in the paper. For example, table 7 documents that there were more delinquencies in 2008 in those MSAs where the market share of lobbying lenders grew most rapidly over the period 2000–2006. This result is intuitive, but it need not imply anything about the causal consequences of lobbying. Instead, in the spirit of the Mozilo analogy, it could simply be that lobbying lenders had more aggressive underwriting practices ex ante, or were located in MSAs where there were more high credit-risk borrowers to begin with. Similarly, when table 8 shows that the stock prices of lobbying lenders fell by more around the time of the Bear Stearns and Lehman failures, and rose by more on announcement of the TARP, this is exactly what one would expect if lobbying lenders had engaged in ex ante riskier lending. There is also likely to be a mega-bank effect at work in table 8 that is not adequately picked up by the linear size controls: the very biggest banks, who are much more prone to lobby, may also be the most exposed to negative spillovers from a systemic meltdown. If so, they would naturally tend to have stock prices that move more sharply on days when there is news that has implications for the probability of such an event.

Finally, the place where I feel that the paper is overreaching the most is in its interpretation of the results in table 9, which asks whether banks that engaged in lobbying were more likely to either receive TARP money, or to get a larger TARP allocation. The authors motivate this analysis by referring to a January 23, 2009 *Wall Street Journal* story that reads in part: "Troubled One United Bank in Boston didn't look much like a candidate for aid from the Treasury Department's bank bailout fund last fall. . . . Nonetheless, in December One United got a $12 million injection from the Treasury's Troubled Asset Relief Program, or TARP. One apparent factor: the intercession of Rep. Barney Frank, the powerful head of the House Financial Services Committee."

Whatever truth there is to this one story, I do not see that table 9 adds much further evidence in terms of making the case that lobbying had a causal effect on TARP allocations. Given that we know that lobbying banks were making riskier loans and as a result had gotten themselves into worse trouble by 2008, we would expect them to be getting more TARP money even if the program were being administered with no political influence whatsoever. Indeed, it would be surprising if the result came out any other way.

There are a couple of other caveats about the analysis in table 9. First, it is not clear to me that it excludes the original group of the nine largest banks who were called into Treasury Secretary Paulson's office on October 13, 2008, and collectively asked to take nondiscretionary TARP allocations totaling $125 billion. If these banks are not excluded from the analysis, this could skew the results, since they are very likely, simply by virtue of their scale, to have been involved in lobbying activity.

A second caveat is specific to the intensive-margin regressions in table 9, which look at total TARP dollars allocated to a given bank. The TARP program was designed so that, conditional on a bank's application to the TARP being approved, the dollar amount that the bank would received was determined by a preset formula, with an upper bound equal to 3% of its risk-weighted assets. Thus, even if there was some favoritism in the approval process, it probably does not make sense to look at dollar amounts as opposed to simply a dummy for receiving TARP funds. Indeed, any incremental results in these columns are likely to be picking up a purely hard-wired effect: big banks lobby more than small banks, and also have higher ratios of risk-weighted assets to raw assets. Given that the regressions only have a linear control for raw assets, this will create the appearance that lobbying is associated with larger dollar allocations, when in fact this is just the workings of the preset formula.

Again, let me emphasize that none of my objections should be taken to imply that I find the authors' premise about political favoritism in the operation of the TARP to be uninteresting or a priori implausible. Quite to the contrary: the concern that there might have been political influence in TARP allocations is obviously one that deserves to be taken very seriously, and subject to careful empirical analysis. However, the data in table 9 are simply not up to the task. It seems to me that to even make a start on this question, one would need to look not just at ex post TARP allocations, but rather at all the applications to the program, both those that were accepted and those that were rejected. In particular, one might ask whether, controlling for the criteria that should have legitimately shaped the decision by regulators to accept or reject an application (e.g., various measures of a bank's health, or its lending opportunities), it is the case that lobbying expenditures, or some other objective measure of political influence, exerted an independent effect on the accept/reject decision. While one can still imagine methodological pitfalls with this approach, it would clearly be a big step in the right direction.

Endnotes

For acknowledgments, sources of research support, and disclosure of the author's material financial relationships, if any, please see http://www.nber.org/chapters/c12417.ack.

1. One caveat to these results is that lobbying firms are much bigger than nonlobbying firms—if I am reading the summary statistics in table 2 correctly, they imply that the median assets of lobbying firms is 600 times bigger ($19B versus $30M). If so, it might be important to control more expansively for firm size than with a simple log of assets term. A hint that this issue could be relevant comes from table 4, where firm fixed effects cut the estimates of the coefficients of interest by a factor of about three.

Reference

Mian, Atif, Amir Sufi, and Francesco Trebbi. 2010. "The Political Economy of the Subprime Mortgage Expansion." Working Paper, University of Chicago.

Comment

Luigi Zingales, *University of Chicago and NBER*

Has lobbying by financial institutions contributed to the financial crisis? The question that Igan, Mishra, and Tressel (IMT) set themselves to address is of the highest importance. They are trying to show, in econometric terms, what Morgenson and Rosner (2011) claim to show in a narrative way in their recent book, *Reckless Endangerment: How Outsized Ambition, Greed, and Corruption Led to Economic Armageddon.* As the title suggests, Morgenson and Rosner claim that the lobbying power of the banking sector has weakened the regulatory environment and that this weakening is one of the main culprits of the financial crisis. Igan et al. are a bit softer in their claim, but the two theses are substantially the same.

To argue that lobbying by financial institutions contributed to/caused the financial crisis, one has to establish four results: (1) that lobbying by financial institutions distorted the policy formation process; (2) that this undue influence was crucial to create a lax regulatory environment; (3) that this lax regulatory environment caused a large number of bad loans; (4) that these bad loans were the major cause of the crisis.

Personally, I believe in all four of these logical steps, with the possible exception of the last one. Still, I am not sure this paper adds much to my conviction. It does, however, strengthen my belief that lobbying firms are generally corrupt and inefficient firms and that lobbying, at least to the extent it takes place now in the United States, is highly distortive. But let's go in order.

Does Lobbying Distort the Policy Formation Process?

Interest groups can legally influence the policy formation process through two main channels: campaign finance contributions and lobbying activities in the executive and legislative branches. Igan et al. purposefully limit themselves to the second channel, since the first has received more attention in the literature. While their assessment is correct, this self-imposed restriction negatively impacts their ability to identify the distortive nature of the lobbying process. When we look at campaign contributions it is easier to identify the quid pro quo aspect (see, for example, Goldberg and Maggi 1999 and Gawande and Bandyopadhyay 2000). It is more difficult to do so when we look at pure lobbying, since this lobbying has a legitimate purpose, which is difficult to separate from the distortionary one.

According to the *American League of Lobbyists* website, "[l]obbying is a legitimate and necessary part of our democratic political process. Government decisions affect both people and organizations, and information must be provided in order to produce informed decisions. Public officials cannot make fair and informed decisions without considering information from a broad range of interested parties. All sides of an issue must be explored in order to produce equitable government policies."[1] So the positive view of lobbying is that it provides necessary information for policymakers to do their job properly.

Is Igan and colleagues' evidence inconsistent with this benign view of lobbying? Because of my role as a discussant, let me play the devil's advocate a bit and try to see whether a coherent information-based story of lobbying is consistent with all their results. Imagine that some new lenders have a proprietary technology to better identify people who are creditworthy. Existing lenders who do not have that technology will lobby to restrict new entrants from the market. Since they cannot ban a new entry directly, they will try to do so indirectly, shutting down the market where the new lenders have the strongest comparative advantage: the market for high-risk borrowers. The newcomers will fight back. In fact, in a very optimistic view of the world, where the more efficient firms will win the lobbying battle because they have more resources to fight (Becker 1983), the new lenders will lobby more on this issue and win. Unfortunately, this technology is introduced during a real estate bubble, and when the bubble bursts, the lenders who specialized in the more risky segment of the market are hit hardest: their technology was better at detecting the idiosyncratic components of risk, but not the systematic ones. Being hit the hardest, they are also the ones that end up receiving more funds from the Troubled Asset Relief Program.

I am not claiming this is an accurate description of what happened, but only that it is a possible alternative story, which is perfectly consistent with Igan and colleagues' findings. Hence their findings, while not inconsistent, do not prove that the first logical step is true.

Igan et al. acknowledge this limitation several times in their paper. Still, they could have done more to address it. At the very least, they could have cited more extensively the growing literature documenting that connections are a big part of lobbying. For example, Blanes i Vidal, Draca, and Fons-Rosen (2010) find that lobbyists who worked in a US senator's office suffer a 24% drop in revenue when that senator leaves office. Since it is hard to imagine that a lobbyist loses 24% of his ability to inform when his former boss loses his senate seat, it must be that at least one-quarter of a lobbyist's value is given by his connections. Similarly, Bertrand, Bombardini, and Trebbi (2011) show that in the issues they work on, lobbyists follow the politicians they were previously connected to, rather than sticking to the issues. Thus, it appears as if the most valuable component of their human capital is *who* they know, not *what* they know, a result hardly consistent with lobbying being mostly about information.

The second, more costly, way Igan et al. could have addressed this problem is by linking the lobbying data to the campaign contributions by the financial industry and the votes representatives and senators cast on the key pieces of legislation. This is what is done in Mian, Sufi, and Trebbi (2010).

Finally, another piece of evidence in favor of a causal link could have been obtained by looking at whether there is a correlation between the lobbying ex ante and the number of legal suits brought against these companies ex post. If lobbying is a sign of corrupt companies and not just of companies that are willing to take more risk, then this should manifest it in the frequency of illegal behavior.

Was Lobbying Crucial in Creating a Lax Regulatory Environment?

Even if I believe that lobbying can and often is distortionary, it is not fair to blame it for all that goes wrong. In other words, the relevant question is whether the regulatory environment would have been significantly different without the lobbying of the financial industry.

Consider the antipredatory law in Georgia, which was designed to protect subprime lenders. As Morgenson and Rosner (2011) describe, what killed the law in Georgia was not lobbying but Standard & Poors, who announced that it would not allow mortgage loans that originated in Georgia into any mortgage-backed securities pool it rated. The reason was that the Georgia law created a liability for any institution that participated in a securitization containing a loan that might be considered predatory. Even Morgenson and Rosner (2011) admit that the lobbyists had only to circulate the S&P press release to overturn the law. This is a clear case where lobbyists' effort might have been inframarginal. The same happened in New Jersey.

The same is also true for the mandatory counseling pilot program introduced in Illinois in September 2006 and terminated only 20 weeks later. An Illinois law firm described the reasons for this premature termination as follows:

The Program came under fire from community organizations and civic leaders, who raised serious concerns that certain individuals were being wrongly targeted, based solely on race. In addition, the initial implementation of HB 4050 resulted in fewer mortgage loans being made in certain zip codes targeted by the Program. A report from the University of Illinois demonstrated that housing sales in the targeted zip codes dropped nearly 50 percent, while those in nontargeted zip codes declined only 20 percent. As a result, Governor Blagojevich suspended the initial Program Jan. 19, 2007.[2]

Was this program killed by lobbyists? According to the Counseling Agencies that participated to the pilot program, it was very successful. "More than half of the borrowers referred for File Review could not afford the loan they were being given by their mortgage broker/loan originator and 9% of the file reviews showed indicia of fraud."[3] Nevertheless, the program was very unpopular. Agarwal et al. (2010) show that in the ten treated zip codes, the legislation caused a 65% drop in the number of mortgage applications, a 35% decline in the number of active lenders, about 47% decline in the number of originated purchase-related mortgages, and 77% decline in the number of originated refinancing mortgages. The reduction in the supply of credit was so extreme, that the program was terminated by popular demand. Mortgage brokers, especially those specialized in subprime mortgages, celebrated the demise of the program. I am quite confident that they also lobbied against it. Are they responsible for its demise? No. The real estate bubble was like a party gone wild, where borrowers were demanding the change to take crazy loans as drunks demand booze. Are just the bartenders responsible if too much alcohol was served? No. The customers have their fair share of responsibility. Furthermore, in a democracy it is difficult for a regulator to lean against the popular consensus. And the customers, not only the bartenders, wanted the party to continue.

In sum, I do not doubt that lobbyists pushed for the party to continue, but would the party have ended much earlier if they did not? I doubt it.

Did This Lax Regulatory Environment Cause the Large Number of Bad Loans?

At some level the response to this question is obvious. If regulation had rigidly enforced a down payment of 50% and a total debt-to-income ratio below 2%, very few loans would have defaulted and even the one that defaulted would not have caused many losses. Yet, such rigid guidelines would have reduced dramatically the number of loans available. Furthermore, even before the subprime bubble the lending standards were much lower than this. The down payment was below 20% and in computing the ratio of annual income to mortgage costs, most lenders used a lower teaser rate, rather than an actual rate.

Thus, the more relevant (and difficult to answer) question is whether the subprime bubble was caused by a relaxation of lending standards below what was common in the United States before. To answer this question, it is useful to distinguish between a macro effect, where we take into consideration the effect that a relaxation of lending standards has on the equilibrium prices of houses, and a micro effect, where prices are exogenously determined.

From a macro point of view, Mian and Sufi (2009) show that the greater availability of credit has contributed to the rise in real estate prices, especially in the subprime areas. They focus on securitization, not relaxation of the lending standards. Keys et al. (2010) show the existence of a connection between securitization and relaxation in lending standards. This relaxation, however, is not caused by reduced regulation, but by the incentive of the underwriter. While it is possible that a more aggressive regulatory stance could have reduced the relaxation of these standards, there is no evidence either in Igan et al. or in Keys et al. (2010) that this is the case. In fact, Keys et al. (2009), who look at the relation between regulatory tightness and lending standards, find that more regulated entities do not relax their lending standards less.

From a micro point of view, the existence of a connection between relaxed regulation and bad loans have been convincingly shown by Jiang, Nelson, and Vytlacil (2010) and Rajan, Seru, and Vig (2010). By looking at one large underwriter Jiang et al. (2010) show that low documentation loans perform significantly worse than full doc loans by the same underwriter, even accounting for all observables. They also find that, unlike for full doc loans, borrower's information for low documentation loans does not predict default well, suggesting it is either inaccurately recorded or intentionally falsified.

Similarly, Rajan et al. (2010), who look at lenders representing more than 90% of the subprime mortgages, find that low doc loans performed worse than full doc loans. They also find that observable information for low doc fails to predict defaults—more so for borrowers for whom "soft" information might be important.

In sum, while logically one could argue that prohibiting low doc loans would have reduced the number of bad loans, there is no evidence that a more lax regulatory environment leads to a higher number of bad loans.

Were These Bad Loans the Major Cause of the Crisis?

Paradoxically, the weakest link in the logical argument is the connection between the bad loans and the overall financial crisis. I say "paradoxically" because this link is a foregone conclusion in most of the popular discussion. Nevertheless, we need to distinguish between the effect of the real estate bubble and the marginal effect due to the bad loans. As before, if all loans required 50% down, even the bursting of a real estate bubble would not have had very dramatic effects. Thus, the crucial dimension to establish this link is the interpretation of the word bad. If by "bad" we mean fraudulent, I posit that the link is far from clear. In the Jiang et al. (2010) paper, for instance, the difference in default between low doc and full doc loans was only 5 to 8 percentage points. Yet the increment in default rates during the crisis was much, much higher.

As figure 1 shows, the difference in cumulative default rates across various default vintages was enormous. After 24 months the 2005 subprime vintage had only 10% of cumulative default, versus almost 30% for 2006 and more than 40% for 2007. The large surge in defaults in 2006–2007 was present also in the full doc loans, albeit the difference between low and full doc defaults increased (see Rajan et al. 2011). Thus, the main cause of the increase in defaults seems to be a macro factor, not a micro one.

We arrive at the same conclusion if we analyze the result of the Illinois experiment. The mandatory counseling pilot program that decreased by 47% the number of purchase-related mortgages and by 77% the refinancing was able to reduce the ex post default rates only by 3 to 4 percentage points. Even with the most aggressive counseling and eradication of liar loans, regulation could have reduced mortgage default rates by less than a third. Fraudulent loans are terrible and people

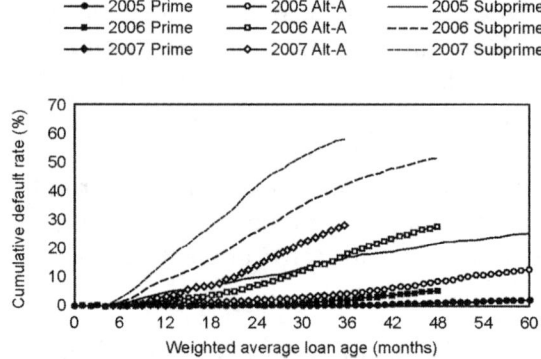

Fig. 1. Overall cumulative defaults (active plus closed defaults) by first-quarter vintage and product type.

Source: Standard & Poor, "U.S. Residential Mortgage Default Index: Defaults Are Waning But Cumulative Default Rates Remain Extremely High for Recent Vintages," May 24, 2010.

who consciously underwrote them should be prosecuted. Still, it is far from clear that they were the main cause of the crisis.

Conclusions

Before the development of modern medicine, every time there was an epidemic a few people were unjustly accused of spreading the disease and ended up lynched or executed in the public square. These killings did not prevent future epidemics, but they did calm public anxiety and fulfilled the desire of public authorities who wanted to be seen as proactive. Economics is not as developed as modern medicine, but fortunately is not as primitive as premodern medicine. With sufficient data we do have methods to identify the potential causes of a phenomenon. Most of the time, the limits are imposed by the data availability, not by our methodology.

The Financial Crisis Inquiry Commission, nominated by Congress, was supposed to collect the necessary data and analyze it so as to provide an accurate report of what happened. Unfortunately, it wasted its time in political squabbles and provided no data. Thus, three years after the crisis we are still wondering should take the most blame.

As with most big trends, the crisis was probably the combination and the interaction of several factors: a very lenient monetary policy, very lax lending standards, and heavy lobbying to keep the previous two in place. Igan et al. do an excellent job in showing how these phenomena are correlated. More micro data are needed to try to tease out the casual link.

Endnotes

For acknowledgments, sources of research support, and disclosure of the author's material financial relationships, if any, please see http://www.nber.org/chapters/c12418.ack.
   1. http://www.alldc.org/publicresources/lobbying.cfm
   2. http://www.reedsmith.com/library/search_library.cfm?FaArea1=CustomWidgets.content_view_1&cit_id=14695
   3. http://www.nlihc.org/doc/repository/IL-Findings.pdf

References

Agarwal, Sumit, Gene Amromin, Itzhak Ben-David, Souphala Chomsiseng-pthet, and Douglas D. Evanoff. 2010. "Do Financial Counseling Mandates Improve Mortgage Choice and Performance?" Chicago Fed Working Paper.
Becker, G. 1983. "A Theory of Competition Among Pressure Groups for Political Influence." *Quarterly Journal of Economics* 98 (3): 371–400.
Bertrand, Marianne, Matilde Bombardini, and Francesco Trebbi. 2011. "Is It Whom You Know Or What You Know? An Empirical Assessment of the Lobbying Process." NBER Working Paper no. 16765. Cambridge, MA: National Bureau of Economic Research, February.
Blanes i Vidal, Jordi, Mirko Draca, and Christian Fons-Rosen. 2010. "Revolving Door Lobbyists." London School of Economics Working Paper.
Gawande, K., and U. Bandyopadhyay. 2000. "Is Protection for Sale? Evidence on the Grossman-Helpman Theory of Endogenous Protection." *Review of Economics and Statistics* 82 (1): 139–52.
Goldberg, P. K., and G. Maggi. 1999. "Protection for Sale: An Empirical Investigation." *American Economic Review* 89 (5): 1135–55.
Keys, Benjamin, Tanmoy Mukherjee, Amit Seru, and Vikrant Vig. 2009. "Financial Regulation and Securitization: Evidence from Subprime Loans." *Journal of Monetary Economics* 56 (5): 700–20.
———. 2010. "Did Securitization Lead to Lax Screening? Evidence from Subprime Loans." *Quarterly Journal of Economics* 125 (1): 307–62.
Jiang, Wei, Ashlyn Aiko Nelson, and Edward Vytlacil. 2010. "Liar's Loan? Effects of Origination Channel and Information Falsification on Mortgage Delinquency." Columbia University Working Paper.
Mian, Atif, and Amir Sufi. 2009. "The Consequences of Mortgage Credit Expansion: Evidence from the U.S. Mortgage Default Crisis." *Quarterly Journal of Economics* 124 (4): 1449–96.
Mian, Atif, Amir Sufi, and Francesco Trebbi. 2010. "The Political Economy of the U.S. Mortgage Default Crisis." *American Economic Review* 100 (5): 1967–98.
Morgenson, Gretchen, and Joshua Rosner. 2011. *Reckless Endangerment: How Outsized Ambition, Greed, and Corruption Led to Economic Armageddon.* New York: Times Books.
Rajan, Uday, Amit Seru, and Vikrant Vig. 2010. "The Failure of Models That Predict Failure: Distance, Incentives and Defaults." Working Paper.

Discussion

Alberto Alesina expanded on Zingales's discussion about Japanese nuclear plants. Alesina argued that in the example, the lobbying in Japan allowed nuclear plants to be built in highly seismic areas and to use outdated technologies, leading to a disaster when the earthquake struck. He argued that similar events happened in the US financial system: lobbying allowed banks to take extreme risks. Then he mentioned that the authors presented their paper as if they had three results: more risk-taking, more default, and more bailouts due to lobbying. He argued that default and bailouts follow naturally from increased risk-taking and should not be regarded as separate results.

Frederic Mishkin proposed that the size of a firm can create a correlation between risk-taking and lobbying. He proposed that a bigger firm is more likely to be bailed out because of the too-big-to-fail problem, leading to greater risk-taking. Hence, bigger firms have more incentives to lobby because they receive the greatest benefits.

Xavier Gabaix gave an example of a possible positive effect of lobbying. He mentioned that genetically modified food is banned under current law in Europe. If the prohibition is due to the irrationally negative public attitude to these products, then allowing modified food could benefit society. If lobbyists were stronger in Europe then they could lobby to repeal the law.

Alesina mentioned that there is a sizable literature that addresses rent-seeking and information revelation issues in lobbying. In the models that consider these issues, lobbyists provide information but have incentives to provide biased information. The question is how to separate the information from bias. Acemoglu agreed that lobbying has a lot to do with expertise. He noted that the reality is more complex

than what is captured in the cheap talk models used to understand informative lobbying. He remarked that in the cheap talk models, the
receiver is always better off ex ante. However, the receiver in a lobbying environment is a politician who may not necessarily care about
the constituency he or she represents. Hence, cheap talk lobbying can
make a constituency worse off because the incentives of the receiver
are not necessarily aligned with his or her constituents. Next, Acemoglu referred to an empirical literature that tries to identify what lobbyists do. He cited Betrand, Bombardini, and Trebbi (2011) as a recent
example from this literature. One of the findings of this literature is that
politicians are very responsive to the views of moneyed interests. He
mentioned that there is some evidence that Democrats seem to have
shifted their positions when campaign financing was very important.
He remarked that Hacker and Pearson argue that a big shift in US politics came as campaign fund-raising become more important. Thus, it is
possible that lobbying was originally informative but has since become
a tool for helping politicians raise money. Prachi Mishra responded by
saying that it is very difficult to rule out the information alternative on
the basis of the lobbying expenditures because they do not have an experiment where firms sent messages without spending money.

Daron Acemoglu commented on the bailout result of the paper. He
mentioned that the evidence has identification issues, but he acknowledged that the authors are upfront about them. He reiterated Stein's
view that the authors add the size of banks as control variable to their
regressions. He thought that it would be interesting if the results sur-
vive under these additional controls. While the results may still not be
causally interpretable, it would show if the authors have just one result
in their paper, or more. Deniz Igan agreed that they have to control for
the size of the banks, but Hall argued that an unidentified result is of
little value.

Igan started her response by stating that they did not interpret their
results as causal. They used the word "contributed" in the text of the
paper in a loose way to mean that lobbying did stop certain regulations
from being adopted while it helped lax regulations to pass. This may
have allowed lenders to make riskier loans. Then, she addressed the
point raised by Stein that one has to think about the mechanism of allocation of bailouts before linking lobbying to bailouts. She believed that
lobbying activities do not necessarily always target politicians. She said
it is possible that the banks were trying to affect the regulators. Next,
Igan replied to Stein about the instrumental variable regression by say-

ing that they were thinking of removing the regression from the paper. Finally, Igan responded to the issue of the lobbying effect on politicians' voting. She said that they have a follow-up paper in which they study how lobbying expenditures affect politicians' voting outcomes. She added that not only did money spent affect the voting outcomes, but also the connection of a politician to a lobbyist. She added that they also study this connection channel in a follow-up paper.

5

Risk, Monetary Policy, and the Exchange Rate

Gianluca Benigno, *London School of Economics*
Pierpaolo Benigno, *LUISS Guido Carli, EIEF, and NBER*
Salvatore Nisticò, *Università di Roma La Sapienza and LUISS Guido Carli*

I. Introduction

One of the main features of the recent financial crisis has been the increase in financial and macroeconomic volatility. Currency markets have not been an exception: foreign exchange rate volatility has surged and large swings in the dollar exchange rate have occurred. How do changes in volatility affect exchange rates? Is the source of volatility, nominal or real, relevant for determining exchange rate fluctuations?

These are the questions that we address in this research by providing an empirical and theoretical analysis on the link between uncertainty and the exchange rate. The focus on uncertainty belongs to the tradition in international finance that has emphasized how variations in risk over time are essential for understanding the exchange rate. In fact, the large biases in the foreign-exchange forward premium that have been documented since Bilson (1981) and Fama (1984) constitute a compelling evidence of variations in risk premia as a rational-expectations explanation of the link between exchange rates and interest rates. Evidence of a time-varying risk component of the excess return in foreign-exchange market is further documented by the recent work of Menkhoff et al. (2011), who show that deviations from Uncovered Interest-rate Parity (UIP) can be accounted for in terms of compensation for risk.[1] They identify global foreign exchange volatility as a key factor.

We propose a theory of exchange rate determination based on exogenous risk factors in which the link between risk and the nominal exchange rate is guided by monetary policy through interest-rate rules.[2] The aim is to understand the role of exogenous risk factors in explaining the main regularities that we observe in international finance. To this purpose, we depart from most of the existing models of exchange rate determination, which study the impact of the first moments of exogenous variables on the nominal exchange rate, and examine the exchange rate's response to changes in the volatility of nominal and real shocks.[3] Moreover, the structure upon which we build our analysis between risk factors and exchange rates is a theory of nominal exchange rate determination based on interest rate rules (Benigno and Benigno 2008).[4]

This research contributes to the literature from an empirical and a theoretical perspective. In our empirical analysis we provide new evidence that justifies our focus on risk factors: the novelty of our contribution is to examine the role of nominal and real stochastic volatilities for the behavior of exchange rates in an otherwise standard open-economy VAR (Vector AutoRegression). We find that volatility shocks do matter for the equilibrium level of interest and exchange rates and that the exchange rate tends to appreciate in response to an increase in nominal volatility (both of the discretionary shock to monetary policy and of the inflation target) and to depreciate following an increase in real volatility (of the productivity shock). Moreover, the stylized facts reported by Eichenbaum and Evans (1995) about the response of interest and exchange rates to a shock to the level of the monetary policy instrument are not affected by the explicit consideration of time-varying volatility elements in the VAR.

In our theoretical model, the key channel through which exchange rates and uncertainty are related is a simple hedging motive. An increase in uncertainty does not necessarily lead to a depreciation of the currency: what matters is whether the currency is relatively safer when there is bad news. In this respect, uncertainty may improve the hedging properties of the currency leading to an increase in its demand and thereby an appreciation.

We develop a two-country open-economy model along the lines of Benigno and Benigno (2008), extended in two dimensions. As in Benigno and Benigno (2008), we assume differentiated home- and foreign-produced goods, international market completeness, nominal price rigidities, and interest rate rules; here, however, we allow for a more general specification of preferences as in Epstein and Zin (1989) and for stochastic volatility in the exogenous processes driving the economy.

In this direction, our contribution to the literature is to provide a general-equilibrium perspective on the ability of currently used models with stochastic volatility to explain international macro-finance facts.[5] From a modeling point of view, the general equilibrium analysis is crucial for examining the transmission mechanism of risk factors and generating a nontrivial interaction between shocks and the variables of interests. From an empirical point of view, the general equilibrium analysis allows us to compare the model's performance with the shocks and factors highlighted in the VAR.

The assumption of time-varying exogenous uncertainty entails nontrivial issues in the solution of the model. To this end, we apply a new method that we have recently developed for general dynamic stochastic models with time-varying uncertainty (Benigno, Benigno, and Nisticò 2010). The main result of our previous work is that a second-order approximation of the model is sufficient to account for a distinct and direct role of time-varying uncertainty on the endogenous variables, provided that the structural shocks are conditionally linear. In contrast, recent works have emphasized the need of relying on a third-order approximation (see Fernandez-Villaverde and Rubio-Ramirez 2010).[6] Our method has several advantages: it simplifies the computational burden, it reduces the degree of freedom that a third-order approximation would generate when evaluating the model performance through a calibration exercise and, finally, it allows us to evaluate time-varying risk premia, which in our case are second-order terms, through just a first-order approximation of the equilibrium conditions.

For a special case of our general model we are able to obtain analytical results. When purchasing power parity holds, prices are flexible and monetary policy is specified as a Taylor rule that reacts to either PPI (Producer Price Index) or CPI (Consumer Price Index) inflation, we obtain that an increase in the domestic volatilities of the nominal shocks appreciate the nominal exchange rate consistently with our empirical findings. Theoretically the excess return on home currency bonds decreases with an increase in nominal risk factors.

While this simple model is partly successful in capturing the link between nominal risk factors and the exchange rate, it fails in replicating other key international finance regularities. In fact, the implied slope coefficient from a UIP regression would still be positive. We then consider the case in which policy authorities smooth interest rates over time and find that, conditional on shocks to the monetary policy instrument, it is possible to obtain a negative coefficient in the UIP regression, which becomes more negative as the smoothing coefficient increases.

From a theoretical point of view we then explore the role of Epstein-

Zin preferences. First, in an open economy, cross-country surprises in utility influence the international distribution of wealth so that equilibrium quantities are also affected by the preference specification, unlike in the closed-economy case. Second, if we focus on the case in which the subjective discount factor is very close to the unitary value, then the surprises to utility depend, up to a first order, only on the stochastic trend in world productivity. The implication is that, in this case, nominal stochastic discount factors are highly correlated across countries, an aspect that is consistent with a global explanation for risk premia.

We then evaluate quantitatively the properties of our model by calibrating it following the recent empirical literature (see, e.g., Lubik and Schorfeide 2005). We focus on a small set of facts that are related to exchange rates. The response of exchange rates and excess returns to volatility shocks is consistent with our empirical findings. Moreover, we show that the specification of monetary policy and the presence of stochastic volatility terms is crucial for obtaining a negative coefficient in the UIP regression (as discussed in Backus et al. 2010).

A.   Related Literature

This paper is related to different strands of literature. From an empirical point of view, we build on the early analysis of Clarida and Gali (1994) and Eichenbaum and Evans (1995), which have examined the effects of monetary shocks on the exchange rate. Our contribution is to assess the role of real and nominal uncertainty on the exchange rate, whereas their focus is on the innovation in real and nominal shocks.

From a theoretical perspective there are two key elements in our analysis: stochastic volatility and monetary policy. The emphasis on exogenous risk factors is not novel in exchange rate economics: early contributions by Frankel and Meese (1987) in a partial equilibrium setting, and Hodrick (1989) in general equilibrium, have pointed out the role of uncertainty in explaining exchange rate determination. More recently Obstfeld and Rogoff (2002) have studied the role of risk factors in a general equilibrium model when nominal prices are sticky, focusing on money supply as the monetary-policy instrument. Our paper follows this tradition in international finance and it is also connected to a more recent macroeconomic literature that has examined the role and the effects that risk or uncertainty have on macroeconomic variables (see, for example, Bloom 2009; Bloom, Floetotto, and Jaimovich 2009; and Fernandez-Villaverde et al. 2009).

The importance of monetary policy using interest-rate rules in exchange rate determination has been analyzed in Benigno and Benigno (2008), while its role for the understanding of the uncovered interest rate parity puzzle has been first highlighted by McCallum (1994) and more recently by Backus et al. (2010). The latter authors have recast McCallum's insight in a microfounded setting endogenizing the currency risk premium that is exogenous in McCallum's model.

Our work is also related to a fast-growing literature in international macro-finance that has developed models of the risk premium based on specifications of the stochastic discount factors derived from alternative preferences. Bansal and Shaliastovich (2010) relies on Epstein-Zin preferences combined with long-run risk, Backus et al. (2010) emphasizes the role of monetary policy for addressing the uncovered interest rate parity puzzle in nominal terms, Gavazzoni (2009) relies on Epstein-Zin preferences combined with stochastic volatility, and Moore and Roche (2010) and Verdelhan (2010) propose models based on external habit with preferences à la Campbell and Cochrane (1999). While we share some of the features of these studies, our analysis follows a general equilibrium approach by combining macro and financial market equilibrium and builds upon a theory of nominal exchange rate determination based on interest rate rules. The latter aspect is important insofar as we want to address, from a model perspective, the UIP puzzle in nominal rather than in real terms, as most of these models do.

II. Empirical Evidence

In this section, we provide new empirical evidence on the importance of time-varying uncertainty in open economies through a simple VAR analysis along the lines of Eichenbaum and Evans (1995), which we take as our empirical benchmark. We aim at providing a quantitative assessment on the effects that innovations to the *volatility* of underlying disturbances may have on the *level* of macro variables of interest. In particular we focus on the conditional time-varying volatilities of three specific shocks that are going to play a relevant role in the theoretical model of the next sections: the conditional volatility of the monetary-policy shock, of the inflation-target shock, and of the productivity shock.[7] Our focus will be mainly to study how these shocks affect the nominal (and real) exchange rate and the foreign currency risk premium, which captures the deviations from UIP. However, we will also look at the responses of output, inflation, and the yield curve. Moreover, we will evaluate whether the results of Eichenbaum and Evans

(1995)—also investigated by a large body of subsequent literature—are robust to the inclusion of time-varying volatility into the picture.

We use monthly data for the G7 countries on the sample period ranging from March 1971 through September 2010, and estimate a VAR with six lags for each pair of countries that includes the United States.[8] We consider a benchmark specification with seven macroeconomic variables, in the spirit of Eichenbaum and Evans (1995). To this set of macro "level" variables, we then add three time series describing the time-varying volatilities of the monetary-policy shock ($u_{\xi,t}$), the inflation-target shock ($u_{\pi,t}$), and the productivity shock ($u_{a,t}$). The "level" variables that we consider are the US nominal Federal Funds Rate (i) indicating the stance of monetary policy, the US and foreign Industrial Production Indexes (y, y^*) measuring the domestic and foreign real activity, the US CPI Index (p) capturing the domestic price level, the foreign short-term nominal interest rate measured by the three-month Treasury Bill rate (i^*), the slope of the US term structure computed as the difference between the ten-year Treasury Constant Maturities rate and the three-month Treasury Bill rate ($i_{sl} \equiv i_{10y} - i_{3m}$), and the real exchange rate, defined as $q \equiv s + p^* - p$, where s denotes the nominal exchange rate, expressed in terms of units of US dollars (USD) needed to buy one unit of foreign currency.[9] As such, an increase in q (or s) denotes a USD real (nominal) depreciation. All variables are in logs, except for the interest rates, which are monthly percentage points.

A. Measuring Time-Varying Volatility

We now explain how we build the three conditional volatilities of interest. For the conditional volatility of the monetary-policy shock we use daily data from the Federal Funds futures markets, following Kuttner (2001), among others.

In particular, denoting with $f^0_{t,d}$ the spot-month futures rate on day d for a contract with delivery in month t (with day d belonging to month t), we can interpret $f^0_{t,d}$ as the conditional time $- d$ expectation of the average funds rate in month t, plus a stochastic risk premium μ:

$$f^0_{t,d} = E_d \frac{1}{m_t} \sum_{j \in t} i_{1,j} + \mu^0_{t,d},$$

where m_t is the number of days in month t and i_1 is the daily interest rate. To extract information about revisions in time $- d$ expectations about future monetary policy actions from data on f, Kuttner (2001) suggests to use the daily change in the futures rate, scaled up to account for the number of days in month t that are affected by the surprise: $(m_t/m_t - d)(f_{t,d}^0 - f_{t,d-1}^0)$. This measure seems particularly appealing because it reduces the distortions associated with the time variation in the risk premium μ.

As to our case, we use data on one-month futures rates rather than spot-month rates, $f_{t,d}^1$, where day d belongs to month $t - 1$ rather than t. As a consequence, any revision in policy expectations reflected in a daily change of the futures rate is related to the full month t, rather than a fraction of it. Therefore, in our case we can measure day $-d$ revisions in expectations about next-month monetary policy actions using the simple daily change in the futures rate: $(f_{t,d}^1 - f_{t,d-1}^1)$. In what follows we will denote with $u_{\xi,t}^2$ the variance of the monetary policy surprise in month $t + 1$ conditionally on information available in month t and we use, as an approximate measure of such conditional variance, the empirical second moment, within month t, of daily revisions in expectations of time $t + 1$ monetary policy actions:

$$ u_{\xi,t} \approx \sqrt{\frac{1}{m_t} \sum_{d=2}^{m_t} (f_{t,d}^1 - f_{t,d-1}^1)^2}. $$

Since data for the Fed funds futures rates are only available starting October 1988, we complete the time series with realized volatilities, within the month, computed using daily data on the effective federal funds rate—net of settlement Wednesdays—standardized to the mean and variance of the measure coming from the futures market, for the period where the two measures overlap (correlation over that period is about .6).

For the inflation-target shock, we measure the conditional volatility with the Merrill Lynch Option Volatility Estimate (MOVE). Movements in the inflation target can produce parallel shifts in the yield curve.[10] Indeed, the MOVE Index can capture the volatility of this level factor since it is a yield curve weighted index of the normalized implied volatility on one-month Treasury options, which are weighted on the 5-, 10-, and 30-year contracts. Since this index starts only in 1989, we complete the time series with the realized volatility, within the month, computed using daily data on US 10-year Treasury bonds; since the MOVE is an index, moreover, we standardize it to the mean and variance of the realized volatility, for the period where the two measures overlap (correlation over that period is about .8).

Finally, we build an approximate measure of the volatility of the pro-

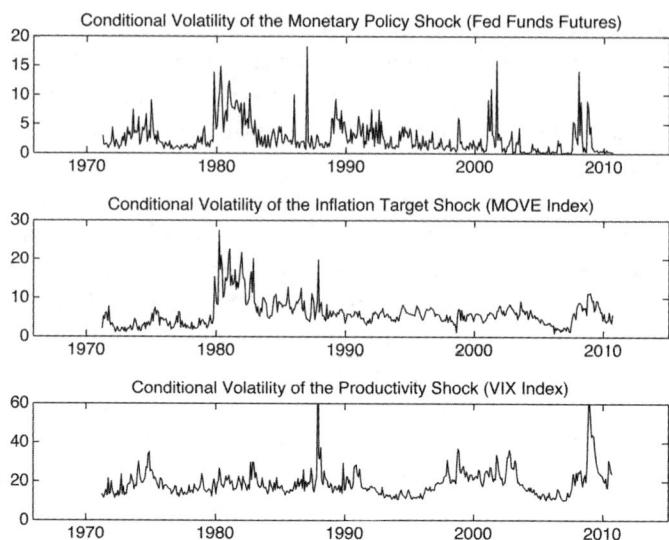

Fig. 1. Time-varying conditional volatilities, standard deviations in percentage points
Note: The y-axis of the bottom panel has been truncated at 60 for the sake of readability; the value of the index around Black Monday is actually about 87.

ductivity shock using the stock market option-based implied volatility, the VIX index (monthly averages of daily data). However, since data for the VIX are only available starting January 1990, we follow the approach of Bloom (2009) and complete the time series with within-month realized volatilities computed using daily returns on the S&P500, standardized to the mean and variance of the VIX, for the period where the two measures overlap (correlation over that period is about .9).

As a last step, since all aforementioned measures are based on implied and realized volatilities, we construct the *conditional* volatilities considering the fitted values of an AR(1) regression for each indicator, similarly to Bekaert and Engstrom (2009). Figure 1 displays the dynamic properties of the obtained indicators.

B.   VAR Analysis

For each pair of the G7 countries that includes the United States, we then estimate the following VAR(p) model

$$\mathbf{y}_t = \mathbf{A}(L)\mathbf{y}_{t-1} + \mathbf{e}_t, \tag{1}$$

where the data vector is defined as $\mathbf{y}_t \equiv [u_{\xi,t}, u_{a,t}, u_{\pi,t}, y_t, p_t, i_t, i_{sl,t}, i_t^*, q_t, y_t^*]'$, and the lag-order is six. This ordering allows for a contemporaneous response of the interest rate to domestic output and the price level, consistently with a Taylor-type monetary policy rule and with our empirical benchmark (see Eichenbaum and Evans 1995). As to the order in which the volatility measures enter the VAR, our choice is driven by how volatility is modeled in the theoretical framework of the next sections. Indeed, we build a model in which volatility shocks are allowed to have contemporaneous effects on the endogenous variables; however, in order to apply the approximation methods developed by Benigno, Benigno, and Nisticò (2010), we restrict our attention to conditionally-linear stochastic processes for the underlying structural disturbances of our theoretical model, implying contemporaneous orthogonality between "level" shocks and volatility measures. In order to be consistent with these features of our theoretical approach, in the VAR we place the volatility measures before all the other variables. As to the volatility measures, since the MOVE index might also be affected by the volatility of monetary policy or productivity shocks, we place it last among the three volatility indexes. On the other hand, since the monetary-policy volatility measure is built directly from data on the Federal Funds Market, we see it as very tightly related to monetary policy: we therefore assume that it is not affected contemporaneously by any other volatility measure and thus place it first.

Figures 2 through 5 display the dynamic response of selected variables to, respectively, a "classic" monetary-policy shock (the orthogonalized innovation to the level of the Federal funds rate), an innovation to the volatility of the monetary-policy shock, an innovation to the volatility of the shock to the inflation target, and an innovation to the volatility of the productivity shock. Each panel reports the point estimate of the impulse response function—the solid line—and the associated one-standard-deviation confidence intervals—the dashed lines. In each figure, the first row displays the dynamic response of the US Federal Funds Rate, the second row the response of the real exchange rate, the third the response of the excess return on foreign currency, and the last one shows the response of the slope of the yield curve.[11] In particular, the excess return on foreign currency is defined as

$$exr_t \equiv i^*_{1,t} - i_{1,t} + E_t \Delta s_{t+1},$$

and measures deviations from the UIP condition.

Figure 2 addresses the robustness of the findings of Eichenbaum and Evans (1995). The responses to a contractionary shock to monetary policy seem virtually unaffected by the explicit consideration of the interplay between time-varying volatility and the "level" variables. In

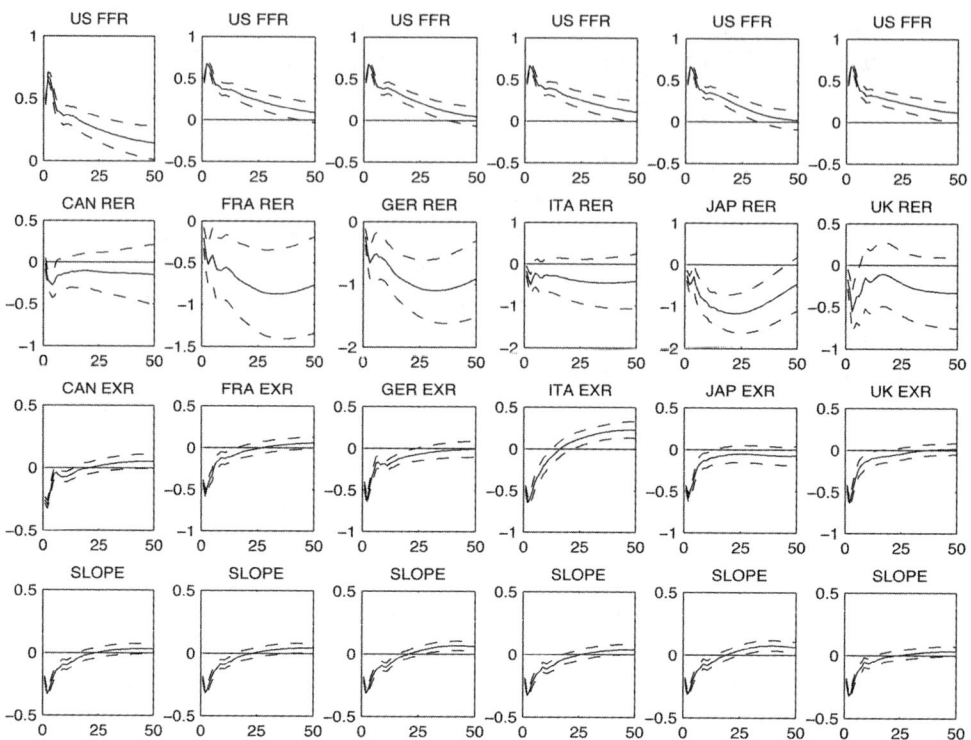

Fig. 2. Dynamic responses to an orthogonalized innovation to the Federal Funds Rate
Notes: Each column reports, for each country pair, the responses of the US Federal Funds
rate (i), the RER (q), the foreign currency risk premium (exr), and the slope of the US term
structure (i_{sl}). x-axes: months, y-axes: annual percentage points. Country pairs are, respectively, US-Canada, US-France, US-Germany, US-Italy, US-Japan, US-UK.

particular, a positive innovation to the Federal Funds Rate implies a
significant appreciation of the USD, on impact. Moreover, the exchange
rate appreciates also in the transition, and starts depreciating only in
the medium run. Second, the spread between foreign and domestic
short-term interest rates decreases gradually through the implied, less-
than-proportional increase in the foreign one (not shown). Finally, the
two previous results drive the persistent deviations from UIP shown
in the third row, in the form of positive excess returns on US securities.
Additionally, figure 2 also shows the negative response of the slope of
the yield curve.

Figures 3, 4, and 5 present our new evidence on the importance
of volatility shocks. The first result, common to all three figures, is that
shocks to volatility indeed do affect the level of the other macro va-

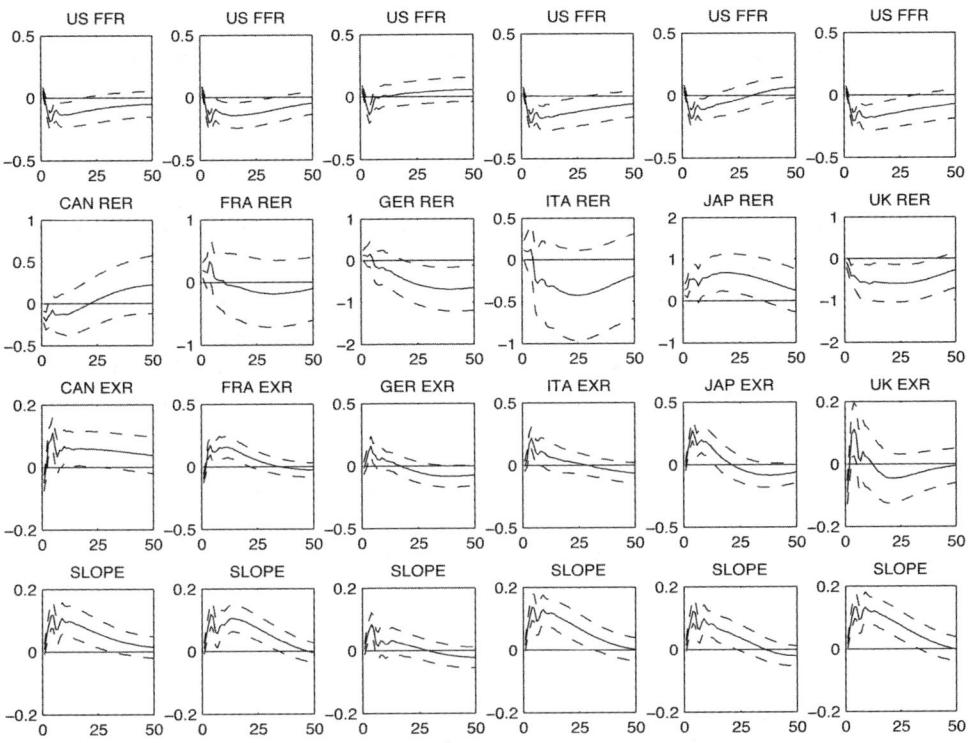

Fig. 3. Dynamic responses to an orthogonalized innovation to the volatility of the monetary-policy shock.

Notes: Each column reports, for each country pair, the responses of the US Federal Funds Rate (i), the RER (q), the foreign currency risk premium (exr), and the slope of the US term structure (i_{sl}). x-axes: months, y-axes: annual percentage points. Country pairs are, respectively, US-Canada, US-France, US-Germany, US-Italy, US-Japan, US-UK.

riables, although with different magnitudes and significance across variables and shocks. Hence volatility does have a *distinct and direct* effect, which will be important in characterizing our theoretical model.

In particular, figure 3 shows the responses to an orthogonalized innovation to the volatility of the monetary-policy shock. The response of the exchange rate (second row) is ambiguous. The point estimate indicates that an increase in the volatility of the monetary-policy shock strengthens the US dollar. However, this is not particularly significant (except for the case of the United Kingdom and, marginally, Germany). Later, we are going to evaluate if results change by exploiting the panel dimension of our data set. The third row shows that an increase in the volatility of the monetary-policy shock induces significant and persistent deviations from UIP, in the form of positive excess returns on foreign securities. This result is mainly driven by the response of the spread in the short-term interest rate: the domestic rate falls significantly, and proportionately more than the foreign one, implying an increase in the spread by a magnitude of 5–10 basis points (not shown). The estimated response of the slope of the US yield curve is positive on impact and keeps rising for a few months before reverting back to mean; it remains, however, significantly above the steady-state level for quite some time, regardless of the pair considered (except for the case of Germany, for which the effect dies out within six months).

Figure 4 shows the response to an orthogonalized innovation to the volatility of the inflation-target shock. Here, the implications for the ex-

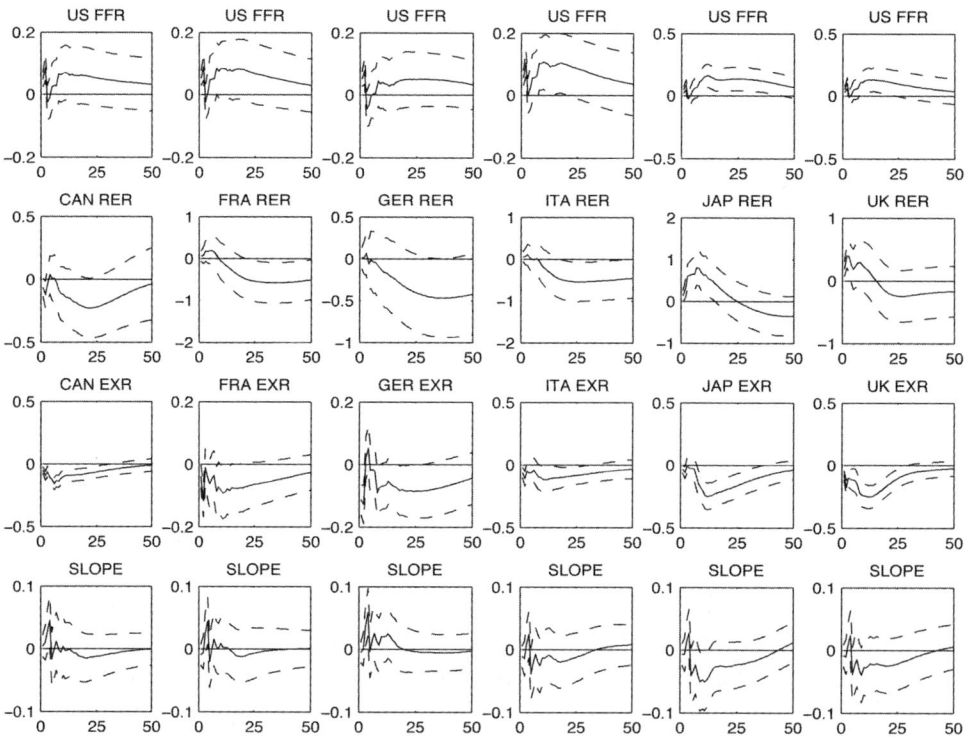

Fig. 4. Dynamic responses to an orthogonalized innovation to the volatility of the inflation-target shock.

Notes: Each column reports, for each country pair, the responses of the US Federal Funds Rate (i), the RER (q), the foreign currency risk premium (exr), and the slope of the US term structure (i_{sl}). x-axes: months, y-axes: annual percentage points. Country pairs are, respectively, US-Canada, US-France, US-Germany, US-Italy, US-Japan, US-UK.

change rate are very interesting. Indeed, while the response is weak on impact and not always significant, the point estimates indicate that an increase in the volatility of the inflation-target shock tends to appreciate the exchange rate (with the notable exception of Japan) in the medium run. This is a particularly appealing result considering the specific nature of the shock, which is indeed related to the medium-run target level for the inflation rate. This pattern is also reflected in the dynamic response of the foreign-currency risk premium: while the short-term response is ambiguous, the estimated impulse-response functions indicate that in the medium run a higher volatility of the inflation-target shock produces a lower foreign currency risk premium, consistently with the appreciation of the domestic currency. Finally, the estimated responses of the nominal interest rate and the slope of the yield curve are not very precise. However, the point estimates suggest a positive response of both the domestic short-term interest rate and the term spread. Again, we will look further into this evidence by exploring the panel dimension of the data.

Figure 5 studies the responses to the conditional volatility of the productivity shock. In particular, the response of the exchange rate is quite clear: although with different timing and magnitude across country pairs, an increase in the volatility of the productivity shock tends to depreciate the exchange rate, mostly on impact. No significant deviation from UIP arises, with the notable exception of Japan. Finally, the estimated response of the slope of the yield curve is muted on impact, but it becomes substantially and significantly positive after about six months and stays significantly positive until about two years after the shock, peaking at about 10–15 basis points after about one year. This response is virtually identical across all considered country pairs.

C. Exploring the Panel Dimension of the Data Set

The empirical evidence of the last section points toward an interesting and nontrivial role of stochastic volatility for macro-financial variables, both domestic (like the short-term interest rate or the term spread) and international (like the exchange rate and deviations from the UIP). Although the point estimates in the pairwise analysis suggest clear trends in the impulse responses of key variables, such trends are sometimes polluted by sampling uncertainty. In order to isolate more effectively the common components across countries, here we exploit the panel dimension of our data set using three methods.[12]

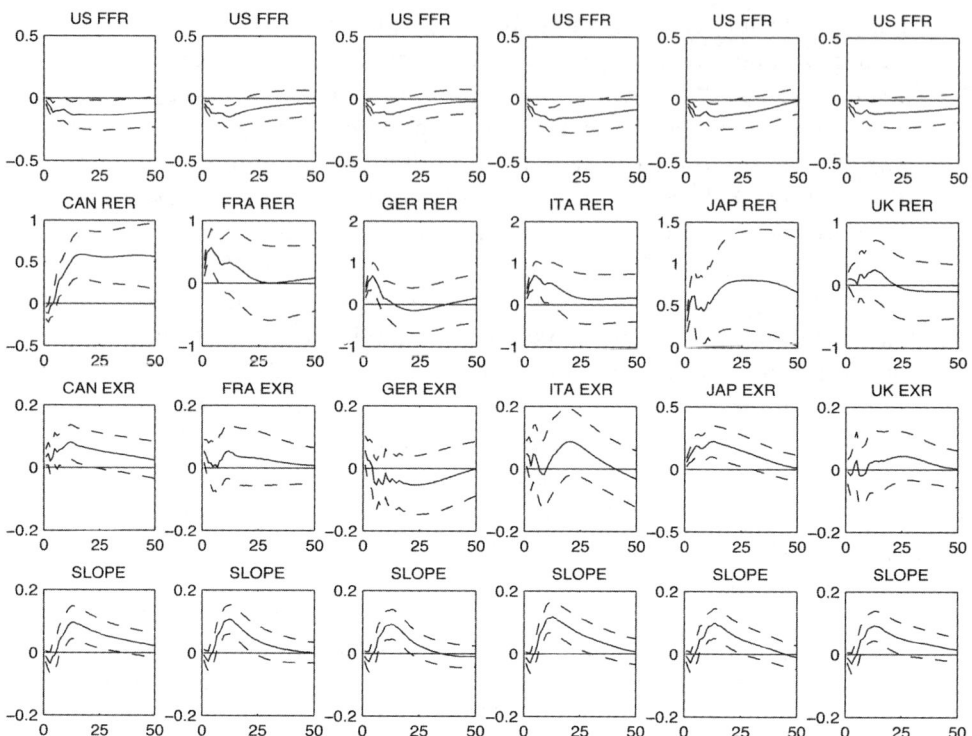

Fig. 5. Dynamic responses to an orthogonalized innovation to the volatility of productivity shocks.

Notes: Each column reports, for each country pair, the responses of the US Federal Funds Rate (i), the RER (q), the foreign currency risk premium (exr), and the slope of the US term structure (i_{sl}). x-axes: months, y-axes: annual percentage points. Country pairs are, respectively, US-Canada, US-France, US-Germany, US-Italy, US-Japan, US-UK.

The first approach is to define a two-country version of our empirical model. We take the home country as describing the US economy, while the foreign country is a GDP-weighted average of the other G7 countries, Japan excluded.[13] The relevant exchange rate is therefore a multilateral exchange rate, while the foreign currency risk premium is actually the expected excess return on a portfolio of several foreign currencies, with the portfolio share of each currency being proportional to the respective country size. The dynamic responses of the four variables of interest are displayed in the first column of figures 6 through 8, labeled "Two-country."[14]

The second approach is a Panel VAR Mean-Group estimation, in the spirit of Pesaran and Smith (1995): we estimate a separate VAR

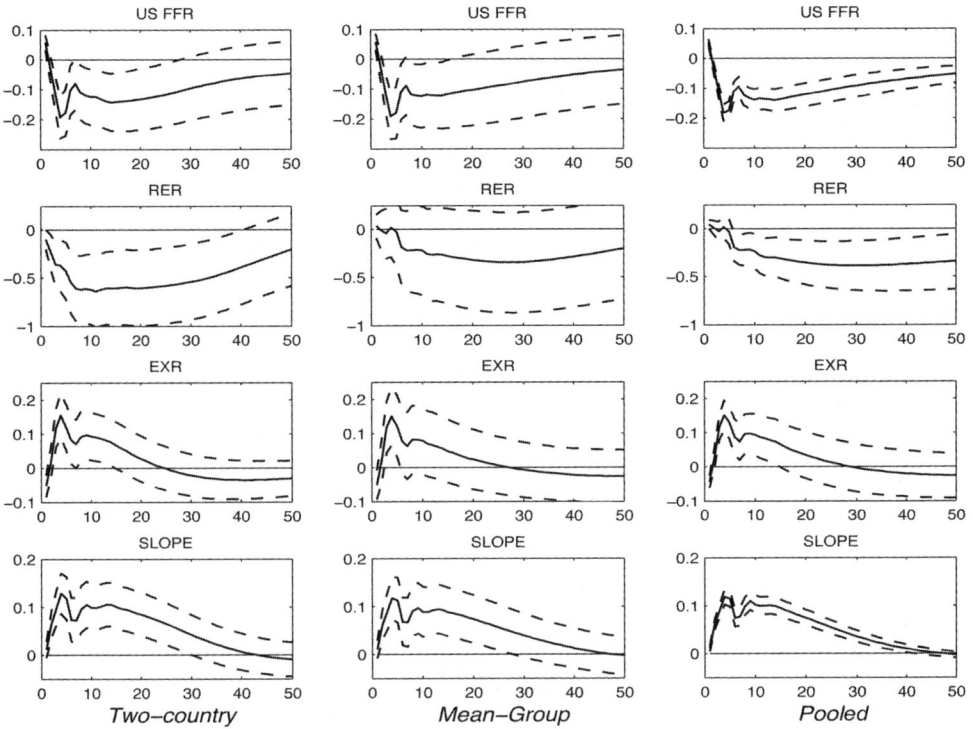

Fig. 6. Dynamic responses to an orthogonalized innovation to the volatility of the monetary-policy shock.

Notes: Each column reports, for each empirical approach, the responses of the US Federal Funds Rate (i), the RER (q), the foreign currency risk premium (exr), and the slope of the US term structure (i_{sl}). x-axes: months, y-axes: annual percentage points. "Two-country": single VAR, US-vs.-G6 countries (Japan excluded); "Mean-Group": average statistics from pair-specific VARs (from Section II, subsection B); "Pooled": single pooled panel VAR estimation.

model for each country-pair and then evaluate the mean of the estimated statistics of interest (namely the impulse-response function) across groups. Our data set is sufficiently long (along the time-series dimension) to support consistency of the Mean-Group estimator. The impulse-responses of interest are displayed in the second column of figures 6 through 8. In this case, the exchange-rate response measures the average response that the dollar bilateral exchange rate displays after a (domestic) level or volatility shock. Similarly, the third panel of the column shows the average response of the foreign currency risk premium, with respect to the US dollar.

The third and final approach that we consider is the traditional Panel

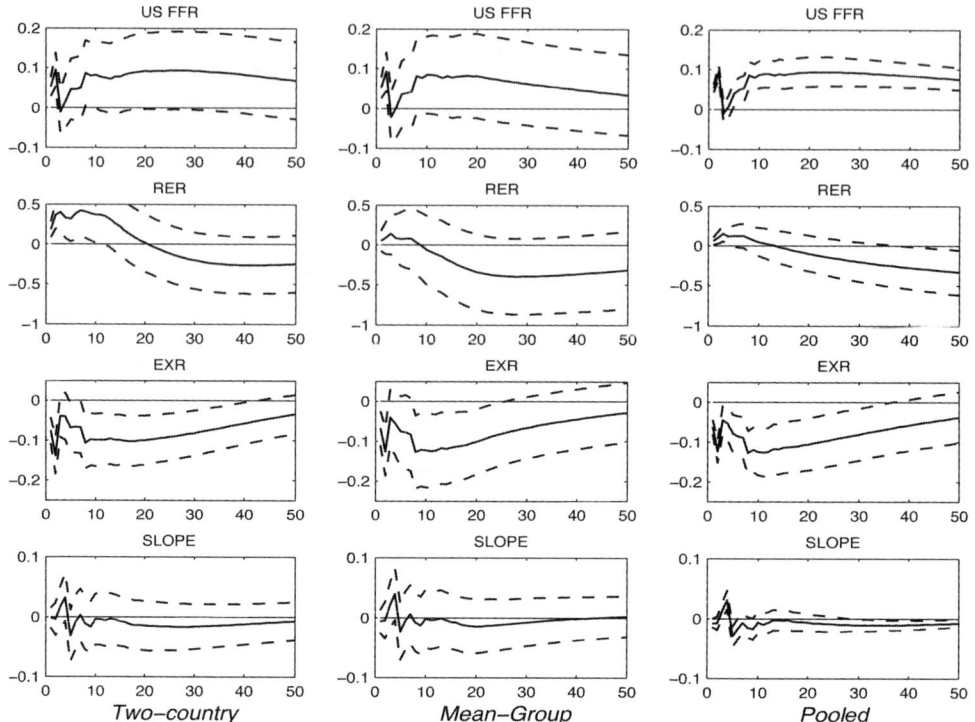

Fig. 7. Dynamic responses to an orthogonalized innovation to the volatility of the inflation-target shock.

Notes: Each column reports, for each empirical approach, the responses of the US Federal Funds Rate (i), the RER (q), the foreign currency risk premium (exr), and the slope of the US term structure (i_{sl}). x-axes: months, y-axes: annual percentage points. "Two-country": single VAR, US-vs.-G6 countries (Japan excluded); "Mean-Group": average statistics from pair-specific VARs (from Section II, subsection B); "Pooled": single pooled panel VAR estimation.

VAR Pooled estimation: we pool cross-section and (demeaned) time series, and estimate and analyze a VAR(p) using the pooled series. This
estimator, by construction, imposes the same dynamic structure to all
countries, vis-à-vis the United States. Accordingly, also in this case the
impulse-response functions show an "average" response, capturing the
common component across countries, of the bilateral USD exchange
rate and foreign risk premium.

Figures 6 through 8 display the dynamic response of selected variables to the three volatility shocks that we analyze, for each method
used. The variables are the US Federal Funds Rate (i), the US Dollar
Real Exchange Rate (q), the expected excess return on foreign currency

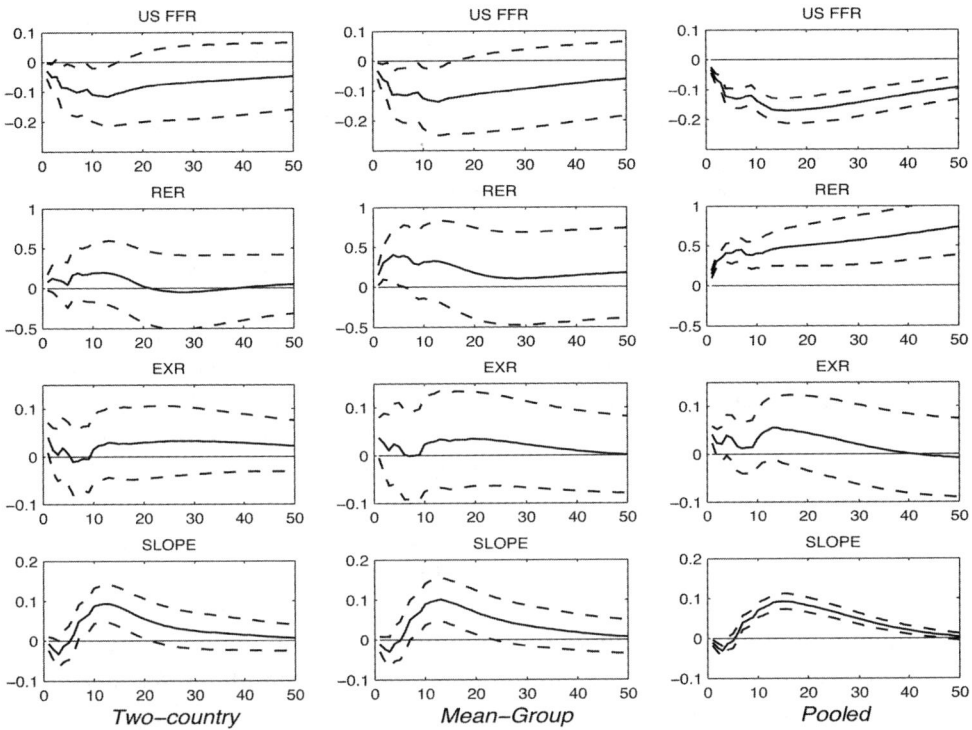

Fig. 8. Dynamic responses to an orthogonalized innovation to the volatility of productivity shocks.

Notes: Each column reports, for each empirical approach, the responses of the US Federal Funds Rate (i), the RER (q), the foreign currency risk premium (exr), and the slope of the US term structure (i_{sl}). x-axes: months, y-axes: annual percentage points. "Two-country": single VAR, US-vs.-G6 countries (Japan excluded); "Mean-Group": average statistics from pair-specific VARs (from Section II, subsection B); "Pooled": single pooled panel VAR estimation.

with respect to the US Dollar (exr), and the slope of the US yield curve (i_{sl}). In particular, the "Pooled" approach, displayed in the third column of each figure, seems quite useful in order to derive more precise impulse responses.

By looking at figures 6 through 8, the overall picture shows that the main results, made in the previous section, are in fact reinforced considering the panel dimension of our data. In particular, in response to an unexpected increase in the volatility of the monetary-policy shock, Figure 6 shows that the US dollar tends to appreciate while the foreign-currency risk premium increases. The latter result is driven by the domestic short-term interest rate falling more than the foreign one (not shown), which more than offsets the negative effect coming from the appreciation of the exchange rate. The yield curve, moreover, becomes significantly steeper.

Following an increase in the volatility of the inflation-target shock, the real exchange rate tends to appreciate in the medium term while the currency premium decreases, mainly as a result of the significant increase in the Federal Funds Rate. The slope of the yield curve, as also implied by the pairwise analysis, does not seem to display any systematic response.

Finally, and again consistently with the evidence suggested by the pairwise analysis of the previous section, an increase in the volatility of the productivity shock depreciates the US dollar and makes the yield curve significantly steeper. No clear effect is displayed by the foreign currency risk premium, regardless of the significant decrease in the domestic interest rate.

The important conclusion that we can draw from this analysis is that indeed volatility does matter. And it does matter also for traditional macro variables like real activity and the price level, as figure 9 shows. In response to an increase in volatility of the monetary-policy shock or to productivity, real activity substantially contracts and the price level falls, while a rise in volatility of the inflation-target shock tends to bring CPI inflation to a permanently higher level in the long run and implies a temporary increase in real output. Finally, not displayed, the impulse responses to an increase in the level of the monetary-policy shock are standard as in the literature, with output falling and the prices rising in the short run, consistently with the standard "price puzzle."[15]

III.   International Finance Regularities

In the previous section, we have provided evidence that volatility shocks have important effects on open-economy macro variables. In the next section, we are going to build a model in which indeed time-varying uncertainty plays a role. To nail down the desiderata that our model should meet, here we summarize the implications of our findings and report other empirical regularities along which we would like our model to perform well. The sense in which we refer to these facts (or puzzles) as international finance regularities relates to our focus on the joint behavior of interest rates and exchange rates.

The empirical evidence on the importance of volatility shocks can be summarized along two facts related respectively to the effects that

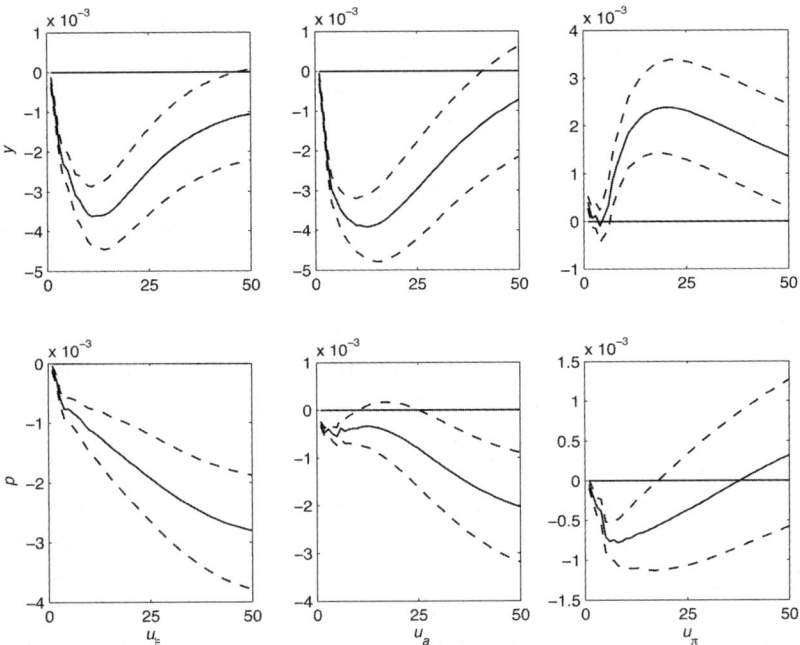

Fig. 9. Dynamic responses of the domestic industrial production index (first row) and the domestic CPI (second row) to, respectively, a shock to the volatility of the monetary-policy instrument (u_ζ) (first column), of the productivity shock (u_a) (second column), and of the inflation-target shock (u_π) (third column).

volatility shocks have on the nominal (and real) exchange rate and the deviations from UIP.

Fact 1: An increase in the volatilities of the US monetary-policy and inflation-target shocks appreciates the dollar exchange rate, especially in the medium run. On the other hand, an increase in the volatility of the productivity shock depreciates the dollar exchange rate.

Fact 2: An increase in the volatilities of both the monetary-policy and the inflation-target shocks generates significant and persistent deviations from UIP; in particular an increase in the excess return of foreign-versus-domestic short-term bonds in the case of the monetary-policy volatility shock and a decrease in the case of the inflation-target volatility shock.

The next fact is in common with our empirical analysis and the evidence reported by Eichenbaum and Evans (1995).

Fact 3: A positive innovation to the level of the monetary-policy shock (contractionary policy shock) produces a persistent appreciation in both the real and nominal exchange rates and a persistent deviation from the UIP in the form of positive excess returns on US securities.

To this list, we add another well-known fact, or puzzle, that we would like to address. While our previous facts are conditional statements about how excess returns and exchange rate co-move following different innovations (level or volatility shocks), another relevant empirical regularity is related to the joint behavior of exchange and interest rates as captured by the negative regression coefficient that arises from the UIP regression.

Fact 4: The regression coefficient between exchange rate changes and the nominal interest rate differential (UIP regression) is negative.

Related to the UIP puzzle, there is another one, recently discussed by Engel (2010), who documents that high real interest rate countries tend to have currencies that are strong in real terms and stronger than what can be explained by the real UIP. In particular, the puzzle comes from the fact that while current international-finance models struggle to account for the negative covariance between interest-rate differentials and exchange rate *changes*, those that succeed invariably miss the negative covariance between the interest-rate differential and the *level* of the exchange rate. Moreover, while the real interest-rate differential is negatively correlated with the real one-step-ahead excess return on foreign-versus-domestic currency, such correlation turns positive if we instead consider the "prospective excess return"; that is, the expected cumulative excess return over the infinite future.

Finally, we would like our model to be also consistent with the responses of output and prices to the volatility shocks documented in figure 9.

IV. A Two-Country Open Economy Model

To study the relationships between time-varying volatility and the exchange rate, we present a two-country open-economy model along the lines of Benigno and Benigno (2008). In particular we consider two extensions, whose relevance will be discussed later, which are important for the model to be able to match the empirical facts discussed earlier: (1) we allow for more general recursive preferences as in the work of Epstein and Zin (1989, 1991) and Weil (1990); and (2) we consider stochastic volatility for the exogenous processes driving the economy. The latter addition, in particular, implies a careful treatment of the solution. To this end, we expound the method developed by Benigno, Benigno, and Nisticò (2010) to show how we can handle in a relatively easy way approximations of dynamic general equilibrium models with time-varying uncertainty and at the same time characterize the effect of uncertainty on the variables of interest.

A. Households

The world economy consists of two countries, Home and Foreign, and is populated by a continuum of agents of measure one: Home households lie on the interval $[0, n]$, while Foreign households on $(n, 1]$ where $n \in (0, 1)$. The population size is set equal to the range of goods produced so that Home firms produce goods on $[0, n]$, Foreign firms produce on $(n, 1]$. Home households are indexed by j, Foreign households by i, C_t^j denotes the level of consumption for household j in period t, and L_t^j denotes its supply of working hours.

Preferences are recursive, as in the framework of Epstein and Zin (1989, 1991) and Weil (1990). In particular, we assume that for a generic household of type j recursive utility can be written as

$$V_t^j = (U(C_t^j, L_t^j)^{1-\rho} + \beta(E_t(V_{t+1}^j)^{1-\gamma})^{(1-\rho)/(1-\gamma)})^{1/(1-\rho)}, \qquad (2)$$

where ρ is a measure of the inverse of the intertemporal elasticity of substitution over the utility flow, $U(\cdot)$, γ represents the risk aversion toward static wealth gambles, and $\beta \in (0, 1)$ is the household's subjective discount factor. The classical expected utility model is nested under the assumption $\rho = \gamma$.

The utility flow is a Cobb-Douglas index of aggregate consumption, C, and leisure, $1 - L$

$$U(C_t^j, L_t^j) = (C_t^j)^\psi (1 - L_t^j)^{1-\psi}, \qquad (3)$$

where $\psi \in (0, 1)$ reflects the preference for consumption versus leisure. As it is well known, this specification of preferences allows us to disentangle the elasticity of substitution, $1/\rho$, from the risk-aversion coefficient.[16]

The aggregate consumption index C is a composite consumption good

$$C = [v^{1/\theta} C_H^{(\theta-1)/\theta} + (1 - v)^{1/\theta} C_F^{(\theta-1)/\theta}]^{\theta/(\theta-1)}, \theta > 0, \qquad (4)$$

where C_H and C_F are the two consumption subindexes that refer, respectively, to the consumption of Home-produced and Foreign-produced goods; θ, with $\theta > 0$, is the elasticity of intratemporal substitution, and

$v \in (0, 1)$ represents the weight given to home-produced goods in the aggregator C. Home bias in consumption arises when the weight given to Home goods is higher than the size of the country; that is, when $v > n$.

In the Foreign country, preferences have the same structure as in (2)

$$V_t^{*i} = (U(C_t^{*i}, L_t^{*i})^{1-\rho} + \beta(E_t(V_{t+1}^{*i})^{1-\gamma})^{(1-\rho)/(1-\gamma)})^{1/(1-\rho)} \qquad (5)$$

where the aggregate consumption bundle is given by

$$C^* = [v^{*1/\theta}C_H^{*(\theta-1)/\theta} + (1 - v^*)^{1/\theta}C_F^{*(\theta-1)/\theta}]^{\theta/(\theta-1)}, \qquad (6)$$

for a different weight $v^* \in (0, 1)$.

We introduce home bias in consumption following Benigno and De Paoli (2010). Specifically, denoting with $\lambda \in (0, 1)$ the (common) degree of openness of the two countries, the weights in the consumption bundle are related to the country sizes through:

$$1 - v = (1 - n)\lambda,$$

$$v^* = n\lambda.$$

The consumption bundles C_H, C_F, C_H^*, C_F^*, are in turn Dixit-Stiglitz aggregators of the goods produced in the two countries and are given by

$$C_H = \left[\left(\frac{1}{n}\right)^{1/\sigma} \int_0^n c(h)^{(\sigma-1)/\sigma} dh\right]^{\sigma/(\sigma-1)} \qquad C_F = \left[\left(\frac{1}{1-n}\right)^{1/\sigma} \int_n^1 c(f)^{(\sigma-1)/\sigma} df\right]^{\sigma/(\sigma-1)}, \quad (7)$$

$$C_H^* = \left[\left(\frac{1}{n}\right)^{1/\sigma} \int_0^n c^*(h)^{(\sigma-1)/\sigma} dh\right]^{\sigma/(\sigma-1)} \qquad C_F^* = \left[\left(\frac{1}{1-n}\right)^{1/\sigma} \int_n^1 c^*(f)^{(\sigma-1)/\sigma} df\right]^{\sigma/(\sigma-1)}, \quad (8)$$

where σ, with σ > 1, is the elasticity of substitution across the consumption goods produced within a country. The appropriate consumption-based price indexes associated with C and C^* are given respectively by

$$P = [vP_H^{1-\theta} + (1 - v)(P_F)^{1-\theta}]^{1/(1-\theta)}, \qquad (9)$$

$$P^* = [v^*P_H^{*1-\theta} + (1 - v^*)(P_F^*)^{1-\theta}]^{1/(1-\theta)}, \qquad (10)$$

where P_H (P_H^*) is the price subindex for Home-produced goods expressed in the Home (Foreign) currency and $P_F(P_H^*)$ is the price subindex for Foreign-produced goods expressed in the Home (Foreign) currency. Moreover,

$$P_H = \left[\left(\frac{1}{n}\right)\int_0^n p(h)^{1-\sigma}dh\right]^{1/(1-\sigma)} \qquad P_F = \left[\left(\frac{1}{1-n}\right)\int_n^1 p(f)^{1-\sigma}dz\right]^{1/(1-\sigma)}, \quad (11)$$

$$P_H^* = \left[\left(\frac{1}{n}\right)\int_0^n p^*(h)^{1-\sigma}dz\right]^{1/(1-\sigma)} \qquad P_F^* = \left[\left(\frac{1}{1-n}\right)\int_n^1 p^*(f)^{1-\sigma}dz\right]^{1/(1-\sigma)}, \quad (12)$$

where $p(h)$ and $p^*(h)$ are the prices of the generic good h produced by the Home country in the currencies of the Home and Foreign country, respectively, while $p(f)$ and $p^*(f)$ are the prices of the generic good f produced by the Foreign country in the currencies of the Home and Foreign country, respectively. The law of one price holds across all individual goods: $p(h) = Sp^*(h)$ and $p(f) = Sp^*(f)$, where S is the nominal exchange rate (the price of foreign currency in terms of domestic currency). Therefore, equations (11) and (12) imply that $P_H = SP_H^*$ and $P_F = SP_F^*$. However, equations (9) and (10) show that, since Home and Foreign agents' preferences are not necessarily identical, there can be deviations from purchasing power parity (PPP) unless $v = v^*$; that is, $P \ne SP^*$. Appropriately we measure the deviations from PPP through the real exchange rate given by $Q \equiv SP^*/P$. We also define the terms of trade in the Home country as $T \equiv P_F/P_H$. Notice the following useful relationships between relative prices, the real exchange rate, and terms of trade

$$1 = \left[v\left(\frac{P_H}{P}\right)^{1-\theta} + (1-v)\left(\frac{P_F}{P}\right)^{1-\theta}\right], \quad (13)$$

$$Q = \frac{[v^* + (1-v^*)(T)^{1-\theta}]^{1/(1-\theta)}}{[v + (1-v)(T)^{1-\theta}]^{1/(1-\theta)}}, \quad (14)$$

$$T = \frac{P_F}{P}\frac{P}{P_H}. \quad (15)$$

Given the above-specified preferences, we can derive total demands of the generic good h, produced in country H, and of the good f, produced in country F:

$$y^d(h) = \left(\frac{p(h)}{P_H}\right)^{-\sigma}Y_H \qquad y^d(f) = \left(\frac{p(f)}{P_F}\right)^{-\sigma}Y_F \quad (16)$$

where output aggregators Y_H and Y_F are appropriately defined

$$Y_H = \left(\frac{P_H}{P}\right)^{-\theta}\left(vC + \frac{v^*(1-n)}{n}Q^\theta C^*\right), \quad (17)$$

$$Y_F = \left(\frac{P_F}{P}\right)^{-\theta} \left(\frac{(1-v)n}{1-n} C + (1-v^*)Q^\theta C^*\right). \qquad (18)$$

We assume that asset markets are complete both at the domestic and international levels. In particular, households can trade in a set of state-contingent nominal securities denominated in the Home currency that span all the uncertainty from one period to another.[17] Each of these securities pays respectively only in one of the possible states of nature in the next period. Let B_{t+1}^j be the state-contingent payoff at time $t+1$ of the portfolio of state-contingent nominal securities held by household in the Home country at the end of period t. The value of this portfolio can be written as $E_t[M_{t,t+1}B_{t+1}^j]$, where $M_{t,t+1}$ represents the nominal stochastic discount factor for discounting units of Home-currency wealth from a state of nature at time $t+1$ back to time t. This stochastic discount factor is unique, because of the complete-market assumption, and equivalent to the price of a state-contingent security standardized by the time-t conditional probability of occurrence of the state of nature at time $t+1$ in which the security pays. We can write the flow budget constraint that the Home households face as

$$E_t[M_{t,t+1}B_{t+1}^j] \le B_t^j + W_t L_t^j + D_t^j - P_t C_t^j,$$

for each j, where W_t is the nominal wage in the Home country, determined in a common labor market, and D_t^j is nominal profits. Each household holds equal shares of all firms (domestic firms are located on the interval $[0, n]$ and the size of the Home population is normalized to n), and there is no trade in firms' shares. Households are subject to a standard limit on their borrowing possibilities.

Households in the Foreign country can also trade in the state-contingent securities denominated in the currency of country H. Let B_{t+1}^i be the state-contingent payoff at time $t+1$ of the portfolio of state-contingent nominal securities held by Foreign households at the end of period t. Since B_{t+1}^i is denominated in units of Home currency, the payoff in Foreign currency is given by $B_{t+1}^{*i} = B_{t+1}^i / S_{t+1}$ and the value of the portfolio in Foreign currency is simply $E_t[M_{t,t+1}B_{t+1}^i]/S_t = E_t[M_{t,t+1}B_{t+1}^{*i}S_{t+1}]/S_t$. We can appropriately define the nominal stochastic discount factor for discounting units of Foreign-currency wealth across time

$$M_{t,t+1}^* = \frac{S_{t+1}}{S_t} M_{t,t+1}, \qquad (19)$$

which is uniquely defined given that $M_{t,t+1}$ is unique. Therefore, the flow budget constraint for the Foreign households can be written as

$$E_t[M^*_{t,t+1}B^{*i}_{t+1}] \le B^{*i}_t + W^*_t L^{*i}_t + D^{*i}_t - P^*_t C^{*i}_t,$$

for each i where the definition of the variables follows from before with the appropriate modifications. A standard borrowing-limit condition also applies here.

Households maximize utility subject to the sequence of the flow budget constraints and the borrowing-limit constraints by choosing aggregate consumption, labor, and asset holdings in terms of the state contingent securities.

At optimum the marginal rate of substitution between labor and consumption is equal to the real wage

$$\frac{W_t}{P_t} = \frac{1-\psi}{\psi}\frac{C^j_t}{1-L^j_t} \tag{20}$$

$$\frac{W^*_t}{P^*_t} = \frac{1-\psi}{\psi}\frac{C^{i*}_t}{1-L^{*i}_t} \tag{21}$$

for each j and i in the respective country.

Optimality conditions with respect to the holdings of the state-contingent securities for the Home household imply

$$\frac{\partial(V^j_t)}{\partial C^j_t}\frac{(V^j_t)^{-\rho}}{P_t}M_{t,t+1} = \beta(E_t(V^j_{t+1})^{1-\gamma})^{\frac{\gamma-\rho}{1-\gamma}}\frac{(V^j_{t+1})^{-\gamma}}{P_{t+1}}\frac{\partial V^j_{t+1}}{\partial C^j_{t+1}},$$

for each contingency at time $t+1$ where the marginal utility of consumption is given by

$$\frac{\partial V^j_t}{\partial C^j_t} = \psi\frac{U(C^j_t,L^j_t)^{1-\rho}}{C^j_t}(V^j_t)^\rho.$$

Combining the two previous equations, we obtain that the nominal stochastic discount factor in the Home country is

$$M_{t,t+1} = \beta\left(\frac{V^{1-\gamma}_{t+1}}{E_t V^{1-\gamma}_{t+1}}\right)^{(\rho-\gamma)/(1-\gamma)}\left(\frac{U(C_{t+1},L_{t+1})}{U(C_t,L_t)}\right)^{1-\rho}\frac{C_t}{C_{t+1}}\frac{1}{\Pi_{t+1}}, \tag{22}$$

where we have also neglected the index j from V, C, L.[18] Moreover, we have defined the gross CPI inflation rate as

$$\Pi_t \equiv \frac{P_t}{P_{t-1}} = \Pi_{H,t}\frac{[v+(1-v)(T_t)^{1-\theta}]^{1/(1-\theta)}}{[v+(1-v)(T_{t-1})^{1-\theta}]^{1/(1-\theta)}}, \tag{23}$$

where $\Pi_{H,t} \equiv P_{H,t}/P_{H,t-1}$.

Similarly, in the Foreign country we obtain

$$M^*_{t,t+1} = \beta \left(\frac{V^{*1-\gamma}_{t+1}}{E_t V^{*1-\gamma}_{t+1}} \right)^{(\rho-\gamma)/(1-\gamma)} \left(\frac{U(C^*_{t+1}, L^*_{t+1})}{U(C^*_t, L^*_t)} \right)^{1-\rho} \frac{C^*_t}{C^*_{t+1}} \frac{1}{\Pi^*_{t+1}}, \qquad (24)$$

where the Foreign gross CPI inflation rate is given by

$$\Pi^*_t = \Pi_t \frac{Q_t}{Q_{t-1}} \frac{S_{t-1}}{S_t}. \qquad (25)$$

The above nominal discount factors correspond to those of the standard expected-utility model, under the assumption $\rho = \gamma$. In this case, they depend on the ratio between the marginal utilities of nominal income across the two periods. With Epstein-Zin preferences, there is an additional term reflecting the preference for an early, in the case of $\rho < \gamma$, or late, in the case of $\rho > \gamma$, resolution of intertemporal uncertainty. This intertemporal uncertainty is captured by the ratio of the utility at time $t + 1$ with respect to its risk-adjusted expected value, where the risk-adjustment occurs through the factor $1 - \gamma$. When agents prefer an early resolution of uncertainty ($\rho < \gamma$), bad realizations of the utility at time $t + 1$ with respect to its risk-adjusted expected value increase the stochastic discount factor and therefore the appetite for state-contingent wealth in that state of nature.

The above nominal stochastic discount factor can be used to price any security in arbitrage-free markets and, in particular, they imply that the short-term nominal interest rates satisfy

$$\frac{1}{1 + i_t} = E_t M_{t+1}, \qquad (26)$$

$$\frac{1}{1 + i^*_t} = E_t M^*_{t+1}, \qquad (27)$$

where i_t and i^*_t are the one-period nominal interest rates in the Home and Foreign country, respectively.

Using (22) and (24) into (19), we can obtain

$$\left(\frac{V^{1-\gamma}_{t+1}(E_t V^{*1-\gamma}_{t+1})}{V^{*1-\gamma}_{t+1}(E_t V^{1-\gamma}_{t+1})} \right)^{(\rho-\gamma)/(1-\gamma)} \left[\frac{U(C_{t+1}, L_{t+1})}{U(C^*_{t+1}, L^*_{t+1})} \right]^{1-\rho} \frac{C^*_{t+1}}{C_{t+1}} Q_{t+1} = \left(\frac{U(C_t, L_t)}{U(C^*_t, L^*_t)} \right)^{1-\rho} \frac{C^*_t}{C_t} Q_t. \qquad (28)$$

To close the assumption of complete markets, we need to specify initial conditions for the holdings of the state-contingent securities. A standard assumption in the literature is to choose initial state-contingent wealth in a way to equalize the ratio between the marginal utilities of nominal income across countries, converted in the same currency. Let G_t denote this ratio at time t; it follows that we can write it as

$$G_t = \frac{(\partial V_t^{1-\rho}/\partial C_t)(1/P_t)}{(\partial V_t^{*1-\rho}/\partial C_t^*)(1/S_t P_t^*)} = \left(\frac{U(C_t, L_t)}{U(C_t^*, L_t^*)}\right)^{1-\rho} \frac{C_t^*}{C_t} Q_t, \tag{29}$$

where we have rescaled utility as $V_t^{1-\rho}$ in order to make a direct comparison with the expected-utility model.[19] Combining (28) and (29) we obtain the following law of motion for G_t

$$G_{t+1} = G_t \left(\frac{V_{t+1}^{1-\gamma}(E_t V_{t+1}^{*1-\gamma})}{V_{t+1}^{*1-\gamma}(E_t V_{t+1}^{1-\gamma})}\right)^{(\gamma-\rho)/(1-\gamma)}. \tag{30}$$

We set $G_{t_0} = 1$ and therefore assume that initial state-contingent wealth equalizes the ratio of the marginal utilities of nominal income across countries in the initial period. Notice that, under the expected-utility model ($\gamma = \rho$), this assumption implies equalization of the ratio at all times and contingencies. With Epstein-Zin preferences, instead, this ratio evolves over time depending on cross-country realizations of utility with respect to their risk-adjusted expected values.

B. Firms

The Home country produces goods on the interval $[0, n]$, while the Foreign country on $(n, 1]$. At first pass we abstract from investment and capital accumulation.[20] A generic firm h producing in the Home country uses the following technology

$$y_t(h) = A_t(L_t(h))^\varphi, \tag{31}$$

where A_t is a productivity shifter common to all the firms in the Home country, φ with $\varphi \in (0, 1]$ measures decreasing return to scale in the labor input $L_t(h)$, which is a composite of all the differentiated labor supplied by households j according to

$$L_t(h) = \frac{1}{n} \int_0^n L_t^j(h) dj,$$

where $L_t^j(h)$ denotes the demand of household j's labor by firm h.

We assume that there are frictions in the price adjustment. In particular, we model price rigidity as in Calvo's (1983) model, but with indexation. In each period, in the Home country, only a fraction $(1 - \alpha)$ of firms, with $0 \leq \alpha < 1$, can reset their prices independently of the last time they had reset them. In this case, the price is chosen to maximize the expected discounted value of the profits under the circumstances that the price, appropriately indexed, still applies. These firms choose prices to maximize the following objective

$$E_t \sum_{T=t}^{\infty} \alpha^{T-t} M_{t,T} \{p_{t,T}(h)y_{t,T}(h) - W_T L_T(h)\}$$

where total demand is:

$$y_{t,T}(h) = \left(\frac{p_{t,T}(h)}{P_{H,T}}\right)^{-\sigma} Y_{H,T}$$

and moreover, $p_{t,T}(h) = \tilde{p}_t(h)\bar{P}_{H,T} / \bar{P}_{H,t}$, where $\tilde{p}_t(h)$ is the price chosen at time t and $\bar{P}_{H,T}/\bar{P}_{H,t}$ is the gross inflation target from t to T to which all prices are automatically adjusted. The optimal price $\tilde{p}_t(h)$ is chosen to satisfy the following first-order condition:

$$\tilde{p}_t(h) = \mu \frac{E_t\sum_{T=t}^{\infty} \alpha^{T-t} M_{t,T} W_T \{[y_{t,T}(h)]/A_T\}^{1/\varphi}}{E_t\sum_{T=t}^{\infty} \alpha^{T-t} M_{t,T} (\bar{P}_{H,T}/\bar{P}_{H,t})y_{t,T}(h)},$$

where the overall mark-up has been defined as $\mu = \sigma/(\varphi(\sigma - 1))$. Using (20) and (22), we can write the previous equation as

$$\left(\frac{\tilde{p}_t(h)}{P_{H,t}}\right)^{1-\sigma+(\sigma/\varphi)} = \mu \frac{1-\psi}{\psi} \frac{E_t\sum_{T=t}^{\infty}(\alpha\beta)^{T-t} N_{t,T} U(C_T, L_T)^{1-\rho} \frac{1}{1-L_T}\left(\frac{P_{H,T}}{P_{H,t}}\frac{\bar{P}_{H,t}}{\bar{P}_{H,T}}\right)^{\sigma/\varphi}\left(\frac{Y_{H,T}}{A_T}\right)^{1/\varphi}}{E_t\sum_{T=t}^{\infty}(\alpha\beta)^{T-t} N_{t,T} U(C_T, L_T)^{1-\rho} C_T^{-1}\left(\frac{P_{H,T}}{P_{H,t}}\frac{\bar{P}_{H,t}}{\bar{P}_{H,T}}\right)^{\sigma-1} \frac{P_{H,T}}{P_T} Y_{H,T}}, \quad (32)$$

where we have defined

$$N_{t,T} = \left(\frac{V_{t+1}^{1-\gamma}V_{t+2}^{1-\gamma}\cdots V_T^{1-\gamma}}{E_t V_{t+1}^{1-\gamma} E_{t+1} V_{t+2}^{1-\gamma}\cdots E_{T-1} V_T^{1-\gamma}}\right)^{(\rho-\gamma)/(1-\gamma)},$$

with $N_{t,t} = 1$.

The remaining fraction of firms of measure α can change their prices only by indexing them to the current inflation index, which does not necessarily coincide with actual inflation. Therefore, we note that Calvo's model implies the following law of motion for the aggregate price index $P_{H,t}$

$$P_{H,t}^{1-\sigma} = \alpha \bar{\Pi}_{H,t}^{1-\sigma} P_{H,t-1}^{1-\sigma} + (1 - \alpha)\tilde{p}_t(h)^{1-\sigma}, \quad (33)$$

where $\bar{\Pi}_{H,t} \equiv \bar{P}_{H,t}/\bar{P}_{H,t-1}$. Using (33), we can write (32) as

$$\left(\frac{1-\alpha(\Pi_{H,t}/\overline{\Pi}_{H,t})^{\sigma-1}}{1-\alpha}\right)^{1/(1-\sigma)} = \left(\frac{F_t}{K_t}\right)^{\varphi/(\phi-\sigma\varphi+\sigma)}, \tag{34}$$

where F_t and K_t can be written recursively as

$$F_t = \mu \frac{1-\psi}{\psi} \frac{U(C_t, L_t)^{1-\rho}}{1-L_t}\left(\frac{Y_{H,t}}{A_t}\right)^{1/\varphi} + \alpha\beta E_t\left\{\left(\frac{\Pi_{H,t+1}}{\overline{\Pi}_{H,t+1}}\right)^{\sigma/\varphi}\left(\frac{V_{t+1}^{1-\gamma}}{E_t V_{t+1}^{1-\gamma}}\right)^{(\rho-\gamma)/(1-\gamma)} F_{t+1}\right\}, \tag{35}$$

$$K_t = U(C_t, L_t)^{1-\rho}\frac{P_{H,t}Y_{H,t}}{P_t C_t} + \alpha\beta E_t\left\{\left(\frac{\Pi_{H,t+1}}{\overline{\Pi}_{H,t+1}}\right)^{\sigma-1}\left(\frac{V_{t+1}^{1-\gamma}}{E_t V_{t+1}^{1-\gamma}}\right)^{(\rho-\gamma)/(1-\gamma)} K_{t+1}\right\}. \tag{36}$$

Notice that equilibrium in the labor market requires

$$L_t = \frac{1}{n}\int_0^n L_t(h)dh = \frac{1}{n}\int_0^n \left(\frac{y_t(h)}{A_t}\right)^{1/\varphi}dh = \Delta_t\left(\frac{Y_{H,t}}{A_t}\right)^{1/\varphi}, \tag{37}$$

where the index of price dispersion Δ_t can be written recursively as

$$\Delta_t \equiv \frac{1}{n}\int_0^n \left(\frac{p_t(h)}{P_{H,t}}\right)^{-(\sigma/\varphi)}dh = \alpha\Delta_{t-1}\left(\frac{\Pi_{H,t}}{\overline{\Pi}_{H,t}}\right)^{\sigma/\varphi} + (1-\alpha)\left(\frac{1-\alpha(\Pi_{H,t}/\overline{\Pi}_{H,t})^{\sigma-1}}{1-\alpha}\right)^{-[\sigma/[\varphi(1-\sigma)]]}. \tag{38}$$

The price-setting mechanism is similar in the Foreign country, where now $(1 - \alpha^*)$ represents the mass of firms, with $0 \le \alpha^* < 1$, that can reset their prices each period. Following similar steps, the Foreign country's aggregate-supply equation can be written as

$$\left(\frac{1-\alpha^*(\Pi_{F,t}^*/\overline{\Pi}_{F,t}^*)^{\sigma-1}}{1-\alpha^*}\right)^{1/(1-\sigma)} = \left(\frac{F_t^*}{K_t^*}\right)^{\varphi/(\varphi-\sigma\varphi+\sigma)}, \tag{39}$$

with

$$F_t^* = \mu \frac{1-\psi}{\psi} \frac{U(C_t^*, L_t^*)^{1-\rho}}{1-L_t^*}\left(\frac{Y_{F,t}^*}{A_t^*}\right)^{1/\varphi} + \alpha^*\beta E_t\left\{\left(\frac{\Pi_{F,t+1}^*}{\overline{\Pi}_{F,t+1}^*}\right)^{\sigma/\varphi}\left(\frac{V_{t+1}^{*1-\gamma}}{E_t V_{t+1}^{*1-\gamma}}\right)^{(\rho-\gamma)/(1-\gamma)} F_{t+1}^*\right\}, \tag{40}$$

$$K_t^* = U(C_t^*, L_t^*)^{1-\rho}\frac{P_{F,t}^*Y_{F,t}^*}{P_t^* Q_t C_t^*} + \alpha^*\beta E_t\left\{\left(\frac{\Pi_{F,t+1}^*}{\overline{\Pi}_{F,t+1}^*}\right)^{\sigma-1}\left(\frac{V_{t+1}^{*1-\gamma}}{E_t V_{t+1}^{*1-\gamma}}\right)^{(\rho-\gamma)/(1-\gamma)} K_{t+1}^*\right\}, \tag{41}$$

where $\Pi_{F,t}^* = P_{F,t}^*/P_{F,t-1}^*$ and $\overline{\Pi}_{F,t}^*$ is the gross inflation target to which foreign prices adjust each period. Equilibrium in the Foreign labor market implies

$$L_t^* = \frac{1}{1-n}\int_n^1 L_t^*(f)df = \frac{1}{1-n}\int_n^1 \left(\frac{y_t^*(f)}{A_t^*}\right)^{1/\varphi}df = \Delta_t^*\left(\frac{Y_{F,t}^*}{A_t^*}\right)^{1/\varphi} \tag{42}$$

where now Δ_t^* is given by

$$\Delta_t^* \equiv \frac{1}{1-n} \int_n^1 \left(\frac{p_t^*(f)}{P_{F,t}^*} \right)^{-(\sigma/\varphi)} df = \alpha^* \Delta_{t-1}^* \left(\frac{\Pi_{F,t}^*}{\bar{\Pi}_{F,t}^*} \right)^{\sigma/\varphi}$$

$$+ (1-\alpha^*) \left(\frac{1-\alpha^* (\Pi_{F,t}^*/\bar{\Pi}_{F,t}^*)^{\sigma-1}}{1-\alpha^*} \right)^{-\{\sigma/[\phi(1-\sigma)]\}}. \tag{43}$$

Finally, we note the following relationship between the terms of trade and producer-price inflation rates

$$T_t = T_{t-1} \frac{S_t}{S_{t-1}} \frac{\Pi_{F,t}^*}{\Pi_{H,t}}. \tag{44}$$

C. Monetary Policy Rules

We close the model by specifying the monetary policy rules. A broad class of policy rules that we consider can be written as

$$(1+i_{1,t}) = (1+i_{1,t-1})^{\phi_i} \left(\frac{\Pi_t}{\tilde{\beta}} \right)^{1-\phi_i} \left(\frac{\Pi_{H,t}}{\bar{\Pi}_t} \right)^{(1-\phi_i)\phi_\pi} \left(\frac{\tilde{Y}_{H,t}}{\tilde{Y}_{H,t-1}} \right)^{(1-\phi_i)\phi_y} \left(\frac{S_t}{S_{t-1}} \right)^{(1-\phi_i)\phi_s} e^{\xi_t} \tag{45}$$

for the Home monetary policymaker where the short-term interest rate reacts to its past value, to the deviation of the gross producer inflation from a target, to domestic output growth and to the changes in the exchange rate;[21] ϕ_i, ϕ_π, ϕ_y, ϕ_s are nonnegative parameters, $\tilde{\beta}$ is an appropriately-defined parameter, ξ_t is the policy shock, and $\bar{\Pi}_t$ represents the inflation target followed by the Home monetary policymaker, which is generally different from the target to which prices are indexed. The link between the two inflation targets could be expressed as

$$\bar{\Pi}_{H,t} = \bar{\Pi}_t^\kappa \Pi_{H,t-1}^{1-\kappa},$$

with a weight $\kappa \in 0,1]$, which can be interpreted as a measure of the credibility of monetary policy in the Home country. When $\kappa = 1$ producer prices are indexed to the inflation target used by the monetary policymaker, otherwise prices are indexed to a weighted average of past realized producer inflation and the current policy target.

In a similar way, we assume that in the Foreign country the short-term nominal interest rate follows

$$(1+i_{1,t}^*) = (1+i_{1,t-1}^*)^{\phi_i^*} \left(\frac{\bar{\Pi}_t^*}{\tilde{\beta}^*}\right)^{1-\phi_i^*} \left(\frac{\Pi_{F,t}^*}{\bar{\Pi}_t^*}\right)^{(1-\phi_i^*)\phi_\pi^*} \left(\frac{\tilde{Y}_{F,t}^*}{\tilde{Y}_{F,t-1}^*}\right)^{(1-\phi_i^*)\phi_y^*} \left(\frac{S_t}{S_{t-1}}\right)^{-(1-\phi_i^*)\phi_s^*} e^{\xi_t^*}, \quad (46)$$

where ϕ_i^*, ϕ_π^*, ϕ_y^*, ϕ_s^* are nonnegative parameters, $\tilde{\beta}^*$ is an appropriately-defined parameter, ξ_t^* is the policy shock, and $\bar{\Pi}_t^*$ represents the inflation target followed by the Foreign monetary policymaker where now

$$\bar{\Pi}_{F,t}^* = (\bar{\Pi}_t^*)^{\kappa^*}(\Pi_{F,t-1}^*)^{1-\kappa^*},$$

with a weight $\kappa^* \in 0,1]$ measuring the credibility of Foreign monetary policy.

D. Equilibrium

We now define the equilibrium of the previous model. Given processes for the exogenous state variables ($\ln A_t$, $\ln \xi_t$, $\ln \bar{\Pi}_{H,t}$, $\ln A_t^*$, $\ln \xi_t^*$, $\ln \bar{\Pi}_{F,t}^*$), an equilibrium is an allocation (V_t, V_t^*, C_t, C_t^*, L_t, L_t^*, $Y_{H,t}$, $Y_{F,t}^*$, $P_{H,t}/P_t$, $P_{F,t}/P_t$, S_t/S_{t-1}, Q_t, T_t, G_t, $\Pi_{H,t}$, $\Pi_{F,t}^*$, Π_t, Π_t^*, Δ_t, Δ_t^*, F_t, F_t^*, K_t, K_t^*, $M_{t,t+1}$, $M_{t,t+1}^*$, $i_{1,t}$, $i_{1,t}^*$) that satisfies the equations (2), (5), (13), (14), (15), (17), (18), (22), (23), (24), (25), (26), (27), (29), (30), (34), (35), (36), (37), (38), (39), (40), (41), (42), (43), (44) given the two policy rules (45) and (46) and the relationships between the inflation targets of the firms and of the monetary policymaker.

We assume that the vector of exogenous variables follows conditionally-linear processes with time-varying volatility. In particular, we assume a general specification of the stochastic productivity processes to take into account the possibility of a trend in productivity. We model the productivity shock in country H as $A_t = A_{W,t}\tilde{A}_t$, and that in country F as $A_t^* = A_{W,t}\tilde{A}_t^*$, where $A_{W,t}$ has a stochastic trend and can be interpreted as a global common productivity shock while $\tilde{A}_t$ and $\tilde{A}_t^*$ are log-stationary processes that are country-specific.[22]

The stochastic processes of the shocks are:

$$\ln A_{W,t+1} = \ln a + \ln A_{W,t} + u_{aw,t}\varepsilon_{aw,t+1}$$

$$\ln \tilde{A}_{t+1} = \delta_a \ln \tilde{A}_t + u_{a,t}\varepsilon_{a,t+1}$$

$$\ln \bar{\Pi}_{t+1} = \ln \bar{\Pi}_t + u_{\pi,t}\varepsilon_{\pi,t+1}$$

$$\xi_{t+1} = u_{\xi,t}\varepsilon_{\xi,t+1},$$

where a is a parameter measuring the deterministic trend in productivity growth and $0 \leq \delta_a \leq 1$. In what follows, all the ε shocks are i.i.d. white-noise processes.

Time-varying volatility is modeled through linear processes for the variances:

$$u^2_{aw,t+1} = (1 - \rho_{aw})\sigma^2_u + \rho_{aw}u^2_{aw,t} + \sigma^2_\zeta \zeta_{aw,t+1}$$

$$u^2_{a,t+1} = (1 - \rho_a)\sigma^2_u + \rho_a u^2_{a,t} + \sigma^2_\zeta \zeta_{a,t+1}$$

$$u^2_{\pi,t+1} = (1 - \rho_\pi)\sigma^2_u + \rho_\pi u^2_{\pi,t} + \sigma^2_\zeta \zeta_{\pi,t+1}$$

$$u^2_{\xi,t+1} = (1 - \rho_\xi)\sigma^2_u + \rho_\xi u^2_{\xi,t} + \sigma^2_\zeta \zeta_{\xi,t+1}$$

in which all the ζ are i.i.d. white-noise processes and $0 \leq \rho_{aw}, \rho_a, \rho_\pi, \rho_\xi, \leq 1$ with $\sigma^2_u, \sigma^2_\zeta > 0$. The processes for the stochastic disturbances hitting the Foreign economy behave similarly:

$$u^2_{a^*,t+1} = (1 - \rho_{a^*})\sigma^2_u + \rho_{a^*}u^2_{a^*,t} + \sigma^2_\zeta \zeta_{a^*,t+1}$$

$$u^2_{\pi^*,t+1} = (1 - \rho_{\pi^*})\sigma^2_u + \rho_{\pi^*}u^2_{\pi^*,t} + \sigma^2_\zeta \zeta_{\pi^*,t+1}$$

$$u^2_{\xi^*,t+1} = (1 - \rho_{\xi^*})\sigma^2_u + \rho_{\xi^*}u^2_{\xi^*,t} + \sigma^2_\zeta \zeta_{\xi^*,t+1}.$$

In what follows we will refer to the shocks to the inflation target and the shock to the policy instruments as *monetary* or *nominal* shocks, while the productivity shock will be the *real* shock.

E.   Solution

Given the aforementioned specification for the processes of the exogenous state variable, we can write them more compactly as

$$z_{t+1} = \Lambda_z z_t + \eta_{t+1}, \qquad (47)$$

where the vector z_t is defined as $z_t \equiv (\Delta \ln A_{W,t} - \ln a)$, $\ln \tilde{A}_t$, ζ_t, $\ln \overline{\Pi}_{H,t}$, $\ln \tilde{A}^*_t$, ξ^*_t, $\ln \overline{\Pi}^*_{F,t}$, and Λ_z is an appropriately-defined square matrix. The vector η_{t+1} is given by

$$\eta_{t+1} = U_t \varepsilon_{z,t+1}, \qquad (48)$$

where $\varepsilon_{z,t+1}$ collects the innovations, which are assumed to have a bounded support and to be independently and identically distributed with mean zero and variance/covariance matrix I_z, where I_z is an identity matrix of the same dimension of the vector z; U_t is a diagonal matrix whose elements on the diagonal are collected into a vector u_t. In particular, u_t follows the exogenous stochastic linear process given by

$$u_{t+1}^2 = \sigma_u^2 (I_z - \Lambda_u) \bar{u}^2 + \Lambda_u u_t^2 + \sigma_\zeta^2 Z \zeta_{u,t+1}. \tag{49}$$

Each element of u_t^2 is the corresponding squared value of each element of u_t, which still corresponds to the diagonal of matrix U_t as in (48); $\bar{u}^2$ is a vector of steady-state variances, Z and Λ_u are appropriately defined square matrices; $\zeta_{u,t+1}$ is a vector of innovation collecting the above ζ, which are assumed to have a bounded support and to be independently and identically distributed with mean zero and variance/covariance matrix I_z; σ_u and σ_ζ are scalars with $\sigma_u, \sigma_\zeta \geq 0$.

Noticing that (47) with (48) and (49) defines a conditionally-linear process, we can write the set of equilibrium conditions of the model together with the conditional expectation of (47) in a more compact form

$$E_t\{f(y_{t+1}, x_{t+1}, y_t, x_t)\} = \mathbf{0}, \tag{50}$$

for an appropriately defined vector of function $f(\cdot)$ where y_t identifies the nonpredetermined variables while the vector x_t of state variables contains also the vector of exogenous predetermined variables z_t. Given the processes (47), with (48) and (49), an equilibrium of our model is a sequence for the vector of endogenous nonpredetermined variables y_t and for the state variables x_t that satisfies (50), given the initial conditions.

Benigno et al. (2010) characterize the solution of (50) and show that a first-order approximation of the solution can be written as

$$\tilde{y}_t = \bar{g}_x \tilde{x}_t,$$

$$\tilde{x}_{t+1} = \bar{h}_x \tilde{x}_t + \bar{h}_\eta \eta_{t+1},$$

for appropriately-defined matrices $\bar{g}_x$, $\bar{h}_x$, and $\bar{h}_\eta$. This approximation does not correspond to a fully linear solution since η_{t+1}, defined, in (48) is nonlinear. However, it is the best conditionally linear approximation and, in particular, the matrices $\bar{g}_x$ and $\bar{h}_x$ coincide with those of a fully linear approximation. Our first-order approximation maintains heteroskedastic shocks but time-varying volatility does not play a distinct role, meaning that the impulse response of the endogenous variables with respect to the shock to volatility, $\zeta_{u,t+1}$, is always zero. The advantage of performing a conditionally-linear approximation instead of a fully-linear approximation, in which η_{t+1} is also linearized, is clear when we look at a second-order approximation of the solution. Benigno et al. (2010) show that this takes the form

$$\tilde{y}_t = \bar{g}_x \tilde{x}_t + \frac{1}{2}(I_y \otimes \tilde{x}_t')\bar{g}_{xx}\tilde{x}_t + \frac{1}{2}\bar{g}_{uu}u_t^2 + \frac{1}{2}\bar{g}_{zz}\sigma_u^2, \tag{51}$$

$$\tilde{x}_{t+1} = \bar{h}_x \tilde{x}_t + \frac{1}{2}(I_x \otimes \tilde{x}_t')\bar{h}_{xx}\tilde{x}_t + \frac{1}{2}\bar{h}_{uu}u_t^2 + \frac{1}{2}\bar{h}_{zz}\sigma_u^2 + \bar{h}_\eta \eta_{t+1}, \tag{52}$$

for appropriately defined matrices $\bar{g}_{xx}$, $\bar{g}_{zz}$, $\bar{g}_{uu}$ and $\bar{h}_{xx}$, $\bar{h}_{zz}$, $\bar{h}_{uu}$. In this second-order approximation, the volatility of the exogenous state variables now plays a distinct and direct role through the matrices $\bar{g}_{uu}$ and $\bar{h}_{uu}$. Indeed, the endogenous variables are now in a linear relationship with the vector of volatilities, u_t^2. Other methods discussed in the literature, as in Fernandez-Villaverde et al. (2010), need instead to rely at least on a third-order approximation to get such a distinct role for volatilities in influencing the endogenous variables.

The second advantage of our conditionally-linear approximation is that risk premia, evaluated using a first-order approximation of the model, will also be time-varying. This feature enables the model to characterize some stylized facts on the role of volatility on international data in a simple way.

V. Exchange Rates and Risk: A Simple Example

In this section, before we turn to the solution of our general model, we present a simplified framework to study whether we can already account for some of the facts that we have underlined in the empirical analysis. The framework of this section, with its analytical solutions, will also be helpful to explain how our solution method works and represent a useful benchmark through which we can later evaluate the effects of relaxing the assumptions of this section. The simplifying assumptions are: (1) monetary policy in each country is modeled through Taylor rules reacting only to the domestic CPI inflation rate with the same coefficients across countries, and later in the section we allow for interest-rate smoothing; (2) purchasing power parity holds ($v = v^* = n$); (3) flexible prices ($\alpha = \alpha^* = 0$) and constant real rates, which make real shocks irrelevant for the analysis of this section. Therefore, we will abstract completely from productivity shocks and give just a monetary explanation of the facts related to the nominal exchange rate and the UIP deviations.

The starting points are the standard arbitrage-free conditions (26) and (27). As discussed more generally in Benigno et al. (2010), we rely on approximation methods to solve our model. In particular we show that it is sufficient to use a second-order approximation of the model to characterize how risk influences the variables of interest and in particular the exchange rate.

By taking a second-order approximation of (26) and (27), we obtain

$$\hat{i}_t = -E_t\hat{M}_{t+1} - \frac{1}{2}Var_t\hat{M}_{t+1} \tag{53}$$

$$\hat{i}_t^* = -E_t\hat{M}_{t+1}^* - \frac{1}{2}Var_t\hat{M}_{t+1}^*, \tag{54}$$

where hats denote log-deviations with respect to the steady state, in which we assume $i = i^* = 1/\beta - 1$, and E_t and Var_t are conditional expectation and variance operators, respectively.[23] In logs, the complete-market assumption (19) implies

$$\hat{M}_{t+1} = \hat{M}_{t+1}^* - \Delta s_{t+1}. \tag{55}$$

We can combine (53), (54), and (55) to write the short-term excess return of investing in the currency of country F with respect to investing in the currency of country H as

$$\hat{i}_t^* + E_t\Delta s_{t+1} - \hat{i}_t = \frac{\vartheta_t^*}{2} - \frac{\vartheta_t}{2} \tag{56}$$

where

$$\vartheta_t = cov_t(\hat{M}_{t+1}, \Delta s_{t+1}) \qquad \vartheta_t^* = cov_t(\hat{M}_{t+1}^*, -\Delta s_{t+1}). \tag{57}$$

The intuition for why there can be or cannot be an excess return on foreign currency with respect to domestic currency depends on whether foreign currency is or is not a bad hedge with respect to risk relatively to domestic currency. The standard principle is that an asset is "risky" when it does not pay well when money is really needed. In this case, investors command a premium to hold it, which shows up in an excess return relatively to other assets. In our context, the stochastic discount factors measure the agents' appetites for state contingent wealth and therefore when money is needed or not. When $\hat{M}_{t+1}$ and $\hat{M}_{t+1}^*$ are high in some contingencies, the appetites for wealth of the Home and Foreign agents are also high in those contingencies. An asset that pays well under this case is a good asset and represents a good hedge with respect to risk. If, for example, the currency of country H depreciates (the nominal exchange rate depreciates, i.e., $\Delta s_{t+1} > 0$) then having invested in the currency of country F is indeed a good investment since it delivers more money when it is really needed. In this case ϑ_t is positive and ϑ_t^* is negative. In general, the expected short-term excess return of investing in the currency of country F with respect to that of investing in the currency of country H is negative simply because the currency of country H is not a good hedge with respect to the appetite for wealth of both agents. In general, to have a negative expected excess return on the Foreign-versus-Home currency it is not necessary that ϑ_t should be positive and ϑ_t^* negative, but just $\vartheta_t > \vartheta_t^*$.

Finally, it is worth stressing that the right-hand side of equation (56) captures the deviations from uncovered interest parity in any model in which no-arbitrage restrictions apply. Indeed, so far, none of the simplifying assumptions (1), (2) and (3) have been used.

A. Simple Taylor Rules

By making assumption (1) ($\phi_i = \phi_i^* = \phi_y = \phi_y^* = \phi_s = \phi_s^* = 0$, $\phi_\pi = \phi_\pi^*$ with interest rate reacting to CPI inflation into [45] and [46]), we can further use (56) to determine the equilibrium nominal exchange rate. In particular, the short-term nominal interest rates follow simple Taylor rules in which

$$\hat{i}_t = \bar{\pi}_t + \phi_\pi(\pi_t - \bar{\pi}_t) + \xi_t \tag{58}$$

$$\hat{i}_t^* = \bar{\pi}_t^* + \phi_\pi(\pi_t^* - \bar{\pi}_t^*) + \xi_t^* \tag{59}$$

where $\bar{\pi}_t$ and $\bar{\pi}_t^*$ represent the logs of Home and Foreign inflation-target shocks and ζ_t and ξ_t^* are the Home and Foreign policy shocks as in (45) and (46).

We now use the simplifying assumption (2), that there is no home bias in consumption, implying that purchasing power parity holds; that is, $\pi_t = \pi_t^* + \Delta s_t$.

1. Exchange Rate Determination

Using PPP and rules (58) and (59) into (56) we obtain a first-order stochastic difference equation in Δs_t

$$E_t \Delta s_{t+1} = \phi_\pi \Delta s_t + (1 - \phi_\pi)(\overline{\pi}_t - \overline{\pi}_t^*) + (\xi_t - \xi_t^*) - \frac{1}{2}(\vartheta_t - \vartheta_t^*),$$

which can be solved forward to deliver a unique bounded solution for the nominal exchange rate of the form

$$\Delta s_t = E_t \sum_{T=t}^{\infty} \left(\frac{1}{\phi_\pi}\right)^{T+1-t} \left[(\phi_\pi - 1)(\overline{\pi}_T - \overline{\pi}_T^*) - (\xi_T - \xi_T^*) + \frac{1}{2}(\vartheta_T - \vartheta_T^*)\right], \quad (60)$$

under the requirement, for determinacy, that the Taylor's principle holds; that is, $\phi_\pi > 1$.[24]

There are several implications of the previous simple model for nominal exchange rate determination. First, the design of the monetary policy rules is important. Indeed, equation (60) holds only under the special policy rules (58) and (59).[25] Within this class of rules, variation in the policy parameter ϕ_π can also change in an important way the relationship between exchange rate and fundamentals. But which are the fundamentals for exchange rate determination under this simple model? Shocks and risk. Given that $\phi_\pi > 1$ is needed for equilibrium determinacy, a shock that increases the inflation target in a country depreciates its currency, whereas a contractionary policy shock in a country appreciates its own currency (the sign of the response to the policy shock is consistent with the empirical findings that we reported in Section II). In particular, a (temporary) contractionary policy shock appreciates permanently the exchange rate, but without producing the hump-shaped curve found in the data.

Current and future shocks matter, but also current and future risk premia. If the currency of country F has relatively good hedge properties with respect to the currency of country H ($\vartheta_t > \vartheta_t^*$), then currency F strengthens and current nominal exchange rate s_t rises.

Equation (60) represents a second-order approximation for the solution of the equilibrium nominal exchange rate, which depends on first-order terms $\{\overline{\pi}_t, \overline{\pi}_t^*, \xi_t, \xi_t^*\}$ and second-order terms $\{\vartheta_t, \vartheta_t^*\}$. However, to get an explicit solution for the exchange rate in terms of the state variables, we need to solve the second-order terms. The simplification comes by observing that these second-order terms can be just evaluated using a first-order approximation.[26] In particular, given (57), to evaluate ϑ_t and ϑ_t^* we need a first-order approximation of the stochastic discount factors $\hat{M}_{t+1}$ and $\hat{M}_{t+1}^*$ and also a first-order approximation of Δs_t, which we already have in (60). In the general model of the previous section, the stochastic discount factors $\hat{M}_{t+1}$ and $\hat{M}_{t+1}^*$ are complex linear functions, in a first-order approximation, of the shocks of the model. In our simple illustrative example, we assume flexible prices and constant real interest rate (assumption 3). In this case, the stochastic discount factors are just exact linear functions of the inflation rates

$$\hat{M}_{t+1} = -\pi_{t+1} \qquad \hat{M}^*_{t+1} = -\pi^*_{t+1}.$$

Moreover, we assume that the inflation-target shocks behave as random walks with stochastic volatility

$$\bar{\pi}_t = \bar{\pi}_{t-1} + u_{\pi,t-1}\varepsilon_{\pi,t}$$

$$\bar{\pi}^*_t = \bar{\pi}^*_{t-1} + u^*_{\pi,t-1}\varepsilon^*_{\pi,t},$$

where $\varepsilon_{\pi,t}$ and $\varepsilon^*_{\pi,t}$ are i.i.d. white-noise processes. For the policy shocks we assume

$$\xi_t = u_{\xi,t-1}\varepsilon_{\xi,t}$$

$$\xi^*_t = u^*_{\xi,t-1}\varepsilon^*_{\xi,t},$$

where $\varepsilon_{\xi,t}$ and $\varepsilon^*_{\xi,t}$ are i.i.d. white-noise processes.[27] The variances of the above processes are all time varying following the linear stochastic processes

$$u^2_{\pi,t} = \sigma^2_u + \rho_\pi(u^2_{\pi,t-1} - \sigma^2_u) + \sigma^2_\zeta\zeta_{\pi,t}$$

$$u^{*2}_{\pi,t} = \sigma^2_u + \rho_\pi(u^{*2}_{\pi,t-1} - \sigma^2_u) + \sigma^2_\zeta\zeta^*_{\pi,t}$$

$$u^2_{\xi,t} = \sigma^2_u + \rho_\xi(u^2_{\xi,t-1} - \sigma^2_u) + \sigma^2_\zeta\zeta_{\xi,t}$$

$$u^{*2}_{\xi,t} = \sigma^2_u + \rho_\xi(u^{*2}_{\xi,t-1} - \sigma^2_u) + \sigma^2_\zeta\zeta^*_{\xi,t},$$

where $0 \le \rho_\pi, \rho_\xi \le 1$ and all the zetas are i.i.d. white-noise processes while σ^2_u and σ^2_ζ are nonnegative parameters.

Given the previously defined processes, and up to a first-order approximation, equation (60) implies

$$\Delta s_t = (\bar{\pi}_t - \bar{\pi}^*_t) - \frac{1}{\phi_\pi}(\xi_t - \xi^*_t), \tag{61}$$

where movements in the inflation-target shocks move one-to-one the nominal exchange rate, while the response of the nominal exchange rate to policy shocks depends on the parameter of the Taylor rules. Using (53) and (58), and (54) and (59), respectively, we can determine the domestic and foreign inflation rates as

$$\pi_t = \bar{\pi}_t - \frac{1}{\phi_\pi} \xi_t \tag{62}$$

$$\pi_t^* = \bar{\pi}_t^* - \frac{1}{\phi_\pi} \xi_t^*, \tag{63}$$

which in this simple example only reflect the influence of their own monetary shocks. We can use (61), (62), and (63) to evaluate the risk premia component in (57)

$$\vartheta_t = cov_t(\hat{M}_{t+1}, \Delta s_{t+1}) = -u_{\pi,t}^2 - \frac{1}{\phi_\pi^2} u_{\xi,t}^2$$

$$\vartheta_t^* = cov_t(\hat{M}_{t+1}^*, -\Delta s_{t+1}) = -u_{\pi,t}^{*2} - \frac{1}{\phi_\pi^2} u_{\xi,t}^{*2},$$

which can be plugged into (60) to obtain the equilibrium exchange rate

$$\Delta s_t = (\bar{\pi}_t - \bar{\pi}_t^*) - \frac{1}{\phi_\pi}(\xi_t - \xi_t^*) - \frac{1}{2}\frac{1}{\phi_\pi - \rho_\pi}(u_{\pi,t}^2 - u_{\pi,t}^{*2})$$
$$-\frac{1}{2}\frac{1}{\phi_\pi - \rho_\xi}\frac{1}{\phi_\pi^2}(u_{\xi,t}^2 - u_{\xi,t}^{*2}). \tag{64}$$

In this solution, the time-varying volatilities of the monetary shocks matter for the determination of the nominal exchange rate.[28] This is the important consequence of the solution method proposed by Benigno et al. (2010), in which a second-order approximation of the model is sufficient to get a distinct role for time-varying uncertainty in affecting the determination of variables of interest. In (64), the higher the variance of the inflation-target and of the policy shocks in country H, the stronger the currency of country H is, and specularly for the volatility of the monetary shocks in country F. These theoretical findings are in part consistent with the empirical results of Section II: there, we reported that an increase in both volatilities leads to an appreciation of the currency (at least in the medium-run with the exception of the USD/Yen bilateral).

The model is then consistent with the view that more uncertainty can be good for the nominal exchange rate, meaning that the exchange rate can even appreciate when volatility rises. The intuition insists on the good or bad hedging properties of the currency. If a currency is a good hedge with respect to a particular risk and this risk increases, then there is more demand of the currency and its exchange rate appreciates. For example, when the Home inflation target shock falls, the appetite for wealth for the Home consumers rises. At the same time, the nominal exchange rate appreciates, therefore Home currency delivers more money when needed, relatively to foreign currency. This is good for hedging purposes. When the variance of the Home inflation-target shock rises, the good hedging properties of Home currency are enhanced and therefore the higher demand of Home currency leads to an appreciation.

The magnitude of the effects on the exchange rate depends obviously on the magnitude of the shock, but also on the persistence. The higher the persistence the higher the response. It is further influenced by the policy parameter of the Taylor rule, the higher ϕ_π, the muted the response of the exchange rate. In this symmetric example, as for the primitive shocks, what matters for the determination of the equilibrium exchange rate is the relative strength between the volatilities of the monetary shocks across countries. However, while a positive inflation-target shock and a positive policy shock produce responses of opposite sign on the equilibrium nominal exchange rate, an increase in the volatility of the inflation-target shock or of the policy shock impacts in the same direction.

2.   UIP Implications

$$\hat{i}_t^* + E_t \Delta s_{t+1} - \hat{i}_t = \frac{1}{2}(u_{\pi,t}^2 - u_{\pi,t}^{*2}) + \frac{1}{2\phi_\pi^2}(u_{\xi,t}^2 - u_{\xi,t}^{*2})$$

The expected excess return of investing in the currency of country F with respect to that of country H rises with the increase in the volatilities of the monetary shocks in country H. Consistently with the discussion of the previous section, a rise in the volatility of both the monetary shocks in country H enhance the hedging properties of currency H and reduces those of currency F. Currency F requires a premium to be held. While the response of the foreign excess return to an increase in volatility of monetary-policy shock $(u_{\xi,t}^2)$ is, at first pass, consistent with the empirical findings in Section II, an increase in the volatility of the inflation-target shock $(u_{\pi,t}^2)$ goes in the opposite direction with what we found in the data.

This is not the only counterfactual result of this section. As discussed in Backus et al. (2010), this stylized framework cannot account for the negative slope coefficient in the UIP regression: the regression of the one-period changes in the nominal exchange rate on the interest rate differential. Using (64), and analogous solutions for the interest rates in the two countries, the coefficient of the UIP regression implied by our model would be

$$\hat{\beta}^{uip} = \frac{Cov(\Delta s_{t+1}, \hat{i}_t - \hat{i}_t^*)}{Var(\hat{i}_t - \hat{i}_t^*)}$$

$$\hat{\beta}^{uip} = \frac{var(\bar{\pi}_t - \bar{\pi}_t^*) + a_{1,u_\pi}^2 (\rho_\pi/\phi_\pi)var(u_{\pi,t}^2 - u_{\pi,t}^{*2}) + a_{1,u_\xi}^2 (\rho_\xi/\phi_\pi)var(u_{\xi,t}^2 - u_{\xi,t}^{*2})}{var(\bar{\pi}_t - \bar{\pi}_t^*) + a_{1,u_\pi}^2 var(u_{\pi,t}^2 - u_{\pi,t}^{*2}) + a_{1,u_\xi}^2 var(u_{\xi,t}^2 - u_{\xi,t}^{*2})},$$

where the assumption of unit-root processes for the inflation-target shocks blows up numerator and denominator, in large samples, to produce a unitary coefficient. However, abstracting from this issue or focusing on small samples, the only possibility for $\hat{\beta}^{uip}$ to be negative is that ρ_ξ/ϕ_π be negative, as shown in Backus et al. (2010). Since assuming $\rho_\xi < 0$ is not plausible, then in our simplified framework $\hat{\beta}^{uip}$ is positive and decreasing with ϕ_π, the inflation's coefficient in the Taylor rule.

B.   Taylor Rules with Interest-Rate Smoothing

One natural extension to the previous setting is to consider a model in which the interest rate set by the policy authority moves gradually (interest rates are smoothed over time as in McCallum 1994 and Backus et al. 2010) so that interest rates depend also on their past value. The modified Taylor's rules take the form

$$\hat{i}_t = \phi_i \hat{i}_{t-1} + (1 - \phi_i)[\bar{\pi}_t + \phi_\pi(\pi_t - \bar{\pi}_t)] + \xi_t,$$

$$\hat{i}_t^* = \phi_i \hat{i}_{t-1}^* + (1 - \phi_i)[\bar{\pi}_t^* + \phi_\pi(\pi_t^* - \bar{\pi}_t^*)] + \xi_t^*,$$

to replace (58) and (59). Following the same steps as before, it is possible to show that the equilibrium exchange rate is given by

$$\Delta s_t = -\frac{\phi_i}{\lambda - \phi_i}(\hat{i}_{t-1} - \hat{i}_{t-1}^*) + \frac{\lambda}{\lambda - \phi_i}(\bar{\pi}_t - \bar{\pi}_t^*) - \frac{1}{\lambda}(\xi_t - \xi_t^*)$$

$$-\frac{1}{2}\frac{1}{\lambda - \rho_u}\left(\frac{\lambda}{\lambda - \phi_i}\right)^2 (u_{\pi,t}^2 - u_{\pi,t}^{*2}) - \frac{1}{2}\frac{1}{\lambda - \rho_u}\frac{1}{\lambda^2}(u_{\xi,t}^2 - u_{\xi,t}^{*2})$$

(65)

where we are restricting ϕ_i to be $0 < \phi_i < 1$ and where $\lambda \equiv \phi_\pi(1 - \phi_i) + \phi_i$ with the requirement $\lambda > 1$ for equilibrium determinacy, implying again $\phi_\pi > 1$. In general, allowing for interest-rate smoothing changes also the short-run responses to the shocks and the volatilities but does not change the sign of the response. Responses are obviously changed at longer horizons given the lagged reaction to the interest rate.

The important contribution of assuming interest-rate smoothing is that the negative dependence on lagged interest rates can be such to reduce the coefficient of the UIP regression and eventually to turn it negative, as discussed in Backus et al. (2010). However, it does not change the sign of the responses of the expected excess return on foreign-versus-domestic currency to the volatilities of the monetary shocks.

VI. Exchange Rates and Risk: The General Case

We now turn to the implications of the more general framework with sticky prices presented in Section IV. First, we investigate the properties of the nominal stochastic discount factor which, as shown in the previous section, is critical to understand the relationship between exchange rate and risk, and to evaluate the risk premia embedded in asset prices.

In our general framework the stochastic discount factor depends on the Epstein-Zin preference specification. Our first result shows a peculiarity of Epstein-Zin preferences in an international context. In closed economy, a standard finding is the irrelevance of Epstein-Zin preferences for quantities and the importance for asset pricing.[29] The irrelevance result can be understood by observing that up to a first-order approximation, Epstein-Zin preferences do not matter for the equilibrium allocation. In contrast, we will show that Epstein-Zin preferences might also be important for quantities in our two-country open-economy model, since, as shown in equation (30), the cross-country surprises in utility affect the international distribution of wealth. Indeed, in a first-order approximation we obtain

$$\hat{G}_{t+1} = \hat{G}_t + (\gamma - \rho)[(\hat{V}_{t+1} - E_t\hat{V}_{t+1}) - (\hat{V}^*_{t+1} - E_t\hat{V}^*_{t+1})]$$

where hats denote log-deviations with respect to the steady state. Under expected utility, $\rho = \gamma$, $\hat{G}_t$ will be constant across time, implying the standard risk-sharing condition that links marginal utilities of nominal income across countries. Instead, with the Epstein-Zin preferences, the cross-country differences in the realization of utility matter for the distribution of wealth. This might have interesting consequences for the equilibrium allocation of quantities.[30]

However, the general-equilibrium flavor of our analysis makes it difficult to keep track of all the effects through analytical solutions. To get further insights and to study the contribution of the Epstein-Zin preferences to the evaluation of risk premia, we now discuss more deeply the properties of the stochastic discount factor. In a first-order approximation of (22), the Home-country nominal discount factor can be written as

$$
\hat{M}_{t,t+1} = -(\gamma - \rho)(\hat{V}_{t+1} - E_t \hat{V}_{t+1}) + (1 - \rho)(1 - \psi)\Delta \hat{L}_{t+1}
$$

$$
-[1 - \psi(1 - \rho)](\Delta \hat{C}_{t+1} + \Delta \hat{A}_{W,t+1}) - \pi_{t+1},
$$

(66)

where we have defined $\hat{L}_t = \ln(1 - L_t)/\ln(1 - L)$ while $\hat{C}_t$ denotes the deviations of detrended consumption with respect to the steady state, $\hat{C}_t \equiv \ln C_t / A_{W,t} - \ln(C/A_W)$.[31] Under the expected-utility model, $\gamma = \rho$, the stochastic discount factor is a function of consumption growth, which can be decomposed in the growth of detrended consumption, and in the growth of world productivity, a function of the CPI inflation rate and of the growth in hours worked. An increase in consumption lowers the stochastic discount factor and the appetite for wealth, for realistic values of the intertemporal elasticity of substitution, ρ. The impact of the growth in hours worked depends on $\rho \lessgtr 1$, while an increase in the inflation rate reduces instead unambiguously the appetite for wealth. On top of affecting the equilibrium allocation and therefore the allocation of consumption and labor, as discussed earlier, Epstein-Zin preferences bring the novelty that also surprises in the indirect utility matter through the term $(\hat{V}_{t+1} - E_t \hat{V}_{t+1})$. To get further insights on this component, we take a first-order approximation of the indirect utility (2) and show that we can relate it to the present discounted value of the surprises in consumption and labor

$$
\hat{V}_{t+1} - E_t \hat{V}_{t+1} = (1 - \beta) \sum_{T=t+1}^{\infty} \beta^{T-t-1}[\Delta E_{t+1}(\psi(\hat{C}_T + \hat{A}_{W,T}) + (1 - \psi)\hat{L}_T)]
$$

where we have defined $\Delta E_{t+1}(\cdot) = E_{t+1}(\cdot) - E_t(\cdot)$. In general equilibrium, interaction terms will be quite complex. However, at the cost of losing generality, we can get further insights by looking at a limiting case in which the discount factor, β, is close to the unitary value. In this case, indeed, we show that Epstein-Zin preferences do not matter for the equilibrium allocation of quantities, up to a first-order approximation. Under the assumption $\beta \to 1$ we can write

$$
\hat{V}_{t+1} - E_t \hat{V}_{t+1} \approx \Delta E_{t+1}(\psi(\hat{C}_\infty + \hat{A}_{W,\infty}) + (1 - \psi)\hat{L}_\infty),
$$

which shows that only the stochastic trend in the respective variables influences the current surprises in utility. However, since $\hat{C}$ and $\hat{L}$ are respectively a detrended and a stationary variable, their stochastic trends are zero. The surprises to indirect utility will therefore only depend on the stochastic trend in world productivity

$$\hat{V}_{t+1} - E_t\hat{V}_{t+1} \approx \psi\Delta E_{t+1}(\hat{A}_{W,\infty}) = \psi u_{a,t}\varepsilon_{a,t+1},$$

which also displays time-varying risk. The importance of this factor in (66) will be higher, the larger the difference between γ and ρ. Under this particular case, the ability of Epstein-Zin preferences to explain risk premia hinges upon the comovements between returns and the nominal stochastic discount factor. In particular, when agents have a preference for an early resolution of uncertainty (i.e., $\gamma > \rho$), a negative shock to world productivity $\varepsilon_{a,t}$ implies bad news with respect to long-run consumption, which is reflected in bad news on utility. In this case, the stochastic discount factor rises and the appetite for state-contingent wealth too. This mechanism would apply also to the country F. Indeed, it is also true that the surprise in the utility of the foreign country depends on the shifts in the long-run component of world productivity

$$\hat{V}^*_{t+1} - E_t\hat{V}^*_{t+1} \approx \psi\Delta E_{t+1}(\hat{A}_{W,\infty}) = u_{a,t}\varepsilon_{a,t+1}.$$

Under the case $\beta \to 1$, Epstein-Zin preferences might therefore contribute to imply highly correlated discount factors across countries and deliver a global explanation for the risk premia, which will be time-varying and driven by the shocks to the common technological process. The consequence of this result is indeed that, up to a first-order approximation, general equilibrium effects will be shut down. Since surprises in the utility of the Home and Foreign country are highly correlated then, using (29) and (30), G_t is approximately constant over time[32]

$$\hat{G}_{t+1} = \hat{G}_t + (\gamma - \rho)[(\hat{V}_{t+1} - E_t\hat{V}_{t+1}) - (\hat{V}^*_{t+1} - E_t\hat{V}^*_{t+1})]$$

$$\approx \hat{G}_t.$$

This is true up to a first-order approximation, but not in a second-order approximation where it might be possible that EZ preferences also have sizable effects on quantities.

A. Quantitative Evaluation

We now move to a quantitative evaluation of the model implications. In particular, a second-order approximation of the model will be relevant to study the relationship between risk and the exchange rate, and provide a quantitative assessment of such links. This will be implicit in the general solution of the nominal and real exchange rate

$$\Delta \hat{S}_t = \bar{g}_x^s \tilde{x}_t + \frac{1}{2} \tilde{x}_t' \bar{g}_{xx}^s \tilde{x}_t + \frac{1}{2} \bar{g}_{uu}^s u_t^2 + \frac{1}{2} \bar{g}_{zz}^s \sigma_u^2$$

$$\hat{Q}_t = \bar{g}_x^q \tilde{x}_t + \frac{1}{2} \tilde{x}_t' \bar{g}_{xx}^q \tilde{x}_t + \frac{1}{2} \bar{g}_{uu}^q u_t^2 + \frac{1}{2} \bar{g}_{zz}^q \sigma_{u'}^2$$

where the index $i = s, q$ selects appropriate elements of the respective vector or matrices. In this solution, time-varying uncertainty for the stochastic disturbances of the model affects linearly the nominal and real exchange rates through the factors $\bar{g}_{uu}^i$.

1. Calibration

In this section we describe our baseline calibration for the general model. The strategy that we adopt for the calibration exercise is to rely as much as possible on standard values for the parameters and conduct a sensitivity analysis on those for which there are divergences in the literature. We assume that the Home and Foreign economy are of equal size and are calibrated in a symmetric fashion. In this calibration section we think about our two-country world as United States versus the Euro area, abstracting then from asymmetries that might be important for understanding some empirical regularities when it comes to small open economies.[33]

   In choosing the parameters of utility function, we set β to 0.994, consistent with other studies with Epstein-Zin preferences (e.g., Fernandez-Villaverde, Guerron-Quintana, and Rubio-Ramirez 2010). We set the inverse of the intertemporal elasticity of substitution ρ to 2, implying an intertemporal elasticity of substitution (IES) in consumption of 0.5, which is consistent with estimates in the micro literature (e.g., Vissing-Jorgensen 2002) and used also in the international real business cycle literature (as in Stockman and Tesar 1995). We set the coefficient of relative risk aversion γ to 5, as in Backus et al. (2010). We set the share of consumption in the utility bundle, ψ, to 1/3 as in Cooley and Prescott (1995) in order to imply that in the steady state households devote one-third of their time to work.

   We calibrate the parameters pertaining to the consumption basket in the following way. The share of home goods in tradable consumption, v, is set to 0.87. The elasticity of substitution between home and foreign traded goods, θ, is assumed equal to 1.5, which is in the range of the plausible values.

We set the firms' output elasticity with respect to labor, ϕ, to 2/3, and the elasticity of substitution among differentiated goods, σ, to 6 (implying a steady state markup of 20%) and $\alpha = 0.66$ and $\alpha^* = 0.75$ (implying an average length of price contracts equal to 3 and 4 quarters), respectively; all these are standard in the literature and consistent with the posterior estimates for the United States and Euro area by Lubik and Schorfeide (2005).

Regarding the policy rules we assume $\phi_i = 0.76$, $\phi_\pi = 1.41$, $\phi_s = 0.03$, and $\phi_y = .66$ for the US economy and $\phi_i^* = 0.84$, $\phi_\pi^* = 1.37$, $\phi_s^* = 0.03$, and $\phi_y^* = 1.27$ for the Euro area that corresponds to the posterior estimates that Lubik and Schorfeide (2005) have found for the US and Euro area, respectively.[34]

We now turn to the calibration of the stochastic processes. For the productivity shocks we use the posterior estimates of Lubik and Schorfeide (2005) for the United States and Euro-area: $\delta_A = 0.83$, $\delta_A^* = 0.85$, with $\sigma_A = 1.66$ and $\sigma_A^* = 2.71$ as the values through which we scale the individual standard deviation for the Home and Foreign shocks, respectively. We assume no persistence for the policy shocks and we scale its standard deviation by $\sigma_\zeta = 0.18$ for both countries based on the estimates of Lubik and Schorfeide (2005). For the inflation-target shocks we follow Ireland (2007) and set it to $\sigma_\pi = 0.1$. For the persistence of the volatility shocks, we calibrate the autocorrelation coefficients at the values implied by fitting an AR(1) process for each of the three time-series employed in the empirical part. As a consequence, we set $\rho_{aw} = \rho_a = \rho_{a^*} = .71$, $\rho_\pi = \rho_{\pi^*} = .67$, and $\rho_\xi = \rho_{\xi^*} = .53$.

2.   Results

In this section we evaluate to what extent our two-country model with recursive preferences and stochastic volatility can replicate the dynamic properties of the data found in Sections II and III. Our analysis is mainly qualitative as we compare our model-based impulse response with the ones generated by the VAR. In what follows, we plot impulse response of the main variables of interest: real exchange rate (RER), real interest rate differential $(r - r^*)$, deviations from real uncovered interest-rate parity (real UIP), nominal exchange rate (NEX), nominal interest rate differential $(i - i^*)$, nominal uncovered interest-rate parity (Nominal UIP), and domestic output (Y_H), producer inflation (π_H), and Home nominal interest rate (i).[35]

In particular, we identified two main regularities on the relationship between exchange rate and risk: (1) an increase in the volatility of both monetary-policy and inflation-target shocks appreciates the exchange rate, while an increase in the volatility of the productivity shock induces an exchange rate depreciation; (2) an increase in the volatility of the monetary-policy shock leads to deviations from UIP in the form of an increase in the excess return on foreign-versus-domestic currency, while an increase in the volatility of the inflation-target shock leads to a fall in the excess return.

An additional regularity, originally documented by Eichenbaum and Evans (1995) and that we also confirm by controlling for the effects of time-varying volatility, is that a contractionary monetary-policy shock produces a persistent appreciation of the exchange rate and persistent deviations from the UIP in the form of positive excess returns on domestic securities.

Figures 10 and 11 display the dynamic response of our variables of interest to volatility shocks hitting the monetary-policy instrument and the inflation target, respectively. The figures show that the model is in-

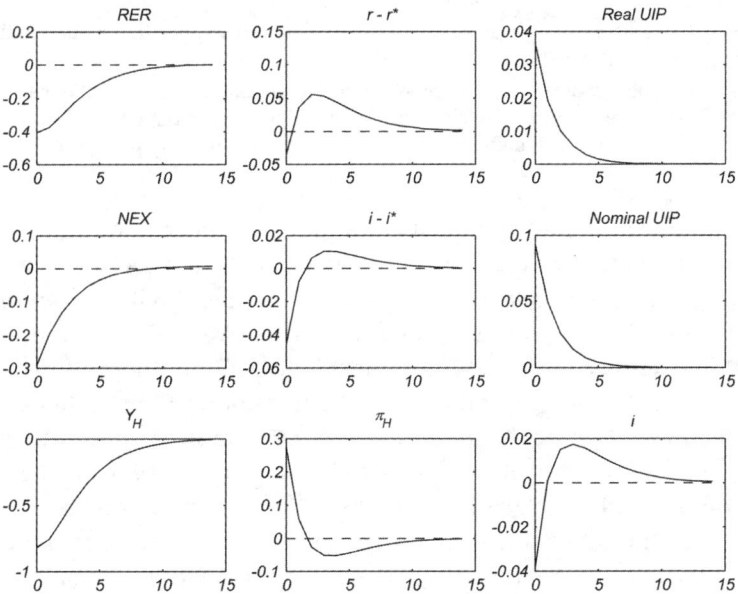

Fig. 10. Dynamic responses to a monetary-policy volatility shock (innovation to the *volatility* of the monetary policy *instrument*).

Notes: The panels show: RER, real interest rate differential ($r - r^*$), deviations from real UIP, NEX, nominal interest rate differential ($i - i^*$), deviations from nominal UIP, domestic output (Y_H), domestic inflation (π_H), and domestic short-term nominal interest rate (i).

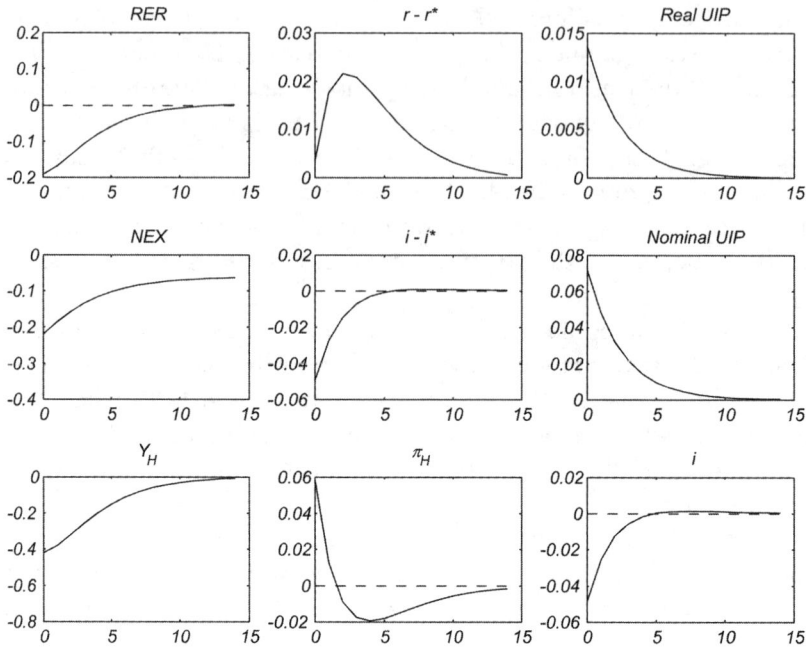

Fig. 11. Dynamic responses to an inflation-target volatility shock (innovation to the volatility of the inflation target).

Notes: The panels show: RER, real interest rate differential ($r - r^*$), deviations from real UIP, NEX, nominal interest rate differential ($i - i^*$), deviations from nominal UIP, domestic output (Y_H), domestic inflation (π_H), and domestic short-term nominal interest rate (i).

deed able to imply an appreciation of the real exchange rate and deviations from the UIP in the form of positive excess returns from investing in foreign-currency denominated bonds, consistent with our empirical findings both in real and in nominal terms. A rise in home nominal volatility tends also to reduce domestic output and increase domestic producer inflation while the domestic nominal interest rate declines proportionately more than the foreign one. An interesting difference among the two nominal shocks arises in the response of the real interest rate differential. In the case of the shock to volatility of the inflation target, the real interest rate differential is positive on impact and increasing in the short run while it is negative on impact following a shock to the volatility of the monetary instrument. This difference arises because the volatility shock to the monetary instrument generates more inflation than the shock to the inflation target.

Figure 12 similarly shows the dynamic response of RER and the de-

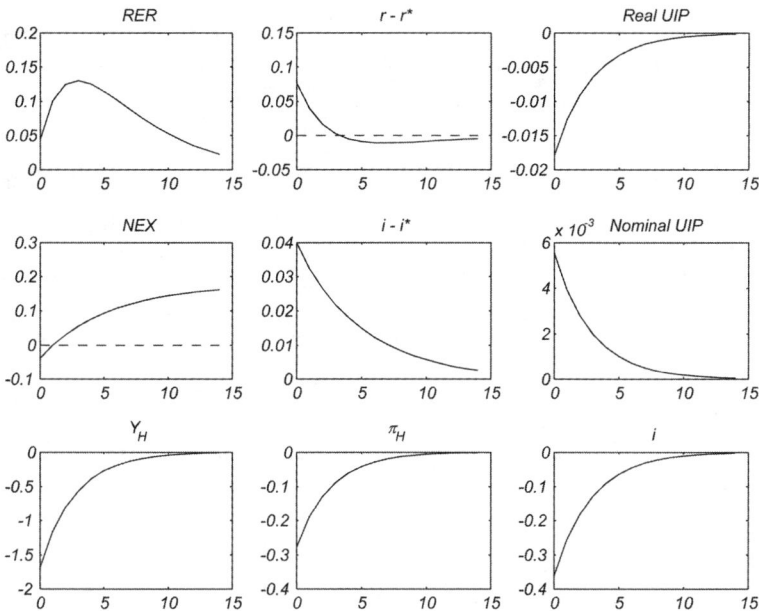

Fig. 12. Dynamic responses to an innovation to the volatility of the productivity shock
Notes: The panels show: RER, real interest rate differential $(r - r^*)$, deviations from real
UIP, NEX, nominal interest rate differential $(i - i^*)$, deviations from nominal UIP, domes-
tic output (Y_H), domestic inflation (π_H), and domestic short-term nominal interest rate (i).

viation from UIP to a volatility shock hitting global productivity. The
asymmetries in the degrees of price stickiness and the response coefficients of the policy rules imply that innovations in the level and/or
volatility of the global productivity shocks are able to produce a non-
zero response on international variables. In particular, in response to
an increase in the volatility of the global productivity shock, the RER
depreciates and we observe positive deviations from nominal UIP consistent with the sign of the response that we observe in our empirical
findings. However, the nominal exchange rate appreciates on impact.
Therefore, the movements in the real exchange rate are mainly driven
by changes in domestic CPI inflation.

All these results are qualitatively consistent with the empirical regularities *Fact 1* and *2*, and also show that our approximation method is
effective to study the link between time-varying volatility and the endogenous variables, like the exchange rate.

As to *Fact 3*, related to the effects of monetary-policy *level* shocks on

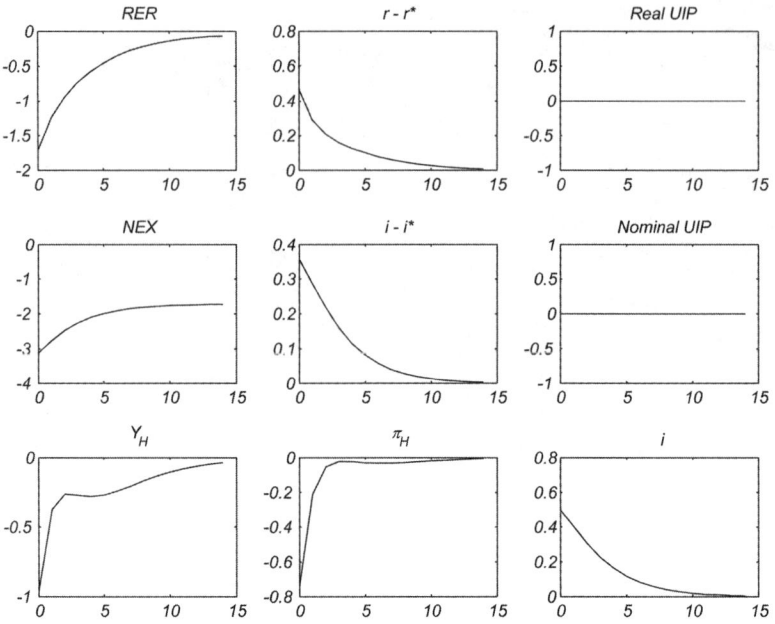

Fig. 13.   Dynamic responses to a monetary policy shock

Notes: The panels show: RER, real interest rate differential $(r - r^*)$, deviations from Real UIP, NEX, nominal interest rate differential $(i - i^*)$, deviations from nominal UIP, domestic output (Y_H), domestic inflation (π_H), and domestic short-term nominal interest rate (i).

the exchange rate and UIP deviations, figure 13 shows that a contractionary monetary-policy shock indeed implies an appreciation of the RER but it is unable to generate the hump-shaped response that we observe in the data, nor deviations from the UIP.

In order to look deeper into this result, we next explore which element of the theoretical model is responsible for this behavior and whether a different calibration would lead to the persistent appreciation observed in the data.

Figures 14 through 16 perform this task by displaying the dynamic responses of the variables of interest to a monetary-policy shock (level shock) and to volatility shocks, respectively, and for different degrees of monetary policy inertia, as measured by the smoothing parameter ϕ_i in equation (45).

Specifically, figure 14 displays the dynamic response of the economy to a monetary-policy *level* shock, which raises the interest rate differential, and it shows that for high enough degrees of interest-rate smoothing, the model is indeed able to imply a substantial degree of persis-

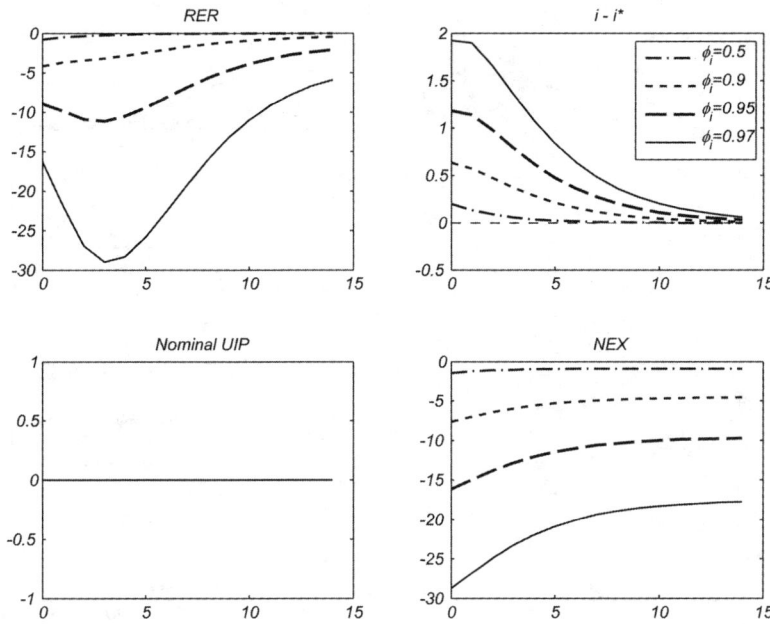

Fig. 14. Dynamic responses to a monetary policy shock (level): The role of interest-rate smoothing.

Note: The panels show: RER, nominal interest rate differential $(i - i^*)$, deviations from nominal UIP, and NEX.

tence in the real appreciation. On the other hand, increasing the inertia in the monetary-policy rules does not imply significant deviations from the UIP. This result, however, is not at all surprising, as it is common to any rational-expectations open-economy model with no financial frictions, where the UIP holds up to a first-order approximation. As a consequence, the increase in the interest rate differential implied by the domestic monetary-policy shock is offset by the nominal depreciation that follows the initial appreciation: UIP holds and the model fails to reproduce the hump-shaped response of the nominal exchange rate.

With respect to this latter point, however, we know that in our model deviations from the UIP can be implied by second-order terms and in particular by stochastic volatility, as shown analytically in the simple case of Section V. Figures 15 and 16, then, show the role of interest-rate smoothing in shaping the response of deviations from the UIP following volatility shocks on the monetary policy instrument and target. As the graphs clearly document, for both cases of volatility shocks, the response of the excess return on foreign-versus-domestic currency mono-

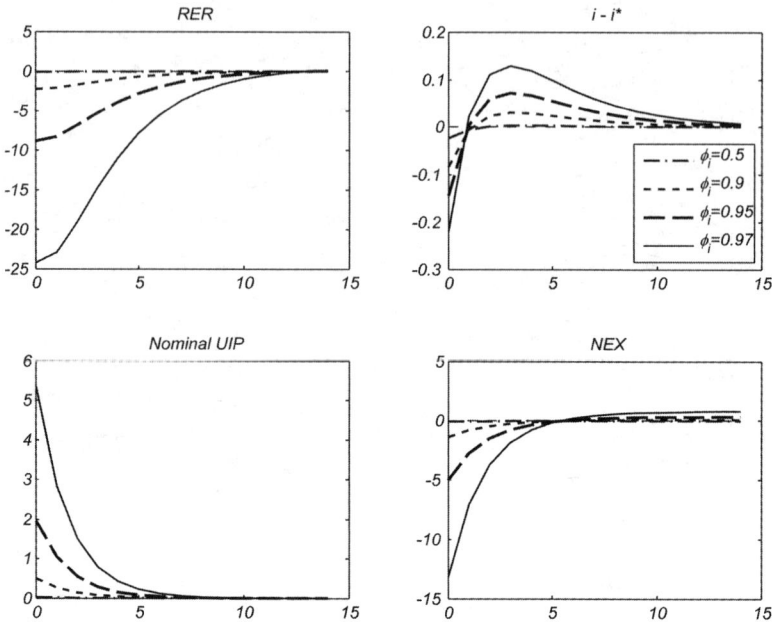

Fig. 15. Dynamic responses to a shock to the monetary-policy volatility (u_ε^2): The role of interest-rate smoothing.

Note: The panels show: RER, nominal interest rate differential ($i - i^*$), deviations from nominal UIP, and NEX.

tonically increases with the coefficient of interest-rate smoothing, as expected. A higher policy inertia, moreover, is also able to amplify the nominal and real exchange rate appreciation.

An additional test for our model would be to see how it performs in terms of the UIP puzzle: the negative slope of the regression between nominal exchange-rate changes and the interest-rate differential.

In figures 15 and 16, we show that the interaction between interest-rate smoothing and stochastic volatility is able to produce persistent deviations from the UIP. The natural next step is to see to what extent such deviations are consistent with a negative slope in the UIP regression, and what are the theoretical factors that, within the model, can have an effect on it. We study this issue by simulating the theoretical model and computing the moments of interest from the simulated time series.

Figure 17 studies the slope of the UIP regression under different parametrizations. The top panels display the interaction among stochastic volatility, interest-rate smoothing, and Epstein-Zin preferences in a flexible-price economy. The bottom panels instead study the role

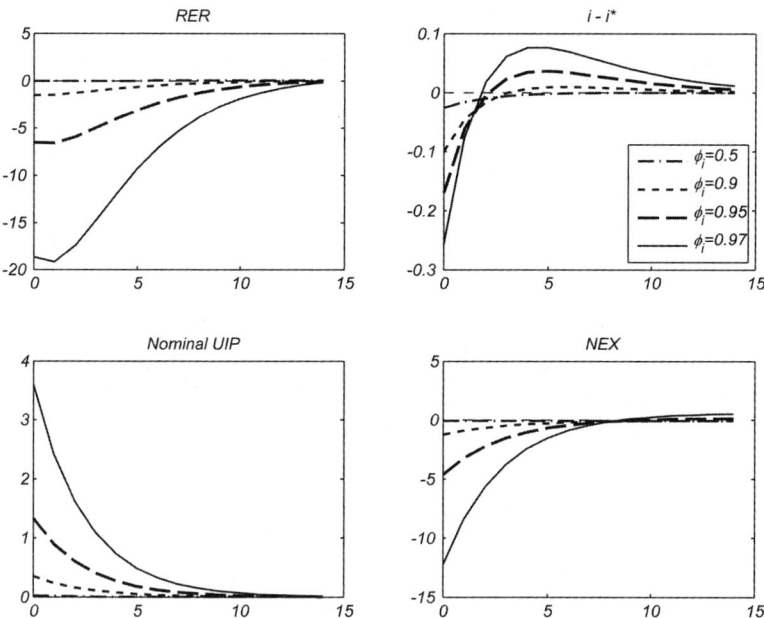

Fig. 16.   Dynamic responses to a shock to the volatility of the inflation target (u_π^2): The role of interest-rate smoothing.

Note: The panels show: RER, nominal interest rate differential ($i - i^*$), deviations from nominal UIP, and NEX.

of price stickiness and its interaction with stochastic volatility and Epstein-Zin preferences, for a given degree of interest-rate smoothing ($\phi_i = 0.95$). The other parameters are calibrated as discussed earlier.

Three main implications arise from figure 17:

1. The interaction between stochastic volatility and interest-rate smoothing can drive the negative covariance between nominal exchange-rate changes and interest-rate differential that is observed in the data. For this result, stochastic volatility is a necessary ingredient of the model. The effect of interest-rate smoothing on the slope of the UIP regression, however, can vary quite a bit depending on the specific type of shock to which we condition the simulation of the model: in particular, the effects of raising monetary-policy inertia on the covariance between nominal-exchange-rate depreciations and interest-rate differentials are stronger conditional on monetary policy and global productivity shocks, while smaller impact is implied by conditioning on inflation-target shocks or idiosyncratic productivity shocks. The result

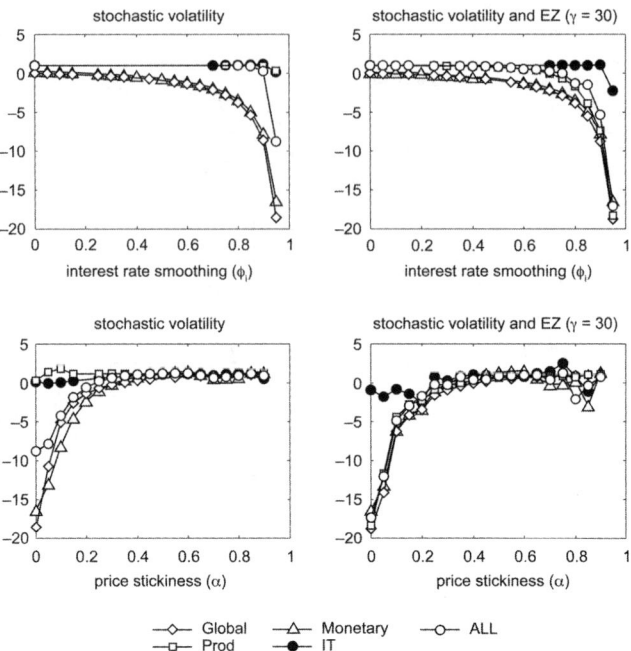

Fig. 17. The slope of the UIP regression: The role of interest-rate smoothing (top panels) and price stickiness (bottom panels).

on monetary-policy and inflation-target shocks are qualitatively consistent with the simple case discussed in Section V: the unit root in the process for the inflation target tends to drive the slope toward unity in large samples, regardless of the degree of interest-rate smoothing, while a negative correlation between exchange-rate changes and interest-rate differentials arises following monetary-policy shocks. The asymmetric calibration of the policy rules implies that even a global productivity shock can have implications for international relative variables. The degree of interest-rate smoothing in the policy rules can again play a key role in driving the slope of the UIP regression.

2. High degrees of price stickiness, on the contrary, tend to drive the slope of the UIP regression toward the unitary value, even for a high degree of interest-rate smoothing (calibrated at 0.95). Moderate degrees of price stickiness, however, are still consistent with a negative covariance between nominal exchange-rate changes and interest-rate differential, provided that the degree of monetary policy inertia is sufficiently

strong. This result holds conditional on monetary and global productivity shocks, and fades away instead if we condition on inflation-target and idiosyncratic productivity shocks, consistent with implication 1.

3. Deviating from expected utility has little but beneficial effects on both respects: the effect of monetary-policy inertia becomes stronger also, conditional on idiosyncratic productivity shocks and even on inflation-target shocks, while moderate degrees of price stickiness are now consistent with a negative slope in the UIP regression, also conditional on country-specific productivity shocks.

It is worth noticing, that none of the aforementioned results would arise in a model without stochastic volatility, in which case the slope of the UIP would always be one: stochastic volatility is therefore a necessary ingredient to understand these regularities.

Another relevant empirical regularity that is connected to the UIP puzzle has been recently pointed out by Engel (2010) and is related to the behavior of the *level* of the *real* exchange rate: Engel (2010) shows that when a country real interest rate is high (relative to the foreign one), then its currency tends to be stronger in real terms than what would be implied by the *real* uncovered interest rate parity. As discussed in Engel (2010), this observation poses a challenge for the models that have been designed to address the UIP puzzle in nominal terms. Indeed, while matching the empirical comovement between real interest-rate differentials and RER expected one-period changes, most of the existing models fail to capture the sign of the covariance between real interest-rate differentials and the *level* of the real exchange rate.

We focus on the impulse response to volatility shocks, since these are the shocks that in our model can generate deviations from nominal or real UIP. Our impulse response analysis suggests that, conditionally on a shock to the volatility of the inflation target, the real exchange rate appreciates on impact while the real interest rate differential is positive (see figure 11): this pattern is consistent with Engel's evidence. However, conditional on the same shock, the exchange rate would depreciate in its adjustment path, contradicting the evidence in Engel (2010). Moreover, the current real interest-rate differential, following a shock to the volatility of the inflation target, is positively related to both current and future deviations from UIP, while in Engel's findings it covaries negatively with the short-run deviations from UIP.

There are three main caveats that are important to keep in mind when looking at our model-based impulse responses to assess our model's ability to replicate Engel's findings. First, Engel's finding in terms of the behavior of the real exchange rate are based on a VAR-estimate of real interest rates, where the VAR model considers only a subset of the variables involved in our theoretical model (Q_t, $i_t - i_t^*$, and $\pi_t - \pi_t^*$). Second, the estimates in Engel (2010) are based on a *linear* projection while our approach emphasizes the importance of *second-order* moments for exchange rate determination. Third, and most important, the puzzle discussed in Engel (2010) is related to *unconditional* covariances—the linear-regression coefficients of the real exchange rate on the interest-rate differential at various time-horizons—while our model-based impulse-response functions only reflect comovements *conditional* on specific shocks.

Therefore, while looking at the model-implied impulse-response functions is useful at first pass, a proper analysis of the evidence discussed by Engel would require us to use our theoretical model to simulate the relevant time series, and then estimate the same VAR and construct the same statistics that are presented and discussed in Engel (2010), and that are at the heart of the puzzle. Also, it would be interesting to check the robustness of Engel's findings from an empirical point of view by augmenting his VAR specification with volatility measures, to make it consistent with the implications of our approach to exchange rate determination. We plan on pursuing this research avenue in future works.

VII. Conclusion

Time variation in uncertainty and risk can be an important source of fluctuations for macroeconomic variables and in particular for the exchange rate. Using a standard open-economy VAR, we have provided new evidence on the importance of both real and nominal volatility shocks for the behavior of the nominal and real exchange rate. These findings complement the well-known evidence, documented by several studies, based on the UIP regression. Under rational expectations, the negative regression coefficients found in these works can be interpreted as variation over time in risk premia. Time variation in uncertainty can also be an important source of the variation over time in risk premia.

Our VAR analysis shows that a rise in the volatilities of the nominal shocks appreciates the dollar exchange rate, especially in the medium run. On the other hand, an increase in the volatility of the real shock (productivity) has the opposite effect. Moreover, a rise in the volatilities of the nominal shocks generates significant and persistent deviations from UIP and in particular an increase in the excess returns of foreign short-term bonds. We also investigate the response of the slope of the term structure to volatility shocks and find that both real and nominal shocks steepen the term structure. Finally, we also confirm the evidence reported by Eichenbaum and Evans (1995) that a positive innovation to the level of the monetary-policy shock (contractionary policy shock) produces a persistent appreciation in both the real and nominal exchange rates and persistent deviations from the UIP in the form of positive excess returns on US securities.

We propose a New Keynesian open economy model as a unifying framework for reconciling these findings in a general equilibrium model with time-varying uncertainty.

Our model is successful along some dimensions. The key element is the specification of monetary policy through interest rate rules and in particular the smoothing coefficient relating current to past interest rates in the rule. The smoothing coefficient, together with price stickiness, is important to produce a hump-shaped response of the real exchange rate to the level interest-rate shock, and combined with time-varying uncertainty can capture a negative coefficient in the UIP regression. Among the other factors that affect critically the coefficient in the UIP regression, higher nominal rigidities do not help, while an increase in risk aversion improves the results. In this sense, allowing for Epstein-Zin preferences that disentangle intertemporal elasticity of substitution and risk aversion is an important feature of our framework. However, at a first look, it is not clear that Epstein-Zin preferences, in a general equilibrium, maintain their appeal to explain some puzzles in asset pricing as in other partial equilibrium analysis. This is an issue that needs further investigation.

We consider this work as a primal approach for the analysis of time-varying uncertainty in open economies because of the methodology that we use for its solution and the general features that we allow for in the model. However, there are several limitations. First, our model, as any framework in which UIP holds up to a first-order approximation, cannot produce a hump-shaped response of the nominal exchange rate to a policy shock, but only of the real exchange rate. Directions to explore could be in the form of financial frictions or departures from rational expectations. Second, there are several tensions between the parameter values of the model relevant to match one fact or another.

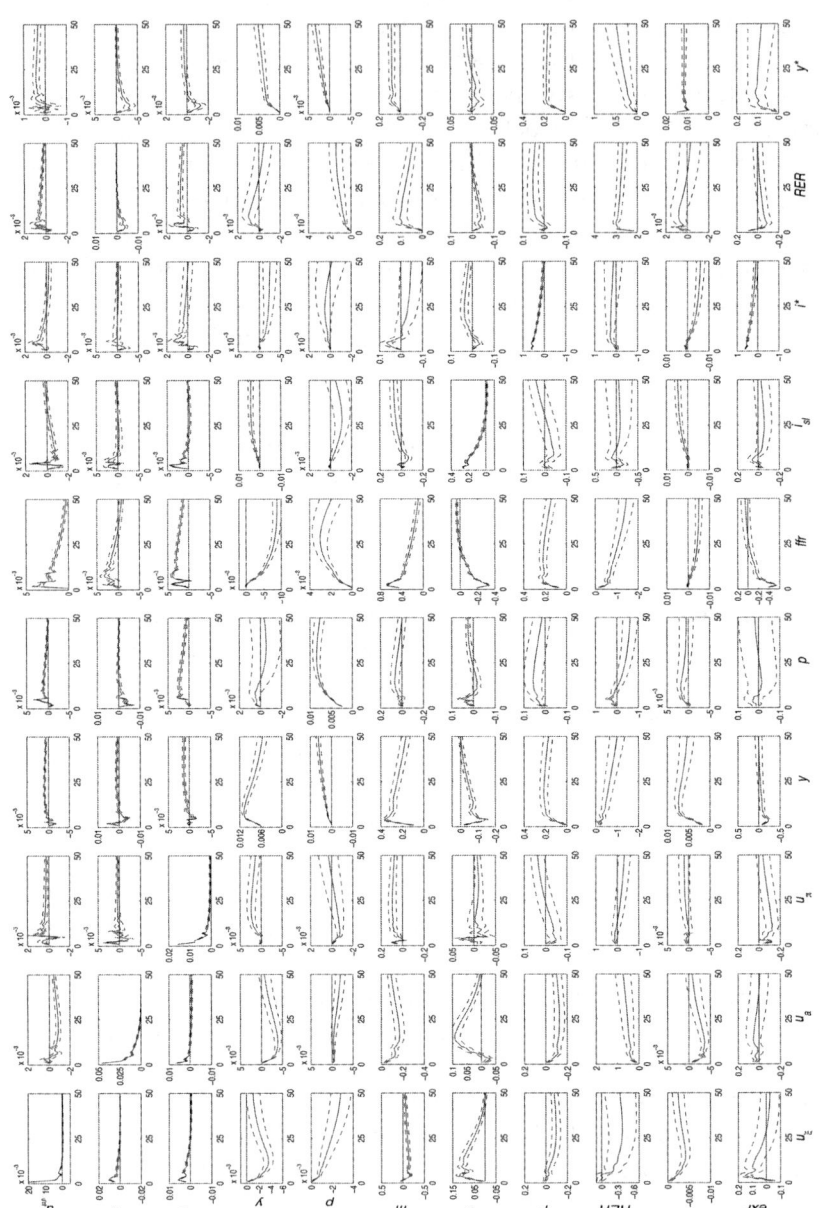

Fig. 18. Impulse response functions: Pooled panel VAR

We cannot claim a complete success on all directions simultaneously nor we did analyze a full match of the model with the data. Finally, related to the latter point, we have calibrated the parameters of our model based on empirical studies building on first-order approximations of the model. This is in contrast with the message of our work that second-order terms are important. Therefore, the estimation of the model is really needed to evaluate its fit. To this purpose, an appropriate methodology should be elaborated to handle the features of our general second-order approximated solutions. We leave this research for future work.

Endnotes

We thank the editors, Daron Acemoglu and Michael Woodford. We also thank Marianna Bellòc, Fabrice Collard, Charles Engel, Max Gillman, Hande Küçük-Tuger, Albert Marcet, Alessandro Rebucci, Martin Uribe, seminar participants at Cardiff Business School and Trinity College Dublin and participants at the NBER's Twenty-Sixth Annual Conference on Macroeconomics for helpful comments, Matteo Ciccarelli for sharing his RATS codes for PanelVAR estimation and analysis, and Federica Romei for excellent research assistance. Financial support from and ERC Starting Independent Grant (Pierpaolo Benigno) and ESRC grant ES/1024174/1 (Gianluca Benigno) is gratefully acknowledged. For acknowledgments, sources of research support, and disclosure of the authors' material financial relationships, if any, please see http://www.nber.org/chapters/c12420 .ack.

1. Engel (2010) provides further evidence on this even by looking at the real version of the UIP and shows that the expected appreciation of high-yield currencies is combined with a relatively stronger currency.

2. In what follows we refer to risk, uncertainty, and stochastic volatility in an interchangeable way.

3. Hodrick (1989) and Obstfeld and Rogoff (2002) in a flexible- and sticky-price environment, respectively, relate the nominal exchange rate to monetary uncertainty through alternative specifications of money demand.

4. This implies that the parameters of the policy rules (as opposed to preferences to money demand) become crucial in shaping exchange rate dynamics and in determining to what extent nominal or real disturbances matter for the nominal (and real) exchange rate.

5. As we will discuss later, most of the models that have been developed recently specify exogenous process for consumption and/or output.

6. The key difference is that our first-order approximation still displays heteroskedasticity and is the best approximation in the class of conditionally-linear processes.

7. In our model, the monetary policy shock represents a shock to the systematic component of the interest rate rule. The inflation target is also part of the interest rate rule and represents the target with respect to which any deviation of actual inflation triggers the policy response.

8. Many specifications of our empirical analysis, like the lag-order of the main VAR, the use of a price-level index instead of inflation, and the choice to display one-standard deviation bands in the impulse-response analysis, are borrowed from our empirical benchmark, Eichenbaum and Evans (1995), to which we seek to relate our results.

9. We depart from Eichenbaum and Evans (1995), besides by including three volatility measures, by considering the slope of the US yield curve $i_{sl,t}$, on the one hand, while disregarding the measure of nonborrowed reserves, on the other hand.

10. This is true in the theoretical model presented later in the paper but we leave the details for future work.

11. We do not report the responses of the nominal exchange rate, since they are very similar to those of the real exchange rate.

12. For a thorough discussion of these and other empirical approaches for the analysis of dynamic macro panels, see Canova (2007, ch. 8).

13. As shown in the previous section, Japan is often an outlier with respect to the dynamic responses of the exchange rate and the foreign currency risk premium. These differences suggest that the Japanese currency behaves in a somewhat peculiar way vis-à-vis the USD, for which the enormous and persistent positions in the yen carry-trade strategy might possibly play a key role. For this reason, we disregard Japan for the remainder of the section.

14. This corresponds to the Aggregate Time Series estimator, as defined by Canova (2007), which we slightly modify by aggregating the time series using a GDP-weighted average (rather than a simple average) as in Benigno and Nisticò (2011), among others.

15. See figure 18 for the complete set of impulse-response functions for the pooled panel VAR.

16. See Swanson (2010) for how to compute risk-aversion toward consumption with Epstein-Zin preferences.

17. See Chari, Kehoe, and McGrattan (2002).

18. Given the assumption that a common labor market exists in each country and that each firm employs all the workers, as it will be discussed later, we can impose symmetry in labor supply and set $L^j = L$ for each j. It follows from (20) that $C^j = C$ for each j. Therefore, also $V^j = V$.

19. When $\gamma = \rho$, utility (2) coincides with the expected utility model where indeed intertemporal utility is defined as $V_t^{1-\rho}$.

20. Otherwise we can assume that each firm is endowed with a fixed amount of nondepreciating capital.

21. We will also consider a target in terms of CPI inflation instead of PPI inflation.

22. In this way our model will allow for a balanced-growth path. As we will show in the next section, the stochastic trend is in particular important for the relevance of the Epstein-Zin assumption.

23. Notice that (53) and (54) do not hold exactly but up to residuals, which are of third-order in an appropriate norm on the stochastic disturbances. Under the assumption of log-normality, as in Backus et al. (2010), they would hold exactly. Our analysis is a local analysis and theirs is a global analysis. Therefore, their approach is limited to the possibility of a closed-form solution. Moreover, the two frameworks will also deliver subtle differences in terms of the conditions needed for the determinancy of the equilibrium.

24. Necessary and sufficient conditions for the local determinancy of equilibrium are discussed more extensively in Benigno and Benigno (2008), for two-country open-economy models.

25. Hodrick (1989) and Obstfeld and Rogoff (2002) restrict their attention to special money-supply rules in which the equilibrium in the money market also becomes relevant for the determination of the exchange rate.

26. See also Lombardo and Sutherland (2007).

27. We could surely generalize to autoregressive process for the policy shock, but the most common assumption in the literature is that of white-noise processes.

28. Notice that the terms in σ_u^2 cancel out because of the symmetry assumed.

29. See, among others, Rudebush and Swanson (2009).

30. Notice, however, that in this first-order approximation $E_t \hat{G}_{t+1} = \hat{G}_t$, and therefore $\hat{G}_t$ is a local martingale.

31. The balance growth path of the model is defined with respect to the common trend in productivity, A_W.

32. The statement is true under the assumption that β is close to the unitary value up to a first-order approximation, and independently of the values assumed by the parameters γ and ρ.

33. Relevant asymmetries could be in terms of a policy rule that reacts to exchange rate for small open economies or different degrees of openess that affect critically the international transmission mechanism of shocks.

34. Although we specified a theoretical model in which monetary-policy credibility might possibly play a role, we disregard this role in the present work, and accordingly parameterize $\kappa = \kappa^* = 1$.

35. For ease of comparison with the empirical analysis, we normalize the size of each shock to the one featured in the VAR analysis.

References

Backus, D., F. Gavazzoni, C. Telmer, and S. E. Zin. 2010. "Monetary Policy and the Uncovered Interest Parity Puzzle." NBER Working Paper no. 16218. Cambridge, MA: National Bureau of Economic Research, July.

Bansal, R., and I. Shaliastovich. 2010. "A Long-Run Risks Explanation of Predictability Puzzles in Bond and Currency Markets." Manuscript, Duke University.

Bekaert, G., and E. Engstrom. 2009. "Asset Return Dynamics under Bad Environment Good Environment Fundamentals." NBER Working Paper no. 15222. Cambridge, MA: National Bureau of Economic Research, August.

Benigno, G., and P. Benigno. 2008. "Exchange Rate Determination under Interest Rate Rules." *Journal of International Money and Finance* 27:971–93.

Benigno, G., P. Benigno, and S. Nisticò. 2010. "Second-Order Approximation of Dynamic Models with Time-Varying Risk." NBER Working Paper no. 16633. Cambridge, MA: National Bureau of Economic Research, December.

Benigno, G., and B. De Paoli. 2010. "On the International Dimension of Fiscal Policy." *Journal of Money, Credit and Banking* 42:1523–42.

Bilson, J. F. 1981. "The Speculative Efficiency Hypothesis." *Journal of Business* 54:435–51.

Bloom, N. 2009. "The Impact of Uncertainty Shocks." *Econometrica* 77:623–85.

Bloom, N., M. Floetotto, and N. Jaimovich. 2009. "Really Uncertain Business Cycles." Manuscript, Stanford University.

Calvo, G. A. 1983. "Staggered Prices in a Utility-Maximizing Framework." *Journal of Monetary Economics* 12:383–98.

Campbell, J. Y., and J. H. Cochrane. 1999. "By Force of Habit: A Consumption-Based Explanation of Aggregate Stock Market Behavior." *Journal of Political Economy* 107 (2): 205–51.

Canova, F. 2007. *Methods for Applied Macroeconomic Research.* Princeton, NJ: Princeton University Press.

Chari, V. V., P. J. Kehoe, and E. R. McGrattan. 2002. "Can Sticky Price Models Generate Volatile and Persistent Real Exchange Rates?" *Review of Economic Studies* 69:533–63.

Clarida, R., and J. Gali. 1994. "Sources of Real Exchange Rate Fluctuations: How Important Are Nominal Shocks?" *Carnegie-Rochester Conference on Public Policy* 41:1–56.

Cooley, T., and E. Prescott. 1995. "Economic Growth and Business Cycles." In *Frontiers of Business Cycle Research,* edited by T. Cooley, 1–38. Princeton, NJ: Princeton University Press.

Eichenbaum, M., and C. L. Evans. 1995. "Some Empirical Evidence on the Effects of Shocks to Monetary Policy on Exchange Rates." *The Quarterly Journal of Economics* 110:975–1009.

Engel, C. 2010. "The Real Exchange Rate, Real Interest Rates, and the Risk Premium." University of Wisconsin.

Epstein, L., and S. E. Zin. 1989. "Substitution, Risk Aversion and the Temporal Behavior of Consumption and Asset Returns: A Theoretical Framework." *Econometrica* 57:937–69.

———. 1991. "The Independence Axiom and Asset Returns." NBER Technical Working Paper no. 0109. Cambridge, MA: National Bureau of Economic Research.

Fama, E. F. 1984. "Forward and Spot Exchange Rates." *Journal of Monetary Economics* 14:319–38.

Fernandez-Villaverde, J., P. Guerron-Quintana, and J. F. Rubio-Ramirez. 2010. "Fortune or Virtue: Time-Variant Volatilities Versus Parameter Drifting in U.S. Data." NBER Working Paper no. 15928. Cambridge, MA: National Bureau of Economic Research, April.

Fernandez-Villaverde, J., P. Guerron-Quintana, J. F. Rubio-Ramirez, and M. Uribe. 2009. "Risk Matters: The Real Effects of Volatility Shocks." NBER Working Paper no. 14875. Cambridge, MA: National Bureau of Economic Research, April.

Frankel, J. A., and R. Meese. 1987. "Are Exchange Rates Excessively Variable?" In *NBER Macroeconomics Annual 1987*, edited by S. Fischer, 117–53. Cambridge, MA: MIT Press.

Gavazzoni, F. 2009. "Uncovered Interest Rate Parity Puzzle: An Explanation Based on Recursive Utility and Stochastic Volatility." Manuscript, Tepper School of Business, Carnegie Mellon University.

Hodrick, R. J. 1989. "Risk, Uncertainty, and Exchange Rates." *Journal of Monetary Economics* 23:433–59.

Kuttner, K. N. 2001. "Monetary Policy Surprises and Interest Rates: Evidence from the Fed Funds Futures Market." *Journal of Monetary Economics* 47:523–44.

Lombardo, G., and A. Sutherland. 2007. "Computing Second-Order-Accurate Solutions for Rational Expectation Models Using Linear Solution Methods." *Journal of Economic Dynamics and Control* 31 (2): 515–30.

Lubik, T., and F. Schorfeide. 2005. "A Bayesian Look at New Open Economy Macroeconomics." Economics Working Paper Archive 521, Johns Hopkins University.

McCallum, B. T. 1994. "A Reconsideration of the Uncovered Interest Parity Relationship." *Journal of Monetary Economics* 33:105–32.

Menkhoff, L., L. Sarno, M. Schmeling, and A. Schrimpf. 2011. "Carry Trades and Global Foreign Exchange Volatility." *Journal of Finance*, forthcoming. European Finance Association (EFA) 2009 Bergen Meetings Paper.

Moore, M. J., and M. J. Roche. 2010. "Solving Exchange Rate Puzzles with Neither Sticky Prices Nor Trade Costs." *Journal of International Money and Finance* 29:1151–70.

Obstfeld, M., and K. Rogoff. 2002. "Risk and Exchange Rates." In *Contemporary Economic Policy: Essays in Honor of Assaf Razin*, edited by Elhanan Helpman and Effraim Sadka. Cambridge: Cambridge University Press.

Pesaran, M. H., and R. P. Smith. 1995. "Estimating Long-Run Relationships from Dynamic Heterogeneous Panels." *Journal of Econometrics* 68:79–113.

Rudebush, G., and E. Swanson. 2009. "The Bond Premium in a DSGE Model with Long-Run Real and Nominal Risks." Federal Reserve Bank of San Francisco Working Paper 2008-31.

Stockman, A. C., and L. L. Tesar. 1995. "Tastes and Technology in a Two-Country Model of the Business Cycle: Explaining International Comovements." *American Economic Review* 85 (1): 168–85.

Swanson, E. 2010. "Risk Aversion and the Labor Margin in Dynamic Equilibium Models." Federal Reserve Bank of San Francisco Working Paper 2009-26.

Verdelhan, A. 2010. "A Habit Based Explanation of the Exchange Rate Risk Premium." *Journal of Finance* 65 (1): 123–46.

Vissing-Jorgensen, A. 2002. "Limited Asset Market Participation and the Elasticity of Intertemporal Substitution." *Journal of Political Economy* 100:825–53.

Weil, P. 1990. "Non-Expected Utility in Macroeconomics." *Quarterly Journal of Economics* 105:29–42.

Comment

Charles Engel, *University of Wisconsin and NBER*

This important contribution to open-economy macroeconomics delivers significant insights in three areas: the empirical response of exchange rates to measures of uncertainty; the incorporation of an endogenous foreign exchange risk premium into a fully-specified New Keynesian dynamic model; and the implementation of a tractable method for solving models with shocks to volatility.

It is not uncommon in the literature to incorporate a time-varying deviation from uncovered interest parity (UIP) into sticky-price open-economy macro models.[1] These deviations help the models to account for real exchange rate volatility. However, to the best of my knowledge, this is the first paper that endogenizes the UIP deviation in a New Keynesian dynamic stochastic general equilibrium (DSGE) model. Assuming Epstein-Zin preferences and time-varying volatility of shocks, the UIP deviation arises as a foreign exchange risk premium in equilibrium. This contrasts to previous literature that takes the UIP deviation as an exogenous shock.

An original insight of the paper is that different types of "uncertainty" shocks—shocks to the variances of exogenous driving processes—can have different impacts on the behavior of exchange rates and interest rates. Because the paper does not treat the UIP deviation as a pure shock, but instead as an endogenous variable, the authors are led to investigate empirically the effects of different types of uncertainty shocks.

The paper applies the methods developed by the same authors for solving models with time-varying volatilities.[2] The neat insight is that when structural shocks are conditionally linear, a second-order approximation to the model is sufficient to incorporate the effects of volatility shocks on the levels of the endogenous variables.

The paper emphasizes four empirical regularities that the model is designed to explain:

1. Volatility shocks influence the level of dollar exchange rates. An increase in the volatility of the inflation-target shock or the monetary policy shock appreciates the dollar, but an increase in the volatility of productivity shocks depreciates the dollar.

2. Shocks to the volatility of inflation or monetary policy lead to persistent deviations from UIP.

3. The well-known delayed overshooting result: A contractionary monetary policy shock leads to an appreciation on impact, but then a continued appreciation that implies a deviation from UIP.

4. The famous UIP puzzle: The change in the exchange rate is negatively related to the interest differential.

The paper shows how a New Keynesian DSGE model with an endogenous risk premium can account for these four regularities.

I have a couple of general comments of a critical nature, and then a specific comment on the model's ability to explain exchange-rate behavior.

First, the paper does not measure time-varying volatility by simultaneously extracting fundamental shocks implied by the model while incorporating a model of stochastic volatility for those shocks. Instead, it infers the variance of those shocks from financial market data.

Shocks to monetary policy are imputed using innovations in daily Fed funds futures rates. The volatility of those shocks is measured as a monthly average of the squared daily innovations. The volatility of inflation-target shocks is imputed from options on the term structure. The volatility index (VIX) is used as a measure of the volatility of productivity shocks.

What does the model imply about the behavior of these variables? I don't believe the model would say that these variables necessarily capture the volatility of the shocks they are supposed to measure. The paper promises in a footnote that future work will draw the link between the inflation-target variance and the measure derived from term-structure options. I am skeptical that VIX is a pure measure of the volatility of productivity shocks. Surely the volatility of nominal stock prices depends on nominal as well as real shocks, and is probably also influenced heavily by things not included in the model, such as default risk and liquidity risk.

In the case of monetary policy shocks, the problem with the measure produced here is that the innovations in the Fed funds futures rates might be measuring innovations in the risk premium instead of shocks to monetary policy. The paper mentions that this problem is minimized by the way the measure of volatility is constructed, but it would be helpful to characterize more fully the nature of this approximation. In the extreme, if the risk premium were highly volatile, it could account for almost all of the movement in the Fed funds futures rate. The risk premium itself must be driven by variances in all of the shocks in the model, so it is not clear what is being assumed about the relative size of the volatility of shocks so that we can approximately interpret innovations in the Fed funds rate as pure policy shocks.

These comments are specific examples of a more general issue—that the paper could do more to link the empirical work (the VAR) to the model. Similarly, further investigation is needed to see how plausibly the model can account for the data. The paper focuses almost entirely on the model's ability to account for the four empirical regularities mentioned earlier. Does the model do a reasonable job accounting for these facts but miss other empirical facts?

If we are really going to buy this as a model of the open economy, we need to know how well the model accounts for many other aspects of the macroeconomy—the volatility, comovement and time-series behavior of, for example, output, inflation, consumption, investment, and many other standard macro variables. Does it meet the same standards as the rest of the quantitative literature on monetary policy models, such as Christiano et. al. (2005)?

One particular concern is whether the model of the paper really can even account for some of the most important empirical regularities of exchange rates. Recently (Engel 2011), I have been trying to understand what it takes to reconcile three well-known empirical exchange-rate regularities: (1) The UIP puzzle (empirical regularity number four in the Benigno, Benigno, and Nisticò paper). This puzzle dates at least as far back as Bilson (1981). (2) An increase in real interest rates tends to appreciate the currency (see, for example, Frankel 1979). (3) Exchange rates are excessively volatile, in the sense that their volatility is greater than would be implied by the variance of interest differentials under UIP (see, for example, Frankel and Meese 1988.)

My paper explores the implications of prominent partial equilibrium models of the foreign exchange risk premium for accounting for these facts (e.g., Verdelhan's 2010 model based on Campbell-Cochrane preferences and Bansal and Shaliastovich's 2010 exploration of the "long-run risks" model that uses Epstein-Zin preferences). These models cannot explain all three regularities. In my paper, I note conditions on a model of the risk premium that must be met to account for all of these facts. A necessary condition is that there may be more than one factor driving the risk premium. On that score, the model in this paper is promising—there are three factors (the variances of monetary-policy shocks, inflation-target shocks, and productivity shocks), and each has different effects on interest rates and exchange rates.

The Benigno et al. paper discusses these empirical regularities, but does not explore directly whether the model can account for them. Explaining these facts is not only a challenge for models but also a challenge to (my) intuition. Here is how my paper puts it. Define the risk premium as $\lambda_t = i_t^* - i_t + E_t s_{t+1} - s_t$. The sum of current and expected future risk premiums is given by $\Lambda_t = E_t \sum_{j=0}^{\infty} \lambda_{t+j}$. The home and foreign real interest rates are r_t and r_t^*, respectively. Engel (2011) shows that the three familiar empirical regularities mentioned before imply $\text{cov}(\lambda_t, r_t - r_t^*) < 0$, but $\text{cov}(\Lambda_t, r_t - r_t^*) > 0$. The first inequality follows from empirical fact A (the UIP puzzle), the second inequality from the next two empirical facts, B and C (currency strengthens when real interest rate rises, but is excessively volatile).

Clearly if $\text{cov}(\Lambda_t, r_t - r_t^*) > 0$, we need $\text{cov}(E_t \lambda_{t+j}, r_t - r_t^*) > 0$ for at least some time horizons j. If we are to account for $\text{cov}(\lambda_t, r_t - r_t^*) < 0$ and $\text{cov}(\Lambda_t, r_t - r_t^*) > 0$ with a model of an endogenous foreign exchange risk premium, we need a plausible story that has two potentially conflicting implications. First, when $r_t - r_t^*$ is high, the home bond is riskier in the short run (λ_t is low), so that $\text{cov}(\lambda_t, r_t - r_t^*) < 0$. At the same time, when $r_t - r_t^*$ is high, the home bond in the future must be considered less risky (Λ_t is low), so that $\text{cov}(\Lambda_t, r_t - r_t^*) > 0$. That is, when $r_t - r_t^*$ rises, the risk premium model requires λ_t to fall but Λ_t to rise.

Maybe this model can generate that behavior. Most convincing would be a model that can not only reproduce these moments mechanically, but also one that has a good story. It is tempting otherwise to look for an alternative mechanism.

The model in Benigno et al. is built on the complete markets assumption with representative agents in each country. There are distortions in goods markets—monopolistic producers and sticky nominal prices—but not in financial markets. It may turn out that a convincing story of interest rate and exchange rate behavior requires a model with financial market distortions as well—liquidity constraints, enforceability problems, or deviations from rational expectations in the form of herding and overreaction.

The types of market inefficiencies matter, and not just for understanding the response of exchange rates to shocks. The monetary DSGE models are constructed to guide monetary policy. The monetary policy implications of a model with financial market distortions may be substantially different than one with only goods-market distortions.

While my opinion is that ultimately we need to incorporate some financial market distortions in open-economy models to make progress both positively and normatively, this does not diminish the contribution of this paper. Surely this paper will play a big role in the field's progress in understanding and modeling exchange rates.

Endnotes

Financial support from ERC Starting Independent Grant (Pierpaolo Benigno) and ESRC grant ES/1024174/1 (Gianluca Benigno) is gratefull acknowledged. For acknowledgments, sources of research support, and disclosure of the author's material financial relationships, if any, please see http://www.nber.org/chapters/c12421.ack.
    1. Kollmann (2002) is an early prominent example.
    2. Benigno, Benigno, and Nisticò (2010).

References

Bansal, Ravi, and Ivan Shaliastovich. 2010. "A Long-Run Risks Explanation of Predictability Puzzles in Bond and Currency Markets." Working Paper, Duke University.
Benigno, Gianluca, Pierpaolo Benigno, and Salvatore Nisticò. 2010. "Second-Order Approximation of Dynamic Models with Time-Varying Risk." NBER Working Paper no. 16633. Cambridge, MA: National Bureau of Economic Research, December.
Bilson, John F. O. 1981. "The 'Speculative Efficiency' Hypothesis." *The Journal of Business* 54:435–51.
Christiano, Lawrence J., Martin Eichenbaum, and Charles L. Evans. 2005. "Nominal Rigidities and the Dynanmic Effects of a Shock to Monetary Policy." *Journal of Political Economy* 113:1–45.
Engel, Charles. 2011. "The Real Exchange Rate, Real Interest Rates, and the Risk Premium." NBER Working Paper no. 17116. Cambridge, MA: National Bureau of Economic Research, June.
Frankel, Jeffrey A. 1979. "On the Mark: A Theory of Floating Exchange Rates Based on Real Interest Differentials." *American Economic Review* 69:610–22.
Frankel, Jeffrey A., and Richard Meese. 1988. "Are Exchange Rates Excessively Variable?" In *NBER Macroeconomics Annual 1987*, edited by Stanley Fischer 117–53. Cambridge, MA: MIT Press.
Kollmann, Robert. 2002. "Monetary Policy Rules in the Open Economy: Effects on Welfare and Business Cycles." *Journal of Monetary Economics* 49:989–1015.
Verdelhan, Adrien. 2010. "A Habit-Based Explanation of the Exchange-Rate Risk Premium." *Journal of Finance* 65:123–46.

Comment

Martín Uribe, Columbia University and NBER

This paper studies the effects of time-varying volatility shocks in the open economy. More specifically, it analyzes the consequences of productivity volatility shocks, monetary-policy volatility shocks, and inflation-target volatility shocks for the dynamics of exchange rates, the yield curve, and cross-country interest-rate differentials.

Spurred in part by significant advances in quantitative economics and computational speed, interest in the macroeconomics of uncertainty shocks has experienced a revival in the past few years. Recent applications include an explanation of the great moderation based on a decline in the volatility of structural shocks (Fernández-Villaverde and Rubio-Ramírez 2007; Justiniano and Primiceri 2008), an evaluation of the role of country-spread uncertainty as a driver of business cycles in emerging countries (Fernández-Villaverde et al. 2011), and uncertainty shocks to productivity as determinants of the demand for factors of production at the firm level (Bloom 2009). The Benigno, Benigno, and Nisticò paper adds to this list by considering the role of uncertainty in a global context.

This is an ambitious project, for it attempts to accomplish three demanding tasks. The first one is to empirically identify the three aforementioned volatility shocks. The second one is to estimate the empirical impulse responses of a number of variables of interest to innovations in the identified volatility shocks. Finally, the paper assesses the ability of a two-country, New Keynsian model to account for the estimated impulse responses.

This paper represents a first pass at what I view as an important research agenda in open economy macroeconomics. As such, it suffers from a number of problems that I will spell out in what follows. Never-

theless, I believe that the present study is bound to become an important reference in this literature.

Identification Issues

The first contribution of the Benigno, Benigno, and Nisticò paper is to
empirically identify three sources of time-varying volatility: monetary-
policy volatility shocks, inflation-target volatility shocks, and total factor productivity (TFP) volatility shocks. To this end, the paper estimates
a VAR system of the form

$$y_t = A(L)y_{t-1} + e_t,$$

where y_t includes ten variables that can be classified in two groups. The
first group consists of three unobserved volatility shocks that form the
focus of the empirical analysis. They are:

$u_{\zeta,t}$ = monetary-policy volatility shock.

$u_{\pi,t}$ = inflation-target volatility shock.

$u_{a,t}$ = TFP volatility shock.

The second group of elements of y_t consists of seven observable
variables typically included in open macro/finance empirical studies.
They are:

i_t = Federal Funds rate.

$i_t - i_t^*$ = cross-country interest-rate differential.

$i_{sl,t}$ = slope of yield curve.

q_t = Real exchange rate $(s + p^* - p)$.

p_t = CPI log level.

y_t = domestic industrial production.

y_t^* = foreign industrial production.

The authors orthogonalize the regression residual e_t using a Choleski
decomposition with the order of the variables just given.

To make the previous VAR system operative, the authors must, of
course, proceed to identify the three unobservable variables. I find this
step of the exercise highly unconvincing. To see why, consider, for example, the identification of $u_{a,t}$, the TFP volatility shock. The authors
proxy this variable with the volatility of the stock market. This is problematic because in principle the volatility of stock prices can be driven

by all of the shocks (e.g., preference volatility shocks, fiscal volatility shocks, monetary volatility shocks, animal spirits volatility shocks) buffeting the economy, not just TFP volatility shocks. Granted, under this identification approach, the VAR does deliver a measure of time-varying volatility. But it does not provide any basis to determine that this measure of time-varying volatility represents time-varying volatility in TFP. Instead, the time-varying volatility shock that comes out of the VAR is in principle a combination of a number of volatility shocks of different natures.

A similar problem arises with the identification of $u_{\pi,t}$, the inflation-target volatility shocks. In this case, the authors use as a proxy the MOVE index of implied volatilities in one-month Treasury options. Again, the volatility of bond option values can in principle be determined by multiple shocks, not just by inflation-target volatility shocks. As a result, the VAR will deliver a measure of time-varying volatility that cannot be reliably associated with innovations in the volatility of the inflation target.

These identification problems are serious for two main reasons. First, the authors use the identified VAR to plot empirical impulse responses to TFP volatility shocks and inflation-target volatility shocks. To the extent that these shocks are poorly identified, the information provided by these impulse responses may be highly misleading. Second, and equally important, the authors will build a DSGE model and will judge the ability of this model to explain the data by comparing the theoretical and empirical impulse responses to TFP volatility shocks and inflation-target volatility shocks. Because the empirical impulse responses correspond not to the desired shock but to an unknown combination of shocks, the conclusions derived from this evaluation exercise can, again, be highly misleading.

The third unobservable variable that requires identification is $u_{\zeta,t}$, the monetary-policy volatility shock. The authors proxy this variable with the (within-month mean square changes in) Federal Funds Futures Rate. In my opinion, this identification strategy is more fortunate than are the previous two. The reason is that the federal funds rate is to a large extent under the control of the monetary authority. It represents, after all, the Fed's central policy instrument. As a result, the measure of volatility constructed by the authors is likely to capture well the uncertainty involved in monetary policy. One caveat could be the fact that monetary policy has two parts, one systematic (which may depend upon variables such as inflation, output, and past interest rates) and one nonsystematic. Ideally, the identification exercise should deliver a measure of innovations in the nonsystematic component of monetary-policy uncertainty. To the extent that the systematic component of monetary policy responds to past values of macroeconomic indicators, the VAR filter could succeed in purging a significant part of the systematic component.

Based on the aforementioned considerations, for the remainder of my discussion I will focus exclusively on the macroeconomic effects of monetary-policy volatility shocks.

Before moving on, I would like to close this section by suggesting an alternative identification approach. It consists of a direct estimation of a DSGE model. Indeed, the DSGE model that the authors build in a later section of the paper includes among its driving forces the three volatility shocks that the authors aim to identify and has precise predictions for the seven observable variables included in the empirical analysis. Admittedly, estimating DSGE models driven by time-varying volatility shocks is not a simple task. One difficulty has to do with the fact that linear approximations are not sufficient to capture the dynamic effects of disturbances in volatility. Therefore, higher-order approximations, which are technically and computationally more demanding, are called for. Another problem is the fact that the convenient Kalman filter cannot be used for constructing the likelihood function of nonlinear models. Instead, researchers have appealed to other methods, such as particle filtering. The good news is that recent significant advances in the formulation, computation, and estimation of nonlinear DSGE models coupled with ever-growing computational speed have made estimation feasible, at least at a small to medium scale. Some of the references cited at the beginning of this discussion represent examples of how this can be accomplished. In this regard, a key technical reference for macroeconomic applications is the recent survey by Fernández-Villaverde and Rubio-Ramírez (2010).

The Macroeconomic Effects of Monetary-Policy Volatility Shocks

Figure 1 represents the central empirical fact documented in this paper. It includes all three of the elements condensed in the title of the paper: "Risk, Monetary Policy, and the Exchange Rate." It displays the response of the real exchange rate to an increase in the volatility of US monetary-policy implied by the estimated VAR system. The real exchange rate, $RER \equiv SP^*/P$, is defined as the number of US dollars re-

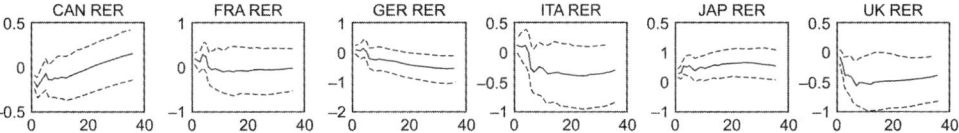

Fig. 1. The response of the real exchange rate to an increase in the volatility of US monetary-policy implied by the estimated VAR system.

Source: Benigno, Benigno, and Nisticò (chapter 5, this volume).

quired to buy a unit of foreign currency, S, adjusted by the ratio of the foreign consumer price index, P^*, to the US consumer price index, P. Therefore, when, for example, the real exchange rate goes down, it means that the US dollar is becoming stronger, or that the foreign country is becoming relatively cheaper. To understand the nature of the monetary-policy volatility shock, think of the monetary authority as following an interest rate rule that has two components. One component is systematic and may depend on variables such as output and inflation. The second component is purely random and is referred to as the monetary-policy shock. The variance of this shock is the monetary-policy volatility shock, and is itself random. Figure 1 shows the effect of an increase in this random volatility on the real exchange rate. Six foreign countries are considered: Canada, France, Germany, Italy, Japan, and the United Kingdom. I note in passing that the impulse response of the nominal exchange rate, S_t, would look very similar to that of the real exchange rate shown in the figure. The reason is that the post Bretton-Woods period, which is the sample period used for the estimation of the VAR, is characterized by much larger movements in the nominal exchange rate, S, than in consumer price indices P and P^*. As a consequence, movements in the real exchange rate are dominated by movements in the nominal exchange rate. Thus, in what follows, when I refer to the exchange rate, the reader can think either of the nominal or of the real exchange rate.

I find figure 1 highly thought-provoking in spite of the fact that, from a purely statistical viewpoint, its validity is questionable. For instance, the broken lines display one-standard-deviation error bands around the point estimates. In macroeconomics, however, the usual practice is to display two-standard-error confidence bands. Such a confidence interval would comfortably include zero for all countries, rendering the responses insignificant. And there are other statistical problems related to disparities in the signs and shapes of the responses across countries, to which I will come back later. But from an economic point of view, the message of this figure is quite striking. To see this, I will ask the reader to do two things. First, forget about Japan. Second, erase from your minds the confidence bands. The picture that emerges is one in which an increase in monetary-policy uncertainty in the United States causes the US dollar to strengthen. This is a very counterintuitive stylized fact. For it states that if a new, more unpredictable Fed chair were to replace the current one, then the reaction of the US dollar would be to become stronger (not weaker)! This implication does not square well with the notion that the Fed is the primary guardian of the purchasing power of the US dollar. An immediate question is what kind of theoretical mechanism could explain this surprising result. I turn to this issue next.

Explaining the Surprising Empirical Relationship between Monetary-Policy Uncertainty and the Exchange Rate

What model could explain the empirical regularity that an increase in the volatility of domestic monetary-policy shocks causes the domestic currency to strengthen? It turns out that a standard two-country extension of the New Keynesian model captures this fact quite well, at least qualitatively. This is a significant finding of the paper under review which the authors do not highlight enough (a problem that hopefully will be fixed in the published version). The theoretical model presented in the paper has the following ingredients:

- Two countries.
- Two goods.
- Complete asset markets.
- Sticky prices.
- Epstein-Zin Preferences.
- Volatility and "level" shocks to the nominal interest rate, the inflation target, and productivity.

As it will become clear shortly, Epstein-Zin preferences are not essential for explaining the empirical link between monetary uncertainty and the exchange rate.

Figure 2 displays the impulse response of the real exchange rate to an increase in the monetary-policy volatility shock. Compare this figure with its empirical counterpart shown in figure 1. Quantitatively, the

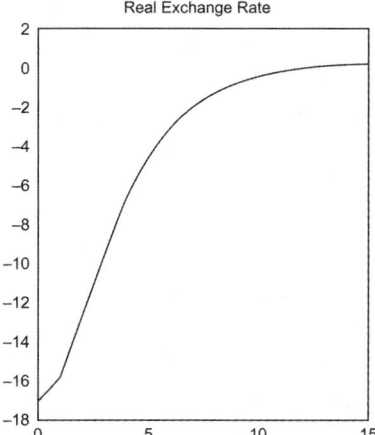

Fig. 2.   The impulse response of the real exchange rate to an increase in the monetary-policy volatility shock.

Source: Benigno, Benigno, and Nisticò (chapter 5, this volume).

model is far from matching the data. For example, the appreciation of the exchange rate predicted by the model is about ten times larger than its empirical counterpart. Also, for most countries, with the exception of Canada and Japan, the response of the exchange rate has a U shape, whereas the theoretical impulse response has a semi-inverted U shape. Finally, in the case of Japan, the empirical and theoretical responses have opposite signs.

But the theoretical response is qualitatively a success, for it captures the counterintuitive empirical finding that in response to an increase in monetary-policy uncertainty the US dollar appreciates. One cannot help but wonder what theoretical mechanism is responsible for this unexpected result. Unfortunately, the version of the present paper that I read does not present an intuitive argument that I find transparent (hopefully this will be not be an issue in the published version). So allow me to present my own intuition. Start with the following well-known Euler equation for pricing dollar-denominated, state-noncontingent bonds:

$$1 = (1 + i_t)\beta Et \left\{ \frac{U'(C_{t+1})}{U'(Ct)} \frac{1}{\pi_{t+1}} \right\},$$

where i_t denotes the nominal interest rate, C_t denotes consumption, π_t denotes the gross rate of inflation, $\beta \in (0,1)$ denotes a subjective discount factor, and U denotes the period utility function. This familiar expression can be interpreted as Fisher's equation stating that the nominal interest rate must equal the sum of the expected rate of inflation and the expected real interest rate.

I will now introduce three simplifying assumptions. First, assume that

$$\frac{U'(C_{t+1})}{U'(C_t)} = 1.$$

This condition will hold in a flexible-price version of the model presented in the paper in which all real shocks (such as productivity shocks, preference shocks, etc.) are shut off. In such an environment, monetary shocks do not affect real quantities in general and consumption in particular. The second simplifying assumption I will introduce is

$$\pi_t = S_t/S_{t-1},$$

where, as mentioned earlier, S_t denotes the nominal exchange rate, defined as the number of US dollars needed to purchase a unit of foreign currency. This assumption essentially states that purchasing power parity (PPP) holds. It will be satisfied in a small open-economy version of the present model with flexible prices and no home bias. Here, the small open-economy feature allows us to ignore foreign inflation in stating the PPP condition, since the focus is on domestic shocks. Finally, the third assumption states that monetary policy is characterized by a Taylor-type interest-rate feedback rule of the form

$$1 + i_t = \phi(\pi_t), \qquad \phi' > 1.$$

Combining these three assumptions with the above Euler equation yields

$$1 = \phi(S_t/S_{t-1})\beta E_t \left\{ \frac{1}{\pi_{t+1}} \right\}. \qquad (1)$$

I will now conjecture that when monetary policy becomes conditionally more volatile (i.e., when the variance of i_{t+1} conditional on information available at t goes up), next period's inflation rate, π_{t+1}, also becomes conditionally more volatile. That is, $\mathrm{var}_t(\pi_{t+1})$ rises. Further, I will assume, rather heroically, that this increase in inflation volatility occurs in a more or less mean preserving fashion. Then, by Jensen's inequality, we have that the conditional expectation of $1/\pi_{t+1}$ must also increase. Finally, by equation (1), the rise in $E_t\{1/\pi_{t+1}\}$ must be associated with an appreciation (a fall) in the nominal exchange rate S_t.

In words, what happens in this model is that the rate at which dollar-denominated assets gain value due to inflation $1/\pi_{t+1} - 1$ (a negative rate when inflation is positive) increases on average with the level of uncertainty. As a result, as the level of monetary uncertainty rises, holders of nominal assets (e.g., treasury bonds) demand a smaller compensation to maintain them in their portfolios. Thus, given the real interest rate, a rise in monetary uncertainty causes the nominal interest rate to fall. In turn, if the monetary authority follows a Taylor-type interest-rate rule, the fall in the interest rate must be associated with a fall in inflation. Finally, if PPP holds, the fall in domestic prices, given foreign prices, must be linked to an appreciation of the domestic currency.

Real Activity: The Disinvited Variable

Both the VAR and theoretical models feature measures of domestic and foreign output. Yet the predicted effects of uncertainty shocks on aggregate activity are reported neither for the empirical model nor for the theoretical model. Instead, the paper focuses exclusively on the effects of volatility shocks on financial variables. This choice is unfortunate because it might be interpreted by some readers as meaning that uncertainty shocks are strong enough to move financial variables but lack the traction to lift real variables such as output, consumption, investment, and employment. This is, of course, not the case, as documented by a number of recent related studies (see, e.g., Fernández-Villaverde et al. 2011; Bloom 2009). Hopefully, the published version of the present paper will remedy this important omission.

Conclusion

This is a promising project. It has the potential to deliver a first step toward understanding the international effects of uncertainty shocks both empirically and theoretically. But there remain a number of issues to be addressed. Among the most important ones are the identification of uncertainty shocks. Ideally, this issue will be tackled by a direct estimation of the proposed theoretical DSGE model. A second pending issue is a more satisfactory investigation of the theoretical model's ability to match the actual data, especially the observed effects of uncertainty shocks. A third priority is to put more effort into developing intuition for the many analytical results contained in the paper. Finally, a revised version of this paper should provide texture to the exposition. The version I reviewed reads mechanical and monotone. All results, large and small, are given the same emphasis and space. A hierarchy of results is highly needed. Overall, I believe that, once finished, this paper has the potential to become an important contribution to the existing related literature.

Endnote

Columbia University and NBER. E-mail: martin.uribe@columbia.edu. For acknowledgments, sources of research support, and disclosure of the author's material financial relationships, if any, please see http://www.nber.org/chapters/c12422.ack.

References

Bloom, Nicholas. 2009. "The Impact of Uncertainty Shocks." *Econometrica* 77: 623–85.
Fernández-Villaverde, Jesús, Pablo Guerrón-Quintana, Juan Rubio-Ramírez, and Martín Uribe. 2011. "Risk Matters: The Real Effects of Volatility Shocks." *American Economic Review* 101 (6): 2530–61.
Fernández-Villaverde, Jesús, and Juan Rubio-Ramírez. 2007. "Estimating Macroeconomic Models: A Likelihood Approach." *Review of Economic Studies* 74:1059–87.
———. 2010. "Macroeconomics and Volatility: Data, Models, and Estimation." Manuscript, Duke University and University of Pennsylvania, December.
Justiniano, Alejandro, and Giorgio E. Primiceri. 2008. "The Time Varying Volatility of Macroeconomic Fluctuations." *American Economic Review* 98:604–41.

Discussion

Francesco Giavazzi opened the discussion by following up on Charles Engel's comment that the response of the nominal and real exchange rates imply that a contractionary monetary shock raises domestic inflation relative to foreign inflation. Giavazzi asked whether this empirical result is simply a manifestation of the price puzzle documented in VAR studies for US data and whether this might be addressed by using other observables to control for price markup shocks. He also noted that changes in fiscal policy are not considered as a possible explanation for monetary policy shocks. Giavazzi suggested that fiscal shocks might explain both monetary shocks and the resulting behavior of the exchange rate.

Lars Hansen suggested that the authors could link their work to a related finance literature using recursive utility to explain other asset-pricing puzzles and examine how their parameter values compare. Hansen also emphasized that stochastic volatility operates through two distinct channels. Stochastic volatility is directly priced and changes risk premia associated with other shocks. He suggested that the authors try to decompose the effect of stochastic volatility through these channels. Lastly, Hansen advocated caution in using volatility indices like the VIX to proxy for real volatility, as some financial shocks are unlikely to spill over to the real economy.

Marjorie Flavin was not surprised by the authors' finding that increased volatility of monetary shocks leads to a dollar appreciation. She argued that the monetary policy shocks identified by the authors may reflect periods of heightened uncertainty that lead to greater deviations of monetary policy from a standard rule. The association of larger monetary policy deviations and a dollar appreciation reflect a flight to quality due to some underlying shocks to the financial markets or global economy.

Albert Marcet noted that two-country models with complete markets often generate counterfactual predictions for capital flows in terms of volatility and direction and asked what predictions the authors' model delivers in terms of flows. Marcet also suggested that, given data with many countries, the authors may be able to estimate a panel VAR to reduce standard errors.

Jordi Galí sought clarification on the quantitative size of the effects of uncertainty shocks. He noted that one of their figures illustrated the effect of a 1 percentage point increase in the variance of monetary shocks and asked how large a typical change in the volatility of monetary shocks might be.

Xavier Gabaix argued that the authors' treatment of monetary policy volatility might be too focused on the United States and that a more symmetrical model could use monetary policy shocks overseas to distinguish between country-specific shocks and the type of global financial shocks described by Flavin. For instance, the shock to the Fed funds rate in 2008 was clearly a response to the credit crisis rather than a pure monetary policy shock. Gabaix also asked about the level of exchange rate volatility in the model, noting that two-country models often exhibit very low levels of exchange rate volatility. He pointed to his work with Emmanuel Farhi that could explain deviations from uncovered interest rate parity using both disaster and business cycle shocks.

Marc Giannoni, reiterating comments by Giavazzi and Flavin, noted that the price puzzle could be addressed by using factor analysis to identify the monetary policy shocks, as shown in Bernanke, Boivin, and Eliasz (2005). He cited his recent work with Jean Boivin and Dalibor Stevanovic using factor-augmented VARs in Canadian data to mitigate the overshooting puzzle and deviations from UIP that are found in standard VAR analyses.

James Kahn asked about how the authors addressed issues raised by a binding zero lower bound. Kahn emphasized that at low interest rates, the distribution of monetary policy shocks is skewed and monetary policy may be operating by channels distinct from changes in the interest rate.

Pierpaolo Benigno responded to Engel's comment that the authors could not explain deviations from UIP using shocks to the *level* of monetary policy. Benigno noted that UIP holds to a first-order approximation in their model, so level shocks could not result in any deviations.

Benigno argued that financial frictions would be needed to break UIP in a first-order approximation, or that a level shock may affect UIP in a third-order approximation. Benigno also noted that US inflation falls on impact with a contractionary monetary policy shock but rises in subsequent periods, which causes difficultly in matching the correlations between interest rate differentials and exchange rate differentials.

Benigno acknowledged the concerns of Martin Uribe and Hansen that the VIX may not be a suitable proxy for the volatility of productivity, but noted that estimating the model would be difficult given the model is nonlinear and emphasized this would be the subject of future work. Benigno further explained the intuition behind the result that increases in monetary policy uncertainty appreciate the dollar. He noted that agents prefer dollars in the event of a dollar appreciation due to a contractionary monetary policy shock. A rise in the volatility of monetary shocks magnifies disproportionately the benefit of holding dollars given a contractionary shock implying a dollar appreciation due to an increase in the volatility of monetary shocks.

Responding to Giavazzi, Benigno stated that the nonsystematic response of monetary policy to fiscal policy should be considered a monetary policy shock, but also acknowledged that fiscal policy may be an important factor behind the inflation target shocks. Responding to Gabaix and Flavin, Benigno emphasized that the flight to quality channel is analogous to the hedging motive driving dollar appreciation in the model. Responding to Hansen, Benigno noted that the role of recursive utility may be quite different in a setting where income is not an exogenous process, in contrast to its use in the finance literature. He noted differences relative to models in finance in the response of the yield curve in their model to changes in the risk aversion parameter, stating that future work would focus on ascertaining differences in the behavior of their model versus standard finance models with Epstein-Zin preferences and an exogenous consumption process. Responding to Marcet, he noted that, even with complete markets, recursive utility posed new challenges for solving the model.

Salvatore Nisticò responded to the discussion by Uribe, noting that the authors used Eichenbaum and Evans (1995) as an empirical benchmark, thereby using the one standard deviation error bands. He agreed with Uribe that their VIX measure might not be the cleanest measure of the volatility of productivity shocks but noted its use in related literature. He justified the use of the MOVE index (Merrill Lynch Option Volatility Estimate) to identify time-varying volatility in the inflation target shocks by citing their theoretical results that inflation target shocks must shift the level of the yield curve. Moreover, to further ensure that their measure of time-varying volatility is capturing changes in the inflation target shock, the authors extract the component of the MOVE index orthogonal to the other volatility measures. Nisticò noted that the ordering of the variables in the VAR is also consistent with their theoretical results since innovations to the level variables can only affect volatility in the next period. As a result, the volatility variables are ordered before the level variables in the VAR. Nisticò closed by acknowledging that Epstein-Zin preferences were not essential for all their results but emphasized that using recursive utility would be necessary for their objective of building a model with realistic asset-pricing behavior that could potentially match multiple facts.

References

Bernanke, Ben S., J. Boivin, and P. S. Eliasz. 2005. "Measuring the Effects of Monetary Policy: A Factor-Augmented Vector Autoregression Approach." *Quarterly Journal of Economics* 120 (1): 387–422.

Eichenbaum, M., and C. L. Evans. 1995. "Some Empirical Evidence on the Effects of Shocks to Monetary Policy on Exchange Rates." *The Quarterly Journal of Economics* 110:975–1009.

6

Unemployment in an Estimated New Keynesian Model

Jordi Galí, *CREI, Universitat Pompeu Fabra, Barcelona GSE, and NBER*
Frank Smets, *European Central Bank, CEPR, and University of Groningen*
Rafael Wouters, *National Bank of Belgium*

I. Introduction

Over the past decade an increasing number of central banks and other policy institutions have developed and estimated medium-scale New Keynesian DSGE models.[1] The combination of a good empirical fit with a sound, microfounded structure makes these models particularly suitable for forecasting and policy analysis. However, as highlighted by Galí and Gertler (2007) and others, one of the shortcomings of these models is the lack of a reference to unemployment. This is unfortunate because unemployment is an important indicator of aggregate resource utilization and a central focus of the policy debate. Recently, a number of papers have started to address this shortcoming by embedding in the basic New Keynesian model various theories of unemployment based on the presence of labor market frictions (e.g., Blanchard and Galí 2010; Christoffel et al. 2009; Gertler, Sala, and Trigari 2008; Christiano, Trabandt, and Walentin 2010, 2011; and de Walque et al. 2009).

The present paper takes a different approach. Following Galí (2011b, 2011c), it reformulates the Smets and Wouters (2003, 2007; henceforth, SW) model to allow for involuntary unemployment, while preserving the convenience of the representative household paradigm. Unemployment in the model results from market power in labor markets, reflected in positive wage markups. Variations in unemployment over time are associated with changes in wage markups, either exogenous or resulting from nominal wage rigidities.[2]

The proposed reformulation allows us to overcome an identification problem pointed out by Chari, Kehoe and McGrattan (2009; henceforth, CKM) and interpreted by these authors as an illustration of the immaturity of New Keynesian models for policy analysis. Their observation is motivated by the SW finding that wage markup shocks account for almost 50% of the variations in real GDP at horizons of more than 10 years. However, without an explicit measure of unemployment (or, alternatively, labor supply), these wage markup shocks cannot be distinguished from preference shocks that shift the marginal disutility of labor. The policy implications of these two sources of fluctuations are, however, very different. Variations in wage markup shocks are inefficient and a welfare-maximizing government should be interested in stabilizing output fluctuations resulting from those shocks (at least partly). In contrast, output and employment fluctuations driven by preference shocks shifting the labor supply schedule should in principle be accommodated. Put differently, the relative importance of those two shocks will influence the extent to which fluctuations in output during a given historical episode should or should not be interpreted as reflecting movements in the welfare-relevant output gap (i.e., the distance between the actual and efficient levels of output). By including unemployment as an observable variable, this identification problem can be overcome, and "correct" measures of the output gap can be constructed, as we show in Section IV.

When we estimate the reformulated SW model using unemployment as an observable variable, we find a much diminished role for wage markup shocks as a source of output and employment fluctuations, even though those shocks preserve a large role as drivers of inflation. Our estimates lead us to classify the multiple shocks in the model in three categories (which we label "demand," "supply," and "labor market" shocks), on the basis of their implied joint comovement among output, employment, the labor force, unemployment, inflation, and the real wage, as captured by their associated impulse response functions (IRFs). In addition, we show how the implied measure of the welfare-relevant output gap is to a large extent the mirror image of the unemployment rate, and resembles conventional measures of the cyclical component of log GDP, based on statistical detrending methods (though the correlation is far from perfect).

Our estimates of the reformulated SW model allow us to address a number of additional questions of interest that could not be dealt with using the model's original formulation. Thus, in Section V we assess quantitatively the relative importance of different shocks as sources of unemployment fluctuations and their role during specific historical episodes, including the recent recession. Also, our approach allows us to uncover a measure of the natural rate of unemployment (i.e., the flexible wage counterfactual) and to study its comovement with actual unemployment. That comovement is shown to be particularly strong at low frequencies, as expected, but the gap between the two caused by wage rigidities is estimated to be large and persistent. We also revisit the evidence on the joint behavior of inflation and unemployment under the lens of our estimated model. This allows us to give a structural interpretation to empirical Phillips curves, both for wage and price inflation. In Section VI we discuss the robustness of our findings to the use of alternative sample period and data. Section VII concludes.

In addition to reformulating the wage equation in terms of unemployment, our model shows a number of small differences with that in SW (2007). First, and regarding the data on which the estimation is based, we use employment rather than hours worked, and redefine the wage as the wage per worker rather than the wage per hour. We do so since the model focuses on variations in labor at the extensive margin, in a way consistent with the conventional definition of unemployment. Given that most of the variation in hours worked over the business cycle is due to changes in employment rather than hours per employee, this change does not have major consequences in itself. We also combine two alternative wage measures in the estimation, compensation and earnings, and model their discrepancy explicitly. Second, we generalize the utility function in a way that allows us to parameterize the strength of the wealth effect on labor supply, as shown in Jaimovich and Rebelo (2009). This generalization yields a better fit of the joint behavior of employment and the labor force, as we discuss in detail. Third, for simplicity, we revert to a Dixit-Stiglitz aggregator rather than the Kimball aggregator used in SW (2007).

The rest of the paper is structured as follows. Section II describes the modified Smets-Wouters model. Next, Section III presents the data and estimation. Section IV contains the discussion of the CKM critique. Section V analyzes different aspects of unemployment fluctuations, which the reformulation of the SW model makes possible. Section VI presents some robustness exercises and, finally, Section VII concludes.

II. Introducing Unemployment in the Smets-Wouters Model

A. Staggered Wage Setting and Wage Inflation Dynamics

This section introduces a variant of the wage-setting block of the SW model, which is in turn an extension of that in Erceg, Henderson, and

Levin (2000; henceforth, EHL). The variant presented here, based on Galí (2011b, 2011c), assumes that labor is indivisible, with all variations in hired labor input taking place at the extensive margin. That feature gives rise to a notion of unemployment consistent with its empirical counterpart.

The model assumes a (large) representative household with a continuum of members represented by the unit square and indexed by a pair $(i, j) \in 0,1] \times 0,1]$. The first dimension, indexed by $i \in 0,1]$, represents the type of labor service in which a given household member is specialized. The second dimension, indexed by $j \in 0,1]$, determines his disutility from work. The latter is given by $\chi_t \Theta_t j^\varphi$ if he is employed, zero otherwise, where $\chi_t > 0$ is an exogenous preference shifter (referred to in the following as a "labor supply shock"), Θ_t is an endogenous preference shifter, taken as given by each individual household and defined in the following, and $\varphi \geq 0$ is a parameter determining the shape of the distribution of work disutilities across individuals.

Individual utility is assumed to be given by:

$$E_0 \sum_{t=0}^{\infty} \beta^t (\log \tilde{C}_t(i, j) - 1_t(i, j)\chi_t \Theta_t j^\varphi)$$

where $\tilde{C}_t(i, j) \equiv C_t(i, j) - h\bar{C}_{t-1}$, with $h \in 0,1]$, and with $\bar{C}_{t-1}$ denoting (lagged) aggregate consumption (taken as given by each household), and where $1_t(i, j)$ is an indicator function taking a value equal to one if individual (i, j) is employed in period t, and zero otherwise. Thus, as in SW and related monetary dynamic stochastic general equilibrium (DSGE) models, we allow for (external) habits in consumption, indexed by h.

As in Merz (1995), full risk sharing of consumption among household members is assumed, implying $C_t(i, j) = C_t$ for all $(i, j) \in 0,1] \times 0,1]$ and t. Thus, we can derive the household utility as the integral over its members' utilities; that is:

$$E_0 \sum_{t=0}^{\infty} \beta^t U_t(C_t, \{N_t(i)\}) \equiv E_0 \sum_{t=0}^{\infty} \beta^t \left(\log \tilde{C}_t - \chi_t \Theta_t \int_0^1 \int_0^{N_t(i)} j^\varphi dj di \right)$$

$$= E_0 \sum_{t=0}^{\infty} \beta^t \left(\log \tilde{C}_t - \chi_t \Theta_t \int_0^1 \frac{N_t(i)^{1+\varphi}}{1 + \varphi} di \right),$$

where $N_t(i) \in 0,1]$ denotes the employment rate in period t among workers specialized in type i labor and $\tilde{C}_t \equiv C_t - h\bar{C}_{t-1}$.[3] We define the endogenous preference shifter Θ_t, as follows:

$$\Theta_t \equiv \frac{Z_t}{\bar{C}_t - h\bar{C}_{t-1}},$$

where Z_t evolves over time according to the difference equation

$$Z_t = Z_{t-1}^{1-\upsilon}(\bar{C}_t - h\bar{C}_{t-1})^{\upsilon}.$$

Thus, Z_t can be interpreted as a "smooth" trend for (quasi-differenced) aggregate consumption. Our preference specification implies a "consumption externality" on individual labor supply: during aggregate consumption booms (i.e., when $\bar{C}_t - h\bar{C}_{t-1}$ is above its trend value Z_t), individual (as well as household-level) marginal disutility from work goes down (at any given level of employment).

The previous specification generalizes the preferences assumed in SW by allowing for an exogenous labor supply shock, χ_t, and by introducing the endogenous shifter Θ_t (just described). The main role of the latter is to reconcile the existence of a long-run balanced growth path with an arbitrarily small *short-term* wealth effect. The latter's importance is determined by the size of parameter $\upsilon \in 0,1]$. As discussed later in detail, that feature is needed in order to match the joint behavior of the labor force, consumption, and the wage over the business cycle. That modification is related to, but not identical to, the one proposed by Jaimovich and Rebelo (2009) as a key ingredient in order to account for the economy's response to news about future productivity increases.[4]

Note that under the previous preferences, the household-relevant marginal rate of substitution between consumption and employment for type i workers in period t is given by:

$$MRS_t(i) \equiv -\frac{U_{n(i),t}}{U_{c,t}}$$

$$= \chi_t \Theta_t \tilde{C}_t N_t(i)^{\varphi}$$

$$= \chi_t Z_t N_t(i)^{\varphi}$$

where the last equality is satisfied in a symmetric equilibrium with $\bar{C}_t = C_t$.

Using lower-case letters to denote the natural logarithms of the original variables, we can derive the average (log) marginal rate of substitution $mrs_t \equiv \int_0^1 mrs_t(i)\, di$ by integrating over all labor types:

$$mrs_t = z_t + \varphi n_t + \xi_t,$$

where $n_t \equiv \int_0^1 n_t(i)\, di$ is (log) aggregate employment and $\xi_t \equiv \log \chi_t$.

We assume nominal wages are set by "unions," each of which represents the workers specialized in a given type of labor, and acting in an uncoordinated way. As in EHL, and following the formalism of Calvo (1983), we assume that the nominal wage for a labor service of a given type can only be reset with probability $1 - \theta_w$ each period. That probability is independent of the time elapsed since the wage for that labor type was last reset, in addition to being independent across labor types. Thus, and by the law of large numbers, a fraction of workers θ_w do not reoptimize their wage in any given period, making that parameter a natural index of nominal wage rigidities. Furthermore, all those who reoptimize their wage choose an identical wage, denoted by W_t^*, since they face an identical problem. Following SW, we allow for partial wage indexation between reoptimization periods, by making the nominal wage adjust mechanically in proportion to past price inflation. Formally, and letting $W_{t+k|t}$ denote the nominal wage in period $t + k$ for workers who last reoptimized their wage in period t, we assume

$$W_{t+k|t} = W_{t+k-1|t} \; \Pi^x (\Pi_{t-1}^p)^{\gamma_w} (\Pi^p)^{1-\gamma_w}$$

for $k = 1, 2, 3, \ldots$ and $W_{t,t} = W_t^*$, and where $\Pi_t^p \equiv P_t/P_{t-1}$ denotes the (gross) rate of price inflation, Π^p is its corresponding steady-state value, Π^x is the steady-state (gross) growth rate of productivity, and $\gamma_w \in 0,1]$ measures the degree of wage indexation to past inflation.

When reoptimizing their wage in period t, workers (or the union representing them) choose a wage W_t^* *in order to maximize their respective households' utility* (as opposed to their individual utility), subject to the usual sequence of household flow budget constraints, as well as a sequence of isoelastic demand schedules of the form $N_{t+k|t} = (W_{t+k|t}/W_{t+k})^{-\epsilon_{w,t}} N_{t+k}$, where $N_{t+k|t}$ denotes period $t + k$ employment among workers whose wage was last reoptimized in period t, and where $\epsilon_{w,t}$ is the period t wage elasticity of the relevant labor demand schedule.[5] We assume that elasticity varies exogenously over time, thus leading to changes in workers' market power.

The first-order condition associated with the wage-setting problem can be written as:

$$\sum_{k=0}^{\infty} (\beta\theta_w)^k E_t \left\{ \left(\frac{N_{t+k|t}}{C_{t+k}}\right) \left(\frac{W_{t+k|t}^*}{P_{t+k}} - \mathcal{M}_{w,t+k}^n MRS_{t+k|t}\right) \right\} = 0, \qquad (1)$$

where, in a symmetric equilibrium, $MRS_{t+k|t} \equiv \chi_t Z_t N_{t+k|t}^\varphi$ is the relevant marginal rate of substitution between consumption and employment in period $t + k$, and $\mathcal{M}_{w,t}^n \equiv \epsilon_{w,t}/(\epsilon_{w,t} - 1)$ is the natural (or desired) wage markup in period t; that is, the one that would obtain under flexible wages.

Under the previous assumptions, we can write the aggregate wage index $W_t \equiv (\int_0^1 W_t(i)^{1-\epsilon_{w,t}} di)[1/(1 - \epsilon_{w,t})]$ as follows:

$$W_t \equiv \{\theta_w(W_{t-1}\Pi^x(\Pi^p_{t-1})^{\gamma_w}(\Pi^p)^{1-\gamma_w})^{1-\epsilon_{w,t}} + (1 - \theta_w)(W_t^*)^{1-\epsilon_{w,t}}\}^{1/1-\epsilon_{w,t}} \quad (2)$$

Log-linearizing (1) and (2) around a perfect foresight steady state and combining the resulting expressions allows us to derive (after some algebra) the following equation for wage inflation $\pi_t^w \equiv w_t - w_{t-1}$:

$$\pi_t^w = \alpha_w + \gamma_w \pi_{t-1}^p + \beta E_t\{\pi_{t+1}^w - \gamma_w \pi_t^p\} - \lambda_w(\mu_{w,t} - \mu_{w,t}^n), \quad (3)$$

where $\alpha_w \equiv (1 - \beta)((1 - \gamma)\pi^p + \pi^x)$, $\lambda_w \equiv \{[(1 - \beta\theta_w)(1 - \theta_w)]/[\theta_w(1 + \epsilon_w\varphi)]\}$, $\mu_{w,t}^n \equiv \log \mathcal{M}_{w,t}^n$ is the (log) natural wage markup, and

$$\mu_{w,t} \equiv (w_t - p_t) - mrs_t \quad (4)$$

is the (log) average wage markup; that is, the log deviation between the average real wage and the average marginal rate of substitution. As equation (3) makes clear, variations in wage inflation above and beyond those resulting from indexation to past price inflation are driven by deviations of average wage markup from its natural level, because those deviations generate pressure on workers currently setting wages to adjust those wages in one direction or another.

One might argue that the previous model provides, if interpreted literally, an unrealistic description of wage setting in the United States. We view it instead as a simple modeling device, consistent with the labor market block of the medium-scale DSGE models currently used for policy analysis (as exemplified by the SW model), and embedding three features of actual labor markets: (1) nominal wage rigidities, (2) staggered wage-setting, and (3) the presence of average wage levels above their perfectly competitive counterparts, resulting from different sources of market power by workers that prevent their underbidding by the unemployed.

B. Introducing Unemployment

Consider an individual specialized in type i labor and with disutility of work $\chi_t \Theta_t j^\varphi$. *Using household welfare as a criterion*, and *taking as given current labor market conditions* (as summarized by the prevailing wage for his labor type), that individual will find it optimal to participate in the labor market in period t if and only if

$$\left(\frac{1}{\tilde{C}_t}\right)\left(\frac{W_t(i)}{P_t}\right) \geq \chi_t \Theta_t j^{\varphi}.$$

Evaluating the previous condition at the symmetric equilibrium, and letting the marginal supplier of type i labor be denoted by $L_t(i)$, we have:

$$\frac{W_t(i)}{P_t} = \chi_t Z_t L_t(i)^{\varphi}.$$

Taking logs and integrating over i we obtain

$$w_t - p_t = z_t + \varphi l_t + \xi_t, \tag{5}$$

where $l_t \equiv \int_0^1 l_t(i)\, di$ can be interpreted as the (log) aggregate participation or labor force.

Following Galí (2011b, 2011c), we define the *unemployment rate* u_t as:

$$u_t \equiv l_t - n_t. \tag{6}$$

Note that under our assumptions, the unemployed thus defined include all the individuals *who would like to be working* (given current labor market conditions, and while internalizing the benefits that this will bring to their households) *but are not currently employed*. It is in that sense that one can view unemployment as involuntary.[6]

Combining (4) with (5) and (6), the following simple linear relation between the average wage markup and the unemployment rate can be derived

$$\mu_{w,t} = \varphi u_t, \tag{7}$$

which is also graphically illustrated in figure 1.

Finally, combining (3) and (7) we obtain an equation relating wage inflation to price inflation, the unemployment rate, and the wage markup.

$$\pi_t^w = \alpha_w + \gamma_w \pi_{t-1}^p + \beta E_t\{\pi_{t+1}^w - \gamma_w \pi_t^p\} - \lambda_w \varphi u_t + \lambda_w \mu_{w,t}^n. \tag{8}$$

Note that in contrast with the representation of the wage equation found in SW and related papers, the error term in (8) captures exclusively shocks to the wage markup, and *not* preference shocks (even though the latter have been allowed for in our model). That feature, made possible by reformulating the wage equation in terms of the (observable) unemployment rate, allows us to overcome the identification problem raised by CKM in their critique of New Keynesian models. We turn to this issue later, when we discuss our empirical findings.

Finally, note that we can define the *natural* rate of unemployment, u_t^n,

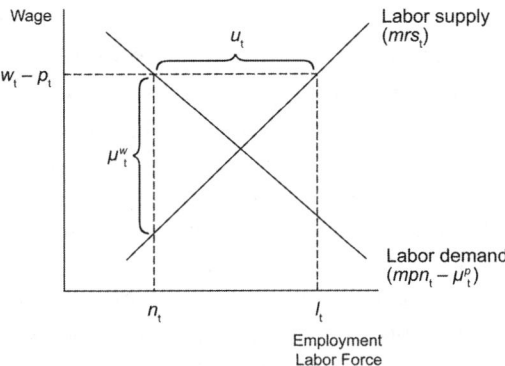

Fig. 1. The wage markup and the unemployment rate

as the unemployment rate that would prevail in the absence of nominal wage rigidities. Under our assumptions, that natural rate will vary exogenously in proportion to the natural wage markup, and can be determined using the simple relation:

$$\mu_{w,t}^n = \varphi u_t^n. \tag{9}$$

The remaining equations describing the log-linearized equilibrium conditions of the model are presented in the appendix. Those equations are identical to a particular case of the specification in SW (2007), corresponding to logarithmic consumption utility. In addition to the wage markup and labor supply shocks just discussed, the model includes six additional shocks: a neutral, factor-augmenting productivity shock; a price markup shock; a risk premium shock; an exogenous spending shock; an investment-specific technology shock; and a monetary policy shock.

III.   Data and Estimation

A.   Data

We estimate our model on US data for the sample period 1966Q1–2007Q4 using Bayesian full-system estimation techniques as in SW (2007). We end our estimation period in 2007Q4 to prevent our estimates from being distorted by the nonlinearities induced by the zero lower bound on the federal funds rate and binding downward nominal wage rigidities during the most recent recession.[7] In Section V we nevertheless use the estimated model to interpret the behavior of unemployment in the recent recession; that is, beyond the estimated period. Section VII on robustness discusses briefly the impact of estimating our model over an extended sample period ending in 2010Q4.

Five of the seven data series used by SW (2007) are also used here: GDP, consumption, investment, GDP deflator inflation, and the federal funds rate, with the first three expressed in per capita terms and log differenced. As the SW model is reformulated in terms of employment (given our interest in explaining unemployment), we use per capita employment rather than hours worked. The main results are not affected if we use hours instead, as discussed in Section VII. In addition, we experiment with two wage concepts. The first one is total compensation per employee obtained from the Bureau of Labor Statistics (BLS) Productivity and Costs Statistics.[8] The second one is "average weekly earnings" from the Current Employment Statistics. Finally, we add the unemployment rate as an additional observable variable. In the following section, we systematically compare the model estimated with and without the latter variable as an observable variable.

The properties of both wage series are quite different.[9] This is illustrated in figure 2, which plots their quarterly nominal growth rates. First, average wage inflation based on compensation per employee is significantly higher than that based on earnings per employee (1.24 versus 1.02). Given average price inflation, the compensation series

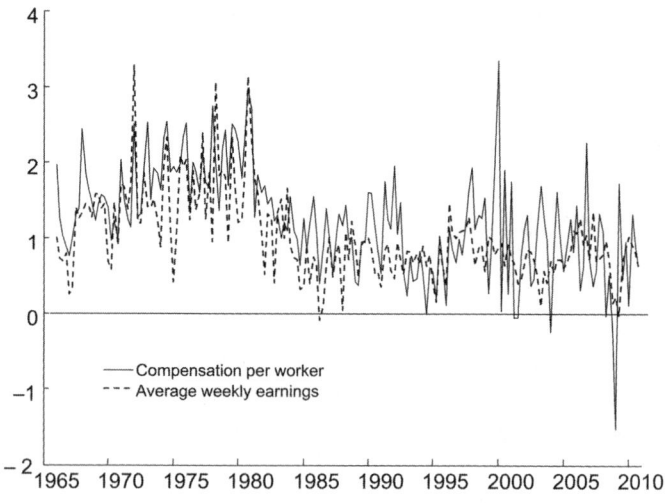

Fig. 2. Two wage inflation measures

appears more compatible with a balanced growth path in which real wages grow at the same rate as real output, consumption, and investment. Second, the compensation series is much more volatile than the earnings series, especially over the past two decades. The standard deviation of wage inflation based on compensation is 0.70, compared to 0.56 for the earnings-based series. Finally, the correlation between both wage inflation measures is surprisingly low at 0.60.

For our baseline estimation, we use both wage series as imperfect measures of the model-based wage concept. This is done by adding measurement error to the corresponding measurement equations and allowing for a separate, smaller trend in the earnings series.[10] In the section on robustness, we briefly discuss the estimation results when we only use the compensation series. In the rest of the paper, we focus on the model with both wage concepts and measurement error.

B. Estimation Results

Table 1 compares the estimated structural parameters of the model obtained with and without unemployment being used as an observable variable. As discussed earlier, adding unemployment allows us to separately identify wage markup and labor supply shocks. In addition, it allows us to exploit the model's prediction of proportionality between the unemployment rate and the wage markup (see equation [7]), in order to identify and estimate the elasticity of substitution between different labor types, which in turn determines the steady-state wage markup. In the model without unemployment this parameter is not identified; instead, we calibrate it to be very similar to the mean of the estimate in the model with observable unemployment.

Overall, most of the estimated structural parameters are very similar in the two models.[11] Focusing on the parameters that are important for the labor market, a number of findings are worth emphasizing.[12] First, the estimated labor supply elasticity is quite similar whether one uses unemployment or not as an observable variable: the inverse of the Frisch elasticity increases slightly from 3.3 to 4.0 as one includes unemployment. In the latter case, the steady-state wage markup is identified and estimated to be slightly below 20%, which is consistent with an average unemployment rate of about 5%.

Second, turning to some of the other parameters that enter the wage Phillips curve, the estimated degree of wage indexation is relatively small (around 0.15) and robust across the two models. The estimated

Table 1

Posterior Estimates for the Model with and without Unemployment as Observed Variable—Complete list of parameters

		Prior Distribution			With UR				Without-UR			
	Type	Mean	St. Dev.	Mode	Mean	5%	95%	Mode	Mean	5%	95%	
St. Dev. of the Innovations[a]												
σ_a	U	2.5	1.44	.41	.42	.37	.46	.42	.42	.37	.46	
σ_b	U	2.5	1.44	1.73	1.60	.56	2.50	.73	.91	.35	1.66	
σ_g	U	2.5	1.44	.47	.48	.43	.52	.47	.48	.43	.52	
σ_q	U	2.5	1.44	.42	.42	.34	.49	.38	.38	.30	.46	
σ_r	U	2.5	1.44	.21	.22	.19	.24	.23	.23	.21	.26	
σ_p	U	2.5	1.44	.05	.11	.03	.18	.06	.32	.02	.73	
σ_w	U	2.5	1.44	.04	.06	.01	.13	.07	.10	.03	.20	
σ_{ls}	U	2.5	1.44	1.07	1.17	.89	1.45	—	—	—	—	
σ_{wC}	U	2.5	1.44	.45	.46	.41	.50	.45	.45	.40	.50	
σ_{wE}	U	2.5	1.44	.34	.36	.32	.41	.33	.34	.29	.39	
Persistence of the Exogenous Processes: ρ = AR(1), μ = MA(1)												
ρ_a	B	.5	.2	.98	.98	.97	.99	.98	.97	.96	.99	
ρ_b	B	.5	.2	.36	.42	.19	.67	.66	.64	.39	.86	
ρ_g	B	.5	.2	.97	.97	.96	.99	.98	.98	.96	.99	
ρ_q	B	.5	.2	.72	.75	.62	.88	.75	.74	.62	.86	
ρ_r	B	.5	.2	.09	.10	.02	.17	.09	.11	.02	.19	
ρ_p	B	.5	.2	.76	.43	.07	.79	.84	.64	.23	.93	
ρ_w	B	.5	.2	.99	.98	.97	1.00	.99	.99	.99	1.00	
μ_p	B	.5	.2	.59	.57	.24	.96	.68	.73	.46	.97	
μ_w	B	.5	.2	.67	.63	.35	.91	.66	.65	.38	.91	
a_g^b	N	.5	.25	.69	.69	.55	.83	.71	.70	.56	.85	
Structural Parameters												
Ψ	N	4.0	1.0	4.09	3.96	2.34	5.58	3.33	3.77	2.32	5.20	
h	B	.7	.10	.78	.75	.65	.85	.66	.68	.57	.81	
φ	N	2.0	1.0	3.99	4.35	3.37	5.32	3.32	3.46	2.27	4.66	
υ	B	.5	.2	.02	.02	.01	.04	.73	.70	.50	.92	
θ_p	B	.5	.15	.58	.62	.53	.71	.60	.71	.56	.84	
θ_w	B	.5	.15	.47	.55	.44	.66	.61	.66	.56	.76	
γ_p	B	.5	.15	.26	.49	.20	.78	.26	.46	.16	.82	
γ_w	B	.5	.15	.16	.18	.07	.29	.17	.20	.08	.31	
ψ	B	.5	.15	.57	.56	.36	.75	.41	.42	.24	.60	
$\mathcal{M}_p$	N	1.25	.12	1.74	1.74	1.61	1.88	1.71	1.73	1.59	1.86	
ρ_r	B	.75	.10	.85	.86	.82	.89	.83	.84	.79	.89	
r_π	N	1.5	.25	1.91	1.89	1.62	2.16	2.03	1.96	1.65	2.26	
r_y	N	.12	.05	.15	.16	.11	.22	.07	.07	.04	.10	
$r\Delta_y$	N	.12	.05	.24	.25	.20	.30	.27	.28	.22	.33	
$\bar{\pi}$	G	.62	.1	.62	.66	.49	.83	.79	.80	.61	.99	
$\$100(\beta^{-1}-1)$	G	.25	.1	.31	.31	.17	.43	.21	.22	.11	.33	
$\bar{l}$	N	.0	2.0	−1.65	−1.52	−3.83	.77	3.56	3.37	1.46	5.29	
τ	N	.4	.1	.34	.34	.30	.37	.40	.39	.36	.43	
τ_{wE}	N	.2	.1	.07	.08	.03	.12	.11	.10	.05	.15	
$\mathcal{M}_w$	N	1.25	.25	1.18	1.22	1.15	1.29	1.25^c	1.25^c	—	—	
α	N	.3	.05	.17	.17	.14	.20	.16	.16	.13	.19	

[a]The IG-distribution is defined by the degree of freedom.
[b]The effect of total factor productivity (TFP) innovations on exogenous demand.
[c]The steady-state wage markup is not identified if the unemployment rate is not observed.

Calvo probability of unchanged wages falls somewhat from 0.61 to 0.47, suggesting relatively flexible wages with average contract durations of two quarters. Overall, the introduction of unemployment as an observable variable leads to a somewhat steeper wage Phillips curve.

Third, the parameter v, governing the short-run wealth effects on labor supply, changes quite dramatically from 0.73 to 0.02. Roughly speaking, this amounts to a change from preferences close to those in King, Plosser, and Rebelo (1988; henceforth, KPR), characterized by strong short-run wealth effects on labor supply, to a specification closer to that in Greenwood, Hercowitz, and Huffman (1988). In the latter case, wealth effects are close to zero in the short run. As discussed later, this helps ensure that not only employment, but also the labor force moves procyclically in response to most shocks.[13]

Finally, it is worth pointing out that the monetary policy reaction coefficient to the output gap (defined as the deviation relative to the constant markup output), doubles from 0.07 to 0.15. As discussed later, this is mainly due to the lower volatility of the output gap once unemployment is used to identify wage markup shocks.

C. Impulse Responses

Figures 3 to 5 show the estimated impulse responses of output, inflation, the real wage, the interest rate, employment, the labor force, the unemployment rate, and the output gap to the eight structural shocks. Figure 3 focuses on the four "demand" shocks, which include the investment-specific technology shock, the risk premium shock, the exogenous spending shock, and the monetary policy shock. We use the label "demand" to refer to those shocks because they all imply a positive comovement beween output, inflation, and the real wage. It is particularly noteworthy that employment and the labor force comove positively in response to all those shocks. Note, however, that the size of the labor force response is typically much smaller than that of employment, so that unemployment fluctuations are mostly driven by changes in employment. This is consistent with the unconditional second moments of detrended data (see, e.g., Galí 2011a, as well as the empirical evidence on the effects of monetary policy shocks as shown in Christiano, Trabandt, and Walentin 2010).

Figure 4 reports the dynamic responses to the labor supply and markup shocks, which we group under the heading of "labor market" shocks. These shocks generate a negative comovement of inflation and

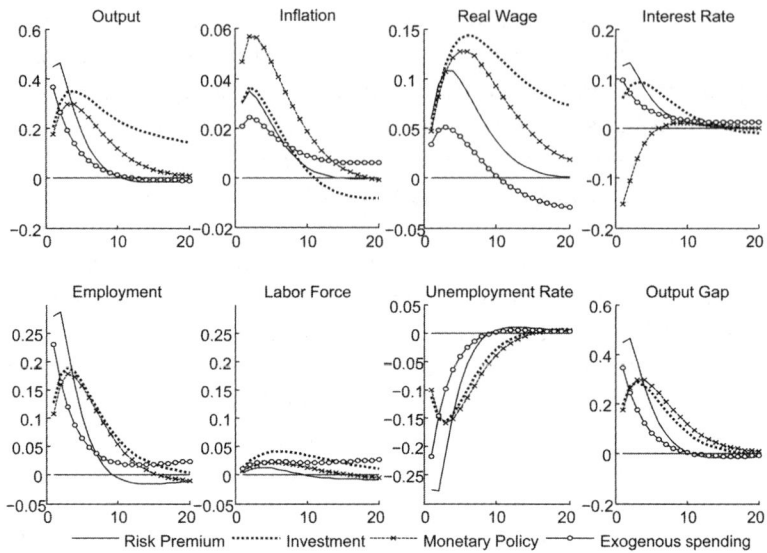

Fig. 3.   Dynamic responses to demand shocks

the real wage with output. An adverse wage markup shock has a sizable positive impact on price inflation and unemployment and a negative one on output, employment, and the output gap, thus generating a clear trade-off for policymakers. On the other hand, an adverse labor supply shock has similar negative effects on output, employment, and the output gap (and positive effects on inflation), but instead leads to a rise in the output gap and a drop in the unemployment rate, so that no significant policy trade-off arises. It is this different effect on unemployment and the output gap associated with the two labor market shocks that makes their separate identification so important from a policy perspective, as further discussed following.

Figure 5 displays the estimated model's implied impulse responses to a positive neutral technology shock and a (negative) price markup shock. We refer to those shocks as "supply" shocks, their distinctive feature being that they generate simultaneously a procyclical real wage response and a countercyclical response of inflation. It is worth noting, that, in line with much of the empirical evidence (e.g. Galí 1999; Barnichon 2010), in our estimated model a positive technology shock leads to a short-run decline in employment and a rise in the unemployment rate. This is in contrast with the predictions of conventionally calibrated real business cycle or search and matching models. Secondly, and in

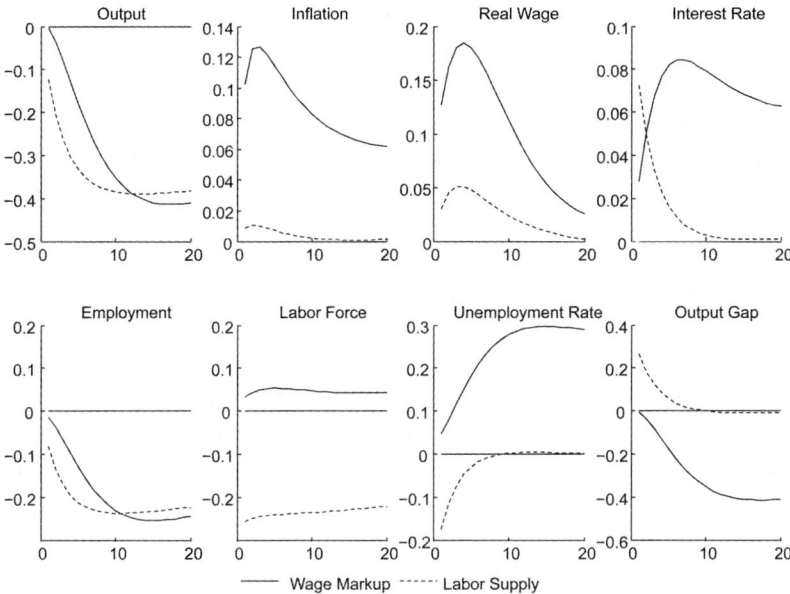

Fig. 4. Dynamic responses to labor market shocks

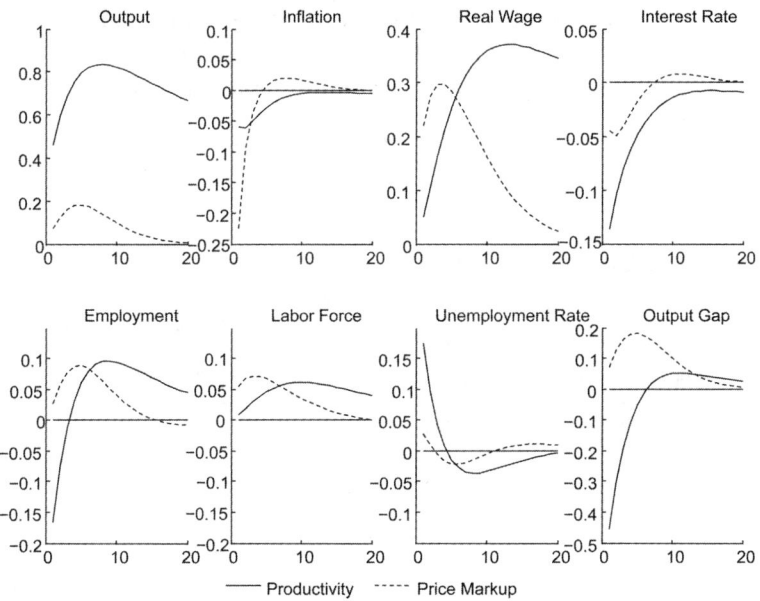

Fig. 5. Dynamic responses to supply shocks

a way analogous to wage markup shocks, we see that price markup shocks also create a policy trade-off between stabilizing inflation and the output gap. This is not the case for technology shocks, since they drive both these variables in the same direction.

Before turning to several interesting questions that can be addressed with our estimated model, we wish to emphasize the importance of departing from conventional KPR preferences in order to match certain aspects of the data. Note that under standard KPR preferences ($v = 1$) the labor supply equation (5) can be written as

$$w_t - p_t = c_t + \varphi l_t + \xi_t,$$

where habit formation is omitted to simplify the argument. As emphasized by Christiano et al. (2010) the previous equation is at odds with their empirical estimates of the effects of monetary policy shocks, which show a countercyclical response of $w_t - p_t - c_t$ coexisting with a procyclical response of the labor force l_t. Instead, under the assumed preferences, a procyclical response of the labor force is consistent with the model as long as the short-run wealth effect is sufficiently weak, implying a small adjustment of z_t and hence a procyclical response of $w_t - p_t - z_t$. This is illustrated in figure 6, which compares the impulse responses of employment, the labor force, and the unemployment rate to a monetary policy shock under (1) our baseline estimated model and (2) an otherwise identical model with KPR preferences (corresponding to $v = 1$). Note that in the latter case, and in contrast with the evidence,

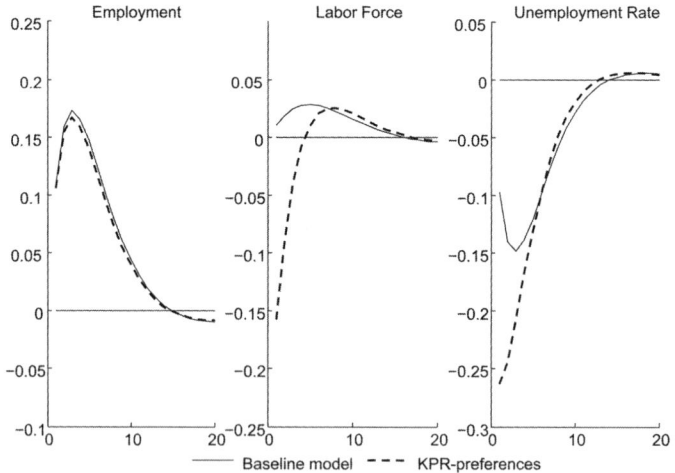

Fig. 6. Monetary policy shocks and the role of wealth effects

the labor force indeed falls significantly following an easing of monetary policy, amplifying the response of the unemployment rate and becoming as important a driver of the latter as employment.

IV.   Wage Markup versus Labor Supply Shocks: Addressing the CKM Critique

In this section we address one of the CKM criticisms pointing to an implausibly large variance of wage markups shocks and a large contribution of the latter to output and employment fluctuations, often implied by estimated DSGE models (e.g., SW 2007). As argued by CKM, that evidence cannot be of much use to policymakers since the SW model is not able to distinguish between wage markup and labor supply shocks. They are effectively "lumped together" as a residual in the wage equation, even though—as discussed earlier—they have very different policy implications.

As discussed before, that problem of incomplete identification is overcome by our reformulation of the SW model using the unemployment rate as an observable variable.[14] In particular, the estimated parameters of the ARMA(1, 1) process for the exogenous wage markup reported in table 1 imply the latter's standard deviation drops from 23 to 12% once unemployment is included as an observable. Based on equation (7) and the estimated inverse labor supply elasticity, this implies a standard deviation of the natural unemployment rate of the order of 3%. This estimate is relatively high, but not unreasonable, especially given that much of that volatility is concentrated at low frequencies, unrelated to business cycles.

How important are wage markup shocks in driving output and employment fluctuations in our estimated model? Table 2 presents the variance decomposition of the forecast errors of the eight observable variables at the 10-quarter and 10-year horizons. The first entry in each cell gives the percent contribution of each shock to fluctuations in each variable in the model with unemployment as an observable, whereas the second entry gives the corresponding share in the model without unemployment. Chari, Kehoe, and McGrattan argue that the contribution of the wage markup shocks to output and employment fluctuations (about 50 and 80% at the 10-year horizon in the model without unemployment) was too high to be plausible. Distinguishing labor supply shocks from wage markup shocks by introducing unemployment helps address this issue. From table 2 it is clear that the contribu-

Table 2
Variance Decomposition

Variance decomposition	Output	Inflation	Real wage	Employment	Labor force	Unemployment
				10-quarter horizon		
Demand shocks						
Risk premium	6/14	2/8	3/6	16/25	0/15	20/25
Exogenous demand	3/5	1/0	1/0	7/10	1/9	8/1
Investment spec. techn.	9/7	3/2	8/2	12/9	2/3	10/2
Monetary policy	5/7	8/8	6/4	11/12	0/4	11/10
Supply shocks						
Productivity	59/46	6/4	40/32	5/2	3/4	4/1
Price markup	2/6	27/33	30/45	3/6	5/3	0/1
Labor market shocks						
Wage markup	6/15	53/46	12/11	18/35	3/61	41/61
Labor supply	11/—	0/—	1/—	29/—	86/—	5/—
				40-quarterhorizon		
Demand shocks						
Risk premium	2/5	1/6	1/3	6/8	0/6	7/7
Exogenous demand	1/2	1/0	1/0	3/5	1/8	3/0
Investment spec. techn.	5/3	2/1	6/3	4/3	1/2	3/0
Monetary policy	2/3	5/7	3/3	4/4	0/2	4/3
Supply shocks						
Productivity	56/39	4/3	71/59	3/1	2/1	1/0
Price markup	1/2	18/26	13/26	1/2	2/1	0/0
Labor market shocks						
Wage markup	17/45	67/57	5/6	39/77	5/81	80/89
Labor supply	17/—	0/—	0/—	40/—	89/—	2/—

Note: Each cell reports the contributions to the forecast error variance of the corresponding variable for the models estimated with and without unemployment, respectively.

tion of the wage markup shocks to output (employment) fluctuations at the 10-year horizon drops substantially, from 45 (77)% to 17 (39)%, in the model with unemployment. Furthermore, in the latter, labor supply shocks (which are now separately identified) account for about 17, 40, and 89% of fluctuations in output, employment, and the labor force, respectively (instead they are ignored in the model without unemployment, as in SW 2007).

As discussed by CKM, the identification of wage markup and labor supply shocks has implications for monetary policy, since those two shocks have very different effects on the efficient level of output and thus on the welfare-relevant output gap. Figure 7 plots the output gap, defined as the log deviation between actual output and the level of output that would prevail with constant markups and flexible prices and

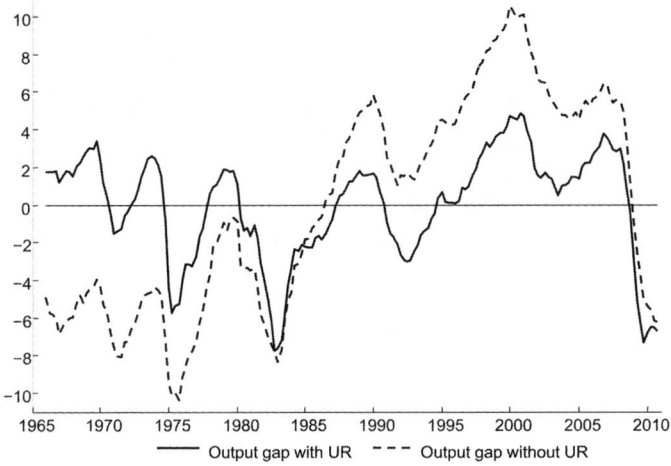

Fig. 7.   Two measures of the output gap

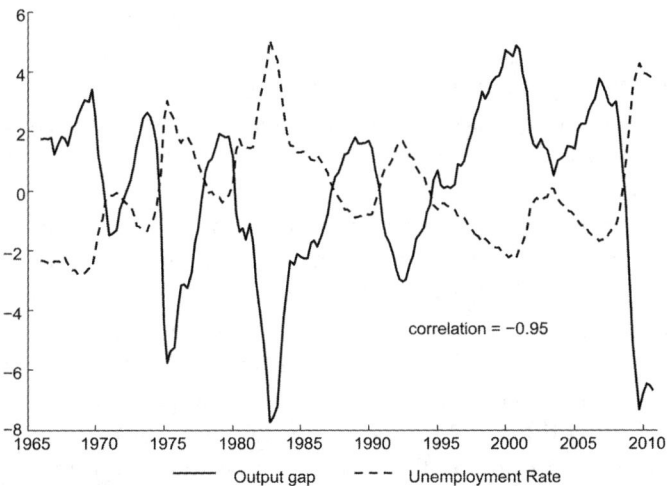

Fig. 8.   The output gap and the unemployment rate

wages. Two versions of the same variable are shown, as implied by the estimated models with and without unemployment, respectively.[15] Figure 7 shows that the separate identification of labor supply shocks allowed by our reformulation has a substantial impact on the estimated output gap, which now looks considerably more stationary.

How does our estimated output gap relate to other variables often used as cyclical indicators? Figure 8 shows that our estimate of the out-

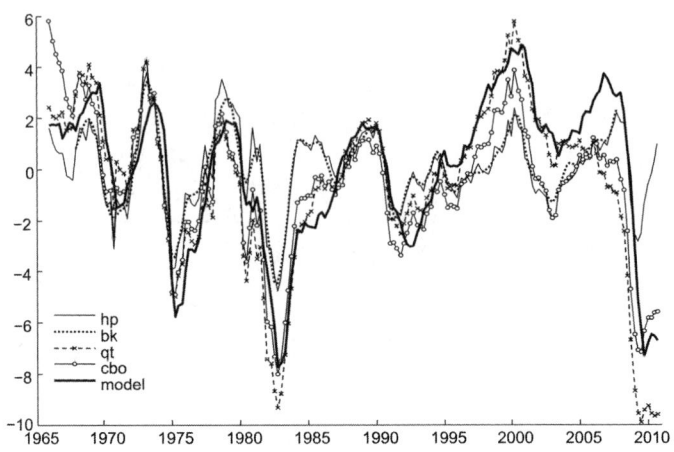

Fig. 9.   The output gap versus detrended GDP

put gap is to a large extent the mirror image of the unemployment rate. The correlation between the two is –0.95. This finding suggests that variations in wage markups, whether exogenous or induced by wage rigidities, are a key factor underlying inefficient output fluctuations.[16] That finding is consistent with the evidence in Galí, Gertler, and López-Salido (2007).[17]

Finally, figure 9 emphasizes that the model-based output gap resembles conventional measures of the cyclical component of log GDP, based on a variety of statistical detrending methods (Hodrick-Prescott [HP] filter, band-pass filter, and quadratic detrending, as well as the Congressional Budget Office [CBO] measure).[18] There are, however, periods such as the 2005–2006 boom period, with substantial deviations from the conventional measures. The output gap correlation with each of the four measures lies in the 0.6 to 0.8 range, with quadratic detrending showing the highest value.

V.   Understanding Unemployment Fluctuations

In the present section we use our estimated model to analyze different aspects of unemployment fluctuations, which the reformulation of the SW model makes possible.

First, we can assess the role of wage rigidities as a factor underlying observed unemployment fluctuations by comparing the observed unemployment rate to its estimated *natural* counterpart, where the latter

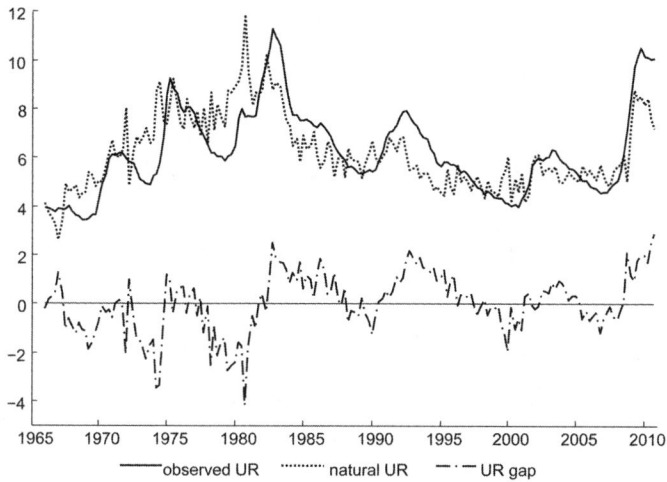

Fig. 10. The natural rate of unemployment

is defined as the unemployment rate that would be observed in the absence of nominal wage rigidities, as determined by equation (9). Figure 10 shows the time series for both variables, together with the gap between the two. The figure makes clear that the natural rate of unemployment accounts for a large fraction of the low-frequency movements in the observed unemployment rate. Yet it is clear that the natural rate cannot account for the bulk of unemployment fluctuations at business-cycle frequencies, which are captured by the unemployment gap. Those fluctuations should thus be attributed to the presence of wage rigidities, interacting with the different shocks.

The variance decomposition reported in table 1 shows that about 50% of unemployment fluctuations at the 10-quarter horizon is due to "demand" shocks, with a prominent role attributed to risk premium shocks. The other half is mostly due to wage markup shocks. In the longer run (10-year horizon), the contribution of demand shocks drops to 17% and wage markup shocks become the dominant driving force. Interestingly, those wage markup shocks also explain a dominant share of the fluctuations in price and wage inflation at all horizons. In contrast, labor supply and other supply shocks have only a limited impact on unemployment. The labor force instead is mostly driven by labor supply shocks, with most other shocks having a very limited impact on that variable.

The importance of demand and wage markup shocks in driving un-

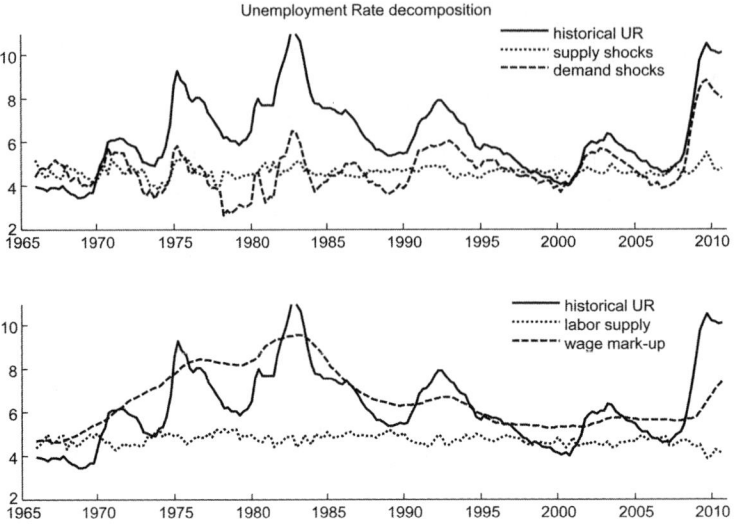

Fig. 11. Sources of unemployment rate fluctuations

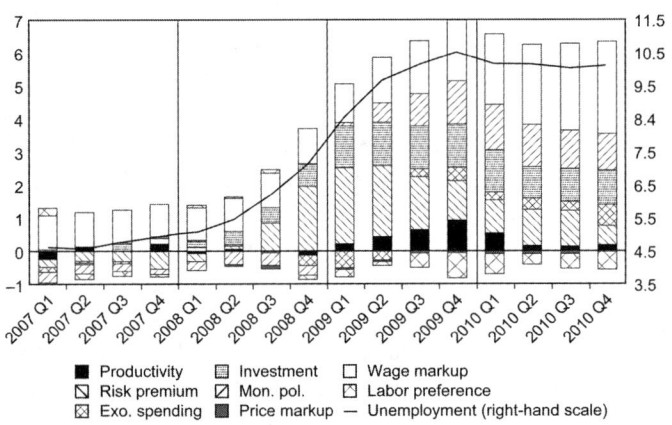

Fig. 12. Unemployment during the Great Recession

employment can also be illustrated by means of the historical decomposition depicted in figure 11. The secular rise of unemployment and inflation in the 1970s and early 1980s is mostly driven by cost-push factors coming from increasing wage markups. This is reversed in the mid-1980s. On the other hand, most of the unemployment fluctuations at business cycle frequencies are seen to be driven by demand shocks. This is particularly the case since the early 1990s. Both the 2001 and 2007–2008 recessions are driven by negative demand shocks. Figure 12 zooms in on the most recent recession, displaying the contribution of

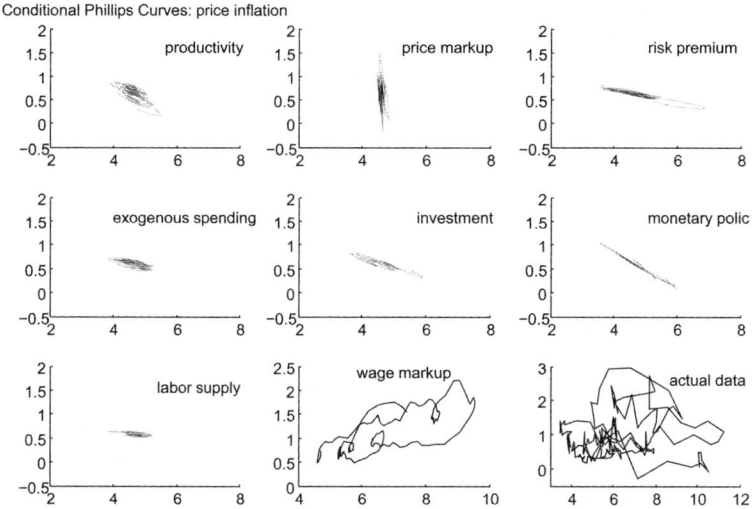

Fig. 13. Unemployment and wage inflation

each individual shock to the rise of unemployment over this period. We see that about three-quarters of the 5 percentage point increase in the unemployment rate is due to demand factors, with adverse risk premium shocks playing a large role at the start of the crisis, thus capturing the tightening of financial conditions. As of 2009 our estimates identify an "effective" tightening of monetary policy, which we attribute to the attainment of the zero lower bound on the federal funds rate, and which is shown to contribute about 1 to 2 percentage points to the rise in the unemployment rate. Finally, it is also worth noting that our estimates suggest a significant contribution of wage markup shocks to the recent rise in the unemployment rate. As conjectured by Galí (2011b), this may be due to downward nominal wage rigidities interacting with very low inflation, which may have prevented the average real wage from adjusting as much as it would be warranted by the decline in inflation and the rise in unemployment.

Finally, we can use the estimated model to interpret the observed comovements between the unemployment rate and measures of wage and price inflation. With that objective, figure 13 displays the joint variation in wage inflation and the unemployment rate conditional on each shock, as well as their unconditional joint variation (bottom-right diagram). The evidence makes clear that whatever Phillips-curve-like negative comovement between wage inflation and unemployment can be found in the data, it is largely the result of the four demand shocks. By contrast, wage markup shocks generate what looks like a positive lower

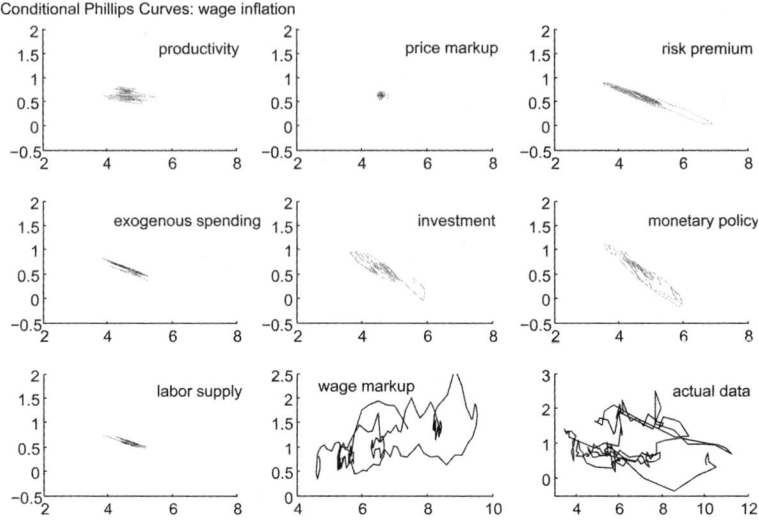

Fig. 14. Unemployment and price inflation

frequency comovement in both variables, and are largely reponsible for the lack of a clean Phillips-curve-like pattern in the observed data. Supply shocks, on the other hand, lead to a near-zero comovement. Note that this is still consistent with wage inflation equation (3) (given the forward-looking nature of the latter), for their implied responses of unemployment display a sign switch (see figure 5), thus leaving wage inflation largely unchanged as a result.

Figure 14 displays analogous evidence for unemployment and price inflation. As in the case of wage inflation, the four demand shocks generate a clear negative comovement between price inflation and the unemployment rate, while wage markup shocks underlie a low frequency positive comovement. Contrary to traditional textbook analyses, productivity shocks are also shown to generate a negative comovement between price inflation and the unemployment rate. On the other hand, price markup shocks produce a nearly vertical Phillips curve, since their impact on the unemployment rate is tiny, while their effect on price inflation is substantial.

VI. Robustness

In this section we briefly summarize the findings based on a number of alternative specifications. First, we use hours worked rather than employment as our measure of labor input. While the benchmark model is written in terms of employment, the actual labor input that enters the production function should be total hours worked. Using employment will therefore distort the estimated productivity process. When we use hours, we leave the unemployment rate unchanged, thus making the implicit assumption that those who are unemployed want to work the same number of hours as those who are employed.[19] In that alternative specification we also use wage per hour. When we leave the model unchanged but use hours worked rather than employment as our measure of labor input, the main results emphasized earlier are not affected. The full set of results is available on request. Two differences are worth mentioning. First, as expected, the contribution of productivity shocks to output fluctuations becomes less important. Second, the degree of wage rigidity is estimated to be higher (0.60) and as a result the slope of the Phillips curve becomes less steep, due to the greater cyclical volatility of wage per worker relative to wage per hour.

We also estimate the model using only the compensation series as a wage measure. Again, the main results are unchanged. The main impact of the higher volatility in the compensation series is to increase the estimate of the inverse Frisch elasticity of the labor supply to 5.6 when unemployment is added. With higher observed volatility of wages, the response of labor supply to real wages is estimated to be less. This has an additional impact on some of the other parameters, such as the degree of habit formation.

Third, we have also estimated the model under KPR preferences (i.e., imposing $v = 0$) and an alternative set of Jaimovich-Rebelo (JR) preferences where the Z_t factor evolves in line with aggregate productivity instead of aggregate consumption. The model with KPR preferences leads to a significant deterioration of the empirical fit by about 15 points. As discussed earlier, in this case the labor force moves countercyclically in response to monetary policy and other demand shocks. However, the modified JR model leads to a significantly improved empirical fit by about 28 points. Moreover, the parameter v rises back to 0.9 (from 0.02 in the baseline model), suggesting that in response to productivity shocks the data prefer stronger short-run wealth effects on labor supply. We still need to think harder about the interpretation of these results.

Finally, we have also re-estimated our model using data up to 2010Q4, thus ignoring the potential problems raised earlier (likely misspecification of the interest rate rule and the wage equation due to nonlinearities at work during this period). The main difference with the benchmark results is that the estimated wage stickiness rises and the overall persistence in the economy as captured by the persistence of the shocks also goes up.

VII.   Conclusion

In this paper we have developed a reformulated version of the Smets-Wouters (2007) framework that embeds the theory of unemployment proposed in Galí (2011b, 2011c). We estimate the resulting model using postwar US data, while treating the unemployment rate as an additional observable variable. This helps overcome the lack of identification of wage markup and labor supply shocks highlighted by Chari, Kehoe, and McGrattan (2008) in their criticism of New Keynesian models. In turn, our approach allows us to estimate a "correct" measure of the output gap. In addition, the estimated model can be used to analyze the sources of unemployment fluctuations.

A number of key results emerge from our analysis. First, we show that wage markup shocks play a smaller role in driving output and employment fluctuations than previously thought. Second, fluctuations in our estimated output gap are shown to be the near mirror image of those experienced by the unemployment rate, and to be well approximated by conventional measures of the cyclical component of GDP. Third, demand shocks are the main driver of unemployment fluctuations at business cycle frequencies, but wage markup shocks are shown to be more important at lower frequencies. Finally, our estimates point to an adverse risk-premium shock as the key force behind the initial rise in unemployment during the Great Recession. The important role uncovered for monetary policy and wage markup shocks at a later stage may be interpreted as capturing the likely effects of the zero lower bound on the nominal rate and of downward wage rigidities (as opposed to those of truly exogenous shocks).

Appendix

In this appendix, we summarize the remaining log-linear equations of the estimated model. For a more detailed presentation, we refer to the discussion in SW.

Consumption Euler equation:

$$\hat{c}_t = c_1 \hat{c}_{t-1} + (1 - c_1) E_t\{\hat{c}_{t+1}\} - c_2(\hat{r}_t - E_t\{\hat{\pi}_{t+1}\} + \hat{\varepsilon}_t^b)$$

with $c_1 \equiv (h/\tau)/(1 + h/\tau)$, $c_2 \equiv (1 - h/\tau)/(1 + h/\tau)$ where h is the external habit parameter and $\tau \equiv \Pi_x$ is the trend growth rate. $\hat{r}_t$ is the nominal interest rate and $\hat{\varepsilon}_t^b$ is the exogenous AR(1) risk premium process.

Investment Euler equation:

$$\hat{i}_t = i_1\hat{i}_{t-1} + (1 - i_1)E_t\{\hat{i}_{t+1}\} + i_2\hat{q}_t + \hat{\varepsilon}_t^q$$

with $i_1 = 1/(1 + \beta)$, $i_2 = i_1/(\tau^2\Psi)$ where β is the household's discount factor, and Ψ is the elasticity of the capital adjustment cost function. $\hat{q}_t$ is the value of installed capital and $\hat{\varepsilon}_t^q$ is the exogenous AR(1) process for the investment specific technology.

Value of the capital stock:

$$\hat{q}_t = -(\hat{r}_t - E_t\{\hat{\pi}_{t+1}\} + \hat{\varepsilon}_t^b) + q_1E_t\{r_{t+1}^k\} + (1 - q_1)E_t\{\hat{q}_{t+1}\}$$

with $q_1 = r^k/(r^k + (1 - \delta))$ where $\hat{r}_t^k$ is the capital rental rate and δ the depreciation rate.

Goods market clearing:

$$\hat{y}_t = c_y\hat{c}_t + i_y\hat{i}_t + \hat{\varepsilon}_t^g + v_y\hat{v}_t$$

$$= \mathcal{M}_p(\alpha\hat{k}_t + (1 - \alpha)\hat{n}_t + \hat{\varepsilon}_t^a)$$

with $c_y \equiv (C/Y)$, $i_y \equiv (I/Y)$, and $v_y \equiv R^kK/Y$. Parameter $\mathcal{M}_p$ denotes the degree of returns to scale which is assumed to correspond to the price markup in steady state. $\hat{\varepsilon}_t^g$ and $\hat{\varepsilon}_t^a$ are the AR(1) processes representing respectiely exogenous demand components and the neutral-technology process.

Price-setting under the Calvo model with indexation:

$$\hat{\pi}_t^p - \gamma_p\hat{\pi}_{t-1}^p = \beta(E_t\{\hat{\pi}_{t+1}^p\} - \gamma_p\hat{\pi}_t^p) - \pi_2(\hat{\mu}_{p,t} - \hat{\mu}_{p,t}^n)$$

with $\pi_1 = (1 - \beta\theta_p)(1 - \theta_p)/[\theta_p(1 + (\mathcal{M}_p - 1)s_p)]$, where θ_p and γ_p respectively denote the Calvo price stickiness and the price indexation parameters, s_p is the curvature of the Kimball aggregator.

Average and natural price markups:

$$\hat{\mu}_{p,t} = -(1 - \alpha)\hat{\omega}_t - \alpha\hat{r}_t^k + \hat{\varepsilon}_t^a$$

$$\hat{\mu}_{p,t}^n = 100 \cdot \hat{\varepsilon}_t^p$$

where $\omega_t \equiv w_t - p_t$ is the real wage.

Wage-setting under the Calvo model with indexation:

$$\hat{\pi}_t^w - \gamma_w\hat{\pi}_{t-1}^p = \beta(E_t\{\hat{\pi}_{t+1}^w\} - \gamma_w\hat{\pi}_t^p) - \lambda_w(\hat{\mu}_{w,t} - \hat{\mu}_{w,t}^n)$$

with $\lambda_w \equiv (1 - \beta\theta_w)(1 - \theta_w)/[\theta_w(1 + \varepsilon_w\varphi)]$.

Average and natural wage markups and unemployment:

$$\hat{\mu}_{w,t} = \hat{\omega}_t - (\hat{z}_t + \hat{\varepsilon}_t^x + \phi\hat{n}_t)$$

$$= \varphi\hat{u}_t$$

$$\hat{\mu}_{w,t}^n = 100 \cdot \hat{\varepsilon}_t^w$$

$$= \varphi\hat{u}_t^n$$

$$\hat{z}_t = (1 - \upsilon)\hat{z}_{t-1} + \upsilon(1/(1 - h/\gamma))\hat{c}_t - ((h / \gamma)/(1 - h/\gamma))\hat{c}_{t-1}]$$

where the exogenous labor supply shock $\hat{\varepsilon}_t^x$ is assumed to follow a highly persistent AR(1) process with autoregressive coefficient fixed at $\rho_x = 0.999$.

Labor force:

$$\hat{l}_t = \hat{n}_t + \hat{u}_t$$

Capital accumulation equation:

$$\hat{k}_t = \kappa_1\hat{k}_{t-1} + (1 - \kappa_1)\hat{i}_t + \kappa_2\hat{\varepsilon}_t^q$$

with $\kappa_1 \equiv 1 - (I/\bar{K})$, $\kappa_2 = (I/\bar{K})(1 + \beta)\tau^2\Psi$. Capital services used in production are defined as: $\hat{k}_t = \hat{\upsilon}_t + \hat{k}_{t-1}$.

Optimal capital utilisation condition:

$$\hat{\upsilon}_t = ((1 - \psi)/\psi)\hat{r}_t^k$$

with ψ is the elasticity of the capital utilization cost function.

Optimal input choice:

$$\hat{k}_t = \hat{\omega}_t - \hat{r}_t^k + \hat{n}_t$$

Monetary policy rule:

$$\hat{r}_t = \rho_r\hat{r}_{t-1} + (1 - \rho_r)(r_\pi\hat{\pi}_t^p + r_y\widehat{(ygap_t)}) + r_{\Delta y}\Delta\widehat{(ygap_t)} + \hat{\varepsilon}_t^r$$

with $ygap_t \equiv \hat{y}_t - \hat{y}_t^{flex}$, is the difference between actual output and the output in the flexible price and wage economy in absence of distorting price and wage markup shocks.

The following parameters are not identified by the estimation procedure and are therefore calibrated: $\delta = 0.025$, $s_p = 10$. The remaining parameters τ_{wE} and a_g in Table 1 denote, respectively, the trend growth rate in real "average weekly earnings" which is allowed to differ from the common trend, and the spillover effect of neutral-technology shocks on the exogenous demand shock in the specification that relaxes the independence assumption.

Endnotes

Prepared for the NBER Macroeconomics Annual 2011 Conference, held in Cambridge, MA, on April 8–9, 2011. We have benefited from comments by Larry Christiano, Marco del Negro, Keith Kuester, Richard Rogerson, Carlos Thomas, and participants at the NBER Summer Institute, SED Conference (Montréal), Banque de France, Harvard, EUI (Florence), Bank of Cyprus, CREI-UPF, ECB, Leuven, Insead, and PSE. Galí acknowledges the financial support from the European Research Council through an Advanced Grant (Project Reference #229650). For acknowledgments, sources of research support, and disclosure of the authors' material financial relationships, if any, please see http://www.nber .org/chapters/c12424.ack.

1. See, for example, Smets et al. (2010) for a short description of the two aggregate euro area models used at the European Central Band (ECB). Two of the DSGE models used at the Federal Reserve are described in Edge, Kiley, and Laforte (2007) and Erceg, Guerrieri, and Gust (2006).

2. The general approach builds on Galí (1996). See also Blanchard and Galí (2007), Casares (2010), and Zanetti (2007) for related applications to the New Keynesian model. After having circulated a first draft of the present paper we became aware of Casares, Moreno, and Vázquez (2011), which contains an exercise close in spirit (but with substantial differences in details) to the one presented here.

3. Alternatively, we can take the consumption utility of the household, $\log \tilde{C}_t$, as a "primitive," without making any assumption on how that consumption is distributed among household members, possibly as a function of employment status.

4. In particular, and leaving aside the presence of habits, our specification assumes that the period utility is separable in consumption and employment, in contrast with that in Jaimovich and Rebelo (2009). This facilitates aggregation of individual utilities into the household utility, and simplifies the analysis by implying equalization of consumption across individuals in the presence of risk-sharing within each household.

5. Details of the derivation of the optimal wage-setting condition can be found in EHL (2000).

6. As noted by one of our discussants, unemployed individuals will enjoy a higher utility ex post, since their consumption will be the same but will not experience any disutility from work. This is, of course, an unavoidable consequence of our assumption of full consumption risk-sharing within the household. Under the latter assumption, and given the infinitesimal weight of each individual in the household, not internalizing the benefits to the latter of an individual's employment would unavoidably lead to no participation.

7. For some discussion on how downward nominal wage rigidity may distort the the estimates of the New Keynesian wage Phillips curve, see Galí (2011b).

8. Note that SW (2007) used compensation per hour instead, in a way consistent with their model specification.

9. See Abraham, Spletzer, and Stewart (1999) and Mehran and Tracy (2001) for a discussion about the sources of some of those differences.

10. A similar strategy is followed by Justiniano, Primiceri, and Tambalotti (2011). They show how using a single series (compensation) and not allowing for measurement error implies a standard deviation for the estimated wage markup shocks that is six times higher than in their baseline model.

11. A robust feature of the model with observed unemployment is that the labor preference shock and the productivity shock are positively correlated. Allowing for such a correlation further improves the fit of the model, but does not affect the estimation results discussed later.

12. Unless otherwise noted, we will consistently refer to the mode of the posterior probability distribution when discussing estimates. Table 1 also reports the mean and 5 and 95 percentiles of the posterior distribution.

13. Jaimovich and Rebelo (2009) have argued that small short-run wealth effects on labor supply are necessary to generate a positive response of output to favorable news about future productivity.

14. Justiniano, Primiceri, and Tambalotti (2011) seek to overcome that problem by as-

suming a different stochastic structure for both driving forces: purely transitory in the case of markup shocks, and potentially persistent (as allowed for by an AR(1) process) for the labor supply shock. Their assumption of a white noise wage markup shock is at odds with our estimated process for that shock, which displays an important low frequency component.

15. Note that, under the assumptions of the model, the output gap thus defined will differ from the gap relative to the efficient level of output by an additive constant.

16. See also the analysis in Galí (2011c) in the context of a much simpler model. A similar qualitative finding is uncovered in Sala, Söderström, and Trigari (2010), though their approach is subject to the CKM critique.

17. It would also appear to be consistent with the evidence on the so-called "labor wedge" (e.g., Chari, Kehoe, and McGrattan 2007; Shimer 2010). Note, however, that the concept of the labor wedge often used in the literature refers to the gap between the marginal rate of substitution and the marginal product of labor (as opposed to the wage). As a result (and despite its name) it captures variations in goods makets distortions, like price markups, in addition to labor market ones.

18. Justiniano, Primiceri, and Tambalotti (2011) obtain a qualitatively similar finding, using an approach that does not exploit the connection between unemployment and wage markups, assuming instead a particular stochastic structure for the latter (white noise).

19. In order to address these issues, ideally we need to explicitly include the intensive margin (i.e., hours worked per employee) in the model and re-estimate it accordingly. That extension is part of our currently ongoing research.

References

Abraham, Katharine G., James R. Spletzer, and Jay C. Stewart. 1999. "Why Do Different Wage Series Tell Different Stories?" *American Economic Review* 89 (2): 34–39.

Barnichon, Regis. 2010. "Productivity and Unemployment over the Business Cycle." *Journal of Monetary Economics* 57 (8): 1013–25.

Blanchard, Olivier J., and Jordi Galí. 2007. "Real Wage Rigidities and the New Keynesian Model." *Journal of Money, Credit, and Banking* 39 (suppl. 1): 35–66.

———. 2010. "Labor Markets and Monetary Policy: A New Keynesian Model with Unemployment." *American Economic Journal: Macroeconomics* 2 (2): 1–33.

Calvo, Guillermo. 1983. "Staggered Prices in a Utility Maximizing Framework." *Journal of Monetary Economics* 12:383–98.

Casares, Miguel. 2010. "Unemployment as Excess Supply of Labor: Implications for Wage and Price Inflation." *Journal of Monetary Economics* 57 (2): 233–43.

Casares, Miguel, Antonio Moreno, and Jesús Vázquez. 2011. "An Estimated New Keynesian Model with Unemployment as Excess Supply of Labor." Unpublished Manuscript, Universidad Pública de Navarra.

Chari, V. V., Patrick J. Kehoe, and Ellen R. McGrattan. 2007. "Business Cycle Accounting." *Econometrica* 75 (3): 781–836.

———. 2009. "New Keynesian Models: Not Yet Useful for Policy Analysis." *American Economic Journal: Macroeconomics* 1 (1): 242–66.

Christiano, Lawrence J., Mathias Trabandt, and Karl Walentin. 2010. "Involuntary Unemployment and the Business Cycle." Unpublished manuscript.

———. 2011. "DSGE Models for Monetary Policy." In *Handbook of Monetary Economics*, edited by B. Friedman and M. Woodford. North Holland: Elsevier.

Christoffel, Kai, Keith Kuester, and Tobias Linzert. 2009. "The Role of Labor Markets for Euro Area Monetary Policy." *European Economic Review* 53: 908–36.

de Walque, Gregory, Olivier Pierrard, Henri Sneessens, and Raf Wouters. 2009.

"Sequential Bargaining in a Neo-Keynesian Model with Frictional Unemployment and Staggered Wage Negotiations." *Annals of Economics and Statistics* 95/96, July/December.

Edge, Rochelle M., Michael T. Kiley, and Jean-Philippe Laforte. 2007. "Documentation of the Research and Statistics Division's Estimated DSGE Model of the U.S. Economy: 2006 Version." Finance and Economics Discussion Series 2007-53. Washington, DC: Federal Reserve Board.

Erceg, Christopher J., Luca Guerrieri, and Christopher Gust. 2006. "SIGMA: A New Open Economy Model for Policy Analysis." *International Journal of Central Banking* 2 (1): 1–50.

Erceg, Christopher J., Dale W. Henderson, and Andrew T. Levin. 2000. "Optimal Monetary Policy with Staggered Wage and Price Contracts." *Journal of Monetary Economics* 46 (2): 281–314.

Galí, Jordi. 1996. "Unemployment in Dynamic General Equilibrium Economies." *European Economic Review* 40:839–45.

———. 1999. "Technology, Employment, and the Business Cycle: Do Technology Shocks Explain Aggregate Fluctuations?" *American Economic Review* 89 (1): 249–71.

———. 2011a. "Monetary Policy and Unemployment." In *Handbook of Monetary Economics*, vol. 3A, edited by B. Friedman and M. Woodford, 487–546. North Holland: Elsevier B.V.

———. 2011b. "The Return of the Wage Phillips Curve." *Journal of the European Economic Association*, forthcoming.

———. 2011c. *Unemployment Fluctuations and Stabilization Policies: A New Keynesian Perspective.* Cambridge, MA: MIT Press.

Galí, Jordi, and Mark Gertler. 2007. "Macroeconomic Modeling for Monetary Policy Evaluation." *Journal of Economic Perspectives* 21 (4): 25–45.

Galí, Jordi, Mark Gertler, and David López-Salido. 2007. "Markups, Gaps, and the Welfare Costs of Business Fluctuations." *Review of Economics and Statistics* 89 (1): 44–59.

Gertler, M., L. Sala, and A. Trigari. 2008. "An Estimated Monetary DSGE Model with Unemployment and Staggered Nominal Wage Bargaining." *Journal of Money, Credit and Banking* 40 (8): 1713–63.

Greenwood, Jeremy, Zvi Hercowitz, and Gregory Huffman. 1988. "Investment, Capacity Utilization and the Real Business Cycle." *American Economic Review* 78 (3): 402–17.

Jaimovich, Nir, and Sergio Rebelo. 2009. "Can News about the Future Drive the Business Cycle?" *American Economic Review* 99 (4): 1097–118.

Justiniano, Alejandro, Giorgio E. Primiceri, and Andrea Tambalotti. 2011. "Is There a Trade-off between Inflation and Output Stabilization?" Unpublished Manuscript.

King, Robert G., Charles I. Plosser, and Sergio Rebelo. 1988. "Production, Growth and Business Cycles I: The Basic Neoclassical Model." *Journal of Monetary Economics* 21 (2/3): 195–232.

Mehran, Hamid, and Joseph Tracy. 2001. "The Effects of Employee Stock Options on the Evolution of Compensation in the 1990s." *FRBNY Economic Policy Review* 2001 (December): 17–33.

Merz, Monika. 1995. "Search in the Labor Market and the Real Business Cycle." *Journal of Monetary Economics* 36:269–300.

Sala, Luca, Ulf Söderström, and Antonella Trigari. 2010. "The Output Gap, the Labor Wedge, and the Dynamic Behavior of Hours." Sveriges Riksbank Working Paper Series no. 246.

Shimer, R. 2010. *Labor Markets and Business Cycles.* Princeton, NJ: Princeton University Press.

Smets, Frank, and Rafael Wouters. 2003. "An Estimated Dynamic Stochastic General Equilibrium Model of the Euro Area." *Journal of the European Economic Association* 1 (5): 1123–75.

———. 2007. "Shocks and Frictions in US Business Cycles: A Bayesian DSGE Approach." *American Economic Review* 97 (3): 586–606.

Smets, Frank, Kai Christoffel, Günter Coenen, Roberto Motto, and Massimo Rostagno. 2010. "DSGE Models and Their Use at the ECB." *SERIEs, Spanish Economic Association* 1 (1): 51–65.

Zanetti, Francesco. 2007. "A Non-Walrasian Labor Market in a Monetary Model of the Business Cycle." *Journal of Economic Dynamics and Control* 31:2413–37.

Comment

Lawrence J. Christiano, *Northwestern and NBER*

This paper represents a valuable statement of a classic theory of unemployment, the "monopoly power" theory of unemployment. It builds on the work by Galí (2011), which identifies a clever reinterpretation of the standard New Keynesian model in which variations in the number of hours worked by the representative household are interpreted as variations in the number of people working. With this reinterpretation of the standard model, the authors are able to address not just the usual list of macroeconomic variables. They are also able to address labor market data such as the labor force and unemployment.[1] The paper undertakes a Bayesian time series analysis of the model, using aggregate data for the United States.

One finding is that with the specification of preferences in the standard model, income effects on labor supply are excessively strong. The authors introduce an externality into preferences to correct this implication. The change implies that when aggregate consumption is high, the individual experiences a smaller disutility of work. I discuss this model change and raise some questions about it.

It is exciting that the authors broaden the range of implications of the standard model beyond the usual set of macroeconomic variables. After reviewing these additional implications, I find four challenges for the model. First, I am skeptical that the people designated as "unemployed" in the model satisfy the offical United States definition of unemployment. Second, the model implies that the unemployed are happier than the employed. The unemployed in the model correspond best to "displaced workers" in the data—those who lose their jobs in mass layoffs and therefore presumably not as a result of their choice or because of poor job performance. Various indicators of health and income for displaced workers suggest that unemployment is in practice not the happy experience envisioned by the model.

Third, the model allows the authors to estimate the strength of labor union power and they find a secular rise from the late 1960s to the mid-1980s, followed by a secular decline. However, data on union density rates suggest that labor union power had been declining throughout this period. Fourth, in a cross-section of countries, the model suggests that the countries with the highest union power should be the ones with the highest levels of unemployment. Using union density as a measure of union power, I find no evidence of a relation between union power and unemployment in a panel of 13 countries.

The following section presents a brief statement of a (simplified) version of the model. That discussion forms the background for my detailed comments, which appear in the subsequent section. I conclude with some brief closing remarks.

Informal Sketch of the Model

A visual representation of the standard model appears in figure 1. The circle at the top of the figure indicates the production of a homogeneous output good by a representative, competitive final good firm. That firm's homogeneous production technology is a function of a continuum of imperfectly-substitutable intermediate goods. Each of these intermediate goods is produced using a Cobb-Douglas function of capital and labor by a monopolist. Each monopolist, while being the sole supplier of its output good, is competitive in markets for homogeneous labor and capital.

The component of the standard model that is of particular interest here is the labor market. The model of the labor market used in the paper is a modified version of the one proposed in Erceg, Henderson, and Levin (2000). The labor market is organized along the same lines as the goods market (figure 1). In particular, a homogeneous labor input is produced by a representative, competitive firm using a linear, homogeneous function of a continuum of imperfectly-substitutable labor types. Each labor type is represented by a monopoly union.

There is a continuum of identical households. Each household has all labor types within it. The relationship between the households and the unions is indicated in figure 2, which displays two arbitrarily selected households, A and B. The figure highlights two types of differentiated labor types: "painters" and "plumbers." The painters from each

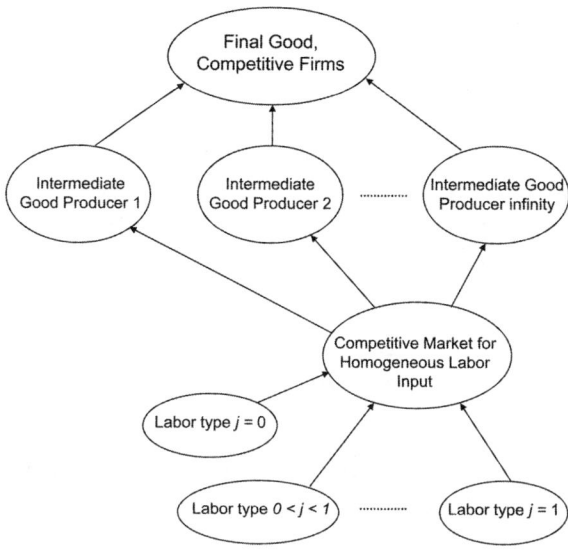

Fig. 1. Goods production and labor market in standard model

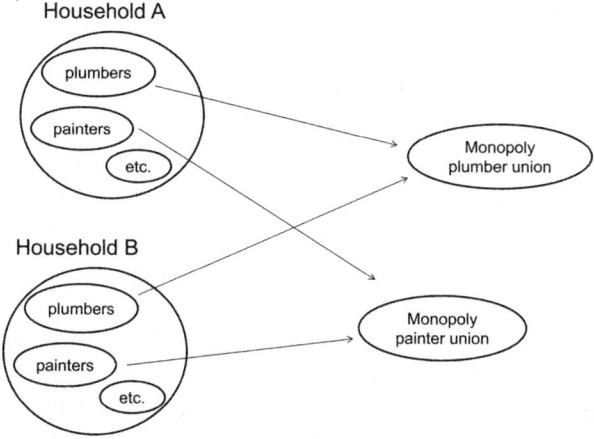

Fig. 2. Relationship between two identical households and monopoly unions

household all gather into a single union that represents all painters in the economy (similarly for the plumbers). Workers in the representative household enjoy perfect consumption insurance. Because utility is separable in consumption and leisure, perfect consumption insurance implies that each worker enjoys the same level of consumption. The

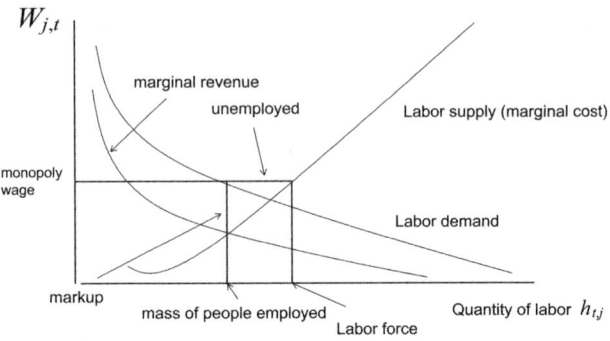

Fig. 3. Type j monopoly union

representative household finances consumption and other expenditures with profits received from the firms that it owns and with wages from employed workers. The household requires employed workers to remit their wages directly to the household. Presumably, the household's ability to require this reflects that it perfectly observes the actions of its workers and that it has leverage over the worker because of its power to withhold consumption insurance.

Differentiated labor types, j, are indexed by the points on the unit interval, $j \in [0, 1]$. The problem of the monopolist ("the jth monopolist") that represents these workers is depicted in figure 3. The downward-sloped demand curve for type j labor implies that if the jth monopolist charges a high nominal wage, $W_{j,t}$, for its type of labor, then quantity demanded is reduced as producers of homogeneous labor substitute away from the jth type of labor. The marginal revenue curve associated with labor demand is also indicated in figure 3.

Now consider the supply of j-type labor. Individual workers are atomistic, can either be employed or not, and differ according to a utility cost of working, $l \in [0, 1]$. The density of workers with any particular value of l is unity. Thus, l is distributed among workers according to a uniform distribution with support $[0, 1]$. If the per-worker level of consumption in the household is C_t, then a j-type worker with utility cost of working, l, enjoys utility

$$\log(C_t) - l^\phi, \phi > 0. \tag{1}$$

A worker that is not employed enjoys utility

$$\log(C_t). \tag{2}$$

Comparing (1) with (2), we see that the utility cost to a worker with work aversion, l, of being employed is l^ϕ. We convert this into consumption units by dividing by λ_t, the multiplier on the household budget constraint when the latter is expressed in consumption units. Thus, the cost of working in consumption units for the household with work aversion l is l^ϕ/λ_t. It is assumed that when a mass, h, of workers is sent to employment, the household sends them out in order, starting with the worker with the lowest value of l. When h workers are sent to employment, the value of l for the marginal worker is $l = h$. To see this, recall that the density of workers with each possible value of l is unity. Thus if all workers with $l \leq h$ are sent to employment, then the total number of employed workers is $h = \int_0^h dl$. These observations imply that h^ϕ/λ_t represents the cost for the marginal worker when h workers are employed. This marginal cost curve is graphed in figure 3.

The jth monopoly union's problem is the standard one, in the absence of wage-setting frictions. It chooses a level of employment, $h_{j,t}$, on the horizontal axis in figure 3 where marginal revenue equals marginal cost of labor. The union then sets the wage rate so that demand equals the chosen level of employment. The authors follow Galí (2011) in defining the total supply of the jth-type of labor as the value of $h^s_{j,t}$ that solves:

$$\frac{W_{j,t}}{P_t} = \frac{(h^s_{j,t})^\phi}{\lambda_t}. \tag{3}$$

this value of $h^s_{j,t}$ is indicated as the labor force in figure 3. Thus, the marginal cost curve is also the labor supply curve in figure 3. The number unemployed, $h^s_{j,t} - h_{j,t}$, is the difference between the labor force and the number of workers employed, and the unemployment rate, $(h^s_{j,t} - h_{j,t})/h^s_{j,t}$, is the ratio of the unemployed to the labor force. Unemployment is positive because the union exploits its power to raise the wage rate by restricting the number of workers that are employed. In the presence of wage-setting frictions, the monopoly union can adjust wages only periodically, subject to Calvo-style frictions. In this case, labor supply is still the solution to (3) and employment is determined by demand at the given wage rate. Unemployment is always positive, as long as shocks are not too large. In the presence of wage-setting frictions the union does not choose $W_{j,t}$ to equate marginal cost and marginal revenue period-by-period—it does so on average instead. In my comments I abstract from the presence of wage-setting frictions in the model.

Is There *Any* Unemployment in the Model?

The unemployment rate for the United States is compiled by the Current Population Survey (CPS), which is a monthly survey of households conducted by the Bureau of Census for the Bureau of Labor Statistics (BLS). If a CPS employee were dropped into the authors' model economy and proceeded to do a survey to determine the unemployment rate in the way that it is done in the United States how much, if any, unemployment would he find? Put differently, does the concept of unemployment in the model match the corresponding concept in the data? To answer this question, note that to be classified as unemployed in the United States, a nonemployed person must report that he or she (a) has actively looked for work in the prior four weeks and (b) is currently available for work.[2] The people designated as unemployed in the model clearly do not satisfy (a), because effort plays no role in acquiring employment. Still, one might suppose that introducing a trivial cost of search might fix this problem, while not changing the model's implications. We will return to this momentarily.

Now consider (b). Suppose the CPS employee encountered one of the people designated as "unemployed" in figure 3, and asked if she were "available for work." What would her answer be? She knows with certainty that she will not be employed in the current period. Privately, she is delighted about this because the nonemployed enjoy higher utility than the employed (more on this in the next subsection). Not only is she happy about not having to work, but the labor union also does not want her to work. From the perspective of the union, her nonemployment is a fundamental component of the union's strategy for promoting the welfare of its membership. Since no one wants her to work, why then would she declare herself "available for work"? Still, since whatever she says has no consequence, perhaps one could simply *assume* that a person designated as unemployed in figure 3 would say she is "available to work." But now recall that (b) is not sufficient for a nonemployed person to be unemployed in practice. Such a person must also satisfy (a). Accordingly, suppose workers must pay a cost (a search cost) to join the labor force, where that cost could be arbitrarily small. However, in the presence of a search cost everyone in the model economy would agree that workers designated as unemployed in figure 3 should definitely *not* search for work. It serves no one—not the worker, not the household, or the labor union—for a worker to pay a search cost, however small, when the probability of finding a job is zero.

In sum, in the model search costs are zero and so no one satisfies the official definition of unemployment. If a tiny search cost were introduced, then the labor force would always equal the number of people employed and once again there would be no unemployment. Thus, a CPS employee dropped into the model economy would conclude that unemployment is zero. Put differently, the concept of unemployment in the model does not match the concept used in the data.

It may be that there exists a minor adjustment to the model under which the authors' concept of unemployment coincides with the one in the United States data. However, one obvious adjustment turns out to be unsuccessful. This adjustment modifies the way the household sends workers to the labor market. Recall that the authors assume the representative household sends workers to the labor market in order of increasing work aversion until labor demand is satisfied. I call this the "efficient labor supply strategy." Suppose that instead the household sends all type j workers into the labor force at the start of the period and instructs all workers who encounter a job opportunity to accept if their work aversion, l, satisfies:

$$\frac{W_j}{P} \geq \frac{l^\phi}{\lambda}, \tag{4}$$

where W_j is the wage rate set by the monopoly union.[3] (I drop the t subscript to simplify notation.) I call this the "inefficient" household labor supply strategy because it leaves open the possibility that some unemployed workers have lower work aversion than some employed workers. The "labor supply" curve in figure 3 continues to deserve that name, since it indicates the mapping from the wage rate, W_j, to h_j^s under the inefficient labor supply strategy (4). Suppose for the moment that the labor supply curve still also measures the marginal cost of employment, as it does in the authors' model. Optimization by the union would then lead to the same quantity of workers employed and unemployed as under the efficient labor supply strategy.[4] An important difference, however, is that the unemployed workers would satisfy condition (b) because they are required to do so by the household. Adding a small cost of being in the labor force seems unlikely to change things, and so under this interpretation the concept of unemployment in figure 3 appears to be consistent with the one used in the CPS. One could ask why the household would impose the inefficient strategy, (4), when the efficient one leads to better outcomes. However, there is a more fundamental problem with this alternative approach.

For pedagogical purposes, the previous discussion assumed that the marginal cost curve coincides with the labor supply curve. Under this assumption, the wage and employment choice of the monpoly union would coincide with what is depicted in figure 3. As it turns out, the monopoly union's behavior is not invariant to labor supply strategy adopted by the household. To see this, suppose jobs are allocated randomly among all the workers in the labor force under the inefficient labor supply strategy. Then the marginal employed worker is not the one with work aversion, $l = h_j$. As a result, marginal cost is not in fact given by (3) under the inefficient labor supply strategy. The marginal cost curve is in fact profoundly different from what it is under the efficient labor supply strategy. The marginal cost of labor has a *negative* slope. To understand this apparently counterintuitive result, consider the incentives of the union as it considers wage rates lower than the one set in figure 3. In contemplating a reduction in the wage, the union is mindful of the fact that among the employed workers there are some with high levels of work aversion, l, taken from the interval $h_j < l \leq h_j^s$. This inefficient state of affairs represents a kind of tax from the point of the union. When the union contemplates raising employment by reducing W_j, the interval, $h_j^s - h_j$, shrinks and some high work-aversion individuals among the employed are replaced with lower work-aversion individuals. In effect, by reducing the wage rate relative to its position in figure 3 the union reduces the size of a tax. Not only does the marginal cost of employment decline with an increase in h_j, but the level of that marginal cost is lower than marginal revenue. As a result, h_j is increased until it reaches its upper bound $h_j = h_j^s$, that is, the point where unemployment is zero even in the authors' sense.[5]

To formally demonstrate the observations in the previous paragraph, I compute the marginal cost of labor by first computing the aggregate utility cost of working and then differentiating with respect to h_j. Consider given values of h_j and h_j^s, the quantity of workers employed and labor supply, respectively. Of course, these values must satisfy

$$h_j \leq h_j^s. \tag{5}$$

Under the assumption that employment is assigned with equal probability to all workers in the labor force, the probability density of any particular worker of type l, $0 \leq l \leq h_j^s$, being employed is h_j / h_j^s. Given that the density of type l workers employed is h_j/h_j^s, for $0 \leq l \leq h_j^s$, the total utility cost of labor is:

$$\frac{(h_j/h_j^s)\int_0^{h_j^s} l^\phi dl}{\lambda} = \frac{(h_j/h_j^s)[(h_j^s)^{1+\phi}/(1+\phi)]}{\lambda} = \frac{h_j}{\lambda}\frac{(h_j^s)^\phi}{1+\phi}.$$

Here, I have divided by λ to convert into consumption units. Under the employment rule, (4), h_j^s satisfies (3). Substituting the utility cost of employment in consumption units turns out to be proportional to total labor revenue:

$$\frac{W_j h_j}{P}\frac{1}{1+\phi}.$$

As usual, marginal revenue, denoted by MR_j, is:

$$MR_j \equiv \frac{d(W_j h_j/P)}{dh_j} = \frac{W_j}{P}\left[1-\frac{1}{\varepsilon}\right],$$

where ε denotes the elasticity of demand for h_j with respect to W_j. I follow the authors in assuming that ε is constant and $\varepsilon > 1$. Specifically, the demand for labor is:

$$\frac{W_j}{P} = \frac{W}{P}\left(\frac{h}{h_j}\right)^{1/\varepsilon},$$

where h and W denote the aggregate level of employment and aggregate wage rate, repectively, both of which are beyond the control of the jth monopolist. Thus, marginal revenue expressed as a function of h_j is

$$MR_j = \frac{W}{P}\left(\frac{h}{h_j}\right)^{1/\varepsilon}\left[1-\frac{1}{\varepsilon}\right].$$

This is the usual downward-sloping function of h_j and lies below the demand for labor by a fixed factor of proportionality, the markup.

From the preceding results, we see that the jth monopolist's marginal cost of labor, denoted by MC_j, is

$$MC_j = \frac{MR_j}{1+\phi}.$$

That is, marginal cost is decreasing and is always lower than marginal revenue. As a result, the jth monopolist sets h_j to its highest possible value. Note from the demand curve that h_j is increased by reducing W_j. This in turn implies, via (3), that h_j^s falls. The highest possible value of h_j is encountered when $h_j = h_j^s$. That is, under the rule (4), the jth monopolist sets the wage to the point where the demand curve intersects the

upward sloping labor supply curve in figure 3. There is no unemployment at all in this case. Ironically, though the inefficient labor supply
strategy leads to an inefficient outcome from the point of view of the
monopolist, from a general equilibrium point of view it leads to the
socially efficient outcome in which there is no unemployment. As noted
before, the reason for this is that under the inefficient labor supply rule
the monopoly union is in effect taxed when there is unemployment
(some high work-aversion workers are employed) and in the model
this gives the monopoly union the incentive to set wages in a way that
avoids unemployment completely.

I state the preceding results in the form of a proposition:

Proposition. *Suppose the labor force is the set of workers with work aversion,*
l, that satisfy (4). Suppose employment is allocated randomly among those
workers. Then, absent wage-setting frictions, optimality by monopolists im-
plies that unemployment is zero in the sense that $h_j^s = h_j$, for all $j \in [0, 1]$.

Utility of the Unemployed

In the model there is perfect consumption insurance among the members of the household. Because of separability in utility, this implies
that consumption is equalized across all workers, whether they are employed or not. Employment is allocated to workers according to their
realized value of *l*. Workers who find that they do not have to work are
unemployed or out of the labor force, and they have cause to rejoice as
a result. Unemployed workers enjoy higher utility than the employed
because they receive the same level of consumption, but without having to work.

There is much evidence that in practice unemployment is not the
happy experience it is for workers in the model. For example, Chetty
and Looney (2006) and Gruber (1997) find that US households suffer
roughly a 10% drop in consumption when they lose their job. According to Couch and Placzek (2010), workers displaced through mass layoffs suffer substantial and extended reductions in earnings. Moreover,
Oreopoulos, Page, and Stevens (2008) present evidence that the children
of displaced workers also suffer reduced earnings. Additional evidence
that unemployed workers suffer a reduction in utility include the results of direct interviews, as well as findings that unemployed workers
experience poor health outcomes. Clark and Oswald (1994), Oswald
(1997), and Schimmack, Schupp, and Wagner (2008) describe evidence

that suggests unemployment has a negative impact on a worker's self-assessment of well-being. Sullivan and von Wachter (2009) report that the mortality rates of high-seniority workers jump 50 to 100% more than would have been expected otherwise in the year after displacement. Cox and Koo (2006) report a significant positive correlation between male suicide and unemployment in Japan and the United States. For additional evidence that unemployment is associated with poor health outcomes, see Fergusson, Horwood, and Lynskey (1997) and Karsten and Moser (2009). Finally, there is a substantial literature which argues that insurance against labor market outcomes is imperfect (for an early example, see Cochrane 1991).

Labor Supply

In the New Keynesian approach to business cycles, labor supply has generally retreated from center stage.[6] This contrasts sharply with the real business cycle approach, in which labor supply was a major preoccupation.[7] In this paper, labor supply is once again central because labor supply corresponds to the labor force, and the latter is a key input to the construction of the unemployment rate. It is therefore not surprising that some of the labor market challenges that were the focus of the real business cycle literature are back. To see this, recall that according to the discussion of equation (3), labor supply has the following form:

$$\frac{(h^s)^\phi}{u'(C)}. \tag{6}$$

For simplicity, in (5) I ignore the distinction between different labor types and I replace λ with $u'(C)$, the marginal utility—to the representative household—of household consumption.[8] Here, $u(C) = \log(C)$ and the prime indicates differentiation. The "labor supply curve" is a graph with h on the horizontal axis and the real wage on the vertical, for given C.

Consider the situation depicted in part A of figure 4, where W denotes the wage rate, which we assume is fixed for the purpose of discussion. Suppose there is an expansionary monetary policy shock and that this results in an increase in aggregate consumption, consistent with the implications of some structural vector autoregression (SVAR) analyses.[9] Then, concavity of preferences implies $u'(C)$ falls and the resulting positive wealth effect shifts labor supply to the left (see part A of figure 4). The only labor market variable included in the standard anal-

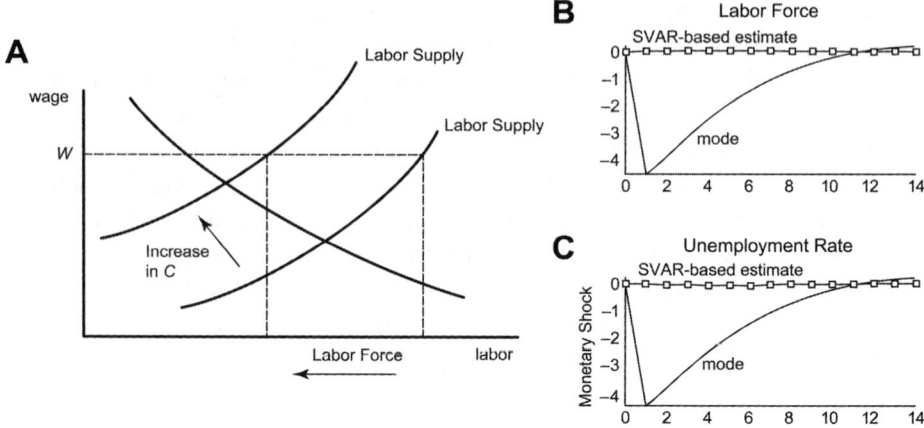

Fig. 4.   Labor market with "Standard Preferences"

ysis of the New Keynesian model is employment and as long as labor is demand determined and W is relatively inflexible, the wealth effect on labor supply has no observable consequence. However, this effect has implications that cannot be ignored when the labor force and unemployment are also included in the analysis.

Note from part A of figure 4 that the labor force falls as the rise in C shifts labor supply to the left. The shift right in labor demand induced by a fall in the price markup (not pictured in figure 4, part A) and shift left in labor supply combine to produce a fall in the unemployment rate. Christiano, Trabandt, and Walentin (2010) simulate a dynamic model that captures the framework discussed here. Figure 4, part B, displays the response of the labor force to an expansionary monetary policy shock in their economic model and in the SVAR analysis that they report. According to their SVAR, the labor force rises a small amount, while—consistent with part A of figure 4—the model implies a substantial drop in the labor force. According to the SVAR result in part C of figure 4, the unemployment rate declines after an expansionary monetary policy shock. However, the dynamic economic model implies a drop in the unemployment rate that is an order of magnitude too large. Evidently, the large income effects on labor supply generate strongly counterfactual implications for unemployment and the labor force.

The fix proposed in the paper to address the aforementioned counterfactual implication modifies the utility cost of working by multiplying it by $u'(\bar{C})$, where $\bar{C}$ denotes the economy-wide level of consumption. With this modification, labor supply in (5) is replaced by:

$$\frac{u'(\bar{C})h^{\phi}}{u(C)}. \tag{6}$$

In equilibrium, $C = \bar{C}$, so that labor supply simply reduces to h^{ϕ} and the income effect is completely gone. With this modification, the troublesome left-shift in the labor supply equation with a rise in C is eliminated. Still, the fix raises several questions.

How is one to interpret the presence of $u'(\bar{C})$ in (6)? Why would the utility cost of working be smaller for individual workers when the aggregate level of consumption is high? The answer is not obvious to me.

The expression for the cost of working in (6) resembles the cost of working implied by the preferences proposed in Greenwood, Hercowitz, and Huffman (1988; henceforth, GHH). With GHH preferences, however, $\bar{C}$ in (6) is actually the household's own consumption. The GHH specification of utility is not adopted in this paper, presumably because it makes consumption and employment nonseparable in utility, making some of the equilibrium computations messy.[10] If the authors have in mind that (6) is a reduced-form approximation to GHH preferences, this raises other questions. For example, GHH preferences imply that labor supply is only a function of the real wage. But, if this is so, then how does one explain that per capita employment has not risen anywhere near as much as the real wage has risen over long periods of time? The wage rate also varies by orders of magnitude in the cross section of the population at a point in time. Is the magnitude of variation in labor supply in the cross section consistent with GHH preferences? A full assessment of the labor market structure in this model requires addressing these questions.

The Wage Markup

The model specifies that the elasticity of demand for labor is constant across the different labor types at a point in time. However, in each period that elasticity is the realization of a stochastic process. This elasticity shock is also referred to as a wage markup shock. This is because there is a one-to-one relation between the elasticity and what the markup of the wage over the marginal cost of labor is in the absence of wage-setting frictions. The monopoly power of unions is high when

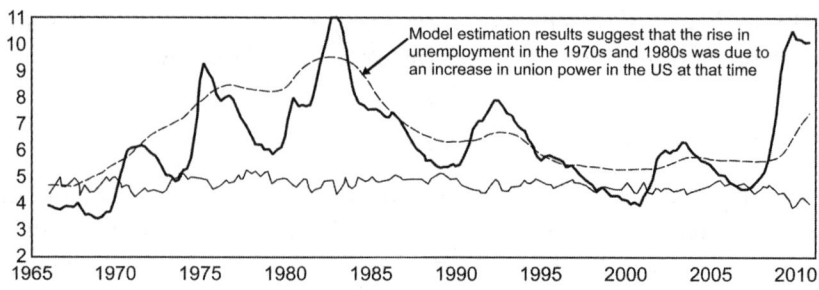

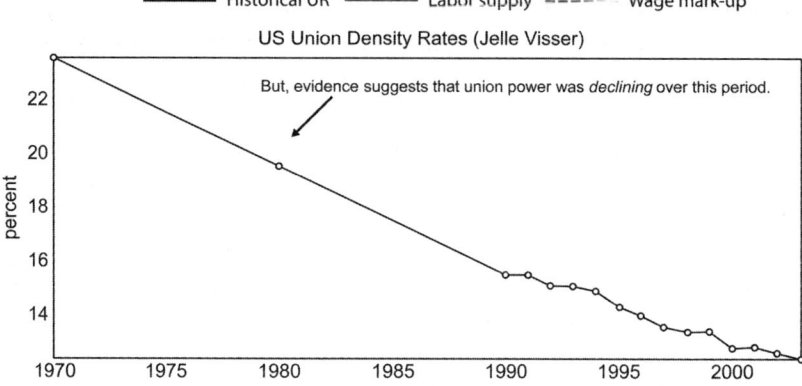

Fig. 5. Union density rates and wage markup over time

the demand elasticity is low—that is, the wage markup is high—and monopoly power of unions is low otherwise. Thus, the model predicts a positive correlation between the wage markup and the unemployment rate. The top panel in figure 5 displays the time series data on the unemployment rate, as well as the historical decomposition of the unemployment rate in terms of the estimated wage markup and labor supply shocks. Labor supply shocks are relatively unimportant for unemployment, while wage markup shocks are important determinants of the low frequency component of unemployment. The portion of unemployment explained by the markup shocks forms an inverted V shape. That is, the model analysis suggests that union monopoly power increased from the late 1960s to around 1984 and declined thereafter.

Measures of the strength of labor unions were not used in the estimation of the model. Such a measure therefore can be used to conduct an "out-of-sample" test of the model. To this end, I obtained data on union density—the fraction of eligible workers who are union members—from Visser (2006). As discussed in Howell et al. (2007) and Visser (2006), union density is an imperfect measure of the strength of labor unions. With this caveat, I use Visser's data to assess the implication of the model analysis for the secular evolution of union power. The bottom panel of figure 5 displays Visser (2006)'s data on union density for the United States, indicated by the solid dots. The data indicate that union density declined since 1970, and shows no evidence of the inverted V predicted by the model. It is important to note that although annual data are available after 1990, the only earlier observations are for 1970 and 1980. Thus, the conclusion that union membership had been declining already since 1970 rests heavily on the accuracy of one observation, the observation for 1970. I conclude that this preliminary evidence appears to go against the model, though a more definitive conclusion requires examining additional evidence on the secular evolution of labor union strength in the United States.

Cross-Country Evidence on the Relation between Union Power and Unemployment

I obtained data on the unemployment rate for 13 countries from the Bureau of Labor Statistics (BLS) and the International Labor Office (ILO).[11] The union density rates for the same 13 countries were taken from table 3 in Visser (2006) (the data pertaining to the United States are displayed in the bottom panel of figure 5). I investigate the model's implication that higher union power (imperfectly measured by union density) produces higher unemployment rates. This implication is referred to as the "Monopoly Power Hypothesis" in figure 6. Although the data are constructed with the aim of preserving international comparability, I nevertheless examine the data in a way that minimizes problems arising from lack of comparability in terms of levels. I do this by focusing on the trends in the levels. Specifically, I test the model implication that in countries where union power is increasing relative to what it is in the United States, unemployment relative to that in the United States should be rising. If this pattern is detected across countries, then the Monopoly Power Hypothesis would fail to be rejected. In this case, the hypothesis is not necessarily supported, of course, because causality could go the other way, from high unemployment stimulating increased unionization as a response. But, in fact I fail to find a systematic positive association in the cross-country data between union power and unemployment, and so this represents a challenge for the model.

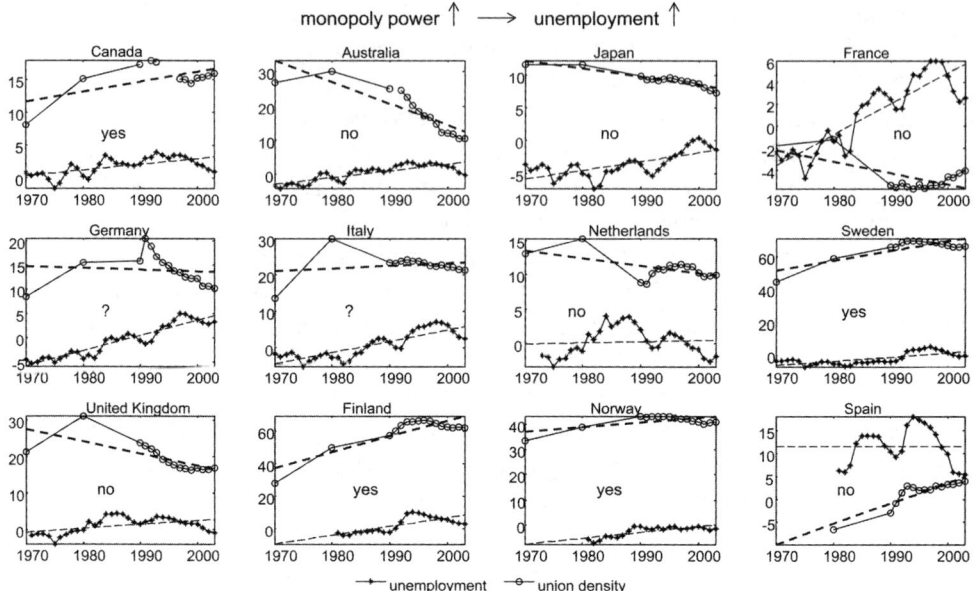

Fig. 6. Data consistent with Monopoly Power Hypothesis

My finding of the absence of a systematic association is consistent with findings reported in the Organization for Economic Cooperation and Development (OECD 2006) and Howell et al. (2007).

Figure 6 contains 12 panels, each of which contains two curves and their associated trend lines (obtained by least squares). One curve displays the unemployment rate for the indicated country, minus the United States unemployment rate. The other curve displays the analogous variable corresponding to union density. If the two trend lines have the same slope, then I conclude that the evidence for that country is consistent with the Monopoly Power Hypothesis and a "yes" is indicated. Otherwise, I indicate a "no." In the case of Germany and Italy, the slope for the trend of the union density differential seems too uncertain, and so I report a "?" , though the reader is free to factor in the evidence from those two countries as he or she sees fit. The figure displays six panels containing a "no" and four panels containing a "yes." I view this as an indication that the cross-country evidence is mixed. In particular, the data do not support the view that high unionization leads to high unemployment.

Conclusion

I have provided a critical assessment of the labor market model analyzed in this paper. I have identified dimensions on which the model
can be challenged. However, a model is an abstraction. A well-crafted
model leaves out features of reality that are not essential for the purposes to which the model is put. So, an assessment of the model shortcomings described here depends on whether they distort the answers to
the policy questions it is used to address. An alternative approach to integrating unemployment into the New Keynesian model is provided in
Christiano, Trabandt, and Walentin (2010). It avoids the problems raised
here. In that model, the unemployed satisfy the official United States
definition of unemployment, the unemployed have lower utility than
the employed, income effects do not create counterfactual implications
for the labor force and unemployment, and there is no prediction for
the relationship between monopoly power and the unemployment rate.

Endnotes

For acknowledgments, sources of research support, and disclosure of the author's material financial relationships, if any, please see http://www.nber.org/chapters/c12425
.ack.
   1. By the standard model, I have in mind the type of structure in, for example, Christiano, Eichenbaum, and Evans (2005), or Smets and Wouters (2007).
   2. See the Bureau of Labor Statistics website, http://www.bls.gov/cps/cps_htgm
.htm#unemployed, for a discussion of the survey questions used to determine a household's employment status.
   3. I continue to assume that the household observes the worker's l and observes all
the worker's actions in the labor market. In addition, the household requires that the
worker remit his or her earnings straight to the household. Finally, it is assumed that the
household has the means to enforce its demands on the worker, perhaps by the threat of
withholding consumption insurance.
   4. Although the quantity of employed and unemployed workers would be the same,
their identities would not be the same. This will play an important role in the following
analysis.
   5. Employment, $h_{j,t}$, cannot be increased beyond $h_{j,t}^s$ because the union is required in
the model to supply all labor demanded at the specified wage. But, the household will not
supply more than $h_{j,t}^s$.
   6. That labor supply plays at best a minor role in the dynamics of New Keynesian
models in part reflects the emphasis on wage-setting frictions and the assumption that
labor is demand determined. The relatively minor role of labor supply also reflecs the
presence of price-setting frictions and the assumption that goods production is demand
determined. This has the effect of amplifying shifts in labor demand through endogenous movements in markups. Examples that highlight the relative unimportance of
labor supply in the New Keynesian model appear in Christiano (2011) and Christiano,
Eichenbaum, and Rebelo (2011). The latter paper shows that in interior equilibria (e.g.,
where the zero lower bound on the nominal rate of interest is nonbinding) of the New

Keynesian model the government consumption multiplier is smaller the more persistent is a given increase in government spending. This persistence property reflects that the negative wealth effect of taxes on private consumption dominates the positive wealth effect on labor supply. This property of the New Keynesian model contrasts sharply with the corresponding property of the standard real business cycle model. In that model, the size of the government spending multiplier is larger, the *more* persistent is the increase in the government spending shock. This reflects the relative importance of wealth effects on labor supply in the real business cycle model (see Christiano and Eichenbaum 1992).

7. That literature was preoccupied with a "labor supply elasticity" puzzle and with an "income effect on labor supply" puzzle. The first puzzle is that according to the aggregate data, employment fluctuates substantially while wages move very little, and in the micro-data employed people do not change their labor supply much in response to changes in the real wage (Hansen 1985 and Rogerson 1988). For a survey, see Christiano, Trabandt, and Walentin (2011). The "income effect" puzzle is that long time series data suggest that income effects roughly cancel the substitution effect arising from the secular rise in the real wage. Yet, the apparently elastic response of employment to small movements in wages over the business cycle suggest that income effects on labor supply are small (for a discussion and proposed resolution, see Benhabib, Rogerson, and Wright 1991).

8. For notational simplicity, I also ignore the fact that the authors assume habit persistence in preferences.

9. See, for example, Christiano, Trabandt, and Walentin (2011).

10. The complications arise from the presence of perfect consumption insurance. The work of Guerron (2008) suggest that, although messy, the calculations are manageable.

11. With the exception of Finland, Norway, and Spain, the unemployment data were taken from the website of the BLS, http://www.bls.gov/fls/flscomparelf/unemployment.htm#table1_2. The BLS data were taken from Table 1-2, "International Comparisons of Annual Labor Force Statistics, Adjusted to U.S. Concepts, 10 Countries, 1970–2010." The unemployment data for Finland, Norway, and Spain were obtained from the ILO document, "Comparable annual employment and unemployment estimates, adjusted averages," available at http://laborsta.ilo.org.

References

Benhabib, Jess, Richard Rogerson, and Randall Wright. 1991. "Homework in Macroeconomics: Household Production and Aggregate Fluctuations." *Journal of Political Economy* 99 (6): 1166–87.

Chetty, Raj, and Adam Looney. 2006. "Income Risk and the Benefits of Social Insurance: Evidence from Indonesia and the United States." NBER Working Paper no. 11708. Cambridge, MA: National Bureau of Economic Research, October.

Christiano, Lawrence J. 2011. Comment on Eggertsson. *NBER Macroeconomics Annual 2010*, vol. 25, edited by Daron Acemoglu and Michael Woodford, 113–24. Chicago: University of Chicago Press.

Christiano, Lawrence J., and Martin Eichenbaum. 1992. "Current Real Business Cycle Theories and Aggregate Labor Market Fluctuations." *American Economic Review* 82 (3): 430–50.

Christiano, Lawrence J., Martin Eichenbaum, and Charles L. Evans. 2005. "Nominal Rigidities and the Dynamic Effects of a Shock to Monetary Policy." *Journal of Political Economy* 113 (1): 1–45.

Christiano, Lawrence J., Martin Eichenbaum, and Sergio Rebelo. 2011. "When Is the Government Spending Multiplier Large?" *The Journal of Political Economy* 119 (1): 78–121.

Christiano, Lawrence J., Mathias Trabandt, and Karl Walentin. 2010. "Involuntary Unemployment and the Business Cycle." NBER Working Paper no. 16074. Cambridge, MA: National Bureau of Economic Research, June.

———. 2011. "DSGE Models for Monetary Policy Analysis." In *Handbook of Monetary Economics*, vol. 3A, edited by Benjamin M. Friedman and Michael Woodford, 285–367. The Netherlands: North-Holland.

Clark, A. E., and A. J. Oswald. 1994. "Unhappiness and Unemployment." *Economic Journal* 104 (424): 648–59.

Cochrane, John H. 1991. "A Simple Test of Consumption Insurance." *The Journal of Political Economy* 99 (5): 957–97.

Couch, Kenneth A., and Dana W. Placzek. 2010. "Earnings Losses of Displaced Workers Revisited." *American Economic Review* 100 (1): 572–89.

Cox, W. M., and J. Koo. 2006. "Miracle to Malaise: What's Next for Japan." Federal Reserve Bank of Dallas Economic letter, January.

Erceg, C. J., D. W. Henderson, and A. T. Levin. 2000. "Optimal Monetary Policy with Staggered Wage and Price Contracts." *Journal of Monetary Economics* 46:281–313.

Fergusson, D. M., L. J. Horwood, and M. T. Lynskey. 1997. "The Effects of Unemployment on Psychiatric Illness during Young Adulthood." *Psychological Medicine* 27 (2): 371–81.

Galí, Jordi. 2011. "The Return of the Wage Phillips Curve." *Journal of the European Economic Association* 9 (3): 436–61.

Greenwood, J., Z. Hercowitz, and G. Huffman. 1988. "Investment, Capacity Utilization, and the Real Business Cycle." *American Economic Review* 78 (3): 402–17.

Guerron, Pablo. 2008. "Refinements on Macroeconomic Modeling: The Role of Non-Separability and Heterogeneous Labor Supply." *Journal of Economic Dynamics and Control* 32: 3613–30.

Gruber, Jonathan. 1997. "The Consumption Smoothing Benefits of Unemployment Insurance." *The American Economic Review* 87 (1): 192–205.

Hansen, Gary D. 1985. "Indivisible Labor and the Business Cycle." *Journal of Monetary Economics* 16:309–27.

Howell, David R., Dean Baker, Andrew Glyn, and John Schmitt. 2007. "Are Protective Labor Market Institutions at the Root of Unemployment? A Critical Review of the Evidence." *Capitalism and Society* 2 (1): 1–71.

Karsten, I. Paul, and Klaus Moser. 2009. "Unemployment Impairs Mental Health: Meta-Analyses." *Journal of Vocational Behavior* 74 (3): 264–82.

Organization of Economic Cooperation and Development (OECD). 2006. "Reassessing the Role of Policies and Institutions for Labour Market Performance: A Quantitative Analysis." In *OECD Economic Outlook, Boosting Jobs and Incomes*, chapter 7. Paris: OECD.

Oreopoulos, Philip, Marianne Page, and Ann Huff Stevens. 2008. "The Intergenerational Effects of Worker Displacement." *Journal of Labor Economics* 26 (3): 455–83.

Oswald, Andrew J. 1997. "Happiness and Economic Performance." *Economic Journal* 107 (445): 1815–31.

Rogerson, Richard. 1988. "Indivisible Labor, Lotteries and Equilibrium." *Journal of Monetary Economics* 21:3–16.

Schimmack, Ulrich, Jurgen Schupp, and Gert G. Wagner. 2008. "The Influence of Environment and Personality on the Affective and Cognitive Component of Subjective Well-Being." *Social Indicators Research* 89:41–60.

Smets, Frank, and Raf Wouters. 2007. "Shocks and Frictions in US Business Cycles." *American Economic Review* 97 (3): 586–606.

Sullivan, D., and T. Von Wachter. 2009. "Job Displacement and Mortality: An Analysis Using Administrative Data." *Quarterly Journal of Economics* 124 (3): 1265–1306.

Visser, Jelle. 2006. "Union Membership Statistics in 24 Countries." *Monthly Labor Review*, January, 38–49.

Comment

Richard Rogerson, Princeton University and NBER

Introduction

This paper embeds the theory of unemployment in Galí (2011a, 2011b) into an otherwise standard medium-scale New Keynesian model and estimates it using the methods of Smets and Wouters (2007). The paper offers one substantive motivation for this merger. Specifically, one of the classic issues in business cycle theory is to identify the quantitatively important shocks that generate these fluctuations. Although Galí's modification to include unemployment does not affect how a given shock affects employment, it turns out that by utilizing data on both employment and unemployment, it can nonetheless be helpful in determining which type of shock might have caused a given change in employment. For example, in standard New Keynesian models, preference shocks and wage markup shocks have similar implications for employment, and existing estimation exercises cannot distinguish between them. But given that these two shocks have very different implications for policy in New Keynesian models, it is important to distinguish between them.

The intuition is straightforward: if employment goes down because of a preference shock that makes households value leisure more highly, one might reasonably expect that the decrease in employment will primarily show up as an increase in nonparticipation, with relatively little effect on unemployment. In contrast, if employment goes down because wage markups have increased and firms reduce their demand for workers, one might reasonably expect that the decrease in employment will primarily show up as an increase in unemployment with relatively little effect on participation. It follows that having an explicit model of unemployment may prove useful in identifying the quantitatively important shocks that lead to business cycles.

The idea that distinguishing between unemployment and nonparticipation might help to identify shocks is a promising one. To the extent that the current paper is intended primarily as a concrete example to illustrate this general point, I think it is largely successful. The analysis is clear and the arguments are clearly exposited. Especially because the introduction of unemployment into the framework does not disturb the workings of the model at all, one can see clearly how adding unemployment as an observable affects the identification of shocks.

The key results of the exercise in the paper are that preference shocks are not very important at business cycle frequencies but are relatively more important at lower frequencies. I do not find these qualitative conclusions objectionable, and I suspect this would be true for most economists. Specifically, I do not view literal preference shocks as a major potential source of business cycle fluctuations. And while the large changes over time in demographics, family structure, and female labor force participation might not correspond literally to preference shocks, in the context of a stand-in household model it may be that preference shocks is a useful way to capture them.

However, even though I find these conclusions reasonable, I do not view the current paper as providing much new evidence to influence my opinion on the matter. To view the exercise in the paper as more than just an illustrative example requires that the authors address two questions. First, is the model of unemployment implicit in this paper a good one for the purposes at hand? Second, is the methodology of Smets and Wouters good at inferring what shocks drive business cycles? Oddly enough, the paper is completely silent on these questions.

One theme that I will stress in these comments concerns the issue of micro-foundations. The authors write in the first paragraph of their paper that one of the appealing features of the class of models that they build on is its "sound, micro-founded structure." I find this statement somewhat curious. To be sure, the model is certainly micro-founded in the sense that the model specifies the economic primitives and is explicit about the behavior of individual agents in the model, implying that the analysis is not subject to the Lucas critique.

However, in my view the desire for micro-foundations goes beyond responding to the Lucas critique. Specifically, the other advantage of providing explicit micro-foundations is to make it possible to connect with micro-data to confirm that the behavior of agents in the model on key dimensions is in line with how these agents respond in the data. I will note specific instances of this in what follows, but in my view a key limitation of this paper, and more generally of the literature to which this paper belongs, is its failure to pursue micro-foundations in this sense.

Using Galí's Theory of Unemployment to Identify Shocks

Two of the virtues of Galí's theory of unemployment are that it is both intuitive and tractable. But given that the goal of this paper—to uncover the relative quantitative importance of various shocks—is very much a quantitative one, I was quite struck by the lack of attempt to argue that this theory of unemployment was in some sense a good quantitative theory of unemployment. "Good" could mean various things in different contexts, depending on the issue being addressed. Given the objective of this paper, I think that "good" should at least mean that it is able to distinguish how unemployment responds to various "labor supply" and "labor demand" forces. Neither this paper nor the previous papers by Galí devote any effort to arguing that this model of unemployment is good in this sense.

Galí's theory takes as given that the only source of unemployment is the market wage being inefficiently high. (The model offers two distinct channels for why the wage may be too high at any particular moment; it could be due to the markup, or it could be due to nominal rigidities that slow down the adjustment of wages to various shocks.) Attributing a significant role to wages in the determination of unemployment is certainly consistent with much other current work on modeling unemployment, including those that follow in the tradition of Mortensen and Pissarides (1994). But two questions arise. First, what is the appropriate theory of wage determination? Second, are there nonwage factors that also have a significant quantitative influence on aggregate movements in unemployment?

Regarding the first question, Galí's theory holds that every type of specialized labor is represented by its own union and that each union sets wages in an uncoordinated fashion. While one can use this as an example to illustrate the workings of the model for one particular wage-setting mechanism, it seems an obvious nonstarter as a theory of wage-setting in the US economy. One would like to see the authors provide some argument based on micro-data that this offers a reasonable foundation for thinking about wage determination.

Next I consider the issue of nonwage factors in influencing unemployment. If nonwage factors sometimes play a significant role in influencing unemployment, then a model that rules them out by assumption will likely not be a good tool for inferring the role of "demand" versus "supply" shocks. The large empirical literature that was started by Davis and Haltiwanger (1992) suggested that the massive reallocation of jobs across establishments is a likely source of some unemployment. Models such as Lucas and Prescott (1974) show that unemployment can result in such settings even with wages set competitively. This literature alone should make one skeptical of the assumption that all unemployment is due to wages being inefficiently high.

But let me also note two prominent contexts of low frequency unemployment changes where nonwage factors seem to potentially be important. The first context is the rise of European unemployment in the 1970s and 1980s. Assessing the relative importance of labor supply responses in accounting for this rise remains an open question. Ljungqvist and Sargent (1998) argue that a significant part of the increase is accounted for by the choices that workers make in the face of an increase in turbulence combined with very generous long-term Unemployment Insurance (UI) benefits. Assuming some element of this story is correct, the framework of Galí and coauthors cannot help us evaluate its importance, since it will simply infer from the rise in unemployment that the wage markup must have increased.[1]

The second context is the rise of US unemployment in the 1970s. Shimer (1998) argued that a large part of the increase in unemployment in the United States during the 1970s could be attributed to the entry of the baby boomers into the labor market, combined with the fact that younger workers have different unemployment dynamics. If forced to account for the data, the framework of Galí and coauthors would again infer that wage markups increased. This would be consistent with Shimer's argument if young workers have different relative unemployment dynamics because of differences in relative wage markups. However, if the matching process works as in Jovanovic (1979), at least some of the difference reflects labor supply channels in the presence of informational frictions.

To summarize the previous discussion, there is currently no consensus on the role that various factors play in accounting for the variation in aggregate unemployment rates over time and across countries, especially at low frequency. It is most certainly of interest to explore the extent to which one given factor (say, for example, wage markups) might help us understand this variation. If one pursues this avenue, a key element of the exercise must surely be to look for independent measures of the movement in wage markups. But what this paper does is to effectively assume that unemployment is entirely due to the wage being too high and then use that assumption to back out what wage markups (gross of nominal rigidities) must have been. In my view this does not offer much of an advance in developing theories of unemployment.

More generally, and in the spirit of my earlier comment about micro-foundations, I find the framework adopted by this paper to be quite limited in its ability to connect with the data. For example, the leading framework used to think about unemployment emphasizes what Blanchard and Diamond (1992) call the flow approach to labor markets. This reflects the fact that most people think that labor market flows reveal useful information. At the most basic level, it seems potentially relevant to decompose unemployment rate differences across time, demographic or skill groups, or countries into parts that are due to differences in duration and frequency of spells. (See, for example, the analysis of Blanchard and Portugal [2001] contrasting unemployment in the United States and Portugal.)

In my view, a model of unemployment that abstracts from flows is not very amenable to confronting various empirical facts that a good theory of unemployment should help us understand. Put somewhat differently, I think a good theory of aggregate unemployment should also offer a good theory of individual unemployment. Of course, it could be that the authors wish to argue that focusing on labor market flows as part of developing a theory of unemployment is misguided. If so, then the authors should articulate this view.

Using the Methods of Smets-Wouters to Identify Shocks

With my remaining space I want to note some issues with using the Smets-Wouters machinery as a way to identify business cycle shocks. A recurrent finding in the literature that estimates medium-scale New Keynesian models is that wage mark-up shocks are a quantitatively important source of business cycle shocks. Central to this finding is the fact that in a stand-in household model with standard functional forms, one finds significant movements in the so-called "labor wedge" at business cycle frequencies. It follows that a method that uses shocks to make this model match the data will necessarily find large shocks to the labor wedge. However, recent work by Chang and Kim (2007) and Chang, Kim, and Schorfheide (2011) show that models with heterogeneity and incomplete markets produce outcomes that look like shocks to the labor wedge in the aggregate data even when the sole driving force is a neutral technology shock.

I believe the assumption of complete insurance markets implicit in the authors' model is motivated by a desire for tractability and the hope that it is not substantively important. That is, I do not think that they are trying to argue that there are (approximately) complete markets for idiosyncratic income shocks. I think many researchers mistakenly interpret the work of Krusell and Smith (1998) to imply that incomplete markets and heterogeneity are not of first-order importance in business cycle settings. What they actually showed is that a few second moments are relatively unaffected by incomplete markets and heterogeneity. But, more importantly, the papers by Chang and coauthors previously noted show that this interpretation of Krusell and Smith's work is definitely not well founded in slightly richer settings.

The current paper contains another result that serves to illustrate the substantive implications of assuming complete insurance markets. When the authors used standard preferences the model implies a negative correlation between employment and participation in the face of some shocks. The mechanism behind this correlation is as follows. Because of complete insurance, when aggregate employment increases, consumption of all individuals increases, including those who remain nonemployed. Because consumption of the nonemployed increases, their desire to work at a given wage level decreases and the participation rate decreases. Because this mechanism generates a counterfactual correlation between employment and participation, the authors adopt an ad hoc and nonstandard specification of preferences in order to minimize the magnitude of this effect.

But intuitively, this counterfactual correlation seems to be an artifact of the assumption of complete insurance. To see why, consider the following scenario under complete and incomplete insurance. There are two individuals who are currently nonemployed, and in the next period one of them becomes employed but the other remains nonemployed. With complete markets, both of the individuals will experience an increase in consumption, and for the individual who remains nonemployed, this increase in consumption (can) lead them to no longer desire employment at the given market wage. But with incomplete markets, only the individual who becomes employed will experience an increase in consumption, and so there will be no effect on the desire of the second individual to be employed.

So while one might argue that one of the benefits of incorporating unemployment into the analysis is that it provides additional discipline on preferences, I think the more appropriate interpretation is to warn researchers about the perverse substantive effects that accompany the assumption of complete insurance in settings with indivisible labor and idiosyncratic income shocks.

As a final comment on the use of these methods to identify business cycle shocks, I would also note the recent work by Eusepi and Preston (2009). They show that moving from the assumption of a stand-in household with separable preferences (over consumption and leisure) and divisible labor to one with nonseparable preferences and indivisible labor has a dramatic effect on what the estimation exercise delivers for the relative importance of various shocks.

By way of summary, let me say the following. The earlier comments should not be taken to imply that we should not perform the types of exercises that Smets and Wouters and many others have carried out, in which we use explicit models to infer the relative importance of various shocks. Instead, they are to remind us that the results of such an exercise can be very sensitive to the details of the model specification and that as a result interpretation of the shocks requires a great deal of care.

Summary

The authors argue that extending standard macroeconomic models to explicitly include three labor market states can prove beneficial in diagnosing the role of various shocks in accounting for aggregate fluctuations. They demonstrate this by embedding Galí's theory of unemployment into an otherwise standard medium-scale New Keynesian model and estimating it using the methods of Smets and Wouters (2007). The analysis is clear and the paper is nicely exposited, and as a concrete example of the general point being made I think the paper is successful. But as either a compelling quantitative theory of the US aggregate labor market or a reliable model to be used to uncover shocks, I think the paper is much less successful. To my mind a key weakness and limitation of the exercise is the lack of attempt to connect with micro-economic data on individual unemployment spells, or wage determination and price setting.

Endnotes

For acknowledgments, sources of research support, and disclosure of the author's material financial relationships, if any, please see http://www.nber.org/chapters/c12426 .ack.

1. As noted earlier, the wage may also be high due to nominal rigidities. In the discussion that follows I will assume that these are not very relevant for low frequency movements, though this is not critical to the arguments being made.

References

Blanchard, O., and P. Diamond. 1992. "The Flow Approach to Labor Markets." *American Economic Review* 82:354–59.

Blanchard, O., and P. Portugal. 2001. "What Hides Behind an Unemployment Rate: Comparing Portuguese and U.S. Labor Markets." *American Economic Review* 91:187–208.

Chang,Y., and S. Kim. 2007. "Heterogeneity and Aggregation: Implications for Labor Market Fluctuations." *American Economic Review* 97:1939–56.

Chang, Y., S. Kim, and F. Schorfheide. 2011. "Labor Market Heterogeneity, Aggregation and the Lucas Critique." RCER Working Paper no. 556. University of Rochester–Center for Economic Research (RCER).

Davis, S., and J. Haltiwanger. 1992. "Gross Job Creation, Gross Job Destruction and Employment Reallocation." *Quarterly Journal of Economics* 107:819–63.

Eusepi, S., and B. Preston. 2009. "Labor Supply Heterogeneity and Macroeconomic Co-movement." NBER Working Paper no. 15561. Cambridge, MA: National Bureau of Economic Research, December.

Galí, J. 2011a. "The Return of the Wage Phillips Curve." *Journal of the European Economic Association*, forthcoming.

———. 2011b. *Unemployment Fluctuations and Stabilization Policies: A New Keynesian Perspective*. Cambridge, MA: MIT Press.

Jovanovic, B. 1979. "Job Matching and the Theory of Turnover." *Journal of Political Economy* 87:972–90.

Krusell, P., and A. Smith Jr. 1998. "Income and Wealth Heterogeneity in the Macroeconomy." *Journal of Political Economy* 106:867–96.

Ljungqvist, L., and T. Sargent. 1998. "The European Unemployment Dilemma." *Journal of Political Economy* 106:514–50.

Lucas, R., and E. Prescott. 1974. "Equilibrium Search and Unemployment." *Journal of Economic Theory* 7:188–209.

Mortensen, D., and C. Pissarides. 1994. "Job Creation and Job Destruction in the Theory of Unemployment." *Review of Economic Studies* 67:397–415.

Shimer, R. 1998. "Why is the U.S. Unemployment Rate So Much Lower?" In *NBER Macroeconomics Annual 1998*, vol. 13, edited by Ben S. Bernanke and Julio J. Rotemberg, 11–61. Cambridge, MA: MIT Press.

Smets, F., and R. Wouters. 2007. "Shocks and Frictions in US Business Cycles: A Bayesian DSGE Approach." *American Economic Review* 97:586–606.

Discussion

Albert Marcet began the discussion by asking whether the model of unemployment (extensive margin adjustment) presented could be expressed as a model of hours worked (intensive margin adjustment). He cited the example of the Hansen (1985) and Rogerson (1988) model of unemployment via lotteries, which is equivalent to a model of hours worked with a linear disutility of labor supply.

Robert Hall commented that a model of wage determination with sticky wages would provide a more appealing amplification mechanism for the underlying shocks of the model. He pointed to the small contribution of estimated contractionary monetary policy shocks to unemployment despite the importance of the zero lower bound. He noted that the authors' estimation attributes much of the rise in unemployment in the Great Recession to exogenous wage markup shocks that are unrelated by any mechanism to the smaller contemporaneous monetary shocks.

Additionally, Hall reiterated comments by the discussants that unemployment in their model should better match the concept as it is defined and measured. Finally, Hall disagreed with Lawrence Christiano's comments that the unemployed agents in the model are happier than the employed agents. He emphasized that value should not be confused with utility—value includes not just today's flow utility but the present value of future earnings that the agent contributes to the household. The contribution of each agent to the household's value function is the right welfare measure for comparing the states of employment and unemployment.

Robert Gordon, citing current experience, emphasized that unemployment is a source of considerable distress and anxiety, highlighting the need for models that capture these facts about unemployment. Gordon agreed with Christiano's view that union power could not explain excessively high wages and pointed to the fact that labor's nearly constant share of national income suggests little variation in market power for workers. Gordon added that the Okun's law relationship between output and unemployment appears unchanged despite the differing nature of shocks in the 1960s and 1970s (demand versus supply, respectively). Thus, any shocks explaining unemployment should preserve this relationship.

George Evans suggested an alternative source of the shocks for the Great Recession. Departing from rational expectations, he noted that the financial and housing market crisis could have triggered a collapse in expectations for future output and inflation that would precipitate a large recession today.

Michael Woodford disagreed with Gordon's view that the labor share should fluctuate with wage markup shocks. He noted that a stable labor share reflects prices in line with average labor costs. Jordi Galí added that a stable price markup should keep the labor share constant despite any markup shocks.

Marjorie Flavin, responding to Christiano's discussion of the definition of unemployment in the authors' model, argued that Christiano's analysis ignores differences between insiders and outsiders in the union. The union may choose to mark up the wage benefiting the insiders, but outsiders would be unhappy, as they would be excluded from the gains secured by the union. These outsiders should be considered unemployed.

Galí began his response by addressing the issue of whether unemployed agents were as happy as the employed agents. He noted that their assumption of risk-sharing among employed and unemployed agents is commonly made to preserve the representative household framework and ensure tractability. He emphasized that agents take into account the utility of the household in making their decisions, since no individual agent has any incentive to work.

Responding to Christiano's comments about efforts to limit the wealth effects in the model, Galí recognized that the limited short-run wealth effect is important for their results but emphasized that the authors adopted a flexible utility specification (similar to Jaimovich-Rebelo). The parameter governing the short-run wealth effect is estimated and the data prefer a parameter value with smaller wealth effects. Galí noted that the parameter in the utility function governing the wealth effect can be interpreted as an external habit.

Galí also addressed concerns about the presence of wage markup shocks given the declining role of unions in the US labor market. Galí emphasized that union density is just one dimension of worker's market power. Factors like unemployment benefits and regulations on hiring and firing are also critical in determining labor's market power. Galí cited the cross-country evidence showing that union density is not a significant predictor for the level of unemployment. In short, data on US union density does not provide evidence for or against variations in the wage markup.

Responding to Rogerson's discussion, Galí acknowledged that many factors of unemployment are ignored as the authors focus on high and rigid wages. However, Galí emphasized that their objective is to augment a standard New Keynesian framework with a simple model of unemployment and examine the implications. Galí also noted that the canonical Diamond-Mortensen-Pissarides model features market power on behalf of workers, and wage rigidities are key for generating large fluctuations in employment. He agreed with Rogerson that an incomplete markets model would be ideal but would introduce substantial technical difficulties, and it is unclear how it would improve on the conclusions derived in a simpler setting.

In response to Marcet's question about whether their labor market model has an intensive margin representation, Galí argued that it is critical for wages to be set collectively but that each individual is a wage-taker, and it is not clear how this corresponds to a model with an intensive margin. In response to Hall's comment on the link between monetary policy shocks and the wage markup shocks, Galí acknowledged that these might not be true shocks and cited downward nominal wage rigidity as a possible reason why the estimation favors simultaneous negative monetary shocks and positive wage markup shocks.